P9-CIW-381

*The Antislavery Debate*

# The Antislavery Debate

*Capitalism and Abolitionism as a*
*Problem in Historical Interpretation*

EDITED AND WITH AN INTRODUCTION
BY THOMAS BENDER
*With Essays by*
*John Ashworth, David Brion Davis,*
*and Thomas L. Haskell*

*University of California Press*
BERKELEY    LOS ANGELES    LONDON

The three chapters in Part I have been reprinted from David Brion Davis, *The Problem of Slavery in the Age of Revolution, 1770–1823*, chapters 1, 5, and 8. Copyright © 1975 by Cornell University. Used by permission of the publisher, Cornell University Press.

The following essays have been reprinted from *The American Historical Review*: Thomas L. Haskell, "Capitalism and the Origins of the Humanitarian Sensibility, Part 1," vol. 90, no. 2 (April 1985), and "Capitalism and the Origins of the Humanitarian Sensibility, Part 2," vol. 90, no. 3 (June 1985); David Brion Davis, "Reflections on Abolitionism and Ideological Hegemony," John Ashworth, "The Relationship between Capitalism and Humanitarianism," and Thomas L. Haskell, "Convention and Hegemonic Interest in the Debate over Antislavery: A Reply to Davis and Ashworth," in *AHR* Forum, vol. 92, no. 4 (October 1987).

University of California Press
Berkeley and Los Angeles, California

University of California Press, Ltd.
London, England

© 1992 by
The Regents of the University of California

**Library of Congress Cataloging-in-Publication Data**

The Antislavery debate : capitalism and abolitionism as a problem in
   historical interpretation / edited by Thomas Bender.
      p.   cm.
   Includes index.
   ISBN 978-0-520-07779-9 (pbk. : alk. paper)
      1. Slavery—Anti-slavery movements.  2. Slavery—United States—
   Anti-slavery movements.  3. Capitalism.  4. Capitalism—United
   States.  I. Bender, Thomas.
   HT1033.A63   1992
   306.3′62—dc20                                              91-21075
                                                              CIP

14  13  12  11  10
12  11  10  9  8

# Contents

# Preface

This volume presents an extended debate about the relationship between capitalism and the antislavery movement initiated by the publication of a two-part essay by Thomas L. Haskell in *The American Historical Review* in 1985. The starting point for Haskell was David Brion Davis's argument in *The Problem of Slavery in the Age of Revolution, 1770–1823* (1975). Since the whole debate is founded upon a few key sections of Davis's study, we begin this book with substantial excerpts from it, followed by Haskell's provocative essay and the responses to it published by Davis and John Ashworth in *The American Historical Review* in 1987. Haskell's response to Davis and Ashworth, also published in *The American Historical Review*, then follows. We conclude with two original essays not before published, one by Ashworth, the other by Davis, responding to the issues raised in the course of the debate. The book begins with an introduction to the debate and its historiographical implications written by me as editor.

I should emphasize at the outset that this book isolates a single thread of argument and a restricted cast of historians from a much larger historiographical inquiry into the relations of slavery and antislavery to capitalism. There have also been important discussions of Davis's claims about the issue at hand that are not reflected here, at least not directly. One thinks particularly of the scholarship of Seymour Drescher, but many other scholars might be named were it appropriate to develop a comprehensive list here. Moreover, this volume falls within the broad field of intellectual and cultural history, and this excludes a very large and important range of scholarship in social and economic history that addresses the question of capitalism and antislavery. But that is beyond the scope of this sharply focused debate.

As editor, I would like to thank my colleagues in this enterprise; it is their book. Indeed, that it is a book at all is a testament to their great skill in conducting a scholarly debate at such a high pitch. I would like to thank *The American Historical Review* for permission to reprint the essays by Haskell, Davis, and Ashworth that first appeared in its pages and Cornell University Press for permission to reprint portions of Davis's *The Problem of Slavery in the Age of Revolution, 1770–1823*. Michael Rogin's encouragement of the project and strongly held view that the debate needed to be continued for another round are much appreciated. David A. Hollinger and Gwendolyn Wright read my introduction with their usual care and insight, and it is better for their efforts. Finally, I would like to thank Sheila Levine of the University of California Press. Her responsiveness to the idea of this project—her intellectual engagement with it, her executive management of it, and her patience and good cheer as we worked to realize it made the task a pleasure.

Thomas Bender

# Contributors

*John Ashworth*, who earned his doctorate from Oxford, has since 1980 been Lecturer in American Studies at the University of East Anglia. Though he is the only Englishman among the authors of this volume, his research is more exclusively concerned with the United States than that of his co-authors. He is the author of *"Agrarians" and "Aristocrats": Party Political Ideology in the United States, 1837–1846* (1983), and he is currently working on a study of American politics in the late 1840s and 1850s, in which he argues that the development of wage labor in the North was a key factor in the growth of sectional antagonisms.

*Thomas Bender*, who is University Professor of the Humanities and Professor of History at New York University, has worked in fields other than the history of abolitionism, but he has both teaching and research interests in the field of historiography. His books include *Toward an Urban Vision* (1975); *Community and Social Change in America* (1978); *New York Intellect* (1987); and, as editor, *The University and the City: From Medieval Origins to the Present* (1988). He is at present writing a book to be titled *History and Public Culture*.

*David Brion Davis* is Sterling Professor of History at Yale University. His books include *Homicide in American Fiction, 1790–1860: A Study in Social Values* (1957); *The Problem of Slavery in Western Culture* (1966); *The Slave Power Conspiracy and the Paranoid Style* (1969); *The Problem of Slavery in the Age of Revolution, 1770–1823* (1975); *Ante-Bellum American Culture: An Interpretive Anthology* (1979); *Slavery and Human Progress* (1984); *From Homicide to Slavery: Studies in American Culture* (1986); *Revolutions: Reflections on American Equality and Foreign Liber-*

*ations* (1990). He is currently writing a two-volume work: *The Problem of Slavery in the Age of Emancipation,* volume 1: *Racial and Transatlantic Dimensions;* volume 2: *Class Conflict and Equality.*

*Thomas L. Haskell* is the Samuel G. McCann Professor of History at Rice University. His principal interest as a historian is in modes of explanation. The essays contained in this volume are part of a larger work in progress on changing conceptions of agency and moral responsibility in Anglo-American culture since 1750. This project will extend to an earlier period the interest in conventions of causal attribution that he began developing in *The Emergence of Professional Social Science: The American Social Science Association and the Nineteenth Century Crisis of Authority* (1977). He is the editor of *The Authority of Experts: Studies in History and Theory* (1984) and co-editor with Richard Teichgraeber of a forthcoming volume of essays on the culture of capitalism. He is also the author of several historiographical articles, including "Objectivity Is Not Neutrality: Rhetoric vs. Practice in Peter Novick's *That Noble Dream,*" which appeared in *History and Theory* (1990), and "Some Doubts about *Time on the Cross*" and "The True and Tragical History of *Time on the Cross,*" which appeared in *The New York Review of Books* (1974, 1975).

# Introduction
*Thomas Bender*

In an intriguing passage in *The Wealth of Nations* (1776), Adam Smith contrasts the energy and dignity of labor motivated by interest with that of the slave. Did Smith here, as in so much else in both *The Wealth of Nations* and *The Theory of Moral Sentiments* (1759), forecast a bit of the future, in this instance the emergence of the antislavery movement out of the dynamic of the rise of an interest-driven commercial society?[1] Is there something to be made of the near simultaneity of the rise of capitalism and the emergence of organized antislavery? Mere chronological conjuncture does not, of course, imply causal connections. Yet it is hard not to wonder about the possibility that there was some connection between the final loss of legitimacy of slave labor after centuries of tolerance, if not always full acceptance, and the process whereby another form of economic production and distribution rather quickly secured itself in the Atlantic world.

Modern historical inquiry into this question, particularly in reference to the English movement to abolish the international slave trade and slavery in the British West Indies, has been on the agenda of professional scholarship for nearly half a century. The line of inquiry was boldly and provocatively opened by Eric Williams in his *Capitalism and Slavery* (1944).[2] Williams, an Oxford-trained historian who became prime minister of postcolonial Trinidad and Tobago, argued that it was economic interest, not any moral claims by abolitionists, that brought slavery to an end in the British West Indies. He claimed that antislavery was a function of the declining importance of West Indian plantations and the concomitant rise of industrial

1. Adam Smith, *An Inquiry into the Nature and Causes of the Wealth of Nations* (1776; New York, 1937), esp. 80, 364–67, 524, 553, 648. Smith attacked slavery rather severely, insisting that it deprived society of the benefit of interest, as well as representing an indefensible form of social power.
2. Eric Williams, *Capitalism and Slavery* (Chapel Hill, N.C., 1944).

1

capitalism to dominance in the British economy (and thus, in Marxist terms, politics).

As all seminal works ought to do, Williams's book stimulated decades of monographic response, but as is often the case with such works, the scholarship it called into existence did not sustain its thesis. It is not at all clear that the plantation economy was in decline, nor is the rather crude explication of interest that Williams employed any longer compelling. Yet the legacy of the work survives. If his formulation of the argument has proven vulnerable, the larger issue of identifying the relationship between the rise of capitalism and the decline of slavery has remained stimulating.[3]

Few historians today discount the possibility of some connection between capitalism and antislavery. The question of the moment is how to phrase that connection and what explanatory weight to give it. The debate over antislavery in this book focuses precisely upon this question, and it does so in a way that illuminates one of the central issues of contemporary historiography—the relation of social structure, practice, and change to culture, ideas, and ideology. More narrowly, it addresses ways of using— indeed the very usefulness of—the notion of cultural hegemony to explain the form of culturally constituted power in modern democracies.

The debate that takes shape here is at once tighter in focus and broader in implication than the debate that has surrounded *Capitalism and Slavery*. What is at issue is not the likelihood of a link between capitalism and antislavery, but rather various theorizations of that association. Although the historical problem being examined here is the emergence of organized antislavery in the late eighteenth and early nineteenth centuries, the discussion is conducted, rather self-consciously, in terms that make it rather easily understood as a general debate about historical explanation. It is clearly a case study of how one might approach questions of the relation of society to consciousness, of interests to ideology, of social practice to cultural formation. Most important of all, the debate puts considerable pressure upon the working assumptions of current historical practice and, especially, upon words and concepts common in historical discourse but not so stable as we might have thought them to be. The debate is about concepts as much as evidence, and the principal harvest is a raised self-consciousness with re-

3. The best book on this is David Eltis, *Economic Growth and the Ending of the Transatlantic Slave Trade* (New York, 1987). See also two other important works: Seymour Drescher, *Econocide: British Slavery in the Era of Abolition* (Pittsburgh, Pa., 1977); and *idem, Capitalism and Antislavery: British Mobilization in Comparative Context* (New York, 1986). There is an outstanding recent symposium on the legacy of Eric Williams: *British Capitalism and Caribbean Slavery*, Barbara Solow and Stanley Engerman, eds. (Cambridge, 1987).

gard to the need for clarity about the concepts and words that are in the tool kit of contemporary historical practice.

All of the contributors to this volume would agree that the debate rests upon the magnificent foundation supplied by David Brion Davis's multivolume inquiry into the meaning and consequences of freedom and slavery in the modern Atlantic world. The first volume, *The Problem of Slavery in Western Culture* (1966), is a wide-ranging exploration of the intellectual (theological and philosophical) sources of the justification and rationalization of slavery throughout Western history, and, then, of emergent antislavery conviction in the eighteenth century. It traces a profound shift in Western moral perception from blindness to insight into the moral problem of slavery. After centuries of either justifying slavery as appropriate to certain classes or kinds of people or of rationalizing it as an unfortunate but tolerable evil, Euro-Americans, or at least a significant number of them, began to insist that slavery was an intolerable evil and a blot on civilized society.

It is, however, the second volume that provides the focal point for the antislavery debate here. *The Problem of Slavery in the Age of Revolution, 1770–1823*, which appeared in 1975, differed from the first volume not only in its chronological framework but also in its mode of historical analysis. Whereas the first volume had been a study in the tradition of the history of ideas and sweeping in its chronological coverage, the second volume concentrated on a quite restricted historical period, about half a century. The second volume is also denser in historical context, and it evidenced a deeper philosophical awareness of interpretive issues, something signaled by an early reference to Hegel's famous discussion of the bondsman and master. It had as well a different explanatory task. Now, rather than tracing and delineating a tradition of ideas, Davis undertook the most difficult burden of historical narration. He sought to explain how ideas, antislavery in this instance, became social facts, cultural attitudes, and motives and means for collective action.

The subtlety with which he addressed this vexing problem of historical explanation made the publication of *The Problem of Slavery in the Age of Revolution* a historiographical event with implications beyond its special field. For all historians who hoped to bring together social and intellectual history on terms more complex and compelling than those of the Progressive historians or the Marxists of the 1940s, both of whom in varying degrees understood ideas as mere reflections of material interest, Davis's book invited close and very exciting scrutiny. Haskell's critique and reformulation of the issue, which represents an even more radical shift in historical analysis of the relationship between social and cultural phenomena, is exciting for the same reason.

*The Problem of Slavery in the Age of Revolution* presents a comparative history of the emerging movement to abolish slavery. Yet the debate in this volume (and much of the initial reaction to the book) has focused upon one particular argument within the book. In terms of the total number of pages, the specific development of the argument may not be a major portion of the book, but it informs the whole book. This argument is the theoretically most interesting part of the book, and as moral commentary, it is its most compelling theme.

Without in any way compromising the religious sources of abolitionism among the English Quakers (a point he had developed in *The Problem of Slavery in Western Culture*), Davis raised the issue of class interest. Rejecting the notion that the cause of antislavery was a transcendent ideal, he announced early in the book that the movement "reflected the ideological needs of various groups and classes" (19, this volume). In the sections of the book reprinted here, Davis suggested that concern for the slave might well have served the hegemonic function of legitimating free labor.

What drew readers to Davis's text on this point was his skill in avoiding both naive idealism and reductive materialism. While he invited his readers to "look at the impulses behind the antislavery phenomenon, asking how they reflected, either consciously or unconsciously, the social orders from which they emerged," he rejected the argument that the "new hostility to human bondage" could be "reduced simply to the needs and interests of particular classes" (25). In his layered analysis, this shift and the new language of humanitarianism were embedded in and partly derived from a cultural context of religious, philosophical, and legal doctrines that he had elaborated in *The Problem of Slavery in Western Culture* and summarized in the first chapter of the sequel (reprinted here). Making a distinction between origin and societal acceptance of antislavery ideas and ideals, he insisted that "the needs and interests of particular classes had much to do with a given society's receptivity to new ideas and thus to the ideas' historical impact." He indicated that much of his new book would "be concerned with the ideological functions and implications of attacking this symbol of the most extreme subordination, exploitation, and dehumanization, at a time when various enlightened elites were experimenting with internalized moral and cultural controls to establish or preserve their own hegemony" (25).

In chapter 5 of *The Problem of Slavery in the Age of Revolution*, "The Quaker Ethic and the Antislavery International" (reprinted here), Davis portrays the English Quakers involved in antislavery as "the very embodiment of the capitalist mentality" and explores the meaning of antislavery principles in the context of an emerging free labor economy (45). Antislavery, he notes, was a "highly selective response to labor exploitation," and in addition it was certainly in the interest of a capitalist class concerned with labor discipline and the legitimation of novel economic practices (61). Moreover, as Davis notices, antislavery enabled an ambitious and previously largely excluded or peripheral group to establish new and more central social connections. But Davis declines to develop this line of argument into a cynical interpretation of their motives. He does not suggest that they consciously manipulated the antislavery issue to their advantage.

He does, however, press the question of consequences for English society. "The paramount question," he observes, "is how antislavery reinforced or legitimized" the hegemony of a developing capitalist elite (70–71). The focus on one kind of human exploitation seems to have sustained a language of social concern that offered less critical perspective on other forms of exploitation, particularly that of workers suffering through the transition to modern capitalism.[4] "At issue," Davis concludes, "are not conscious intentions but the social functions of ideology; not individual motives but shifting patterns of thought and value which focused attention on new problems, which camouflaged others, and which defined new conceptions of social reality" (71).

If, for Davis, class interest provides the link that connects capitalism to antislavery (though not, he would argue, a sufficient causal explanation), Haskell asks whether the Gramscian notion of hegemony, to which Davis refers, is conceptually coherent and empirically warranted. He acknowledges that the "rise of capitalism" may have had an influence on "ideas and values through the medium of class interest," but he is not persuaded that such a linkage is developed adequately by Davis. The force of his argument, moreover, invites some reconsideration of whether the concept of hegemony, quite underdeveloped in Antonio Gramsci's *Prison Notebooks*, can bear the particular interpretive burden that many historians today place on the notion.[5]

---

4. This point has been made in a different context and in a different form in Eric Foner's *Free Soil, Free Labor, Free Men: The Ideology of the Republican Party before the Civil War* (New York, 1970). More indirectly, but powerfully, the point is made by Eugene Genovese's work. See, especially, his *The Political Economy of Slavery* (New York, 1965) and *Roll, Jordan, Roll* (New York, 1976).
5. See *Selections from the Prison Notebooks of Antonio Gramsci*, Quintin Hoare and Geoffrey Nowell Smith, eds. and trans. (New York, 1971); and T. J. Jackson Lears, "The Concept of Cultural Hegemony," *AHR*, 92 (1985): 567–93. Although he refers to Gramsci, it is not at all clear to me that the multicausal interpretation Davis offers either depends upon Gramsci or has been sufficiently developed to ex-

But Haskell is, in fact, interested in another sort of association of culture and capitalism, which has hitherto received little attention. Defining the pertinent aspect of capitalism to be a market economy (rather than a system of class relations), Haskell argues that capitalism had a "more telling influence on the origins of humanitarianism through changes the market wrought in *perception* or *cognitive style*" (111). If Davis's emphasis on class points toward a consideration of interest, Haskell's focus on the market introduces the concept of "conventions" and habitual modes of understanding causation and responsibility.

Haskell acknowledges that "by insisting that the reformers were unaware of the hegemonic function served by their ideology, Davis opened a crucially important space between their intentions and the long-term consequences of their ideas and activities." It is here, in this "zone of indeterminacy," that Davis rejects the reductionism of an argument for the direct expression of class interest (116). Many readers were drawn to Davis's interpretation precisely because of the complexity of this narrative strategy, but not Haskell. He worries that Davis is trying to have it both ways. What some see as flexibility, Haskell sees as incoherence. He insists that the idea of "interest" implies intention, whether conscious or unconscious. Davis's interpretation relies on "self-deception," or unconscious intention, which Haskell regards as difficult to verify in any case and not successfully verified in this one.

Rejecting the terms of class interest and hegemony proposed by Davis, Haskell commends Max Weber's notion of "elective affinity." As an explanatory device, elective affinity, which also posits a zone of indeterminacy, is not far from the structure, though not the phrasing, of Davis's explanation. One of the questions to be pondered here is whether the issue is analytical or about the moral vocabulary of the historian. Davis's rhetoric has a moral edge that dissolves in the notion of elective affinity. Is that the implication of Haskell's rephrasing of the issue?

Since Haskell considers all humane action to be inescapably "selective," a notion both Ashworth and Davis reject, he holds reformers blameless for the fact that their efforts were almost exclusively in aid of chattel slaves, who were, after all, the most oppressed class of their era.[6] The intensity of

---

emplify Gramscian analysis, which is concerned more to explain consent than to delineate ruling-class motivation, or the relation of interest to act.

6. Lest Haskell be misunderstood here as a moral relativist, it is worth noting his interest in theorizing a secure moral foundation in the midst of an intellectual culture skeptical of moral claims, whether on historicist, nihilist, or just plain cynical grounds. See, e.g., his "The Curious Persistence of Rights Talk in the 'Age of Interpretation,' " *Journal of American History*, 74 (1987): 984–1012.

the debate about interest ought not divert our attention from the importance of Haskell's novel vocabulary and his provocative interpretation of the cultural meaning of the social practices inherent in commercial society or capitalism. He asks us to shift our attention from class relations under capitalism to the cultural or cognitive style associated with the capitalist market.

Capitalism, he argues, has a subliminal curriculum, and one of the principal lessons one learns is perceptual: a "widening of causal horizons," a heightened awareness of the remote consequences of both one's acts and (equally important in moral matters) one's inactions. The premium the market notoriously placed on such bourgeois virtues as forethought, calculation, and delay of gratification habituated English and American reformers in the late eighteenth and early nineteenth centuries to thinking and acting within a temporally and spatially enlarged sphere. They lived not only in the present but also in the future, which they felt able to shape in accordance with their wills. The resulting sense of empowerment meant for most people only an expansion of the realm within which they pursued self-interest, but for the scrupulous it meant something quite different: a new consciousness of power to relieve suffering and, correspondingly, unprecedented feelings of guilt and responsibility for evils that had previously seemed remote and irremediable. What had once been a tolerable or "necessary" evil might, with new perceptions of causation and responsibility, become intolerable.

Haskell's resort to such an argumentative mode in itself bears remark. Such ease with philosophical argument and theory is rare in historiographical discourse, especially among Americanists. Haskell not only draws upon philosophy but constructs a self-consciously theoretical argument. While Davis and Ashworth are evidently comfortable with conceptual issues, they ground themselves, more conventionally, in historical sources. The content of the culture—rather than the logic (or possible logic) of the culture—is central not simply to their theses but to their mode of thinking and arguing. Haskell, by contrast, is less inclined to quote from sources. His argument, like his historical work generally, does not rely on the "interestingness" or revelatory power of archival sources. Rather he writes a theoretical and conceptual history, a history not too far from the historical sociology of Max Weber, whose substantive leads Haskell pursues here. This debate, then, combines two modes of argumentation, producing a rich mix of historical data and philosophical reflection.

The question one has for Haskell is just how far he wishes to press his argument. Is the market-driven transformation of conventions of causal attribution and the consequent extension of what he calls "recipe" knowledge

a sufficient explanation for the rise of a humanitarian sensibility that focused particularly on slavery, or merely a necessary condition? In his first
essay, Haskell seemed to argue that the role of capitalism in antislavery was
fundamental but limited. It contributed "a *precondition,* albeit a vital one:
a proliferation of recipe knowledge and consequent expansion of the conventional limits of causal perception and moral responsibility that compelled some exceptionally scrupulous individuals to attack slavery and
prepared others to listen and comprehend" (155–56). Hence the market and
a new structure of perception account for the emergence of the movement
and its reception, without any recourse to interest. Yet if we are really
speaking of a precondition, there may yet be room for interest as well as
elective affinity in the selection of a focus for this extended humanitarian
concern. Later in his argument, however, Haskell seems to want to foreclose
this possibility.

Haskell's argument is liable to misunderstanding, and it is important to
recognize that he is not arguing that either capitalism or the market is inherently humane. Nor is this an effort to "defend" capitalism. Indeed, he
explicitly acknowledges the terrible forms of exploitation that have occurred
under capitalism. He is seeking to make an analytical rather than a moral
point, to explain a connection between capitalism and cultural perception.
To do so does not necessarily deny the possibility of a connection between
capitalism and consciousness through the medium of class relations. But he
does argue that historians who would link consciousness to capitalism
through the notion of interest will have a difficult empirical task before
them. There is no evidence in his essays that Haskell rejects Davis's account
in *The Problem of Slavery in Western Culture* of the creation of new values,
though his focus is consistently elsewhere. What he does argue, however,
is that capitalism created a new circumstance that changed the relation of
moral values to action in the world.

At this point John Ashworth joins the debate. He doubts that the links
that Haskell postulates "between capitalism and humanitarianism via the
market" can explain why the "conscientious reformer" selected slavery but
not "wage labor" as the focus of concern. The South, for example, was
"connected very firmly with the international market," but antislavery was
not the result (184, 187). Class interest, Ashworth insists, was surely involved. Like Davis, he also rejects Haskell's notion that intentionality,
whether conscious or unconscious, must be specified before one can incorporate class interest into an explanatory narrative. He suggests that one
need only recognize that a partial social experience based on a specified social location, which implies a pattern of interest, can nourish a "partial

view" in one's moral and social outlook. From such a partial experience and with such a partial view, one might overlook the seriousness of the injustices involved in wage labor while agitating against slavery. He, unlike Haskell, would consider this an interested act.

The heart of Ashworth's argument, however, rests upon a fuller analysis of the moral history of capitalism. He criticizes Haskell's narrow focus on the market as the essential experience of capitalism, arguing that wage labor and commodification were understood as novel and worrisome aspects of the new economy. The rise of wage labor, with its acknowledgment of self-interest, made the foundations of public and private morality uncertain. Those who embraced the new economy needed a theory of social morality for a self-interested world. Ashworth, who directs his attention to the antebellum American case rather than to Britain, argues that Americans dealt with this problem by establishing "a rigid separation between those areas of life where the market could rule and those where it was forbidden" (194). People awash in a sea of commerce, where the labor market determined the social relations of a community, turned to home, family, and individual conscience as a new foundation for morality.

The celebration of this triptych is a common theme in the historiography of the period, but Ashworth vastly expands its implication. He proposes that it enabled Americans to accept wage labor and commodification generally in the developing capitalist society. These comforting commitments in the North, however, made Southern slavery, which so blatantly violated them, an increasingly unacceptable evil. Moreover, the crusade against slavery had the effect of reinforcing these values—and thus the development of capitalism in the North. What Ashworth finds in the rhetoric of the abolitionists is a theory of capitalist morality, a morality that depended upon a set of family values and a notion of free agency denied by slavery. The same cluster of values that made wage labor or capitalism possible made slavery impossible.

The distinctive positions of Davis, Haskell, and Ashworth are established early. They are then developed with such richness of historiographical invention and dialectical skill that it would be a disservice on my part to propose a summary. The reader needs no road map and should find no difficulty tracking the debate from these starting positions.

There is, however, one new issue introduced later in the debate that ought to be noted here, for it brings a new body of historical material to the discussion. Davis raises the question of the Dutch, and as all comparative history should, it forces a sharpening of the issues. But Davis raises it for a more specific reason. Were Haskell's thesis valid, he argues, this people, the most advanced capitalists (and slavetraders) in the world, ought to have nourished a strong antislavery movement. Yet they did not. Haskell finds the suggestion intriguing, even acknowledging that close study of the Dutch case might indeed cause complications for his own argument. In his final reply, Davis takes up the challenge, and he uses the Dutch case to deflect some of Haskell's criticism, to sharpen the meaning of key terms, and to challenge Haskell's argument.

With this turn, the debate shifts from concepts, abstractions, and analogues to an actual historical case. For historians such evidence is always the court of final appeal. Yet, as with appeals courts, the case brought before the bar is often resolved in ways that miss some of the animating purpose that sent the case to the high court in the first place. In this instance, many of the wider implications that made Haskell's position so provocative and so rich are necessarily set aside. So the Dutch evidence does not resolve the issue; the complex and pressing questions about the relations between consciousness, moral action, and social change raised at the outset remain very much open to further historiographical discussion. They have been enriched, but not resolved by the antislavery debate.

As Davis, Haskell, and Ashworth were drawn more and more fully into the logic of debate, they focused more and more on fine lines of distinction and flanks to be protected in the interest of sustaining their positions. One might argue that the debate format encourages a cognitive style of its own, one that emphasizes skill in splitting as opposed to lumping. By so effectively making such distinctions, Davis, Haskell, and Ashworth force us to critical reflection upon many words, concepts, and assumptions common to historical discourse in our time.

But if debate encourages splitting, perhaps the writing of a general introduction to a debate encourages a spirit of mediation or lumping. At the risk of damaging the purity of the positions taken and of taking too lightly the distinctions made by the rigorous splitters, let me suggest a strategy that might pull these three perspectives together into one interpretation that is fuller than any of the parts.

The different emphases of each historian's definition of capitalism provide the starting point. Although he does not elaborate upon the point, Davis seems to understand capitalism as a system of class relations. Ashworth, who is quite explicit about the matter, would agree, though he would give more focused attention to the mechanism of this relationship—the commodification of labor in the wage system. Davis and Ashworth thus share a great deal in their definitions of capitalism as a system of class relations, and both take the same "side" in the debate. Both see class interest deeply implicated in antislavery (or two key episodes of its development), and they do this without in any way denying the religious sources of the movement and without denigrating the moral intensity or honesty of abolitionists.

Haskell, by contrast, says little about class relations. Yet he nowhere denies that capitalism is—among other things—a class system. He chooses to emphasize a different aspect of capitalism: the market. It is not entirely clear what he means by a market, but the burden of his position is that there were specific lessons to be learned by participating in the capitalist market in its eighteenth- and early nineteenth-century form. The most important lesson was an enlargement of one's capacity for recognizing remote causes and extended chains of moral responsibility.

A lumper like myself cannot resist the possibility that just as the three conceptions of capitalism can be unified, so might the consequent interpretations of antislavery's relation to capitalism. At one point, though not at others, Haskell seems to invite such a move. His aim, he writes, "has not been to supplant the concept of interest . . . but to supplement it and suggest that its explanatory power may be exaggerated" (237).

Haskell's concept of "conventions" of causal attribution and moral responsibility advances and enriches the historian's craft. Although the concept itself is not novel—Haskell frankly imports it from moral philosophy and jurisprudence—it is new to historical discourse and promises to be very fruitful. His claim that conventions were fundamentally altered in the early history of capitalism is quite compelling. With the work of Max Weber and Robert Merton now well absorbed by historians, we can imagine a novel cognitive style being associated with capitalism in concert with religious sources.[7] What Haskell offers, then, and it is a very exciting new prospect, is an extension of the Weberian project, a cultural history of capitalism.[8]

Yet my inclination in this case is to consider reciprocity. If Haskell proposes to supplement the concept of interest, the concept of interest might similarly supplement his own reformulation of the analytical problem. The emergence of market discipline, upon which Haskell relies so heavily in his theory of causation, seems too global to explain the receptivity to antislav-

7. I refer here, of course, to Max Weber, *The Protestant Ethic and the Spirit of Capitalism*, Talcott Parsons, trans. (1930; New York, 1958); and Robert K. Merton, *Science, Technology and Society in Seventeenth Century England* (1938; New York, 1970).
8. One cannot fail to notice, even *en passant*, that in important respects this debate reinscribes the classical debate between social commentators working within or even in the penumbra of the Marxist tradition (especially Ashworth, but Davis too, at least on the specific issue at hand) and the Weberian tradition of social theory (Haskell, rather explicitly).

ery of a particular political culture. The incorporation of some version of interest along with the moral beliefs that Davis describes in *The Problem of Slavery in Western Culture* seems to bring us closer to a sufficient cause. Yet the resort to interest must be measured. An exclusionary reliance on interest would obscure the objective iniquity of slavery, and it would fail to recognize that a person with a conscious or unconscious interest in the advance of industrial capitalism might simultaneously feel a new sense of extended responsibility (generated by market participation as described by Haskell) that resulted in a sense of complicity in a remediable evil. A sufficient explanation might well be a compounded one that relies upon both convention and interest.

If Haskell really means to invite the incorporation of interest into his concept of convention, I would propose a vital, if tightly bounded, role for it. The claims of class are still operative within the new structure of perception he describes. There is no incompatibility here. Nor is there any bar to Davis's argument that the larger and perhaps even indirect consequence of antislavery was to advance the interests of those who were transforming the British economy (not all of whom were abolitionists and some of whom were wage-earners). What Ashworth adds is an insight into the substance and breadth of moral concern. By attending to the specific language of the abolitionist critique, especially the values at the core of the critique, reinforced in the course of the antislavery agitation in public, he shows both the larger usefulness of the movement and how it helped to sustain the new capitalist society.

Early in his critique Haskell portrays himself as a "stowaway" presumptuous enough to propose a change in course. Other images come to mind. Rather than as a stowaway, I am inclined to think of Haskell as a wise sailor who urges upon the captain better riggings and navigational equipment for a journey to a destination fairly well agreed upon. The new rigging and equipment promise to make the journey safer and surer, but they do not require dismantling all the older technology. With the new ways of managing the ship, the journey will be experienced differently and it will be different in some of its implications. But it will be the same journey. Best of all, there is the prospect that the new equipment and rigging will be of use in other journeys as well.

For those considering other journeys, the value of this debate extends far beyond any discussion of possible winners here. Three gifted historians have exemplified the historical mind at work addressing (and considerably clarifying) the pressing historiographical issue of the relationship of consciousness to society, or the way consciousness works in society, or, further, how social change and ideology are related. There is no more sophisticated conversation among historians on this cluster of issues, and we are collectively indebted to David Brion Davis, Thomas L. Haskell, and John Ashworth.

No historian who has read this debate will again casually or unthinkingly use such words as "class," "interest," "self-deception," "market," "capitalism," "intention," "unconscious," "hegemony," or, of course, "base" and "superstructure." And such historians might find themselves using some new words that represent novel analytical concepts, particularly Haskell's notion of convention.

One convention invites notice in conclusion. For all of their differences, for all the passionate commitments that divide these historians, they share a commitment in practice to a conventional (in Haskell's sense of the word) notion of historical objectivity, the marshaling of evidence, and the elaboration of rational, logical arguments that make no subjective claims.[9]

There is always a tendency in the discipline to become habitual in the use of very complex words and concepts. Debates conducted with the intensity and rigor that mark this one provide an indispensable service by demanding that habit be continually interrogated by thought. The historian's armamentarium is thus re-thought and re-stocked.

9. See Thomas L. Haskell, "Objectivity Is Not Neutrality: Rhetoric vs. Practice in Peter Novick's *That Noble Dream*," *History and Theory*, 29 (1990): 129–57.

# Part 1

## THE PROBLEM OF SLAVERY IN
## THE AGE OF REVOLUTION, 1770–1823

*David Brion Davis*

*Chapter 1*

# What the Abolitionists
# Were Up Against

*"The Problem of Slavery in Western Culture":*
*The Argument Summarized*

The concept of chattel slavery, which must be distinguished from historical varieties of servitude and dependence, has always embodied a profound though subtle contradiction. Since man has a remarkable capacity to imagine abstract states of perfection, he very early imagined a perfect form of subordination. Plato compared the slave to the human body, the master to the body's soul. Slaves incarnated the irrationality and chaos of the material universe, as distinct from the masterlike Demiurge. There was thus a cosmic justification behind Aristotle's dictum that "from the hour of their birth, some men are marked out for subjection, others for rule." The true slave, according to Aristotle, could have no will or interests of his own; he was merely a tool or instrument—the extension of his owner's physical nature.

But even metaphysics had to recognize the slave as a conscious being. Aristotle allowed the bondsman a lower form of virtue, consisting, as one might expect, in the perfect fulfillment of his assigned function. The slave could affirm his consciousness, in other words, by partaking of his master's consciousness and by becoming one with his master's desires. The perfect slave, therefore, would be a paradigm of that ideal submission never quite approximated by the most obedient children, wives, subjects, students, or patients: he would be the automatic agent of his creator's will (not an autonomous Adam free to disobey).

At this point we arrive at the root of the "problem" of slavery. The more perfect the slave, as Hegel later observed, the more enslaved becomes the master. For the master's identity depends on having a slave who recognizes

17

him as master: the truth of the master's independent consciousness lies in the dependent and supposedly unessential consciousness of the bondsman.[1]

This psychological paradox was not unknown to the ancient world. "It would be absurd," Diogenes of Sinope reportedly said, when his own slave had run away, "if Manes can live without Diogenes, but Diogenes cannot get on without Manes." When pirates captured Diogenes and took him to a slave market in Crete, he pointed to a spectator wearing rich purple robes and said, "Sell me to this man; he needs a master."

There is no need here to review the history of slave systems or to discuss the sociological gradations between various forms of servitude. It is sufficient to make three brief points about the concept and reality of slavery. First, the ancient ideal of personal subordination was modified by Christianity but continued to influence medieval and early modern thought, even in countries where chattel bondage had disappeared. In medieval England, for example, Bracton identified villeins with Roman slaves, and carefully distinguished them from other kinds of dependent laborers whose rights were protected by the state. Second, insofar as actual forms of servitude approximated the concept of slavery, as elaborated, for example, in Roman law, they represented the extreme example of treating men as objects to be manipulated, humiliated, and exploited. Hence the term "slavery" continued to acquire metaphorical associations implying the ultimate in dependence, disability, powerlessness, sinfulness, and negation of autonomous self-consciousness. Third, the internal contradictions of slavery were not confined to theory, but arose ultimately from historical attempts to keep and govern slaves, a situation which always necessitated compromise. No lawgivers could forget that tools and instruments do not run away, rebel, commit crimes, or help protect the state from external danger. No masters, whether in ancient Rome, medieval Tuscany, or seventeenth-century Brazil, could forget that the obsequious servant might also be a "domestic enemy" bent on theft, poisoning, or arson. Throughout history it has been said that slaves, if occasionally as loyal and faithful as good dogs, were for the most part lazy, irresponsible, cunning, rebellious, untrustworthy, and sexually promiscuous.

The institution of slavery, then, has always given rise to conflict, fear, and accommodation. The settlement of the New World magnified these liabilities, since the slaves now came from an alien and unfamiliar culture; they often outnumbered their European rulers; and many colonial settlements were vulnerable to military attack or close to wilderness areas that

1. G. W. F. Hegel, *The Phenomenology of Mind*, J. B. Baillie, trans., 2d edn. (New York, 1964), 235–37. The other references upon which this section is based can be found in *The Problem of Slavery in Western Culture* (Ithaca, N.Y., 1966).

offered easy refuge. Accordingly, the introduction of Negro slavery to the Americas brought spasmodic cries of warning, anxiety, and racial repugnance. But the grandiose visions of New World wealth—once the Spanish had plundered the Aztecs and Incas—seemed always to require slave labor. The Negro slave thus became an intrinsic part of the American experience.

The economics of slavery have no bearing on the argument at this point. It is obvious that the various colonizing nations, whatever their domestic traditions of servitude, seized upon Africans as the cheapest and most expedient labor supply to meet the immediate demands of mining and tropical agriculture. The institution took on a variety of forms as a result of European cultural differences, the character of the work performed, geographic and ecological conditions, and a host of other variables. But Anglo-American slavery was not unique in defining the bondsman as chattel property endowed with elements of human personality. Nor was Anglo-American society unusual in having to accommodate the underlying contradictions of the master-slave relationship.

The diversities of New World slavery should not blind us to the central point. In the 1760s there was nothing unprecedented about chattel slavery, even the slavery of one ethnic group to another. What was unprecedented by the 1760s and early 1770s was the emergence of a widespread conviction that New World slavery symbolized all the forces that threatened the true destiny of man. How does one explain this remarkable shift in moral consciousness if it was not a direct response to an innovation of unparalleled iniquity? Presumably men of the mid-eighteenth century were no more virtuous than men of earlier times, although something might have altered their perceptions of virtue. No doubt the new antislavery opinion drew on the misgivings and anxieties which slavery had always engendered, but which had been checked by the desire for independence and wealth. Yet the slave systems of the New World, far from being in decay, had never appeared so prosperous, so secure, or so full of promise.

The emergence of an international antislavery opinion represented a momentous turning point in the evolution of man's moral perception, and thus in man's image of himself. The continuing "evolution" did not spring from transcendent sources: as a historical artifact, it reflected the ideological needs of various groups and classes. The explanation must begin, however, with the heritage of religious, legal, and philosophical tensions associated with slavery—or in other words, with the ways in which Western culture had organized man's experience with lordship and bondage.

From antiquity slavery has embodied symbolic meanings connected with the condition and destiny of man. For the Greeks (as for Saint Augustine and other early Christian theologians) physical bondage was part of the cosmic hierarchy, of the divine scheme for ordering and governing the forces of evil and rebellion. For the ancient Hebrews, slavery could be a divine punishment; a time of trial and self-purification prior to deliverance; and the starting point for a historical mission. The literature of Hellenistic and early Christian times is saturated with the paradoxes of human bondage: man was a slave to sin or to his own passions; his incapacity for virtuous self-government justified his external bondage; yet he might escape his internal slavery by becoming the servant of universal reason—or of the Lord. Emancipation from one form of slavery depended on the acceptance of a higher and more righteous bondage.

If Plato and Aristotle provided an ideology for masters, the Cynics, Sophists, and Stoics provided an ideology for slaves. Externally, the servant might be the instrument of his master's will, but internally, in his own self-consciousness, he remained a free soul. And he could affirm the truth of this subjective reality by denying the importance of the world of flesh and human convention. Physical constraint could never bar a man from true virtue. Hence the master, imagining himself to be free and omnipotent, might well be the true slave—at least in the eyes of the slave.

This transvaluation had profound and enduring consequences when absorbed by Christian theology. The early Church Fathers, living in a slave society, accommodated the institution's contradictions by synthesizing Greek and Hebrew notions of freedom. No human master could usurp God's role and demand absolute and unconditional submission from another man. The only slavery that mattered was slavery to sin, from which no man was exempt. Christianity thus harbored a negative equalitarianism, proclaiming that God was no respecter of persons, that lords and servants were equally subject to His wrath and forgiveness. For masters, paradoxically, a submission to God could mean a lessening dependence on their slaves' acceptance of lordship. Christianity also recognized the grievances and longings of slaves, but sublimated them into another realm of time and space. Any man might become truly free, but only by becoming an unconditional slave to the only true Master. The lowliest slave could look forward to emancipation, but only in another life. In this life, "he that was called in the Lord being a bondservant, is the Lord's freeman: likewise he that was called being free, is Christ's bondservant." Slaves should therefore bear their worldly condition for the glory of God, obeying their masters "with fear and trembling, in a singleness of your heart, as unto Christ." In one sense, the Epistle to the Ephesians gave an ingenious solution to the problem posed by Aristotle: a slave could be virtuous by conforming to his master's will, but only if he served the master "as unto Christ."

The early Christian view of slavery was of central importance in reconciling the masses to the existing social order. It constituted the core of an ideology that encouraged hope, patience, endurance, and submission, while reminding the powerful of their own fallibility. It would be a mistake to think of an immanent Christian equalitarianism that was certain to develop, on the analogy of a seed or root, into an unequivocal denunciation of physical slavery. Christianity represented one means of responding to the contradictions of lordship and bondage, and it wove those contradictions into its fundamental views of man and the world. Thus Saint Thomas Aquinas could affirm that slavery was contrary to the first and highest intent of nature, and yet insist that it conformed to the second intent of nature, which was adjusted to man's limited capacities. He could therefore suggest that slavery was a necessary part of the governing pattern of the universe, speak of the slave as the physical instrument of his owner, and find scholastic justifications for the Roman rule that the child of a free man and bond-woman should be a slave. Neither Luther nor Calvin, one may note, had any notion that Christian liberty could alter the fact that some men are born free and others slaves. Indeed, as a result of the verdict of many centuries, one could not begin to assert the universal sinfulness of slavery without questioning the doctrine of original sin and challenging the entire network of rationalization for every form of subordination.

The first groups to denounce the principle of slavery, and all that it implied, were the perfectionist and millennialist sects who sought to live their lives free from sin. In essence, their ideal involved a form of mutual love and recognition that precluded treating men as objects, even as objects with souls. The sectarians, whatever their distinctive beliefs and practices, looked for a form of authentic service, or selflessness, which could not be used as a lever for exploitation. For us their importance does not lie in the transmission of ideas, but in their attempts to realize a mode of interpersonal life that was the precise antithesis of chattel slavery. To the social order, of course, the sectarians were an intolerable affront. They were thus either annihilated or reduced to spiritualistic withdrawal.

The notable exception was the Society of Friends, which early found the means of compromise and thus survival. The Quakers not only contained and stabilized their quest for a purified life, but institutionalized methods for bearing witness to their faith. In other words, the Quakers achieved a dynamic balance between the impulse to perfection and the "reality principle." They also acquired considerable economic and political power, and were the only sect to become deeply involved with Negro slavery.

At the outset, it appeared that the Quakers would accommodate the contradictions of slavery much as Catholics and Protestants had done before them. By the early eighteenth century there were Quaker planters in the

West Indies and Quaker slave merchants in London, Philadelphia, and New-port. But partly because of the Friends' testimony against war, slaveholding occasioned moral tensions that were less common among other denomina-tions. For critics and deviants within the sect, the wealthy masters and slavetrading merchants presented a flagrant symbol of worldly compromise and an ideal target for attack. For a variety of reasons the Seven Years' War brought a spiritual crisis for the Society of Friends, resulting in much soul-searching, attempts at self-purification, and a final commitment to disen-gage themselves, collectively, from the Atlantic slave system.

The Quakers' growing anguish coincided with four complex and inter-related developments in Western culture, particularly the culture of British Protestantism. First, the emergence of secular social philosophy necessi-tated a redefinition of the place of human bondage in the rational order of being. With the exception of Jean Bodin, the great political theorists of the sixteenth and seventeenth centuries all found justifications for chattel slav-ery. On the other hand, by appealing to utility and social order, and by di-vorcing the subject from theological conceptions of sin, they narrowed the grounds of sanction. Thomas Hobbes, for example, gave his blessings to a form of bondage so absolute that a master could kill his servant with im-punity. But by reducing the relationship to fear, power, and self-interest, Hobbes removed any ethical basis for condemning a successful revolt. He also swept away traditional distinctions based on natural merit and assigned status, and thus undermined both the classical and Christian justifications for unquestioned dominion. Because John Locke celebrated the importance of natural liberty, he had to place slavery outside the social compact, which was designed to protect man's inalienable rights. Locke thus imagined slav-ery as *"the state of War continued, between a lawful Conquerour, and a Captive."* Even by the 1730s such arguments were beginning to appear ab-surd to a generation of English and French writers who had learned from Locke to take an irreverent view of past authority and to subject all ques-tions to the test of reason. It was Montesquieu, more than any other thinker, who put the subject of Negro slavery on the agenda of the European Enlightenment, weighing the institution against the general laws or prin-ciples that promoted human happiness, and encouraging the imaginative experiment of a reversal of roles in a world turned upside down. And by the 1760s the arguments of Montesquieu and Francis Hutcheson were being re-peated, developed, and propagated by the cognoscenti of the enlightened world. John Locke, the great enemy of all absolute and arbitrary power, was the last major philosopher to seek a justification for absolute and perpetual slavery.

A second and closely related transformation was the popularization of an ethic of benevolence, personified in the "man of feeling." This ideal first appeared as an answer to the Calvinist and Hobbesian views of man's incapacity for virtue. The insistence on man's inner goodness, identified with his power of sympathy, became part of a gradual secularizing tendency in British Protestantism, a tendency awkwardly designated as "latitudinarianism." Ultimately, this liberal spirit led in two directions, described by the titles of Adam Smith's two books: *The Theory of Moral Sentiments* and *The Wealth of Nations*. If there were unresolved tensions between sympathetic benevolence and individual enterprise, both theories condemned slavery as an intolerable obstacle to human progress. The man of sensibility needed to objectify his virtue by relieving the sufferings of innocent victims. The economic man required a social order that allowed and morally vindicated the free play of individual self-interest. By definition, the slave was both innocent and a victim, since he could not be held responsible for his own condition. The Negro's enslavement, unlike the legitimate restraints of society, seemed wholly undeserved. He represented innocent nature, and hence corresponded, psychologically, to the natural and spontaneous impulses of the man of feeling. Accordingly, the key to progress lay in the controlled emancipation of innocent nature as found both in the objective slave and in the subjective affections of the reformer. The latter's compassion would evoke compassion in the slave, and the reciprocal love would slowly free the world from corruption and illicit self-seeking. The slave would be lifted to a level of independent action and social obligation. The reformer would be assured of the beneficence of his own self-interest by merging himself in a transcendent cause. These results, at least, were the expectation of philanthropists who increasingly transformed the quest for salvation from a sinful world into a mission to cleanse the world of sin.

A third source of the antislavery impulse was the evangelical faith in instantaneous conversion and demonstrative sanctification. One must hasten to add that many Methodists, Anglican Evangelicals, and American revivalists subscribed to the traditional Christian justifications for human bondage. Leading Anglican Evangelicals, like Bishop Beilby Porteus, came to see the African slave trade as an unmitigated sin but recoiled from condemning any form of servitude so clearly sanctioned by Scripture. Yet the evangelical movement, traditional in overall theology and world view, emphasized man's burden of personal responsibility, dramatized the dangers of moral complacency, and magnified the rewards for an authentic change of heart. And by 1774 John Wesley had not only made it clear that the sins of the world would soon be judged, but that every slaveholder, slave merchant, and investor in slave property was deeply stained with blood and guilt. John Newton, who as a sailor had seen the full horrors of slave ships and West

Indian plantations, could testify that "inattention and interest" had so blinded him to sin that he had never doubted the legitimacy of Negro slavery even after his religious conversion. Newton's decision to denounce slavery as a crime and to confess his former depravity became a model, for his pious admirers, of authentic sanctification.

Evangelical religion also gave a new thrust to the ancient desire to Christianize human bondage by imbuing both master and servant with a spirit of charity and forbearance. It thus led to sincere and continuing efforts to teach slaves the Christian hopes and virtues, and to persuade their owners that neither profits nor security could be endangered by the true faith. Yet by 1770 the Quakers were not alone in concluding that the institution was invulnerable to reform and exempt from the laws of Christian progress. The Negro's cultural difference commonly served as the justification for his enslavement, reinforcing the myth that he had been rescued from heathen darkness and taken to a land of spiritual light. But to be validated, this argument ultimately required religious conversion and an assimilation of slavery to the Christian model of benign and paternalistic service. As John Woolman pointed out, no master was saintly enough to avoid the temptations of absolute power; slavery, instead of being ameliorated by Christianity, corrupted the wellsprings of true religion.

The Negro's cultural difference, which served as an excuse for the failures at Christianization, acquired a positive image at the hands of eighteenth-century primitivists who searched through travel accounts and descriptions of exotic lands for examples of man's inherent virtue and creativity. I can only touch on a few of the complexities of this fourth source of antislavery sentiment. For the most part, the "noble savage" was little more than a literary convention that conflated the Iroquois and South Sea islander with sable Venuses, dusky swains, and tear-bedewed daughters of "injur'd Afric." The convention did, however, modify Europe's arrogant ethnocentrism and provide expression for at least a momentary ambivalence toward the human costs of modern civilization. It also tended to counteract the many fears and prejudices that had long cut the Negro off from the normal mechanisms of sympathy and identification. There is no evidence that literary primitivism made Americans any more inclined to view blacks as autonomous human beings. But for many Europeans, as diverse as John Wesley and the Abbé Raynal, the African was an innocent child of nature whose enslavement in America betrayed the very notion of the New World as a land of natural innocence and new hope for mankind. By the early 1770s such writers portrayed the Negro slave as a man of natural virtue and sensitivity who was at once oppressed by the worst vices of civilization and yet capable of receiving its greatest benefits.

These cultural transformations by no means explain, by themselves, the appearance of organized efforts to rid the world of slavery. The secular Enlightenment, for example, contained countervailing tendencies which encouraged the defense of Negro slavery on grounds of utility, racial inferiority, ethical relativism, or the presumed rationality of wealth-giving institutions. Christianity, for the most part, continued to distinguish worldly subordination from spiritual freedom, although there were increasing strains in the balanced dualisms that gave sanction to hereditary bondage. I have not been concerned, however, with immediate causation but rather with the conditions which weakened the traditional screening mechanisms of Western culture; which removed slavery from the list of supposedly inevitable misfortunes of life; and which made it easier to perceive—in a moral sense—the inherent contradictions of human bondage.

By the eve of the American Revolution there was a remarkable convergence of cultural and intellectual developments which at once undercut traditional rationalizations for slavery and offered new modes of sensibility for identifying with its victims. It is at this point that *The Problem of Slavery in Western Culture* concludes: with a rash of antislavery books, sermons, poems, plays, pamphlets; with the economic reassessments of empire occasioned by the Seven Years' War; with the initiative taken by individual reformers in America, France, and England, whose international communication led to an awareness of shared concerns and expectations. But what were the more material considerations which helped both to shape the new moral consciousness and to define its historical effects? If the growth of antislavery opinion signified a profound cultural change, what difference did it make in the end?

There are two sides to such questions. One could take the institution of slavery for granted and look at the impulses behind the antislavery phenomenon, asking how they reflected, either consciously or unconsciously, the social orders from which they emerged. The new hostility to human bondage cannot be reduced simply to the needs and interests of particular classes. Yet the needs and interests of particular classes had much to do with a given society's receptivity to new ideas and thus to the ideas' historical impact. Much of this book will be concerned with the ideological functions and implications of attacking this symbol of the most extreme subordination, exploitation, and dehumanization, at a time when various enlightened elites were experimenting with internalized moral and cultural controls to establish or preserve their own hegemony.

But one cannot ignore a second aspect, which has to do with the strength or vulnerability of slavery itself. There were many planters in Virginia, Jamaica, and St. Domingue who were open to the spirit of the Enlightenment.

They did not, however, decide to give up their slave property after reading Montesquieu, *The Virginia Gazette*, or *The Weekly Magazine or Edinburgh Amusement*. The question of abolishing slavery was ultimately a question of power. In the broadest outline, one therefore needs to know what the abolitionists were up against, in the more obvious meaning of the pun. The first antislavery movements arose in an era of war, revolution, and rapid economic change. In what ways did these forces undermine or strengthen the slave systems of the New World? In what ways did shifts in economic, political, or military power help to shape the consequences of moral condemnation?

Chapter 2

# The Quaker Ethic and the
# Antislavery International

## The Quaker Initiative

The Quakers, more than any other religious group, had long expressed misgivings over the possible sinfulness of buying and selling men. During the first half of the eighteenth century, however, they had been content to issue cautionary warnings about the African slave trade; to exhort Quaker masters to treat their black servants with Christian charity; and to ignore or disown the few deviants, like Benjamin Lay, who shrilly proclaimed that "all slave-keepers" were "apostates." The Quaker commitment to bear collective testimony against slavery came surprisingly late and coincided with the publication of secular antislavery arguments from jurists, philosophers, moralists, and men of letters.[1] Quaker writers did not play a conspicuous

1. See Davis, *The Problem of Slavery in Western Culture* (Ithaca, N.Y., 1966), chap. 10 and epilogue. My discussion of Quakerism in general draws on William C. Braithwaite, *The Beginnings of Quakerism* (London, 1912); Braithwaite, *The Second Period of Quakerism* (London, 1919); Rufus M. Jones, *The Later Periods of Quakerism* (London, 1921); Thomas Drake, *Quakers and Slavery in America* (New Haven, 1950); Sydney V. James, *A People among Peoples: Quaker Benevolence in Eighteenth-Century America* (Cambridge, Mass., 1963); Richard Bauman, *For the Reputation of Truth: Politics, Religion, and Conflict among the Pennsylvania Quakers, 1750–1800* (Baltimore, 1971); Anne T. Gary, "The Political and Economic Relations of English and American Quakers" (D.Phil. thesis, Oxford University, 1935). Most of these and other secondary accounts give the impression of an immanent unfolding of Quaker antislavery testimony, as if there were an unbroken continuity from George Fox to Anthony Benezet, and as if Quaker leaders simply waited until the time was ripe. There are a number of arguments that cast strong doubt on this view: (1) The Quakers in the West Indies did no more than attempt to Christianize their slaves, and even this aroused fierce resistance and persecution

part in creating this international body of antislavery literature, although Anthony Benezet helped to anthologize and disseminate it. Indeed, it was the emergence of an enlightened climate of opinion, defining liberty as a natural and fundamental right, that brought outside sanction to Quaker reformers like Benezet and John Woolman.[2] But then climates of opinion do

---

(Richard S. Dunn, *Sugar and Slaves: The Rise of the Planter Class in the English West Indies, 1624–1713* [Chapel Hill, N.C., 1972], 104–6, 184, 249, 339). (2) The Quaker-dominated government of colonial Pennsylvania enacted a harsh slave code, and as late as 1730, Quaker merchants in Philadelphia were actively importing and selling West Indian Negroes; as late as the 1760s, the Rhode Island slave trade involved leading Quaker families; some of the most powerful English Friends were members of the Royal African Company (Darold D. Wax, "Quaker Merchants and the Slave Trade in Colonial Pennsylvania," *Pennsylvania Magazine of History and Biography*, 86 [April 1962]: 144–59; Gary, "Political and Economic Relations," 194–97). (3) During the Seven Years' War, when the Quaker leaders of Philadelphia agreed to take active measures to discourage slaveholding among their brethren, the city faced a growing shortage of white indentured servants, a shortage which increased the demand for slaves. Gary B. Nash has estimated that by 1767 Quakers "were somewhat overrepresented among Philadelphia slaveholders in proportion to their numbers" and has concluded that "when faced with a direct choice between forgoing the human labor they needed or ignoring the principles enunciated by their leaders and officially sanctioned by the Society through its Quarterly and Yearly Meetings, the rank and file of Philadelphia Friends chose the latter course." Quaker ideology did not become effective until the supply of white indentured servants increased and the supply of slaves decreased in the years immediately prior to the Revolution (Nash, "Slaves and Slaveholders in Colonial Philadelphia," *William and Mary Quarterly*, 3d ser., 30 [April 1973]: 252–54). (4) The early Quaker doubts over the African trade were not so clear-cut as the earlier doubts of the seventeenth-century Dutch clergy, who advised the Dutch West India Company to keep clear of the slave trade; and in neither case did the doubts prevent involvement (Johannes Postma, "Slaving Techniques and Treatment of Slaves: The Dutch Activities on the Guinea Coast" [paper presented at the M.S.S.B. Conference on Systems of Slavery, University of Rochester, March 1972]). (5) The Moravians' ethical and religious views were similar to those of the Quakers, and the Moravians expressed a similar sensitivity to the possible corruptions of slaveholding; but though the Moravians of North Carolina made attempts at communal supervision of slaveholders, they continued into the nineteenth century to buy and hire slave labor. My point, then, is that the Quakers' decision to disengage themselves from slavery was not an inevitable outgrowth of George Fox's cautious advice in 1657 to treat slaves with Christian mercy and if possible limit their terms of bondage to thirty years.
2. For example, in 1783 and 1784, the *Gentleman's Magazine* reported Lord North's compliments to Quaker humanitarianism; published the epistle of the Yearly Meeting in angry response to an anti-Quaker parody; and printed the American Quaker petition to the Continental Congress (53 [June 1783]: 524; 53 [November 1783]: 919; 54 [February 1784]: 121). Even from Liverpool, John Pemberton reported to his wife on 16 July 1783 that the Quaker petition was generally well spoken of, and he thus felt encouraged over the prospects of further efforts to enlighten the English public (Pemberton papers, 39, Historical Society of Pennsylvania [hereafter HSP]). As early as the 1730s, Voltaire had idealized the "Good Quaker" as a symbol of re-

not give virgin birth to social movements. By the 1780s the British and American Quakers could provide what no other group seemed capable of: decision, commitment, and, most important, organization.

It would be difficult to exaggerate the central role Quakers played in initiating and sustaining the first antislavery movements. During the Seven Years' War, Philadelphia Yearly Meeting moved from the ideal of Christianizing the master-slave relationship to the ideal of preparing slaves for freedom. By 1758 official committees were visiting and prodding individual slaveowners, although a shortage of white servants, occasioned by the war, put a premium on the value of slaves. In 1760, New England Yearly Meeting ruled that the importers of slaves would be subject to discipline. The following year London Yearly Meeting, under some pressure from Philadelphia, took the decisive move of authorizing disownment for Quakers still engaged in the slave trade. In 1774, Philadelphia Yearly Meeting finally adopted rules that threatened disownment for any buying or transfer of slave property, that barred Quakers from serving as executors of estates involving slaves, and that required masters to treat Negroes like other servants and to manumit them at the earliest opportunity.[3]

These efforts at self-reform, especially in Pennsylvania and Delaware, soon involved the Quakers in legal battles to protect slaves who claimed to be free. For example, Israel Pemberton and Thomas Harrison tried to defend an Indian woman and her children who had been brought from Virginia to Philadelphia; because Harrison had given the family shelter, the court forced him to pay heavy damages, for which he was later reimbursed £25 in Anthony Benezet's will. It was this contest that led in 1775 to the formation of the Society for the Relief of Free Negroes Unlawfully Held in Bondage.[4] The Revolutionary War soon disrupted the organization, but early in 1784

---

ligious tolerance, and the legend continued to grow in France, receiving nourishment from some of the physiocrats and especially from Crèvecoeur.
3. In 1757, London Meeting for Sufferings appointed a committee to investigate the problem of Quaker engagement in the slave trade. On 1 February 1759, Philadelphia Meeting for Sufferings took comfort and satisfaction in the warnings from London against dealing in Negroes and other slaves. By 22 August 1766, however, London Meeting for Sufferings had grown more cautious about political involvement in general: "If above all things we make the great work of Religion our chief Concern, every other Circumstance will be so directed, or permitted, as to conduce the most effectually to our real Happiness and Security. . . . If we honestly labour to mind our proper Business and truly study to be quiet, we shall be found in a State both safe and acceptable (MS Letterbook, Friends House, London).
4. W. J. Buck, MS History of the Pennsylvania Abolition Society, Pennsylvania Abolition Society MSS, HSP (this section of the history was based on an earlier MS account by Thomas Harrison).

the reported suicides of two blacks who had been illegally enslaved prompted the restoration of what was to become the Pennsylvania Society, for Promoting the Abolition of Slavery, for the Relief of Free Negroes Unlawfully Held in Bondage, and for Improving the Condition of the African Race. The phrase "abolition of slavery" reflected the new state law of 1780 providing for mandatory gradual emancipation. In New York, where no such law had yet been passed, an organization formed in January 1785 bore the title Society for Promoting the Manumission of Slaves in New York City.[5]

The Pennsylvania Abolition Society served as the model and inspiration for the various state societies which began in 1794 to send representatives to Philadelphia for the annual Convention of Delegates from the Abolition Societies. Prominent non-Quakers, like Benjamin Franklin and Benjamin Rush, served at one time or another as presidents of the Pennsylvania Society. But from the outset it was a predominantly Quaker organization. After selecting sixty-eight of the Society's most active members during its first twenty-five years of existence, I have identified more than three-quarters as Friends. I have also identified as Quakers about one-half of the most active members of the New York Manumission Society. In 1805 seven of the ten officers of the same Society were Friends. Except in Connecticut and Kentucky, Quakers were the chief organizers and most active supporters of the early American antislavery societies. In the North Carolina movement the proportion of Quakers ran as high as 80 percent.[6]

5. The New Jersey Society for Promoting the Abolition of Slavery was formed at Burlington in 1793, at the instigation of the Pennsylvania Society, well before New Jersey had passed a gradual emancipation act (Pennsylvania Abolition Society MSS, 3: 15, HSP; *The Constitution of the New-Jersey Society, for Promoting the Abolition of Slavery* . . . [Burlington, 1793]). On the other hand, the Rhode Island organization was simply the Providence Society for Abolishing the Slave-Trade, and in Connecticut the title was Society for the Promotion of Freedom and the Relief of Persons Unlawfully Holden in Bondage. Anthony Benezet referred to the Negroes' suicides in a letter of 10 August 1783 to James Pemberton (George S. Brookes, *Friend Anthony Benezet* [Philadelphia, 1937], 397).
6. Thomas Drake notes that twelve of the original eighteen members attending the New York Manumission Society were Friends (*Quakers and Slavery*, 98). I have checked the MS membership lists against a large number of directories and genealogical guides. The problem is complicated by the number of Quakers who were disowned or who left the Society as a result of outside marriage or active participation in the war against England. John Michael Shay estimates that 80 percent of the participants in the North Carolina antislavery organizations were from Quaker families ("The Anti-Slavery Movement in North Carolina" [Ph.D. thesis, Princeton University, 1971]). The initiative in Kentucky came from Baptist and Methodist ministers.

In Rhode Island and Connecticut, Quakers were the moving spirit behind antislavery organization. As early as 1784, Moses Brown issued a circular letter, trying

For reasons I shall soon discuss, the American Revolution not only stimulated the antislavery zeal of American Quakers but encouraged them to exert pressure on the British and American governments for the abolition of the slave trade. Even before the war had ended, Philadelphia Meeting for Sufferings, an executive committee concerned with political and legal de-

to win support from the New England Congregationalist clergy, but was deterred by anti-Quaker feeling from organizing a society in Providence. In the same year, Samuel Hopkins, a Congregationalist minister and leading opponent of the slave trade in Newport, said he was pleased by Brown's zeal and perseverance, but confessed that he was "apt to sink under discouragements which you seem easily to surmount." Hopkins anticipated a strong movement to repeal Rhode Island's recent emancipation act, since the towns resented the prospect of maintaining the freeborn children of slaves. Although he hastened to add that his own church had condemned slavery, he feared that present circumstances would prevent Congregationalists from taking effective political action (Friends' Moses Brown pamphlets, MBV Austin, 5, Rhode Island Historical Society [hereafter RIHS]; Samuel Hopkins to Moses Brown, 29 April 1784, Moses Brown papers, 4: 1130, RIHS; *The Works of Samuel Hopkins*, E. A. Park, ed. [Boston, 1853], 1: 119–20; *The Literary Diary of Ezra Stiles*, Franklin B. Dexter, ed. [ New York, 1901], 1: 174; David S. Lovejoy, "Samuel Hopkins: Religion, Slavery, and the Revolution," *New England Quarterly* [June 1967]: 227–43; Mack Thompson, *Moses Brown, Reluctant Reformer* [Chapel Hill, N.C., 1962], *passim*; James F. Reilly, "The Providence Abolition Society," *Rhode Island History*, 21 [April 1962]: 33–48). Hopkins's fears were not unfounded. Peter Ecles, a Newport printer, wrote Moses Brown that while he personally hated slavery, he could not print Hopkins's "Crito" essay without ruining his business and bringing disaster upon himself and his family (Hopkins papers, 6: 1537, RIHS).

Quaker antislavery leaders outside New England, such as James Pemberton of Philadelphia and John Murray, Jr., of New York, encouraged Brown to organize an antislavery society. Brown, in turn, sent Hopkins pamphlets he had received from British Quakers, observing that the English Dissenting clergy were "uniting their Endeavours for the removal of slavery from the British Domineouns [sic] & for the suppression of the African Trade for Slaves." After expressing his wish that the American clergy could unite in a similar effort, he offered to donate $20 toward a prize essay on the evils of slavery, in imitation of the Cambridge University prize won by Thomas Clarkson, to be offered to the students at Yale, Princeton, or Harvard. Brown feared that the officers of the Providence college, Brown, were too involved in the slave trade to consider such a prize (Brown papers, 5: 1300, 1344, RIHS).

By 1788, Brown and Hopkins had succeeded in arousing the Connecticut Congregationalists, whose General Assembly petitioned the state legislature to outlaw the slave trade. Early in 1789, Brown could assure the Philadelphia Quakers that lobbyists were at work in Connecticut and Massachusetts, and that he had helped to organize an abolitionist society in Providence (Friends' Moses Brown pamphlets, MBV Austin 5, RIHS; Moses Brown papers, 6: 1614, 1635, RIHS). [ . . . ] in New Haven [antislavery] organizational activity was weak and short-lived, and [ . . . ] in Providence it depended on continuing Quaker initiative. Elsewhere in New England, the zeal inspired by the Revolution died very early.

Although John Murray of the New York Society proposed the idea of an annual convention of delegates, he also recognized the Philadelphia Society as the unofficial leader of the movement (Pennsylvania Abolition Society MSS, 3: 17–18). The

fense, urged its counterpart body in London to organize efforts against the African trade. As a result of this correspondence, Philadelphia and London Quakers succeeded in coordinating petitions in 1783 both to Parliament and to the Continental Congress. Partly in response to pressure from visiting American Quakers, London Meeting for Sufferings appointed in 1783 a special committee on the slave trade. Some of the members of this committee had already formed an unofficial committee of six to consider steps "for the Relief & Liberation of the Negro Slaves in the West Indies, & for the Discouragement of the Slave Trade on the Coast of Africa." This small public-relations committee soon began collecting and reprinting a wide range of antislavery literature, making arrangements especially to submit regular contributions to the London and provincial press.[7]

Between 1783 and 1787 there were thus two overlapping Quaker abolition committees in London. By 1785 the slave-trade committee of the Meeting for Sufferings had expanded its goals to include gradual emancipation and had pressed its parent body to request detailed information from Philadelphia on the good effects of slave manumission.[8] It was the same com-

---

Pennsylvania Society not only corresponded actively with the societies in London and Paris, but sent letters to the governors of such states as Connecticut and Delaware.

7. MS Minutes, Committee on the Slave Trade, Meeting for Sufferings, 1783–92, Box F, Friends House, London; MS Minutes of informal slave-trade committee, Thompson-Clarkson scrapbook, 2: 9, Friends House. The latter committee consisted of Thomas Knowles, Joseph Woods, Samuel Hoare, Jr., William Dillwyn, John Lloyd, and George Harrison, all of whom became active members of the famous 1787 Abolition Committee. Dillwyn was an American, and the movement within London Meeting for Sufferings was clearly inspired by visiting American ministers, including John Pemberton; by epistles from Philadelphia Meeting for Sufferings; and perhaps most important, by renewed prodding from the aged Anthony Benezet, who prior to the Revolution had urged the leading English Quakers to take decisive action to end the slave trade. Through John Lloyd, the publicity committee submitted weekly antislavery extracts to *Lloyds' Evening Post*; they soon secured access to papers in Liverpool, Cork, Dublin, Bristol, Bath, Norwich, York, Newcastle-upon-Tyne, and numerous other cities and towns.

8. The minute for 30 September 1785 contains the crossed-out words "to promote the overthrow" of slavery and also "to abolish slavery"; but the committee recorded that steps had already been taken "to discourage the practice of keeping slaves" (MS Minutes, Box F, Friends House). London Meeting for Sufferings did request the information from Philadelphia Meeting for Sufferings, but the Philadelphians feared that any evidence they could send on the condition of free blacks might be used against the cause of emancipation (London Meeting for Sufferings to Philadelphia Meeting for Sufferings, 2 December 1785; Philadelphia Meeting for Sufferings to London Meeting for Sufferings, 18 May 1786, MS Letterbook, Friends House). London's request could not have been unrelated to the worsening plight of the London black population, much of it made up of refugees from the American war. In 1786 a non-Quaker Committee for the Relief of the Black Poor succeeded in sending three

mittee which decided on 26 February 1787 that the time had arrived for a renewed application to Parliament for the abolition of the slave trade. Since the sequence of related events highlights the importance of Quaker initiative, I shall briefly summarize the chronology.

In 1774, during his first trip from America to England, William Dillwyn had made the acquaintance of Granville Sharp and other non-Quakers with whom Anthony Benezet had corresponded on the subject of slavery. On 25 April 1783, after Dillwyn had returned to England and several months before he helped organize the two Quaker committees, Sharp answered his request for arguments and new evidence against the slave trade. The two men soon engaged in long conferences and continued to meet during the next few years.[9] In 1784, James Phillips, the Quakers' official printer and a member of the slave-trade committee of the Meeting for Sufferings, published James Ramsay's *An Essay on the Treatment and Conversion of African Slaves in the British West Indies*. Ramsay, an Anglican clergyman who had spent many years in the West Indies, sent Phillips instructions on how to get copies of his book to the king and queen, and continued to suggest names of others who should receive antislavery literature. Meanwhile, Thomas Clarkson, who was eager to publish the essay on the slave trade which had won him a prize at Cambridge in 1785, found his way to Phillips's shop, where he soon met Dillwyn and the other Quaker activists.[10] It was well before 1787, therefore, that the Quaker abolitionists had established cooperative ties with outsiders like Sharp, Ramsay, and Clarkson. On 14 May 1787, after frequent previous meetings, the committee of the Meeting for Sufferings concluded that it was too late in the term to petition Parliament. But in determining to mount a campaign directed at the next session of Parliament, they had apparently decided to broaden the membership of the informal publicity group. For on 19 May, Dillwyn recorded a

---

shiploads of blacks to Sierra Leone (James Walvin, *Black and White: The Negro and English Society, 1555–1945* [London, 1973], chap. 9).

9.  William Dillwyn, MS Diaries, 23 and 27 July 1774; 27 January 1781; 23 May 1783; 21 May 1784, National Library of Wales, Aberystwyth (hereafter NLW); Sharp to Dillwyn, 25 April 1783, British and Foreign Bible Society. In the latter communication, Sharp enclosed material on the shocking *Zong* incident, in which 133 slaves had been thrown overboard after the *Zong's* rations had run low. Dillwyn had been especially interested in having information on Spanish slave regulations and on West Indian laws.

10.  James Ramsay to James Phillips, 12 July 1784; 26 November 1785, Misc. MSS R, New York Historical Society (hereafter NYHS); Dillwyn, MS Diaries, 12 December 1786; 30 March 1787; 3 April 1787, NLW. In 1808, Clarkson said he had conversed with Dillwyn as early as 13 March 1786 (*The History of the Rise, Progress and Accomplishment of the Abolition of the African Slave-Trade by the British Parliament* [London, 1808], 1: 218).

meeting at James Phillips's shop of a committee on the slave trade "now instituted." Two nights later Clarkson met William Wilberforce and other dignitaries at the famous anti-slave-trade dinner at the home of Bennet Langton, a host who moved in London's highest social circles. The next day, 22 May, twelve men met at Phillips's shop and officially organized the Society Instituted in 1787 for Effecting the Abolition of the Slave Trade. Except for Sharp, Clarkson, and Philip Sansom, all were Quakers and all were veterans of the earlier Quaker abolitionist efforts. Five were members of the informal publicity group, and at least four were on the Meeting for Suffering's slave-trade committee.[11]

Quakers always predominated as the most regular attenders and active workers of the nominally non-Quaker Abolition Committee, even after Evangelicals had begun to take over political leadership of the movement. Moreover, Quakers played a leading role in organizing anti-slave-trade societies in most of the provincial cities and towns. It was through Quaker example and Quaker encouragement that figures like Sharp and Clarkson became involved in abolitionist organization; it was the Society of Friends that the Parisian Amis des noirs sought to imitate.

Although Quakers in general shared a similar heritage and subculture, they lived in very different environments, which inevitably affected the outcome of their antislavery views. In the southern states there were severe obstacles that delayed implementation of the sect's emerging policy of self-purification. In the South, even more than in England or in the North, the Quaker governing bodies were anxious to dissociate themselves from any official link with manumission societies or with the antislavery movement as a whole.[12] In the Middle Atlantic states, however, some of the "weighti-

---

11. MS Minutes, Box F, Friends House; Dillwyn, MS Diaries, 19 May 1787, NLW; MS Proceedings of the Committee for the Abolition of the Slave Trade, 1787–1819, 1: 2, British Museum Add. MSS 21254–56 (hereafter Abolition Committee Minutes). Dr. Thomas Knowles, the only member of the original publicity group who was not at the 22 May meeting, soon joined and became an active member of the Abolition Committee. In 1788 the men who really seem to have run the Committee and to have directed Clarkson's evidence-gathering activities were: Dillwyn, John Lloyd, James Phillips, Richard Phillips (James's cousin and a soliciter at Lincoln's Inn), Dr. Thomas Knowles, Samuel Hoare, Jr., Joseph Woods, and George Harrison. Late in 1786, George Dillwyn candidly informed Moses Brown that the British clergy were not sufficiently united against the slave trade, and observed that the Quakers had superior advantages over the Dissenting clergy with respect to unpopular movements (George Dillwyn to Moses Brown, 29 November 1786, Friends' Moses Brown pamphlets, MBV Austin 5 and MBV Austin 12, RIHS).
12. Shay, "Antislavery Movement in North Carolina," 431–32; Stephen B. Weeks, *Southern Quakers and Slavery* (Baltimore, 1896), *passim*.

est'' religious leaders were among the minority of reformers who wished to go beyond the Society's official stand.

Pennsylvania Friends were of course the heirs of William Penn's Holy Experiment; they could draw on traditions of leadership and power. It is true that the immigration of non-Quakers had slowly undermined their political dominance, and that the Seven Years' War had forced many conscientious Quakers to withdraw from the colonial legislature. The American Revolution, coming so soon after the war with France, reinforced popular suspicion that the pacifist Quakers were loyalist sympathizers if not outright traitors. Yet as Sydney V. James has perceptively shown, the Pennsylvania Quakers did not abandon their traditions of social leadership as a result of persecution and lessening political power. On the contrary, they took the lead in a variety of benevolent causes, including antislavery, partly as a means of reasserting their influence, of vindicating their reputation, and of restoring cooperative ties with revolutionary patriots like Franklin and Rush. Social reform helped to give Quakers the sense of being ''a people among peoples,'' and thus a part of the sovereign people. Even when fearing and disapproving violence, American Quakers could appeal to the principles of natural rights or to the Declaration of Independence. When Quaker merchants called for an end to the slave trade, they were in effect supporting colonial grievances against British imperial policy.[13] For their English brethren, the same move not only implied a challenge to an institution sanctioned by church and state, but had to be addressed to a traditional order that denied them political rights.

There is evidence that antislavery activity brought American Quakers into sharp conflict with rival ethnic groups, such as the Germans in Pennsylvania and the Dutch in New York.[14] Yet it also served to rehabilitate former leaders like James Pemberton. Pemberton was a Quaker merchant who belonged to one of Philadelphia's wealthiest and most powerful families. He

13. James, *A People among Peoples*, 193–213, 240–58, 282–83, and *passim*; Benezet to Robert Pleasants, 8 April 1773; Benjamin Franklin to Benezet, 22 August 1772, in Brookes, *Friend Anthony Benezet*, 298–302, 422; Philadelphia Meeting for Sufferings to London Meeting for Sufferings, 22 April 1773, MS Letterbook, Friends House; Richard K. MacMaster, ''Arthur Lee's 'Address on Slavery': An Aspect of Virginia's Struggle to End the Slave Trade, 1765–1774,'' *Virginia Magazine*, 80 (April 1972): 141–53.
14. Owen S. Ireland, ''Germans against Abolition: A Minority's View of Slavery in Revolutionary Pennsylvania,'' *Journal of Interdisciplinary History*, 3 (Spring 1973): 685–706. The Germans were not, for the most part, slaveholders. Ireland suggests that their political opposition to emancipation sprang from ethnic rivalry, from uncertain identity, and from a deep and possibly unconscious fear of further radical social change.

was also one of the Quakers who had resigned from the Assembly during the Seven Years' War. After returning to the legislature during the brief interim of peace, Pemberton was arrested during the Revolution as a security risk and sent, along with nineteen other Friends, to Virginia for detention. After the war, however, Pemberton regained prestige as an antislavery leader. He was one of the principal founders of the Pennsylvania Abolition Society, over which he presided in place of the nominal chairman, Benjamin Franklin. He then succeeded Franklin as the Society's president, and was succeeded himself by the illustrious Rush.[15]

Unlike their brethren in Pennsylvania, English Quakers had always been outsiders. As Dissenters they were excluded from public office and from the universities. The professions were virtually closed to them, and they were barred by religious scruples from many other employments that could have been sources of influence and power. On the other hand, they had achieved a pragmatic accommodation with the British political order and were acutely sensitive to any public actions which might rekindle prejudice or jeopardize their informal mechanisms of influence. Thus David Barclay, whose wealthy and eminent family had entertained the king, sent an angry letter to James Pemberton in 1783, complaining of the impetuosity of the American *"Reformers"* who had recently arrived in England and who had agitated the slave-trade question at London Yearly Meeting. The Americans had presumed to tell Barclay that he should not quote William Penn because Penn "had dealt or approved the dealing in slaves!" Even worse, they had pressed the English Quakers to address the king "to *use his influence* with his Parliament to discountenance that trade," a move not only highly improper but self-defeating. Barclay, who said he spoke for "some of our most weighty valuable Friends," told the American leader that he hoped "Friends will be wise enough to submit with propriety to the powers placed over them or that such as do not approve thereof will leave the country!"[16]

Barclay had actually deflected the move to petition the king and had persuaded London Yearly Meeting of the propriety of sending a delegation to Parliament, which was about to consider a measure prohibiting servants of the African Company from engaging in the slave trade "to the detriment of their masters." As a result of Barclay's strategy, Lord North and Lord John Cavendish courteously received the Quaker delegation; Sir Cecil Wray praised Quaker benevolence when he introduced in the Commons their pe-

15. Janet Whitney, *John Woolman: American Quaker* (Boston, 1942), 36; John Woolman, *The Journal and Essays of John Woolman*, Amelia Mott Gummere, ed. (New York, 1922), 513.
16. MS Minutes, London Yearly Meeting, 17 (16 June 1783): 298–307, Friends House; David Barclay to James Pemberton, 2 July 1783, Pemberton papers, 39, HSP.

tition to end the slave trade; and though Parliament tabled the proposal, since it went so far beyond the measure before them, the Quakers received favorable publicity in the public press. It was this occasion that prompted both London Yearly Meeting and Meeting for Sufferings to give official approval to a pamphlet drafted by William Dillwyn and John Lloyd, *The Case of Our Fellow Creatures, the Oppressed Africans, Respectfully Recommended to the Serious Consideration of the Legislature of Great-Britain, by the People Called Quakers.* The slave-trade committee of the Meeting for Sufferings succeeded in getting copies to the king, the queen, the secretaries of state, and then to M.P.'s. Following this achievement, the slave-trade committee printed more than ten thousand copies and devised an elaborate plan for personal distribution to virtually every institution, office holder, and influential man in the realm. By 1786 it was not accidental that the Quaker testimony was commonplace knowledge in Great Britain, or that a pamphlet by Benezet should be readily accessible to anyone who cared to read it.[17]

The availability of such channels and media of persuasion was only one of the circumstances that differentiated British and American Quakers. English Quakers had been mainly concerned with freeing their expanding commercial enterprises from any direct involvement with the slave trade, especially since so much Quaker capital had been invested in colonial commerce. London Yearly Meeting exhorted the various colonial meetings to "clean" themselves from the unrighteous practice of keeping bondsmen, but few English Friends had had any direct experience with slaveholding. Thus when David Barclay discovered that he and his brother had acquired thirty-two Jamaican slaves as payment for a debt, he was ultimately forced

---

17. Barclay to Pemberton, 2 July 1783, Pemberton papers, 39, HSP; MS Minutes, 26 September 1783; 14 May 1784; 23 July 1784, Box F, Friends House; London Meeting for Sufferings, MS Minutes, 37 (18 June 1784): 65; Clarkson, *History*, 1: 121; *Gentleman's Magazine*, 53 (November 1783): 919; Russell S. Mortimer, "Quaker Printers, 1750–1850," *Journal of the Friends' Historical Society*, 50 (1963): 103–6. According to Patrick Cleburne Lipscomb, the London Quakers not only retained a standing committee to review Parliamentary legislation, but regularly paid doorkeepers at both Houses of Parliament to distribute Quaker propaganda ("William Pitt and the Abolition of the Slave Trade" [Ph.D. thesis, University of Texas, 1960], 74–76). Dillwyn indicated that the Quakers had qualms over printing certain antislavery material that contained ideas to which they could not subscribe (Dillwyn to John Pemberton, 6 December 1783, Pemberton papers, 40, HSP). Yet there can be no question that the Quakers' dissemination of antislavery literature had tremendous impact; by 1787 the slave trade had become a lively issue for a considerable segment of the English reading public, and an audience had been prepared for the 51,432 copies of books and pamphlets and the 26,526 briefer reports that the Abolition Committee would print by mid-July 1788 (Clarkson, *History*, 1: 571).

to rely on the assistance of James Pemberton and the Philadelphia Quakers. His own Jamaican agent refused to emancipate the blacks in Jamaica, because the example would be "unpopular in the island." Barclay finally had to send another agent to Jamaica, who with some difficulty persuaded the blacks to embark with him to Philadelphia, where they were apprenticed under the supervision of the Abolition Society, after a committee had decided "what they are fit for."[18]

If the British Quakers were attuned to publicity campaigns and to the subtle means of reaching men of power, they were unfamiliar with the problems of committees appointed to "free Negroes unlawfully held in bondage," or for "improving the condition of free blacks." In the North, at least, American Quakers acquired their main knowledge of slavery through experience with domestic servitude and through their commercial activities in port cities like Philadelphia, New York, and Newport. Understandably, their main antislavery interests focused on stopping the further importation of Negroes, on removing legal obstacles to private manumission, on preventing the re-enslavement of free blacks, and on providing education, apprenticeship, and old age assistance for the objects of their benevolence. Far more than their English brethren, the Americans understood the extent and depth of racial prejudice, as well as the painful complexities of converting domestic servants into free men. They tended to assume, however, that their English correspondents, being free of such obstacles and being closer to the centers of imperial power, could take the leadership in eradicating the Atlantic slave system.[19]

18. London Yearly Meeting, Epistles Sent, 1 (1774–90): 1, 9, 95, 321–22, Friends House; David Barclay, *An Account of the Emancipation of the Slaves of Unity Valley Pen, in Jamaica*, 2d edn. (London, 1801). In the latter work a chart (pp. 13–14) shows that children from four to seven were bound to masters who took no black adults. Caesar, age six, was bound for fifteen years but immediately died and was buried in the potter's field. Several of the blacks were said to be very grateful to the Quakers, although they complained of the cold.
19. Philadelphia Meeting for Sufferings to London Meeting for Sufferings, 18 May 1786, MS Letterbook, Friends House; Benezet to William Dillwyn, 20 August 1783, Misc. MSS, B, NYHS. Of course, many Philadelphia Quakers had seen plantation slavery in the Deep South (John F. Watson, *Annals of Philadelphia and Pennsylvania, in the Olden Time* [Philadelphia, 1845], 1: 595–96). We have already noted that Quakers who remained in the West Indies had difficulty even in giving their slaves religious instruction. Dr. John Coakley Lettsom, a native of Tortola, rendered medical service to hundreds of slaves, but finally emigrated to England. In 1791 and 1792, Richard Nisbet wrote rather plaintive letters to James Pemberton from St. Kitts and Nevis expressing a wish to join the Quakers, since of all religions they most closely approximated the primitive Christian church. Yet Nisbet insisted that Christianity did not forbid slaveholding. He professed an abhorrence for the African trade, but thought that the relatively mild servitude in the West Indies was the only "means of improvement & happiness." He assured Pemberton that he was trying to

Despite the diversity of Quaker experience and the lack of a central ecclesiastical authority, the Society of Friends maintained unity by a communications network unparalleled in the eighteenth century. This achievement was partly the cause and partly the result of the incredible commercial success of enterprising Quakers. The network's growth had also been encouraged by persecution, which had led not only to transatlantic migration, but to institutions for communal discipline and mutual aid. Above all, the communications network drew strength from the Quaker ethic, which gave its adherents the confident sense of being members of an extended family whose business and personal affairs were united in a seamless sphere. The decisions of London Yearly Meeting radiated outward through an intricate structure of regional Yearly, Quarterly, Monthly, and local meetings, affecting the personal and economic lives of Friends from North Carolina to Ireland.

A word about the nature and scope of the Quaker communication system reveals some of the social implications of the Quaker antislavery initiative. Although Friends relied heavily on informal correspondence and on official epistles between the various meetings, it was the traveling ministry that brought distant congregations into living fellowship. By gently rebuking the families they visited for retaining Negro slaves or for displaying worldly vanities, the itinerants also helped to define as well as to apply the consensual values of the Society. Theoretically, any Friend of either sex might feel called to a traveling mission and receive the assent of the appropriate meetings. In practice, however, traveling ministers won recognition only if they could serve as models of authentic religious purity, proving themselves "acceptable" to the various congregations they visited. Though far lesser known than the Wesleys and Whitefields, they were a powerful arm of the international Great Awakening.

The eighteenth-century Quaker revival had two overlapping phases. Many of the early traveling ministers were imbued with a quietistic yearning for self-effacement. Often inclined toward mysticism, they developed spiritual exercises to cleanse themselves of every taint of worldliness. Both in England and America, the quietists' appeal for absolute purity and selflessness struck the consciences of Friends who were dismayed by bloody Indian wars on the American frontier or by their own indirect complicity in the wars with France. John Churchman, for example, saw the Indian raids on the Pennsylvania frontier as a sign of divine disapproval for slaveholding. Churchman, a saintly American quietist, was the mentor and friend of John

give religious instruction to his own slaves (Nisbet to Pemberton, 1 August 1791; 30 May 1792, Misc. MSS, N, NYHS).

Woolman. At times Churchman joined Woolman in visiting and expostulating with Quaker slaveholders. And in a sense, Woolman's continuing and lonely crusade against slavery was an objectification of the older minister's spiritual quest for purity.[20]

The second phase of Quaker revivalism came closer to the evangelicalism of the major Protestant denominations, and coincided with Quaker efforts to enlist outsiders in various benevolent causes. Like Anglican and Methodist evangelicals, the younger Quakers stressed the sinfulness of natural man and the mercies of Christ the Redeemer. Among the leading Quaker preachers of this Christ-centered faith was Rebecca Jones, a convert from Philadelphia's Anglican church. A close friend of Benezet, the Pembertons, and the Dillwyns, Rebecca Jones achieved various triumphs on a mission to England, not the least of which was the conversion of young William Allen to a life of "serious" religion. Later on, in the early nineteenth century, Allen's serious interest in religion led him to work closely with British diplomats on the international suppression of the slave trade, and to confer personally on that subject with Emperor Alexander I of Russia.[21]

Rebecca Jones's most noted co-worker was her fellow Philadelphian William Savery, who converted both Isaac Hopper and Elizabeth Gurney (later Fry) to serious religion, thereby channeling the former toward a life of abolitionism and the latter toward worldwide fame as a prison reformer. Savery even tried to bring off the *coup* of the century by laboring in France to persuade Thomas Paine, the Great Infidel himself, to return to his parental faith.[22]

The distinction between quietistic and evangelical ministers, however, is less important than the role both played as catalysts of antislavery commitment. It is true that the journals of the great itinerants are almost wholly preoccupied with religion. Yet there can be no question that virtually all the early Quaker antislavery leaders were profoundly influenced by the same traveling ministers. Woolman and Churchman, for example, were intimate

20. For expressions of Benezet's quietistic yearnings, see Brookes, *Friend Anthony Benezet*, 210, 222–23.
21. *Memorials of Rebecca Jones*, William J. Allinson, comp. (London, n.d.); Jones, *Later Periods, passim*. I have mentioned only a few of the influential traveling ministers; Thomas Shillitoe, Stephen Grellet, Mary Dudley, and several others were part of the same movement.
22. Jones, *Later Periods*, 1: 280. Benjamin Rush, who cooperated with Benezet and other Quaker abolitionists in Philadelphia, met Paine in 1775 and was much pleased that Paine's first published work was an attack on slavery. Antislavery, coupled with a defense of the colonists' rights, served to unite the two men; but Rush was later much put off by Paine's *Age of Reason* (*Letters of Benjamin Rush*, L. H. Butterfield, ed. [Princeton, 1951], 2: 1007, 1009; *The Autobiography of Benjamin Rush . . .* , George W. Corner, ed. [Princeton, 1948], 113–14).

with the Pemberton brothers, Israel, James, and John, whose family not only owned slaves but had amassed a fortune from the West India trade and from the sale in Europe of slave-produced sugar, rum, tobacco, and rice. Notwithstanding their worldly interests, the Pembertons became deeply moved by the spirit of the revival. Partly at the instigation of Samuel Fothergill, a visiting English minister, they threw their powerful support behind the Quaker withdrawal, in 1756, from the Pennsylvania Assembly. They helped to create and manage Philadelphia Meeting for Sufferings. And while the Pembertons continued to draw wealth from the produce of West Indian slaves, they freed their own Negroes and became leaders in a variety of philanthropic activities. It was on a Pemberton ship that Woolman planned to sail to the West Indies in 1769 to preach against slavery.[23]

Meanwhile, in the early 1750s John Churchman had persuaded young John Pemberton to give up business for a religious life. For three years the two men traveled together through Britain and the Continent, struggling against Quaker declensions in faith. John Pemberton's strictures against card playing and violations of the Sabbath anticipated the mood of evangelical "puritanism." He was so shocked by the visibility of English drunkards, whores, and "profane swearers" that he thought divine punishment must be at hand. For ministers like Pemberton, involvement with slavery was simply one of many worldly sins; and "queries" about slavery could be taken as a prime test of how "clear" Quakers were of contamination. When Woolman himself finally arrived in England twenty years later, he expressed astonishment that many Friends were still indirectly connected with the African trade, a fact he interpreted as the prime symbol of their worldliness and degeneracy.[24]

The mainspring of the Quaker revival lay in such transatlantic lines of influence and personal acquaintance. As the highest official in Philadelphia Meeting for Sufferings, John Pemberton could put considerable weight behind the coordination of antislavery activity. Through commercial as well as religious correspondence, he and his brother James were close to Quaker planters like Robert Pleasants and to Quaker merchants like Moses Brown, the leader of the antislavery cause in Rhode Island. Beginning in 1770 the Pembertons aided and spread news about Benezet's school for Negro children. Even before the American Revolution ended, John Pemberton sailed again for England, where he joined his cousin William Dillwyn in urging

23. Gummere, introduction to *Journal and Essays of John Woolman*, 110; Theodore Thayer, *Israel Pemberton, King of the Quakers* (Philadelphia, 1943), *passim*; Pemberton papers, *passim*, HSP.
24. John Pemberton, MS Journal, 1 June 1752–27 November 1752, Pemberton papers, HSP; *Journal and Essays of John Woolman*, 307–8.

London Meeting for Sufferings to take action against the slave trade. When Rebecca Jones arrived in London in 1784, she was delighted to encounter six American Quaker ministers, in addition to Pemberton, most of whom were actively engaged in the antislavery cause.[25]

The revival moved both ways across the Atlantic. In 1755, two years before Woolman's most famous mission through the South, Israel Pemberton and Samuel Fothergill had traveled the same route, quietly preaching against slavery. A leader of the revival in England, Fothergill also quickened the move for self-purification among Philadelphia Friends. Upon returning to England, he helped to indoctrinate future English abolitionists like George Harrison and the Gurneys of Norwich. It was Samuel's brother John, an internationally renowned physician, who welcomed John Woolman to England. A member of London Meeting for Sufferings, Dr. Fothergill moved in the highest circles of enlightened culture. He was a close friend of Benjamin Franklin and a Licentiate of the Royal College of Physicians (though excluded, as a Quaker, from being a Fellow). Dr. Fothergill's interests ranged from projects for prison reform to a plan for colonizing emancipated Negroes in Africa, a plan for which he said he would contribute £10,000. A correspondent of Benezet's, he also had a link through Joseph Priestley, whom he aided with money and apparatus, with the Nonconformist radicals of the Birmingham Lunar Society. It is tempting, therefore, to see a stream of antislavery influence running from the Quaker revival through Fothergill to men like Priestley, Richard Price, Thomas Day, and Josiah Wedgwood, who laid the foundations for a more secular and radical abolitionism in Birmingham and Manchester. One can speak with more confidence about Fothergill's influence on younger Quaker physicians like Thomas Knowles, Joseph Hooper, John Coakley Lettsom, and George Vaux, all of whom became involved in the British antislavery movement. Although Quaker physicians were few in number, since they could seek degrees only in Scotland or on the Continent, they gave representation, in the ranks of British aboli-

25. James Pemberton to Robert Pleasants, 14 August 1788; 16 November 1789; 20 April 1790, Brock collection, Henry E. Huntington Library (hereafter HEH); Moses Brown to James Pemberton, 14 September 1781; 20 March 1784, Pemberton papers, 36, 40, HSP; James, *A People among Peoples*, 235–37; *Memorials of Rebecca Jones*, 65. On 20 August 1783, Benezet wrote Dillwyn about the plight of Philadelphia's blacks and the need for funds to give them legal protection against being unlawfully enslaved. He reminded Dillwyn of the large unappropriated fund that Quakers had raised in England and Ireland for the relief of their American brethren during the war (Brookes, *Friend Anthony Benezet*, 382–83). Dillwyn wrote John Pemberton on 7 June 1784 that the London Quakers had agreed to send some of the money to Philadelphia (he wished that the amount had been doubled), but had not yet decided whether it should be for Benezet's plan or for the Negro school (Pemberton papers, 41, HSP). In 1787, David Barclay sent the sum of £500 for the school.

tionists, to a profession that seems generally to have been indifferent or hostile to reform.[26]

The traveling ministers prepared the way by exhorting influential Friends to cast off worldly contaminations, which included ties with slavery. The transatlantic connections provided a framework for coordinated action. The deepening imperial crisis, however, precipitated the first Quaker efforts to shift from internal reform to a program for changing the course of history. In the years immediately following the Stamp Act crisis, American Quakers sought to use the leverage of their English connections as a means of modifying British imperial policy. There were mixed motives behind the colonial attempts to tax or prohibit the importation of slaves. But for American Quakers like Benezet and Robert Pleasants, the actions of the Virginia General Assembly—coupled with Arthur Lee's much-quoted "Address on Slavery"—could be used to show that the colonial cause was not only sincere but embodied the noblest principles of an enlightened age. The Americans exhorted the more influential British Friends to use the slave-trade issue as an instrument of reconciliation. In 1773, after considerable prodding from the Americans, David Barclay led a delegation to visit the Lord of Trade in futile support of Virginia's attempts to levy a prohibitive tax on imported Africans. By then, British Friends recognized that a political breach with the colonies would pose grave threats to business as well as to religion.[27]

Between English and American Quakers there was a subtle competition in registering antislavery influence. Writing soon after the Somerset decision had removed any legal basis for slavery in England, London Yearly

26. James, *A People among Peoples*, 137; Arthur Raistrick, *Quakers in Science and Industry: Being an Account of the Quaker Contributions to Science and Industry during the 17th and 18th Centuries* (London, 1950), 264, 278, 292, 295–99. On 13 October 1788, Granville Sharp gave John Coakley Lettsom a report on the new settlement at Sierra Leone, saying that he shared the opinion Dr. William Thornton had adopted from the late Dr. Fothergill: namely, that establishing a free settlement on the coast of Africa would be the most effectual way to destroy the slave trade. Thornton, a Quaker physician and associate of Fothergill and Lettsom, had emigrated to Philadelphia, where he had begun to promote the cause of Negro colonization (Sharp to Lettsom, N147, HEH).
27. Philadelphia Meeting for Sufferings to London Meeting for Sufferings, 21 November 1777, MS Letterbook, Friends House; Gary, "Political and Economic Relations," 221–22; MacMaster, "Arthur Lee's 'Address on Slavery,' " 143–53. Lee's "Address," which appeared in the *Virginia Gazette* in 1767, was later widely publicized by Robert Pleasants and Benezet; but when Benezet reprinted it, he removed the strongest passages, which warned that the slaves might with justice rise in mass insurrection. One should add that Benezet's letters to Granville Sharp from 1772 to 1774 gave a candid and realistic assessment of the self-interested motives behind Maryland and Virginia's opposition to the slave trade.

Meeting rejoiced in the growing testimony against slavery in America but expressed a rather paternalistic hope that the colonies would work harder at enacting laws that discouraged the institution. In 1782, Philadelphia Meeting for Sufferings proudly cited Virginia's law allowing private manumissions as a sign that "through the favour of divine Providence the Light of Truth hath evidently broken forth in many places amongst those whom temporal Considerations, and long accustomed prejudices have held in obdurate blindness." Yet British authority still supported the "Crying Enormity" of the slave trade (as well as the war against America). The Philadelphians hoped that "divine Wisdom will be afforded to qualify you as Instruments in the hand of the Lord . . . to the gradual Extirpation" of the slave trade. In reply, London Meeting for Sufferings promised to put Philadelphia's request before the Yearly Meeting, but warned of the great opposition that could be expected from "interested parties" in the government. Philadelphia then responded, perhaps with intentional irony, that if the "temper of humanity" was gradually prevailing among British statesmen—as the London Quakers had claimed in a letter of 1773—then there should be grounds for hope, notwithstanding the power of interested parties. With the end of hostilities, the Philadelphia Quakers actually shifted their major hopes to the personal influence of Americans like William Dillwyn and John Pemberton, who had arrived in England. As James Pemberton pointed out to his brother, John, the Americans were more familiar with slavery than were their English brethren; they could obviate the objections which timidity or "ill-founded fears" might suggest. Some of the English leaders were annoyed by the Americans' rashness and disregard for political proprieties, but through the 1780s the British and American Quakers continued to spur each other on, proudly reporting their antislavery gains on both sides of the Atlantic.[28]

28. London Meeting for Sufferings to Philadelphia Meeting for Sufferings, 2 October 1772; 4 April 1783; 5 December 1783; 28 January 1785; 3 November 1787; 28 February 1788; Philadelphia to London, 21 November 1777; 15 August 1782; 17 July 1783; 19 August 1784; 2 December 1785; 18 October 1787, MS Letterbook, Friends House; London Yearly Meeting, Epistles Sent, 5 (1774–90): 1, 9, 95, 321–22; London Yearly Meeting, Epistles Received, 5 (1788–1801): 234, 272–73, 317–18, Friends House; James Pemberton to John Pemberton, 19 July 1783; to Daniel Mildred, July 1783, Pemberton papers, 39 HSP. The Philadelphia Quakers were extremely reluctant to send London detailed information on the condition of emancipated blacks, arguing that the cause of emancipation must be defended on its own grounds, not on a possibly misleading study of the consequences. When London Meeting for Sufferings finally received the information they sought, early in 1788, they rejoiced over the progress made by certain free blacks, and indicated that the heart-warming stories sent from Philadelphia had resolved various doubts.

## The Solvent of Wealth

Few accounts of early Quaker abolitionists give any indication of their most conspicuous characteristic, which was, quite simply, their incredible economic success. Although it is generally acknowledged that Quakers epitomized the "Protestant ethic," the central role they played in eighteenth-century commerce, banking, and industry is seldom appreciated. Cut off from traditional sources of wealth and power, the English Friends searched for new opportunities in "innocent" trades. To a variety of small-scale enterprises, ranging from pottery and china to iron production, they brought a seriousness of purpose, a discipline of mind, and a compelling commitment to "useful" work. They were natural innovators, fascinated by the possibility of "useful improvements." Their sectarian exclusiveness, resulting in an intricate web of intermarriages, linked one successful enterprise with many others. By the second half of the eighteenth century the English Quakers had established themselves as the founders and managers of great firms manufacturing porcelain, clocks, instruments, drugs, and china; they were leaders in mining, particularly of lead, and in the production of brass, zinc, copper, and other metals. According to Paul Mantoux, the history of three generations of the great Quaker Darby dynasty "sums up that of the whole English metalworking industry." Nor was it accidental that the names of two great Quaker families, the Lloyds and the Barclays, should ultimately come to designate two of the world's greatest banks. The very embodiment of the capitalist mentality, the English Quakers were in the vanguard of the industrial revolution.[29]

One gets some sense of the linkage of Quaker interests from the diaries of William Dillwyn, whom Thomas Clarkson praised as the chief organizer of the British antislavery movement. Born in Philadelphia in 1738, Dillwyn was a pupil of Anthony Benezet and then a merchant associated with the Pembertons. In 1773 he wrote his cousin James Pemberton from Charleston, reporting his success in exchanging West Indian rum for Carolina rice; in the same year he published a cautious and anonymous pamphlet suggesting the "expediency" of gradual emancipation, and also joined a Quaker delegation petitioning the New Jersey Assembly for a more liberal law regu-

29. Raistrick, *Quakers in Science and Industry, passim*; Paul H. Emden, *Quakers in Commerce: A Record of Business Accomplishment* (London, n.d.), *passim*; Isabel Grubb, *Quakerism in Industry before 1800* (London, 1930), *passim*; Frederick B. Tolles, *Meeting House and Counting House: The Quaker Merchants of Colonial Philadelphia, 1682–1763* (Chapel Hill, N.C., 1948), *passim*; Paul Mantoux, *The Industrial Revolution in the Eighteenth Century*, rev. ed., Marjorie Vernon, trans. (New York, 1929), 307.

lating slave manumissions. In 1774, Dillwyn sailed for England, carrying with him letters from Benezet to a variety of people, including Granville Sharp and John Wesley. Soon after arriving, Dillwyn called upon Sharp, Benjamin Franklin, the Fothergills, and Samuel Hoare. The latter, a wealthy Quaker merchant, had recently formed a banking firm that would eventually merge, as a result of intermarriages, with the Gurney and Barclay banking houses, forming the nucleus of Barclays Bank. Dillwyn went with John Gurney and George Harrison to drink tea at David Barclay's, where he also met Joseph Bevan and John and Ambrose Lloyd. John Gurney was the co-founder of the famous Gurney bank at Norwich; Harrison was a barrister-at-law; Bevan was a leading drug manufacturer; and the Lloyds, who had family connections with the Pembertons, had already expanded from their Birmingham iron and metal trades into banking and industry. Samuel Darby, of the great iron family, took Dillwyn on a tour of the Liverpool docks. In the same city he visited William Rathbone, a rich timber merchant and later a Quaker abolitionist.[30]

It was Manchester, however, that seems to have excited Dillwyn the most. In that "thriving populous Town" he inspected the warehouses filled with domestic manufactures, and spent hours marveling at the linens, cottons, velvets, fustians, hats, and threads. In Birmingham, he dined with Sampson Lloyd, who has been called the true father of Lloyds Bank, and then toured "Taylor's famous Beltt Manufacturies where abundance of Women are employed." He described the pump machinery used to draw water from Quaker-owned lead mines, and in Dorset he viewed

> the curious Silk Mill for winding raw silk in and about which [I] was informed near 300 Persons were constantly employed but many of them are young Children who watch the winding of the silk of the Reels and twisting it. The Machinery is admirable and consists of many thousand wheels of different sizes.[31]

As Dillwyn continued to make notes on British industry and on his business meetings with leading entrepreneurs, he also grew increasingly gloomy over the news that "a bad Ministry is resolving to enslave my Country." He attended meetings of merchants who were angered by British policy and by Parliament's refusal to heed their petitions. After a seventeen-month stay in England, Dillwyn received a certificate from London, ad-

30. Dillwyn to James Pemberton, 27 January 1773; 10 July 1774, Pemberton papers, 24, 26, HSP; Sharp to Dillwyn, 25 July 1774, British and Foreign Bible Society; Dillwyn, MS Diaries, NLW. Here and elsewhere I have drawn on the invaluable MS Dictionary of Quaker Biography at Friends House, and on the Emlen-Dillwyn papers, Library Company of Philadelphia (hereafter LCP).
31. Dillwyn, MS Diaries, October and November 1774, NLW.

dressed to his own Monthly Meeting in West Jersey, attesting to his good conduct while abroad. When he departed for America in 1775 he was on intimate terms with the men who would launch the British antislavery movement: Joseph Woods, Thomas Knowles, John Lloyd, George Harrison, Samuel Hoare, Jr., Joseph Gurney Bevan, Philip Sansom, and Granville Sharp. He had also met the families that would found some of England's greatest industries, banks, railroads, and insurance companies. When Dillwyn returned to England for good, in 1781, he called on Sharp to discuss the slave trade; having married Sarah Weston, a wealthy heiress, he also joined the firm of Weston, James & Dillwyn. He later bought the Cambrian pottery works at Swansea, which produced china of international fame.[32]

The family connections between Quaker business and reform were extraordinarily complex. One of the centers of early British antislavery activity was the home of Joseph Gurney Bevan, at Plough Court, London. As apothecaries and chemists, the Bevans had built up a prosperous pharmaceutical concern at Plough Court (through Dr. John Fothergill, they won the contract to supply Pennsylvania Hospital). By the 1780s the firm had grown sufficiently to allow Joseph Gurney Bevan the leisure to dabble at poetry, to write a refutation of "the misrepresentations of the Quakers," and to devote considerable time to the Quaker slave-trade committee and then to the London Abolition Society. When Rebecca Jones visited the Bevan home, she was welcomed by Bevan's close friend, William Dillwyn, whom she found living "elegantly." Bevan was also an intimate friend of the Quakers' official publisher and bookseller, James Phillips. On Lombard Street, close to David Barclay's house and to such Quaker banking firms as Hanbury, Taylor, Lloyd and Bowman, Phillips printed the thousands of antislavery pamphlets authorized by the Quaker committee and the later Abolition Society.[33]

The Bevans were related by marriage to both the Barclays and the Gurneys. Joseph Gurney Bevan was a cousin of Elizabeth Gurney Fry; his half-brother was a banking partner of the Barclays. His own production of drugs and chemicals soon led into the chemistry of brewing. In 1781 a Bevan and a Barclay bought the Anchor Brewery for £30,000 and, with help from members of the Gurney clan, converted it into a highly profitable enter-

32. In 1785, Dillwyn purchased a summer house and forty acres of land, some of which he began to farm (Dillwyn to Susannah Dillwyn, 16 June 1785; 16 July 1786, Emlen-Dillwyn papers, LCP).
33. Raistrick, *Quakers in Science and Industry*, 283–85; R. S. Sayers, *Lloyds Bank in the History of English Banking* (Oxford, 1957), *passim*; *Memorials of Rebecca Jones*, 63. Lombard Street became London's great banking street. Phillips's shop was a short walk from the Old Jewry, where Granville Sharp lived until 1786 and where the Abolition Committee found a permanent office.

prise. The brewery soon passed into the hands of Robert Barclay of Clapham, whose mother was a Gurney and who was himself an active member of the Abolition Committee, along with his good friends John Lloyd and William Dillwyn.[34]

Thomas Fowell Buxton, of the next generation, led the Parliamentary struggle against slavery in the 1820s. Although Buxton was not a Friend himself, his mother belonged to the Quaker Hanbury family, which had founded a tobacco empire prior to the American Revolution and had then turned to banking, brewing, and iron before eventually launching the age of chocolate. Buxton's wife was the daughter of the banker John Gurney, and was thus the sister of both Elizabeth Fry and of the abolitionist Joseph John Gurney. When in 1808 Buxton joined the brewing firm of Truman, Hanbury & Co., he helped to consolidate, according to Arthur Raistrick, the Hanbury iron interests with both the iron and banking interests of the Lloyd dynasty and the banking and brewing interests of the Barclay group. Buxton later became associated with a great insurance firm founded by Samuel Gurney, Alexander Baring, and Sir Moses Montefiore. Buxton's wife, I may add, was the niece of Samuel Hoare, Jr., one of the most diligent members of the Abolition Committee. Hoare, whose father was a wealthy banker, had worked at Henry Gurney's bank in Norwich before entering the London firm that eventually became the core of Barclays Bank. To round matters off, Hoare was related by marriage to the merchant and woolen draper Joseph Woods, who was also in the nucleus of the Abolition Committee.[35]

I need not labor the point that Quaker antislavery activity was closely associated with complex ties of intermarriage and with fortunes made from shipping, banking, mining, insurance, and industry. And despite the Quakers' valiant efforts to stay clear of the African slave trade, their quest for profit sometimes compromised their quest for innocence. William Rathbone, one of the few abolitionists in Liverpool, was also one of the city's wealthiest merchants. Although he dealt in timber instead of slaves, his firm was the first in England to receive a consignment of cotton grown in the United States. Such historical ironies were common wherever Quakers took the leadership in the economic revolution. Thus Moses Brown, the organizer of the Providence Society for Abolishing the Slave Trade and a leader of the antislavery movement in New England, supported various philan-

34. MS Dictionary of Quaker Biography, Friends House; Raistrick, *Quakers in Science and Industry*, 286–88; William Dillwyn to Thomas Parke, 13 September 1781, Cox, Parrish, Wharton papers, HSP.
35. MS Dictionary of Quaker Biography, Friends House; Emden, *Quakers in Commerce, passim*; Raistrick, *Quakers in Science and Industry*, 147.

thropic causes with a fortune made from the West India trade and from the distillation of rum. In 1773, just before his formal conversion to Quakerism, Brown freed his own slaves and began active work against the African trade, hoping to atone for his sin of eight years before when he had fitted out a slave ship as a quick way to secure profits for investment in an iron furnace. Yet for all of Brown's attempts to dissociate himself from slavery and to make up for a guilty past, he was the great promoter of early New England cotton manufacturing and the patron of Samuel Slater, whose reconstructed spinning frame prepared the way for the American cotton textile industry.[36]

Like their English brethren, the American Quaker abolitionists were distinguished by their mercantile wealth and above all by their entrepreneurial leadership. The Pemberton fortune arose from international trade that depended on slave-produced sugar, molasses, rice, and tobacco, as well as on Caribbean markets for North American commodities. But even by the 1750s the elder Israel Pemberton was discovering that speculation in land, mortgages, and bonds was safer and less time-consuming than investment in commercial shipping. Robert Waln, an active abolitionist and a great Philadelphia merchant of the next generation, moved from the China and East India trade to insurance, cotton manufacturing, and iron. Both in his worldly success and in the diversity of his economic and philanthropic interests Waln was typical of the Quaker leaders of the Philadelphia and New York abolition societies.

There were a number of such influential personages. Among them was Samuel Coates, considered an old-style Philadelphia merchant, a man who was a business correspondent of Moses Brown, a manager of Pennsylvania Hospital, and a director of the First Bank of the United States. Thomas Pym Cope, a promoter of the Chesapeake-Delaware canal, had drawn his wealth from a Philadelphia-to-Liverpool packet line. Isaac Hicks, a prominent New York banker, was close to the merchant interests represented politically by John Jay. John Murray, Sr., was a great New York shipowner and importer, whose insurance, banking, and real estate interests (Murray Hill) helped him to accumulate a fortune of one-half million dollars. John Murray, Jr., a nephew of the latter and an affluent brewer, gave $10,000 in relief to the yellow-fever victims of 1798. Thomas Eddy, who moved from Philadelphia to New York after making a fortune in insurance and speculation in the public debt, turned to various public services, becoming a governor of New York Hospital, the chief founder of Newgate prison, and a promoter of the Bible

36. Friends' Moses Brown pamphlets, MBV Austin 5, RIHS; Moses Brown papers, 2: 328, 331, RIHS. Rathbone, it should be added, was disowned in 1805, four years before his death, but not for importing cotton. Moses Brown had been much influenced by reading the religious testimony of Samuel Fothergill.

Society, the Historical Society, the New York Savings Bank, and the Erie Canal. The younger generation of urban Quakers included Jeremiah Thompson, who by 1827 was said to be the largest shipowner in the United States and one of the leading cotton dealers in the world.[37]

The Quakers constituted the largest identifiable group in the Philadelphia and New York abolition societies, but it is important to ask what kinds of outsiders they attracted to their pioneering efforts. It would be useful to have a comprehensive and quantitative analysis of the active membership of all the abolition societies. Here I can only venture a few general and preliminary observations.

Except in Philadelphia, the major abolition societies represented an extremely narrow and affluent cross section of any given population. The English provincial societies often included artisans, tradesmen, and shopkeepers, many of whom were Quakers or Dissenters, along with a striking number of clergymen, a group conspicuously underrepresented in the American societies, except in Connecticut, Rhode Island, and Kentucky.[38] Among the more active members of the Pennsylvania Abolition Society, during its first twenty years of existence, I have identified a saddler, a hatter, a tanner-currier, a tailor, a ladies' shoemaker, a cooper, three carpenters (probably), two clock and watchmakers, and a number of teachers, booksellers, and printer-stationers. Although most of these skilled workers were probably Quakers and may have been relatively well-to-do, they represent a class that was unseen among the Parisian Amis des noirs, the London Abolition Society, or, with two or three exceptions, among the New York Manumission Society. In any event, the committees of the Pennsylvania Society were clearly dominated by merchants, lawyers, doctors, and the holders of high public office. Because the Society was oriented toward enforcement of the emancipation law, in a city close to neighboring slaveholding states, it retained a large legal counsel and counted among its members an unusually high proportion of attorneys. A study of forty-nine of the more active New York abolitionists shows that at least twenty-three were merchants and shipowners; eight were bankers, including several bank presidents and directors; eight were lawyers and judges; the remaining

37. In sketching profiles of both Quaker and non-Quaker abolition society members in New York and Philadelphia I have drawn on many city directories and biographical guides, far too many to be listed here.
38. For the English provincial societies, the best guide is E. M. Hunt, "The North of England Agitation for the Abolition of the Slave Trade, 1780–1800" (M.A. thesis, University of Manchester, 1959). Except in Scotland, the clergymen were mostly Dissenters. West of the Pennines, the abolition societies contained more wealthy manufacturers and were also, especially in Manchester and Birmingham, more independent of the London Abolition Society.

number included a few ministers, doctors, and college professors, along with a scattered assortment of canal promoters, land speculators, and the owners of drug firms, dry-goods stores, sawmills, and boardinghouses.[39]

Although the overwhelming majority of Americans were farmers, the abolition societies contained virtually no members with agricultural "interests," unless one counts those involved in speculation in confiscated Tory estates and western lands. German, Dutch, and French names are conspicuously scarce in the membership rosters. The New York Society included, at least nominally, the high command of the Federalist party: Hamilton, Jay, Colonel Robert Troup, General Matthew Clarkson, John B. Murray, and many others. But neither the New York nor the Pennsylvania society was a Federalist club. They contained prominent anti-Federalists, Clintonian and Jeffersonian Democrats, former Liberty Boys, and the sons of Tory families. The striking point is not party affiliation but the number of active abolitionists who held important offices. Among the members of both societies were U.S. senators, congressmen, federal judges and diplomats, federal and state attorneys general, members of state legislatures, of constitutional conventions, and of city councils. The abolition societies were, in short, one of the municipal meeting grounds for men of wealth, influence, and political power.

During the post-Revolutionary decades, American municipal life was invigorated by a movement for cooperative organization in the public interest. This spirit partly reflected the commercial and philanthropic ideals of the European Enlightenment, which had led to similar planning and civic organization in cities like Edinburgh. In America, however, there were special circumstances that quickened the sense of local responsibility. Political independence forced merchants to find new markets and routes of trade, while simultaneously opening new opportunities in business, banking, and manufacturing. Interurban rivalry spurred local leaders to improve transportation facilities and to found, by various charters and acts of incorporation, institutions for public service (the Pennsylvania Abolition Society was officially incorporated in 1789). In both Philadelphia and New York, the

---

39. The New York Manumission Society initially required dues of 8 shillings upon joining and 4 shillings every quarter. In 1789 the average skilled carpenter or mason in New York earned about 4 shillings a day, which was twice the wages of an unskilled laborer. I have identified one hatter and one tanner-currier among the New York members. There was at least one Jewish member, Moses Judah, a merchant, Revolutionary War veteran, and active Freemason. Unlike the Pennsylvania Society, the New York Society did admit slaveholders, a fact which resulted in tense debate and which may have strained relationships between Quaker and non-Quaker members (see especially the minutes for 10 November 1785; 8 February 1786; 9 November 1786; 15 February 1787, New York Manumission Society MS Minutes, NYHS).

abolition societies were thus parts of an interlocking network of public and private organizations designed to give order and direction to municipal life. In both cities the leading abolitionists could also be found in the chambers of commerce and in companies promoting canals and improved inland navigation; on the boards of savings banks, libraries, hospitals, Bible societies, and Sunday School societies; as the commissioners and directors of almshouses, poorhouses, and prisons. The London abolitionists exhibited a similar profile, except for the affiliation of many non-Quakers with the Evangelical movement.[40]

In one sense these interlocking directorates can be taken as evidence of the civic pride and philanthropic spirit of successful men who met in the same social clubs and in the same banks and exchanges, and who shared a common interest in the collective health and welfare of their fellow townsmen. Their concern for the Negro cannot be dismissed as a substitute for broader social concerns: the members of the abolition societies worked to extend and improve the education of the poor, to help imprisoned debtors, to provide free smallpox vaccination for the indigent, and to give information and assistance to newly arrived immigrants. And unlike the London and Parisian abolitionists, the reformers of New York and Philadelphia were an unrivaled elite, free from the restraints of an established aristocracy and from the fear of what Jefferson termed the *canaille*.

On the other hand, by the 1790s America's two largest cities were hardly immune from labor conflict. Immigration from Europe was on the rise, the old apprenticeship system continued to decay, and skilled artisans and mechanics complained of cheapened standards and of unfair competition from poorly trained and underpaid workers. In the face of unemployment and a growing pool of cheap labor, some skilled workers saw the manumission of slaves as a further threat to their former dignity and independence.[41] There is no reason to suspect that the entrepreneurial abolitionists were conspiring to lower wages by increasing the free labor force or by preventing the southward drain of Negroes. They were concerned, however, with the broader question of labor discipline and with devising efficient institutions to replace older methods of social control. For example, in both Philadelphia and New York they helped to create the modern prison system, dedicated to

40. Sidney I. Pomerantz, *New York: An American City, 1783–1803* (New York, 1938), *passim*; Louis Hartz, *Economic Policy and American Democratic Thought in Pennsylvania, 1776–1860* (Cambridge, Mass., 1948), 9 and *passim*. In order to avoid losing some members, the New York Manumission Society changed the night of its quarterly meeting so there would be no conflict with the Hand-in-Hand Fire Company (MS Minutes, 6: 57).
41. Pomerantz, *New York*, 209–10, 223, and *passim*; Jackson Turner Main, *The Social Structure of Revolutionary America* (Princeton, 1965), 35–37, 73.

the rehabilitation of deviants by means of steady work, habit-shaping regimen, and strict control over all aspects of life. Instead of being whipped or branded and then set free with an unchanged heart, the offender would now be placed behind walls, ostensibly for his own good as well as that of society, and transformed into a dependable and willing worker. Most of the philanthropies linked with the abolition cause had two broad aims: to protect an urban population from disease and disorder, thereby ensuring the smooth functioning of the social and economic system; and to inculcate the lower classes with various moral and economic virtues, so that workers would want to do what the emerging economy required. Slavery seemed entirely antithetical to this public-spirited ideology. Like sanguinary punishments, it seemed to be a relic of the barbarous past. And if slaves could be converted into sober, self-disciplined workers, the same could presumably be done with vagabonds, whores, felons, and deviants of every kind.

The point to be stressed is that the Quaker example included considerably more than a decision to manumit their slaves. Both in England and in the northern states, the Quakers worked tirelessly for improved credit and insurance facilities; for canal systems and better roads; for transatlantic mail packets; for chambers of commerce and, ultimately, for railroads. And they linked such "useful improvements" with a variety of civic and philanthropic projects. For in the Quaker world view there were no disparities between business enterprise and devoting one's leisure time to the dissemination of Bibles, to the promotion of science, to the building of hospitals and prisons, and to the eradication of slavery. God's plan for human progress, revealed through reason and natural law, was all of a piece. The canals, banks, and technological improvements would be of little use unless workers understood the dynamic core of the Quaker ethic: responsibility. It was not by chance that Franklin issued his famed homilies from the Quaker City.

## William Allen and the Limitations of Quaker Philanthropy

William Allen, a key figure in the British antislavery movement, epitomizes the meaning of Quaker science and philanthropy in the face of revolutionary change. I have already mentioned that Rebecca Jones, the missionary from Philadelphia, imbued young Allen with the spirit of the evangelical revival. Much earlier Allen had developed a keen interest in chemistry and astronomy, and at fourteen had built his own telescope. At eighteen, however, Allen's mind became absorbed with religious introspection and with a daily struggle, recorded in his spiritual diary, against self-indulgence. At that time, in 1788, his models of Quaker piety included Rebecca Jones, George Dillwyn, and John Pemberton. He was deeply moved by Pemberton's account of Quaker committees visiting and helping Negroes in Philadelphia. As a symbol of his own quest·for purity, Allen resolved to abstain from sugar until its West Indian cultivators had been emancipated—a vow he kept for forty-three years.[42]

It happened that Allen was born and grew up in one of the first parts of London to feel the more devastating effects of the economic revolution. His father had moved from Scrooby, the home of the Plymouth Pilgrims, to become a silk manufacturer in Spitalfields, which had a long tradition, in E. P. Thompson's words, of "anti-authoritarian turbulence." According to Thompson, the Spitalfields silk weavers were the first "large group of domestic workers . . . whose conditions anticipate those of the semi-employed proletarian out-workers of the 19th century." As a result of exploitive innovations in management and of increasing competition from Lancashire cottons, the Spitalfields silk weavers were degraded to a ghastly level of poverty and overcrowding.[43] In short, young Allen lived in the midst of a noxious ghetto which threatened at any moment to explode into violence. Much to his father's disappointment, he left the family silk mill at the age of twenty-two and began working at Plough Court for Joseph Gurney Bevan. By 1786 he was on the slave-trade committee of the London Meeting for Sufferings. He married a Hanbury of the tinplate industry and soon became proprietor of Bevan's pharmaceutical concern, which ultimately became Allen & Hanburys.[44]

It might be tempting to conclude that Allen's antislavery activities were a hypocritical effort to divert attention from the sufferings of English workingmen. Thompson, for example, quotes a remarkable address to the public from an anonymous Manchester journeyman cotton spinner who seemed to suspect that humanitarians had contrived a double standard for judging the condition of English workers and West Indian slaves. English workers supposedly enjoyed the equal protection of law and were free to leave their places of employment. Yet:

> The negro slave in the West Indies, if he works under a scorching sun, has probably a little breeze of air sometimes to fan him: he has

42. My account of Allen draws mainly on *Life of William Allen, with Selections from His Correspondence* (London, 1846), and from his papers at Allen & Hanburys, Ltd., London.
43. E. P. Thompson, *The Making of the English Working Class* (New York, 1963), 21, 69, 143, 261, 266.
44. MS Minutes, 14 August 1786, Box F, Friends House. Allen's third wife was a Birkbeck, and was related to Morris Birkbeck, who in 1788 was a correspondent of the Abolition Committee and who in 1817 emigrated to the United States, where he promoted English settlement as well as antislavery doctrine in Illinois.

a space of ground, and a time allowed to cultivate it. The English spinner slave has no enjoyment of the open atmosphere and breezes of heaven. Locked up in factories eight stories high, he has no relaxation till the ponderous engine stops, and then he goes home to get refreshed for the next day; no time for sweet association with his family; they are all alike fatigued and exhausted.[45]

The difficulty is that William Allen was fully aware of the human misery in Spitalfields and of the later degradation of English mill workers. As a rich entrepreneur who had close ties with Evangelicals like William Wilberforce and Henry Thornton, he would probably have endorsed the first part of Burke's famous message of 1795 to the starving poor: "Patience, labour, sobriety, frugality, and religion, should be recommended to them; all the rest is downright *fraud*." But Allen was also heir to the Quaker variant of Dissent, which, for all its inward-turning spirituality and its dilution by wealth, still contained both a latent dissatisfaction with the social order and the vision of a more harmonious and equalitarian world. Beginning in 1797, he helped to organize a committee to distribute soup to the ragged masses of Spitalfields. By 1812 his reorganized "Soup Society" was conducting street-by-street surveys of the area, recording data on population, age, literacy, religion, and families without Bibles. Allen may have considered the possession of a Bible as important as the possession of a job and the doles of soup as an antidote to revolution. The fact remains that Allen's journal, *The Philanthropist*, designed to stimulate "virtue and active benevolence," combined information on West Indian and American slavery with detailed reports on the plight of the English poor.[46]

Except for limitations of time and energy, there is no inherent reason that a concern for one species of injustice should blind a man to other species of injustice. Indeed, Allen probably weakened his effectiveness by engaging in such an incredible number of benevolent activities. And his passion for philanthropy was partly a way of justifying his active hobby of science. As a student of science Allen faced a growing conflict between his faith in God's intelligible design and his fear of French and German natural philosophy (late in life, while writing a paper for the Royal Society on the respiration of pigeons, he threatened Henry Brougham that he would withdraw his sponsorship from the Library of Useful Knowledge unless Kant's works were suppressed!). A friend of Sir Humphrey Davy, Allen gave popular lectures at the Royal Institution, helped write a notable paper on carbonic acid,

45. Thompson, *Making of the English Working Class*, 201.
46. *Life of William Allen*, 1: 33–34; *The Philanthropist: or Repository for Hints and Suggestions Calculated to Promote the Comfort and Happiness of Man*, 2 (1812): 173–96, 395–404, and *passim*.

and was elected Fellow of the Linnaean and Royal Societies. He was confident that "the pursuits of science, properly conducted, tend to enlarge our views, to banish narrow prejudices, to increase our love of truth and order, and give tone and vigour to the mind." Nevertheless, throughout his life Allen kept reminding himself, "beware, lest chemistry and natural philosophy usurp the highest seat in thy heart." Discovery of truth in natural science only "exalted the creature," whereas spiritual truth always "lays him low." In 1812, Allen comforted himself by the thought that his main object had been the good of others, "for if, instead of these things, my time were devoted to philosophical pursuits and experiments, to which I am so naturally prone, the path to honour and distinction stands far above me. May the sacrifice be accepted above!"[47]

These inner conflicts provide insight into the goals Allen sought in philanthropy. Social reform, though secular by traditional standards, was a "spiritual" outlet that balanced worldly success in business and science. It also furnished an inner test of moral worthiness. Allen hoped that his efforts to do good did not spring merely from "benevolent intentions," but also from the humble sense that he was an instrument in the hand of the Lord.[48] Above all, reform led to acceptable external ties with the non-Quaker world. An analysis of the nature and limitations of such external ties will help illuminate the subtle connections between class ideology and the Quaker evangelical faith.

The early Quaker revivalists foreshadowed the moralistic concerns of the great evangelical awakening of the late eighteenth and early nineteenth centuries—the Evangelical crusade within the Church of England, the triumphs of Methodism on both sides of the Atlantic, and parallel movements within the Baptist and Presbyterian churches. Apart from important theological differences, the Quaker itinerants called for the moral uplift of the common people, inveighing against drunkenness, sexual immorality, ignorance of religion, and desecration of the Sabbath. If the Quaker ethic could lead to more radical and secular critiques of the social order—and one may cite Thomas Paine as a witness—the Quaker evangelicals were as horrified by Paine and by the French Revolution as were Wilberforce and Hannah More.[49] Like the Evangelicals within the Church of England, their program for reforming the nation's morals had two goals: to produce a sober, self-disciplined, and industrious working population; and to persuade the upper classes to devote their time and wealth to ennobling causes rather

47. *Life of William Allen*, 1: 143, and *passim*.
48. *Ibid.*, 1: 180.
49. Jones, *Later Periods*, 1: 243, 265–75, 280.

than to gay parties, gambling, and other conspicuous forms of waste and self-indulgence. The result of such reforms, even if not uppermost in the reformers' minds, would be a society free from the threat of class conflict and revolution.

This ideology had considerable appeal for the young Quakers of Allen's generation, born into an affluent environment but surrounded by the boredom and erosion of wealth. Allen's friend Elizabeth Gurney frankly confessed that she had been leading a frivolous and un-Quaker social life before her conversion to serious religion. To families like the Gurneys, Barclays, and Hoares, wealth had brought a slackening of Quaker discipline, exogamous marriage, and a drift away from religious identity. But paradoxically, the same communications network that helped to create the toxin of wealth also accelerated the movement for self-purification. A further paradox was that the Quaker revival, while restoring a sense of religious identity and purpose, also brought Quakers into cooperative alliance with outsiders, most notably with the Wilberforce-Thornton syndicate of reformers. In a sense, it was this latter group that appropriated Quaker programs and Quaker modes of organization as a means of reforming and "saving" the nation. But for Quakers, both in Britain and America, membership in nondenominational societies provided a means of confirming economic success with social acceptability. When a man like Allen collaborated with the British ruling elite in the African Institution, the British and Foreign Bible Society, and the British and Foreign School Society, he became at least a halfway member of the moral establishment, and he assimilated many of its values. The great benevolent societies helped to shape a consciousness of class identity and purpose, and, when leading merchants, bankers, and manufacturers met together in reform societies, they were not unmindful of useful contacts for business purposes.

On the other hand, such alliances could not altogether surmount religious prejudice. Granville Sharp once remarked that Anthony Benezet, his antislavery correspondent, was "unhappily involved in the errors of Quakerism." Wilberforce bluntly wrote Allen that he wished "for your own sake, and that of the world [that] . . . your religious principles and my own were more entirely accordant." Allen's Quaker friend Richard Reynolds commented bitterly on such condescension: after all that Quakers had done for the Bible Society and to secure Wilberforce's election in Yorkshire, Reynolds hoped "that class to which he, Thornton, and Stephen belong, should be convinced that we are, as we are willing to admit they may be, real genuine Christians." Yet for Wilberforce and his associates, the interests of "true" Christianity took precedence over any benevolent cause, and Nonconformists like Allen could only be looked upon pathetically as "poor creatures."[50]

If Allen's ties with liberal reformers were limited, they also qualify any conclusion that he was solely interested in preserving the social order through moral regeneration.[51] Whereas Hannah More's Sunday Schools were intended to produce a dutiful and tractable working population, whose "education" would stop with religious indoctrination, Allen was genuinely dedicated to the cause of educating the public. Despite their close cooperation in the antislavery cause, Wilberforce declined Allen's invitation to join the committee of subscribers to the Lancasterian Society, an organization that included such Utilitarian associates of Allen's as James Mill and David Ricardo. Allen was undisturbed by the democratic implications of the Lancasterian system, which was intended to multiply the effectiveness of knowledge by converting pupils into participating teachers. Unlike the Evangelical leader Charles Simeon, Allen did not think that the movement to reform the penal code was unsuitable for "religious people" so long as a rationalist like Samuel Romilly led the cause. Allen also campaigned against capital punishment, exchanging information with American Quaker philanthropists like John Murray, Jr., as well as with European monarchs.[52] But Allen's most revealing involvement with secular reform came with his en-

50. Prince Hoare, *Memoirs of Granville Sharp, Esq., Composed from His Own Manuscripts* . . . (London, 1820), 97; *Life of William Allen*, 1: 178–79. Similarly, Granville Sharp could praise Benezet in a letter to Benjamin Rush, but also say that he could speak more frankly and candidly to Rush because of religion (Sharp to Rush, 2 July 1774, Rush papers, HSP). Samuel Hopkins admitted that even though Quakers did not celebrate the Lord's Supper, they had led other Christians in freeing their slaves; who could say, he asked, whether the Quakers' neglect of church institutions was worse than keeping slaves? (*Works*, 2: 594).
51. As early as 1811 *The Philanthropist* printed a remarkable essay on "the most rational means of promoting civilization in barbarous states" (in the British Museum copy someone has attributed it to Clarkson), which argued that missionaries should not denounce customs like infanticide and abandonment of the aged if conformity to Christian ethics would simply lead to starvation; the first step toward Christianizing a barbarous people should be "to furnish them with a permanent supply of food"; "You must first improve the worldly condition of those, whom you mean thus morally to serve. You must produce, with this view, a change in their character and habits." In other words, Christian values depended on Western civilization, and the plow and "mechanic" should precede the Bible and priest (*Philanthropist*, 1: 16–21).
52. Although Wilberforce displayed a more liberal or at least a more pragmatic spirit on such subjects than did most of the Evangelicals, he wrote Buxton on 12 February 1819 that he did not think the principles regarding capital punishment had as yet been "clearly ascertained," and that he had long disdained the idea of himself bringing forward any proposition on the subject. He thought that Sir James Mackintosh was ideally suited for the cause, but regretted that Mackintosh was so infected by party spirit (Gurney papers, Friends House).

couragement of Robert Owen's paternalistic experiments at New Lanark. In Allen's eyes, Owen's experiments promised to solve the otherwise catastrophic problems of industrialism. He therefore furnished substantial funds that helped Owen take over the mill town and carry out his reforms. As one of the proprietors of New Lanark, Allen was delighted by the unmistakable improvements in working and social conditions.

The rupture came when it began to dawn on the devout Quaker that Owen was a "determined enemy" of all revealed religion. Indeed, at New Lanark, Owen seemed bent on proving that human happiness required emancipation from the belief in the divinity of the Bible. "We came into the concern," Allen wrote Owen in 1815, "not to form a manufactory of infidels, but to support a benevolent character in plans of a very different nature, in which the happiness of millions, and the cause of morality and virtue, are deeply concerned." Together with Joseph Fox, Allen forced Owen to introduce the Bible in New Lanark schools; he himself lectured the workers on the importance of revealed religion. Allen perfectly trusted the Russian Emperor's professions of humanitarianism and his promises to promote public education—presumably in line with Quaker principles—while, in contrast, Allen threatened to withdraw from New Lanark unless Owen surrendered all control over educating the children, who had proved to be deficient in scriptural knowledge. It was precisely because the eyes of the enlightened world were fastened upon New Lanark that Allen resolved to do anything in his power, even if it meant removing Owen as manager, to prevent the model town from becoming "an infidel establishment."[53] The more contact Allen had with secular radicalism, the more importance he attached to religious orthodoxy. Among the "sound" causes that increasingly absorbed his energies were the dissemination of Bibles and of antislavery doctrine.

## A Preliminary Assessment: The Symbolism of Slave and Free Labor

Quaker testimony against slavery was an extension the sect's traditional stand against war and violence. Such testimony also served, in time of crisis and persecution, both as a test of purity and as an emblem of distinctive identity. But the early Quaker revival, which spawned collective efforts to rid the Society of Friends of slaveholding, issued a broader challenge to the ethical basis of capital accumulation. Unlike their antislavery disciples and successors, Woolman and Benezet were content to live in the most humble

53. *Life of William Allen*, 1: 96–97, 130–32, 180–81, 209, 244–45, 324–25, 344–46, 349–53; 2: 226, 236–37, 362–63.

circumstances. Benezet, whom wealthy friends described as extremely un-prepossessing in appearance, expressed skepticism over the "cant" he heard about the stewardship of wealth. Writing to Samuel Fothergill in 1755, he questioned the rationalizations by which Quaker capitalists justified their success:

> And there are some who, though they have already a large affluence of wealth, yet are toiling hard to add thereto, without knowing wherefore they thus toil, and whether a wise man or a fool shall possess it after them. . . . Why do so many suffer the God of this world so to blind their eyes, and vitiate their reasonable as well as religious senses, as to suffer them to toil after gain, and think it is a mighty thing, and themselves notably employed, if they can add £1,000 to £1,000, or £10,000 to £10,000, and that often by a trade far from being pure from defilement, as such gain often arises chiefly from the purchase and sale of things at least needless and vain, if not of a defiling nature; an instance of which I have often painfully observed amongst us, where it is frequent to see even Friends, toiling year after year, enriching themselves, and thus gathering fuel for their own and their children's vanity and corruption, by the importation and sale of large quantities of rum, &c. . . . Now, that such a person shall esteem himself, and be esteemed, a religious man, and perhaps be the more regarded, even by religious people, because he is rich and great, is a mere paradox; yet is it too often the case. . . . Shall we desire to be great and rich, when our Saviour has so plainly declared it a situation so very dangerous; and that his predominant choice is of the poor of this world?[54]

Such words, warning against the allure of security and accommodation, echo the spirit of seventeenth-century religious radicalism. Insofar as Benezet's critique represented the spirit of the Quaker revival, the revival itself struck at the heart of the business ethic that was enriching families like the Pembertons, Hoares, Gurneys, and Barclays, on whose consciences the revival had a profound impact. From the Benezets, Fothergills, and Churchmans, the wealthy Friends acquired their zeal for education, temperance, and antislavery. They showed little inclination, however, of abandoning their ideology of progress, which justified toiling hard "to add £10,000 to £10,000."

No one should expect the Quaker capitalists to have renounced their wealth; and the possession of wealth does not cast doubt on the moral sin-

54. *Memoirs of the Life and Gospel Labours of Samuel Fothergill, with Selections from his Correspondence* . . . , George Crossfield, ed. (New York, 1844), 363–65.

cerity of Quaker abolitionists. They were, after all, a pioneering minority who were among the first modern capitalists to recognize both the social responsibilities of wealth and the social consequences of economic action. Yet it is essential to distinguish individual motive from the larger ideological functions of a movement like antislavery.

The Society of Friends interpreted each step toward a total disengagement from slaveholding as a tangible sign of growing religious purity. For men disturbed by the revival's strictures against wealth, antislavery suggested the compromise of limited sacrifice, though obviously a sacrifice of keener anguish for a few Quaker planters in the South.[55] Abolitionist activity allowed many of Benezet's "rich and great" Quakers to "be esteemed" religious men, and in accordance with moral criteria which Benezet himself had helped establish. It also brought them into contact with the rich and great of other denominations, enabling them to escape some of the exclusiveness and inwardness of their sect. To moralists and reformers of other faiths, the Quakers demonstrated that testimony against slavery could be a social correlative of inner purity which seemed to pose no threat to the social order—at least to that capitalist order in which the Quakers had won so enviable a "stake." As a social force, antislavery was a highly selective response to labor exploitation. It provided an outlet for demonstrating a Christian concern for human suffering and injustice, and yet thereby gave a certain moral insulation to economic activities less visibly dependent on human suffering and injustice. Viewed from one perspective, the Quakers were at the headwaters of a widening stream of philanthropy and social reform. From another viewpoint, they created the liberal tradition of being "kind" to Negroes as proof of one's humanitarianism.

The simplistic thesis that Quaker abolitionists were governed by "economic interest" in the sense that they stood to profit from the destruction of the slave trade or a weakening of the plantation system cannot bear examination.[56] But Negro slavery was a system of labor which raised fundamental questions about the meanings of freedom, dependability, and

55. Some prominent Quakers refused to make even a limited sacrifice, and either left the Society of Friends or were disowned, like Stephen Hopkins, former governor of Rhode Island. Even in Pennsylvania, some Quaker families had to free as many as ten or fifteen slaves, and often helped to compensate the blacks for past services. In Virginia, Warner Mifflin's father manumitted nearly one hundred slaves (Drake, *Quakers and Slavery*, 75–77). Yet as Stephen B. Weeks shows, there was soon a conservative reaction among Virginia Quakers, many of whom opposed the policy of emancipation and many of whom left the Society of Friends (*Southern Quakers and Slavery*, 216).
56. Although there were a few exceptions, like James Cropper, the Liverpool importer of East India sugar, it would appear that many eighteenth-century Quaker merchants actually stood to lose by any weakening of the Atlantic slave-trade system.

discipline; the Quaker reformers represented an entrepreneurial class which confronted, at least in Great Britain, an unruly labor force, much of it recently uprooted from village or rural life—a labor force which even in the early nineteenth century had not yet been disciplined to the factory system, and which expressed its frustrations in riots, crime, sabotage, and other acts of uninhibited violence.

The Quakers engaged in the antislavery cause were also deeply concerned over domestic problems of labor discipline. William Dillwyn, for example, praised Quaker manufacturers for being more attentive to the welfare of the children in their mills, and for being careful "to preserve good order among them, and employ a man to instruct them in reading, &c., during certain hours, for which no deduction is made from their wages." The wider adoption of such practices, Dillwyn thought, would reduce the public complaints that factories were nurseries of vice. David Barclay circulated large broadsides giving "advice to servants," some of which echoed the sermons of American slaveholders: "Be not what is called an eye-servant, appearing diligent in sight, but neglectful when out of it." "Avoid pert answers; for civil language is cheap, and impertinence provoking." "Never stay when sent on a message; waiting long is painful to a Master, and a quick return shows diligence." Barclay's central message, however, was that "a good character" should be the supreme goal of servants, "for it is their bread." Therefore, servants should watch the company they keep and never provoke their superiors. As for their freedom to change employers, "the Servant that often changes his place works only to be poor."[57]

Consider also the following specimen. On 15 July 1787, Dr. John Coakley Lettsom wrote Dr. Benjamin Rush on the subjects of prisons and slavery. Rush, who read Lettsom's letter to the Philadelphia Prison Society, had become convinced that "a prison sometimes supplies the place of a church and out-preaches the preacher in conveying useful instruction to the heart." Lettsom reported that "villainy" was accumulating so fast in England that "necessity" would soon cure the prejudice against prisons. He had himself favored condemning convicts to public labor out of doors, assuming that the beneficial example to spectators would be more permanent than that of the gallows. Lettsom was struck, however, by Rush's argument that the example might serve to render any physical labor "ignominious." On the other hand, he cited an instance of convicts who were chained at night on a ship and who worked on the land in day. Although voluntary laborers performed the same drudgery within sight of the convicts, the proximity en-

57. *Memoir of the Life and Religious Labors of Henry Hull* (Philadelphia, 1873), 203; David Barclay, "Advice to Servants" (broadside, Friends House).

hanced their appreciation of their own liberty, "for however the body may be occupied alike, the mind is impressed very differently, as differently as voluntary labour, and condemned slavery can impress the mind." Hence "the example of the latter may be beneficial to the morality of the community, without entailing disgrace upon any species of voluntary industry." Without pause, Lettsom then proceeded to express his joy over the joint British and American efforts to abolish the slave trade.[58]

What distinguished the Quakers from earlier mercantilist writers, who had also pondered schemes for suppressing "villainy" and for putting the unruly poor to work, was the Quakers' gift for assimilating utility and national interest to a humanitarian ethic. The Quakers, unlike the mercantilists, deplored visible or overt forms of social cruelty, such as the slave trade. But they also helped to create a moral climate in which a highly ethical purpose could disguise the effects of power. Although eighteenth-century Quakers were not responsible for the consequences of a nineteenth-century free labor market—or for the consequences of British efforts to stamp out the slave trade in the heart of Africa—they unwittingly drew distinctions and boundaries which opened the way, under a guise of moral rectitude, for unprecedented forms of oppression.

Clearly, for Rush and Lettsom there was no comparability between "condemned slavery" and Negro slavery, except for the possibility that both might render voluntary labor ignominious. For Barclay, it was inconceivable that English servants were in any sense unfree. For Dillwyn, the children in the English mines and factories were the beneficiaries of wholesome discipline, except where the factories had become nurseries of vice; the children of American slaves, who seldom endured such regular work or supervision, were the victims of unquestioned oppression. Despite what we have said concerning William Allen's Soup Society and educational reforms, antislavery ideology served to isolate specific forms of human misery, allowing issues of freedom and discipline to be faced in a relatively simplified model. And by defining slavery as a unique *moral* aberration, the ideology tended to give sanction to the prevailing economic order. If we look on antislavery as a game certain people played—which as a conceptual device implies no lack of seriousness on the players' parts, but simply points to the definition and acceptance of arbitrary rules—then we can appreciate how the movement helped to reshape attitudes toward work, liberty, exploitation, and proper discipline.

What made the Negro slave ideally suited as a counter in such a game was his lack of responsibility for his own status. By definition, he was inno-

58. Lettsom to Rush, 15 July 1787, Rush MSS, 32, LCP.

cent of the burdens and coercions of the Protestant work ethic, almost as if his forced labor had freed him from the unhappy legacy of Adam's curse. Accordingly, Quakers and others could commiserate with his sufferings and attack his exploiters while reaffirming both the validity of economic law and God's wisdom in assigning men unequal stations in life.

Yet there can be no greater disparity of power than that between a man convinced of his own disinterested service and another man who is defined as a helpless object. As representatives of the emerging capitalist order, extending charity to the lowliest segment of laborers, Quaker reformers could not view Negroes as even potentially autonomous beings. Most of the Negroes freed by Quaker masters were quietly dissuaded from trying to join the Society of Friends. Liberation from slavery did not mean freedom to live as one chose, but rather freedom to become a diligent, sober, dependable worker who gratefully accepted his position in society. Freedom required the internalization of moral precepts in the place of less subtle forms of external coercion. No doubt it was a sign of progessive enlightenment when Moses Brown showed concern over providing secure savings deposits for his freed slaves; William Allen promoted the same idea for the workers of New Lanark. Yet neither man doubted that he knew the best interests of the laboring class, or that saving from wages was an act of freedom.

Chapter 3

# The Preservation of
# English Liberty, I

## The English Context Compared with
## That of America and France

The ideology of the American Revolution was largely British in origin, and
the arguments that American reformers used against Negro slavery had
long been commonplace in British political and moral philosophy. Yet by the
1770s antislavery thought had considerably different implications in the two
countries.

In England there was no "fundamental shift in values" that mobilized
the society into revolution. There was no counterpart to the American need
for self-justification. No new hopes or obligations arose from an attempt to
build a virtuous republic. Such phrases as "created equal," "inalienable
rights," and "the pursuit of happiness"—all of which had appeared in classic liberal texts—were qualified by a reverent constitutionalism that looked
to Saxon precedent to legitimize ideals of freedom. The notion of man's inherent rights, when assimilated to the historical concept of British "liberty," implied little challenge to traditional laws and authorities. And by the
1790s the very idea of inherent rights was giving way to radical and conservative forms of Utilitarianism. Like the Americans of a later generation,
most Englishmen looked back to a long-sanctified revolution—the Glorious
Revolution of 1688—which had supposedly restored the foundations of a
free society. Reformers and critics often expressed alarm over the corruption of that "revolutionary" heritage. But even when they called for an extension of political liberties, it was usually in the name of purifying or
restoring balance to the existing political order.

The stability of English institutions made antislavery appear less dangerous than in revolutionary America or France. In the latter two countries,

65

where leaders at least thought of themselves as creating new social orders, there was the possibility of judging any institution against the abstract ideals of liberty and equal rights. Since slavery epitomized hereditary power, it could be denounced as one of the vestiges of a barbarous past, along with royalty, primogeniture, feudal dues (in France), or an established church. The creation of new political authorities opened the way for sweeping change that could easily overleap national or continental boundaries.

In the words of the Abbé Grégoire: "Le volcan de la liberté allumé en France amènera bientôt une explosion générale et changera le sort de l'espèce humaine dans les deux hémisphères."[1] Yet even enthusiasts like Grégoire knew that revolutions require priorities and that "higher law" ideals must be selectively applied. What Grégoire had in mind, in the passage just quoted, was a revolutionary alliance of colonial mulattoes and nonslaveholding whites. In order to win full civil rights for free blacks and mulattoes, he was quite willing to postpone the question of slavery. There was a wide discrepancy between the Amis des noirs' declaration of principles and their belief that any "sudden" emancipation would be disastrous for the colonies. In both France and America there was a notable gap between antislavery rhetoric and the realities of revolutionary politics. The slavery issue could not be allowed to divide revolutionary alliances or to take precedence over such critical questions as military defense and political reconstruction. And in both countries, there was a need for qualifying the immediate implications of manifestoes concerned with man's natural equality. Within the context of revolution, the postponement of Negro emancipation could be one of various checks against an uncontrolled assault upon private property.

In France, unlike America, few men had ever seen a Negro slave, except perhaps in Paris and the port cities, and fewer still had grown accustomed to slavery as part of their immediate universe. The antislavery cause could easily be applauded by any enlightened man who had no personal or economic ties with the colonial system. Yet precisely because the French colonies were so remote, the plight of slaves could remain low on the agenda of reform. As the Revolution widened, the agitation of the Amis des noirs seemed at best a pious irrelevancy, at worst a dangerous distraction, inspired no doubt by the British in order to divide the colonies from France. In addition, the bewildering pace of revolutionary events left little time for

1. Quoted in Paul Grunebaum-Ballin, *Henri Grégoire, l'ami des hommes de toutes les couleurs, la lutte pour la suppression de la traite et l'abolition de l'esclavage, 1789–1831* (Paris, 1948), 27. Grégoire's words can be translated as follows: "The volcanic eruption of freedom in France will soon bring on a general explosion which will transform the destiny of mankind in both hemispheres."

antislavery organization, and it was soon too late for white reformers to decide the destiny of the St. Domingue blacks.

In England, however, the remoteness of the colonies had profoundly different implications. As in France, only a few men who had lived in the West Indies had become habituated to slavery as one of the necessary realities of life. They and their proslave trade allies did their best to evoke fears that any humanitarian tampering with the slave system would open Pandora's box, as the earl of Abingdon put it, and let loose democratic forces that would ultimately destroy both monarchy and rank: "The Order, and Subordination, the Happiness of the whole habitable Globe is threatened," Abingdon warned. "What anarchy, confusion, and bloodshed," Gilbert Francklyn asked, "may follow too nice and critical an enquiry into the exact portion of each man's particular liberty, the society of which he is a member may have a right to deprive him of?" He added:

> What would the people of England think of men, who, under a similar pretext of zeal for the rights of humanity, should erect themselves into a society, and endeavour, by preaching, writing, and publishing, to stir up the soldier, the artisan, and the peasant, to assert their rights to an equal portion of liberty with those who now lord it over them? Could any religious man amongst the present petitioners [against the slave trade] object to, or decline promoting an agrarian law, in favour of the distressed poor of Great Britain?[2]

But equality had never been a goal of the earlier petition campaigns for "Wilkes and Liberty," for annual Parliaments, for enlarging the membership of the House of Commons, or for reducing the court's influence in the legislature. English reformers, with the exception of a few isolated radicals, had shown no enthusiasm for the American doctrines of direct representation and continuous public "consent." And since most Englishmen looked upon existing institutions as effective safeguards of liberty, it seemed improbable, except perhaps in 1792 and 1793, that antislavery arguments could be extended to domestic forms of oppression and inequality. On the contrary, for men who sincerely believed that the English workers were a free and contented people, there could be little hazard in cautiously extending to the colonies Whiggish notions of liberty. Antislavery, far from being

2. *Speech of the Earl of Abingdon on His Lordship's Motion for Postponing the Further Consideration of the Question for the Abolition of the Slave Trade* . . . (London, 1793), 5–6; Gilbert Francklyn, *Observations, Occasioned by the Attempts Made in England to Effect the Abolition of the Slave Trade* . . . (Kingston, Jamaica, 1788; reprint, London, 1789), xvii–xviii.

an innovation justified by a Declaration of Independence or a Declaration of the Rights of Man, could be embraced as a reinforcement of tradition.

## Some Political and Ideological Implications

In 1838 an English critic pondered the remarkable discrepancy between the public's apathy toward the most critical political and economic issues of the day, and the public "convulsions upon the question, whether the Black Apprentices [in the West Indies] shall have their indentures cancelled in August next, or be compelled to serve out their time!" Matters of politics and finance, he noted, appeared as lifeless abstractions; local evils became blurred by familiarity. "But slavery *proves* itself; its evils are embodied, and animated by a living spirit. It has action, actors, and horrors. . . . Ordinary home questions, in short, are as dull as lectures or sermons— slavery has the excitement of a tragedy." Moreover,

> except with planters, activity on this subject is followed by no injury or ill-will. A Tory or a Whig aristocrat may call a tenant or a tradesman, who agitates for "instant abolition" . . . an enthusiast, but he does not withdraw his custom or turn a man out of his farm. Individuals, who are disgusted with the state of home politics, but dare not move in them lest they should "bring in the Tories," find here a safe opportunity to "take an interest in public affairs."[3]

When applied retroactively, these remarks suggest that British leaders had much to gain, in ensuring stability, if reform energies could be channeled outward toward a symbol of unparalleled oppression. The critic of 1838 implied nothing about conscious motive. There is no evidence that politicians like William Pitt cannily supported abolition of the slave trade as a means of evading domestic reform or dampening radical discontent. Nor can one ignore the political risks that inhibited Edmund Burke, for example, from taking an early leadership in the antislavery cause. It would be naïve, however, to overlook the political and ideological context within which British antislavery emerged as an organized force.

Adam Smith, who was much esteemed by Pitt and the abolitionists, provides us with a classical precedent for asking what "interests" antislavery might have served. Here is Smith's evaluation of the first achievement of antislavery in America:

> The late resolution of the Quakers in Pennsylvania to set at liberty all their negro slaves, may satisfy us that their number cannot be very great. Had they made any considerable part of their property,

---

3. "Sources of English Zeal for the Blacks," *Spectator*, No. 509 (31 March 1838): 301.

such a resolution could never have been agreed to. In our sugar colonies, on the contrary, the whole work is done by slaves, and in our tobacco colonies a very great part of it. The profits of a sugar-plantation in any of our West Indian colonies are generally much greater than those of any other cultivation that is known either in Europe or America: And the profits of a tobacco plantation, though inferior to those of sugar, are superior to those of corn, as has already been observed.[4]

Since Smith considered self-interest to be the governing principle of life, it was inconceivable that Quakers or any other group would emancipate their slaves if slaves constituted "any considerable part of their property." Of course, Smith heartily favored the reform of a colonial system of labor that was artificially subsidized and that drained capital from more productive investment at home. There could be no "natural identity of interests" between English consumers and American planters unless the latter were subjected to free market forces.

Today even the authority of Adam Smith is likely to raise the bugaboo of "economic interpretation" and the specter of Eric Williams's controversial book *Capitalism and Slavery*. The shortcomings of Williams's thesis, which argues that British self-interest led to the abolition of the slave trade and to West Indian emancipation, have been exposed by a host of historians. In one of the most convincing rebuttals, Roger Anstey has pointed to the absence of any organized or self-conscious group in Parliament that represented the "developing economic forces"; to the fact that a bill for immediate abolition of the slave trade nearly passed in the House of Commons in 1796, at the very peak of the sugar boom; and to the lack of evidence that English reformers or politicians thought of the overproduction of sugar as a reason for slave-trade abolition. Anstey's most intriguing argument concerns the abolitionists' first major breakthrough, in 1806, when as a tactical maneuver they deliberately suppressed humanitarian arguments and concentrated their fire on the neutral (mainly American) slave trade to enemy colonies, and on the British slave trade to foreign and temporarily conquered territories. Anstey appears to turn Williams upside down. Appeals to the national interest cloaked hidden humanitarian motives, and succeeded "by a side wind," as Colonel Banastre Tarleton put it, in annihilating more than half of the total British slave trade. And the precedent of 1806 meant that a total abolition, even if demanded for true humanitarian motives, would not be regarded as a dangerous innovation.[5]

4. Adam Smith, *An Inquiry into the Nature and Causes of the Wealth of Nations* (1776; New York, 1937), 366.
5. Roger Anstey, "A Re-interpretation of the Abolition of the British Slave Trade,

Williams's critics have shown us the inadequacy of a naïve determinism and of too literal a conception of "self-interest." On the other hand, if the majority in Parliament feared the consequences of "any innovation upon a long-established practice," and shifted ground only when aroused to the danger and short-sightedness of supplying slaves to foreign colonies, it is of little importance that few M.P.'s had direct personal ties with the West Indies. And if the most powerful political leaders later championed abolition as the cause of national interest as well as of moral righteousness, it is hardly crucial that they represented the large English landholders—for whom Adam Smith was also a spokesman—more than the rising manufacturers.

The key questions concern the relationship between antislavery and the social system as a whole. Why did a seemingly liberal movement emerge and continue to win support from major government leaders in the period from 1790 to 1832, a period characterized by both political reaction and industrial revolution? How could such a movement be embraced by aristocratic statesmen and yet serve eventually as a vehicle for the triumphant middle class, who regarded West Indian emancipation as the confirmation of the Reform Bill of 1832, and who used antislavery rhetoric and strategy as models for their assault upon the Corn Laws? How could antislavery help to ensure stability while also accommodating society to political and economic change? Antonio Gramsci defined "hegemony," in the words of his biographer, as "the predominance, obtained by consent rather than force, of one class or group over other classes"; or more precisely, as "the 'spontaneous' loyalty that any dominant social group obtains from the masses by virtue of its social and intellectual prestige and its supposedly superior function in the world of production."[6] The paramount question, which sub-

---

1806–1807," *English Historical Review*, 87 (April 1972): 304–32; Anstey, "Capitalism and Slavery: A Critique," *Economic History Review*, 2d ser., 21 (1968): 307–20. I am also indebted to Anstey for allowing me to read chapters of his forthcoming study of British abolition.

6. John M. Cammett, *Antonio Gramsci and the Origins of Italian Communism* (Stanford, 1967), 204–5. Gramsci distinguishes "the apparatus of state coercive power which 'legally' enforces discipline on those groups who do not 'consent' either actively or passively" from "the 'spontaneous' consent given by the great masses of the population to the general direction imposed on social life by the dominant fundamental group" (*Selections from the Prison Notebooks of Antonio Gramsci*, Quintin Hoare and Geoffrey Nowell Smith, eds. and trans. [London, 1971], 12). In his illuminating essay, "On Antonio Gramsci," Eugene D. Genovese stresses that "the success of a ruling class in establishing its hegemony depends entirely on its ability to convince the lower classes that its interests are those of society at large—that it defends the common sensibility and stands for a natural and proper social order" (Genovese, *In Red and Black: Marxian Explorations in Southern and Afro-American History* [New York, 1971], 407). In other words, hegemony rests on a credible

sumes the others, is how antislavery reinforced or legitimized such hegemony.

Ideological hegemony is not the product of conscious choice and seldom involves insincerity or deliberate deception. As Peter Berger has written,  "deliberate deception requires a degree of psychological self-control that few people are capable of. . . . It is much easier to deceive oneself. It is, therefore, important to keep the concept of ideology distinct from notions of lying, deception, propaganda or legerdemain." Ideology is a mode of consciousness, rooted in but not reducible to the needs of a social group; indeed, it helps to define those very needs and interests, as well as to frame the boundaries of conscious tactics and objectives. As phrased by Berger, ideology "both justifies what is done by the group whose vested interest is served and interprets social reality in such a way that the justification is made plausible."[7] At issue, then, are not conscious intentions but the social functions of ideology; not individual motives but shifting patterns of thought and value which focused attention on new problems, which camouflaged others, and which defined new conceptions of social reality.

The antislavery movement, like Smith's political economy, reflected the needs and values of the emerging capitalist order. Smith provided theoretical justification for the belief that all classes and segments of society share a natural identity of interest. The antislavery movement, while absorbing the ambivalent emotions of the age, was essentially dedicated to a practical demonstration of the same reassuring message. It appealed, of course, to the highest ideals of man. Yet the very effectiveness of ideals requires a certain blindness to their social power and social consequences. They must be taken as pure and transcendent, free of ambiguous implication. Thus for abolitionists it was unthinkable that an attack on a specific system of labor and domination might also validate other forms of oppression and test the boundaries of legitimate reform. But from the perspective of our different world view—which no doubt equally restricts our vision in ways we cannot suspect—we can see that abolitionism helped to define the permissible character of a "popular" or "spontaneous" social movement. Antislavery not only reflected the needs and tensions of a transitional social system, but provided a new conceptual and categorical framework that imposed its own "logic" on events. As abolitionists sought support from men in power and

and adaptable *Weltanschauung*. For a brilliant application of Gramsci's theory of hegemony to American history, see Aileen S. Kraditor, "American Radical Historians on Their Heritage," *Past and Present* (August 1972) 56: 136–53.

7. Peter Berger, *Invitation to Sociology: A Humanistic Perspective* (Garden City, N.Y., 1963), 109, 112. In framing these general propositions, I am heavily indebted to the generous and perceptive criticism of Aileen S. Kraditor.

from middle-class opinion, they discovered, though not without travail, the common denominators that gave both zeal and limits to an emerging consensus. In a more positive sense, they succeeded in making a sincere humanitarianism an integral part of class ideology, and thus of British culture.

These themes can be approached initially on three levels of analysis: the relationship between antislavery and economic theory; the significance of antislavery as a channel for political action; and the use of antislavery literature as a medium for resolving conflicts inherent in the emerging system of liberal values. Let me try to spell out the implications of each "level."

By 1776 England was well-prepared for a marshaling of argument and evidence against the mercantilist system, and *The Wealth of Nations* acquired immediate popularity. Adam Smith's great mentors, Hutcheson and Hume, had both questioned the economic utility of Negro slavery. The Physiocrats had linked antislavery with the ideal of laissez faire. In a negative way, the defenders of the slave trade confirmed this association of ideas by invoking mercantilist dogma: the slave trade was a source of naval power and a great "nursery" for seamen; as a form of state-regulated exploitation, the slave colonies were essential to a favorable balance of trade and were the main source of the nation's economic surplus. No statesman had doubted the value of the slave system during those decades of war and competition with Spain and France which had resulted in England's unquestioned supremacy. Yet these backward-looking arguments missed the significance of Smith's challenge: after supremacy has been achieved, the means of achieving it may become obsolete.[8]

Smith's views on slavery present a paradox. He complains that

> We see frequently societies of merchants in London and other trading towns, purchase waste lands in our sugar colonies, which they expect to improve and cultivate with profit by means of factors and agents; notwithstanding the great distance and the uncertain returns, from the defective administration of justice in those coun-

8. Joseph A. Schumpeter, *History of Economic Analysis*, Elizabeth Boody Schumpeter, ed. (New York, 1954), 185–86, 210–20, 267–68; E. A. J. Johnson, *Predecessors of Adam Smith: The Growth of British Economic Thought* (New York, 1937), *passim*; Ronald Hamowy, "Adam Smith, Adam Ferguson, and the Division of Labour," *Economica*, n.s., 35 (August 1968): 249–59; Jacob Viner, "Adam Smith and Laissez Faire," *Journal of Political Economy*, 35 (April 1927): 198–232; Edward Mead Earle, "Adam Smith, Alexander Hamilton, Friedrich List: The Economic Foundations of Military Power," in *Makers of Modern Strategy*, Edward Mead Earle, ed. (Princeton, 1941), 117–28. As Earle notes, Smith favored state intervention whenever essential for military security, and defended navigation acts for preserving the strength of the British navy and merchant marine. Similar arguments would be used in defense of the slave trade. However, Smith considered overseas colonies a liability, in part because of the costs of military defense.

tries. Nobody will attempt to improve and cultivate in the same manner the most fertile lands of Scotland, Ireland, or the corn provinces of North America, though from the more exact administration of justice in these countries, more regular returns might be expected.

Slave-grown sugar is not only more profitable than other crops, but "it is commonly said, that a sugar planter expects that the rum and the molasses should defray the whole expence of his cultivation, and that his sugar should be all clear profit." On the other hand, "the experience of all ages and nations" demonstrates that the labor of slaves, "though it appears to cost only their maintenance, is in the end the dearest of any. A person who can acquire no property, can have no other interest but to eat as much, and to labour as little as possible."[9]

The question of incentive brings us to Smith's central concern, which is the price and productivity of labor as the source of national wealth. For Smith a commodity's price is not the real measure of its value (and he thought the price of sugar artificially inflated); rather, a commodity's value lies in the amount of labor it enables a purchaser to command, in a kind of balancing of pains and pleasures. English consumers of sugar were not getting their money's worth of labor, and the surplus from cheap English labor was paying for the extravagance of slavery: "The prosperity of the English sugar colonies has been, in great measure, owing to the great riches of England, of which a part has overflowed . . . upon those colonies." Even worse, the duties on sugar fell chiefly on people of "middling or more than middling fortune."[10]

The slave system, then, epitomized those artificial market conditions which multiplied conflicts of interest. The heavy losses of English seamen engaged in the slave trade, together with the depopulation of the slave-labor force (at a time when the demand for labor in England was increasing), were sufficient proof of the impediments to authentic self-interest.[11] For Smith

9. Smith, *Wealth of Nations*, 157, 364–67.
10. *Ibid.*, 547–56, 625–26, 837; Elie Halévy, *The Growth of Philosophic Radicalism*, Mary Morris, trans. (London, 1949), 88–120; Schumpeter, *History of Economic Analysis*, 267–69; Ronald L. Meek, "Physiocracy and Classicism in Britain," *Economic Journal*, 61 (March 1951): 26–47. In 1788, Arthur Young argued that Britain would enjoy far greater prosperity if half of the capital invested in the West Indies were reinvested in domestic industry ("On the Abolition of Slavery in the West Indies," *Annals of Agriculture*, 9 [1788]: 96).
11. On 24 May 1787, Thomas Clarkson presented the newly formed Committee for the Abolition of the Slave Trade with evidence and arguments on the unprofitability of the slave trade (the papers included an outline of his own forthcoming and highly influential *Essay on the Impolicy of the African Slave Trade*). From this point on, abolitionists emphasized the following arguments: an end to the slave trade would

and his disciples, the abolition of the slave trade and gradual emancipation could be justified on the same grounds as the removal of other artificial restrictions on enterprise, such as the Poor Laws and Laws of Settlement, or regulations governing wages, apprenticeship, food prices, and usury rates (Jeremy Bentham's early cause).

This philosophy left no room for opposing a hypothetical slave trade resulting from free-market conditions. And if one could show that the enslavement of a minority group increased the sum of total happiness, it is difficult to see how Smith—or Bentham and Burke, Smith's followers on economic questions—could raise any objections. Although the three thinkers stood together as emancipationists, they also denounced all forms of "false charity" that limited the free exercise of individual self-interest. For unless the egoistic principle were given free play, there could be no natural identity of interests. Moreover, in adopting Hume's defense of private property, Bentham echoed the most powerful argument of slave traders: government, by sanctioning private property, creates the expectation that such property will bring future pleasure; to negate such expectation not only inflicts great pain—greater, that is, than the denial of immediate gratifications—but destroys the psychological basis for all security. Burke pushed the argument from utility still further when he insisted that time validates laws and property of illegitimate origin. [12]

Logically, the rapid growth of Utilitarianism should have been a boon to the defenders of colonial slavery, who had long needed weapons that could demolish the champions of sentiment and natural rights. [13] But given the in-

---

greatly benefit the national economy by preventing the annual loss of thousands of seamen; by encouraging the development of the cheapest market for the raw materials needed by industry; by opening new markets for British manufactured goods; by eliminating a wasteful drain of capital and a cumbersome system of credit (Clarkson pointed out that trade in produce would bring returns two or three times a year to merchants and manufacturers, whereas the slave trade required as much as three years' credit); and by creating in the colonies a self-sustaining labor force that would in time consume more British produce (MS Proceedings of the Committee for the Abolition of the Slave Trade, 1787–1819 [hereafter Abolition Committee Minutes], 1: 4; 3: 4–6, British Museum Add. MSS 21254–56).

12. Halévy, *Growth of Philosophic Radicalism*, 17–18, 46–47, 88–120, 174–76. Bentham saw both the American Declaration of Independence and the French Declaration of Rights as revivals of metaphysical "scholasticism"; every law, he pointed out, is a restriction on human liberty; every fine or tax is an attack on property; all human interaction involves a balancing of pains and pleasures.

13. Utilitarian arguments appeared, of course, in various antiabolition pamphlets. An especially interesting specimen is "A West India Planter," *Considerations on the Emancipation of Negroes and on the Abolition of the Slave Trade* (London, 1788). It was not accidental, however, that the main stream of Utilitarian thought, beginning with Bentham and William Paley, was profoundly antithetical to West Indian slavery. Henry Brougham thought that it was "a gross and intolerable perversion of the

tellectual climate of the late eighteenth century, any serious attempt to accommodate slavery to the doctrine of natural identity of interests could only have succeeded in exposing the self-serving character of the doctrine. Or put the other way, an invalidation of slavery would help prove the beneficence of the doctrine of self-interest.

One of the striking features of British intellectual history, in the decades following *The Wealth of Nations,* is the sharp divergence of the standards of utility and moral sentiment. Francis Hutcheson, among others, had assumed that the Creator had perfectly synchronized utility with man's moral sentiment; but Smith, his pupil, could never reconcile *The Theory of Moral Sentiments* (1759) with *The Wealth of Nations* (1776). Indeed, the latter work makes it perfectly clear that man's benevolent feelings can be disastrous if allowed to interfere with public policy. As Elie Halévy and other historians have shown, a dominant theme that connects the writings of Smith, Burke, Joseph Townsend, Bentham, Godwin, and Malthus, is the need to free social philosophy from sentimental notions of charity and human rights. John Millar, a pupil and later colleague of Smith, and an influential opponent of slavery, actually undercut the governing premises of the antislavery movement. Progress, Millar insisted, was always the "natural" consequence of impersonal economic forces. It was never the result of benevolent intent, individual goodwill, or a changed disposition of the people.[14]

---

most liberal and enlightened in modern policy" when slaveholders appealed to the principles of laissez faire. One might as well, he argued, extend the principles of liberty to the destruction of criminal jurisprudence (*An Inquiry into the Colonial Policy of the European Powers* [Edinburgh, 1803],2: 472).

14. Halévy, *Growth of Philosophic Radicalism,* 153–54 and *passim*; J. R. Poynter, *Society and Pauperism: English Ideas on Poor Relief, 1795–1834* (London, 1969), 23–27, 53, 138; Duncan Forbes, " 'Scientific' Whiggism: Adam Smith and John Millar," *Cambridge Journal,* 7 (August 1954): 643–70. Viner, in "Adam Smith and Laissez Faire," notes the discrepancy between Smith's *Theory of Moral Sentiments* and *Wealth of Nations.* One of Smith's anonymous converts published some advice to the abolitionists which embodied the hard realism of the Utilitarians: "Instead of employing the money of your subscribers in paying people for collecting instances of cruelty and oppression, which, if true, only prove what no one denies, that *slaves are slaves,*" the abolitionists should gather evidence to show "that the West Indian islands, so far from being of the importance commonly ascribed to them, have . . . long been, and while the present system remains, must continue to be, a dead weight about the neck of this country, to stifle its efforts and distract its strength." Humanitarian zeal, the author predicted, would only lead "the man of reflection to distrust a cause undertaken by such missionaries." Any legislative attempts to prohibit the slave trade would be as unenforceable as were the early Spanish efforts to prohibit the export of gold and silver. But if the West Indies were deprived of monopolistic privileges and subjected to the forces of free competition, the artificial demand for slaves would cease, and the islands would be inhabited and

Yet paradoxically, the age of early Utilitarianism was also dominated by the cult of sensibility and by evangelical benevolence. Nor did a divergence of the two mentalities lead to ideological warfare. Bentham once confided that he would have been a Methodist "had I not been what I am." He added, significantly, "If to be an anti-slavist is to be a saint, saintship for me. I am a saint!" Halévy has helped to explain why Christian philanthropy could for a time be compatible with antireligious Utilitarianism. Both schools of thought looked upon life as a perpetual struggle; both stressed the need to sacrifice present pleasure for the hope of future happiness; both valued efficiency and practical technique, and preached a form of socially oriented individualism.[15] One may add that both Utilitarian intellectuals and Christian missionaries were experimenting with new methods that would have the effect of ensuring the hegemony of an emerging ruling class.

Eventually, Utilitarianism would become a "radical" instrument in the hands of middle-class reformers, and the landed aristocracy would come to symbolize the retrogressive forces of monopoly. But during the early stages of the antislavery movement, no one could envision the meaning of an industrial society or predict the full implications of utility and laissez faire. The wars of the French Revolution helped to delay any sense of sharp division between industrialists and landlords, between free traders and protectionists, or between Utilitarian reformers and Evangelicals. William Wilberforce, for example, who represented the Christian paternalism of the landed aristocracy, could good-naturedly act as Bentham's intermediary with cabinet ministers, and conclude, after the government had finally abandoned Bentham's plan for a "Panopticon" prison, that "never was any one worse used than Bentham."

Such philanthropic causes as prison reform and antislavery provided a meeting ground for Utilitarians and Christian "Saints." And if few of the early abolitionists were advocates of unqualified laissez faire, their popular movement served as a vehicle for the economic doctrines of Smith's disciples. It was perhaps accidental that Smith's influence on public policy, beginning with Lord North's tax reforms and Lord Shelburne's short ministry of 1782, coincided with the emergence of antislavery activism. Less coincidentally, Pitt, who personally consulted Smith in 1787 on an unknown economic matter, supported Smith's doctrines along with antislavery. Charles James Fox, Burke, and Wilberforce, all eloquent opponents of the

---

cultivated by "a much more useful body of men" (*A Letter to Granville Sharp, Esq., on the Proposed Abolition of the Slave Trade* [London, 1788], 32–43).
15. Elie Halévy, *England in 1815*, vol. 1 of *A History of the English People in the Nineteenth Century*), E. I. Watkin and D. A. Barker, trans. (London, 1949), 586–87.

slave trade, enhanced Smith's reputation in the House of Commons. By 1797, W. N. Pultney could assure the House that Smith would persuade the living generation and govern the next.[16]

More striking, however, are the parallels between the rise of antislavery and a profound transformation in attitudes toward the English poor, a transformation that reflected the growing contradiction between paternalistic traditions of local charity and the demands of a free-market economy. The first two decades of antislavery agitation were times of confusing contrasts: manufacturing towns grew in the midst of an agricultural and aristocratic society; famine and unemployment coexisted with a rising demand for industrial labor; for a time, cotton manufacturers profited from the Old Poor Law which supplied them with parish apprentices and which threw most of the burden of supporting paupers on the country squires; a staggering increase in welfare costs (the poor rates) was offset by lingering paternalism and by the fear of hungry Jacobin mobs. Karl Polanyi has documented the slow and painful emergence of the ideal of a self-regulating labor market, in which the avoidance of starvation and the pursuit of self-gain would be the only incentives for work. The English squirearchy, in particular, resisted any measures that would erode their authority, disrupt the paternalistic order of the countryside, or destroy a sense of reciprocity and personal obligation as economic incentives. It was not until 1795 that Parliament loosened the restrictions of the 1662 Act of Settlement, which had virtually bound certain categories of workers to a parish. But this move toward a national labor market was counterbalanced by the famous Speenhamland Law, also of 1795, which established an allowance system designed to assure the poor of a minimum income, irrespective of earnings, and to prevent a further drain of rural labor. The allowance system had the effect of depressing wages, of guaranteeing a public subsidy to employers, and of exacerbating the problem of pauperism. As late as the 1820s, British statesmen feared any sudden removal of the allowance system—much as they feared an immediate emancipation of West Indian slaves. By then, however, the English middle class had become increasingly dissatisfied with piecemeal reforms. In 1834, the same year that witnessed the nominal emancipation of West Indian slaves, the Poor Law Amendment liberated the English workers from

16. For the difficulties in assessing Smith's influence, see E. G. West, *Adam Smith* (New Rochelle, N.Y., 1969), 165–73; Jacob H. Hollander, "The Founder of a School," in *Adam Smith, 1776–1926: Lectures to Commemorate the Sesquicentennial of the Publication of "Wealth of Nations"* (New York, 1966 [reprint]), 22–52; Halévy, *Growth of Philosophic Radicalism*, 107; Wesley C. Mitchell, *Types of Economic Theory: From Mercantilism to Institutionalism*, Joseph Dorfman, ed. (New York, 1967), 152–62; C. R. Fay, "Adam Smith: A Bicentenary Appreciation," *Dalhousie Review*, 3 (January 1924): 403–22.

public welfare and offered the unemployed a choice between starvation and
the humiliating workhouse. Both "emancipations" had been made possible
by the political triumph, in 1832, of the middle class.[17]

There was no consistent or inevitable connection between antislavery
doctrine and the laissez-faire ideal of a competitive labor market. The early
abolitionists reflected the ambivalent attitudes of a transitional age and
economy. Wilberforce and the Evangelicals tried to preserve traditional notions of deference and paternalism. The Quakers, on the other hand, had
long taken the leadership in proposing labor reforms that would provide relief for the unemployed while making pauperism profitable for enlightened
entrepreneurs. Yet the tension between forward- and backward-looking desires should not obscure a significant fact: the first decades of antislavery
agitation also witnessed an outpouring of tracts on the problem of labor discipline. And the chief figures who helped to revise the traditional paternalism toward the "laboring poor" were all outspoken opponents of Negro
slavery: Pitt, Burke, Samuel Romilly, Bentham, William Paley, Hannah
More, and Thomas Malthus.

In 1786, the year of Thomas Clarkson's famous *Essay on the Slavery and
Commerce of the Human Species*, the Reverend Joseph Townsend suggested
the relationship between antislavery and the ideal of a free and self-regulating market for labor. In his influential attack on the Poor Laws, Townsend
wrote:

> The poor know little of the motives which stimulate the higher
> ranks to action—pride, honour, and ambition. In general it is only
> hunger which can spur and goad them on to labour; yet our laws

17. Karl Polanyi, *The Great Transformation* (New York, 1944), 68–102. John Clive
has pointed to the first post-Reform Bill election in Leeds "as a microcosm of the
social and economic forces in conflict during the 1830s." On the Tory side was Michael Thomas Sadler, a champion of maximum-hours legislation for working children. The Whig opposition consisted of a prominent mill owner and Thomas
Babington Macaulay, the son of the abolitionist and a rising spokesman for laissez-
faire and middle-class ideology. William Cobbett and working-class radicals supported Sadler. Macaulay, who had savagely reviewed a book by Sadler attacking Malthusian economics, maintained that "the lower orders" (he discreetly redefined the
group as "the labouring class") would benefit far more from free trade than from a
ten-hour-day law for persons under eighteen. As Clive perceptively observes, "the
views of Sadler and Macaulay illustrate the differing directions in which tributaries
from the stream of evangelical social teaching could flow in the course of the nineteenth century." Sadler had retained both his Evangelical faith (he had been a friend
of Wilberforce's) and a paternalistic sense of social responsibility "that could eventually lead to a dutiful acceptance of the need for state intervention." Macaulay, who
had moved away from his Evangelical upbringing, had adapted "the doctrine of a
providentially ordered class system . . . to the iron decrees of the classical economists. The laws of supply and demand were no less ineluctable than the divine edicts,
and both seemed to be dependent for their working on a reserve army of labor" (John
Clive, *Macaulay: The Shaping of the Historian* [New York, 1973], 221–25).

have said, they shall never hunger. The laws, it must be confessed, have likewise said that they shall be compelled to work. But then legal constraint is attended with too much trouble, violence, and noise; creates ill will, and never can be productive of good and acceptable service: whereas hunger is not only a peaceable, silent, unremitted pressure, but, as the most natural motive to industry and labour, it calls forth the most powerful exertions. . . . The slave must be compelled to work; but the freeman should be left to his own judgment and discretion; should be protected in the full enjoyment of his own, be it much or little; and punished when he invades his neighbor's property. By recurring to those base motives which influence the slave, and trusting only to compulsion, all the benefits of free service, both to the servant and to the master, must be lost.[18]

Sir Frederick Morton Eden, one of Adam Smith's many disciples, followed the precedents of the slave-trade investigations when he gathered empirical data on "the state of the poor." Paley, in his *Reasons for Contentment* (1795), echoed the West Indian planters by contending that poor workers were much happier than their rich employers, since they were spared from so many cares. The abolitionist Burke, in his *Thoughts and Details on Scarcity, Originally Presented to the Right Honourable William Pitt* (1795), pointed out that "the labouring people are only poor, because they are numerous. Numbers in their nature imply poverty. . . . Patience, labour, sobriety, frugality, and religion, should be recommended to them; all the rest is downright *fraud*. It is horrible to call them 'The *once happy* labourer.' " Malthus asserted that no public relief should be given to illegitimate or deserted children; only the threat of starvation would teach the poor to depend on themselves. Yet Malthus became highly indignant when William Cobbett's *Political Register* used his "profound work" to defend both the slave trade and West Indian slavery![19] The central point for Townsend, Burke, Paley, and Malthus was that the problem of English labor should be seen as entirely distinct from West Indian slavery, except in so far as "false charity" had kept the English poor in bondage.

The *Edinburgh Review*, a leading organ for antislavery propaganda, also disseminated Malthusian economics (the rival Tory journal, the *Quarterly*

18. [Joseph Townsend], "A Dissertation on the Poor Laws," in [J. R. McCulloch], *A Select Collection of Scarce and Valuable Economical Tracts* (London, 1859), 404.
19. *The Works of the Right Honourable Edmund Burke* (London, 1889), 5: 84; Poynter, *Society and Pauperism*, 20–24, 53, 157, 166; *Cobbett's Political Register*, 7 (16 February 1805): 229–32; 9 (18 January 1806), 72–76. Unlike later reformers, Burke thought that alcohol would be of some help to the poor: "It is not nutritive in *any great* degree. But, if not food, it greatly alleviates the want of it. It invigorates the stomach for the digestion of poor meagre diet, not easily alliable to the human constitution. Wine the poor cannot touch. Beer . . . will by no means do the business" (*Works*, 5: 106).

*Review*, attacked Malthus and defended the West Indian planters). Henry Brougham, one of the founders of the *Edinburgh Review*, first won national attention by attacking the slave trade and by demanding a total reformation of the colonial system. Although his abolitionism gave Brougham entrée to the Wilberforce circle, he remained independent of their Tory sympathies and helped to revitalize a Whig Opposition based on the values and aspirations of the new middle class. In 1812 he borrowed and perfected abolitionist methods when he mobilized a vast petition campaign against the Orders-in-Council that had attempted to control the trade of neutral nations (mainly the United States). Brougham's victory was hailed as a triumph for free-trade principles, as a triumph for the new industrialists, and above all, as a triumph for public opinion. According to Asa Briggs, the campaign of 1812 was as instrumental in organizing middle-class self-consciousness as was the Luddite movement in organizing working-class resistance to the bourgeoisie. Briggs has also shown how Brougham's success in shaping middle-class opinion culminated in the anti–Corn Law movement, which was heavily indebted to the precedents of antislavery agitation. The 1826 *Catechism on the Corn Laws*, for example, not only followed the familiar question-and-answer format of abolitionist literature, but included this exchange: *Q.* asserts that the relation between landlords and others, arising out of the Corn Laws, is a "source of kindly feelings and mutual virtues"; *A.* replies, "Exactly the same was said of slavery." No more needed to be said.[20]

20. Halévy, *England in 1815*, 574; Asa Briggs, "The Language of 'Class' in Early Nineteenth-Century England," in *Essays in Labour History: In Memory of G. D. H. Cole*, Asa Briggs and John Saville, eds. (London, 1960), 55–60; Chester W. New, *The Life of Henry Brougham, to 1830* (Oxford, 1961), 36–44, 59, 67–70. Brougham was anything but doctrinaire; he easily bridged the worlds of the Utilitarian reformer James Mill and the evangelical reformer Zachary Macaulay. His personal loyalty to abolitionists transcended partisan politics, as he evidenced when appointed Lord Chancellor, in dispensing patronage. He was perfectly attuned to the causes—antislavery, Catholic Emancipation, parliamentary reform, education, and free trade—which defined the emerging self-consciousness of the middle class. It was Brougham's antislavery alliance with Zachary Macaulay that helped to pave the way for the latter's son, Thomas Babington, to rise to prominence as a writer and public speaker. As John Clive suggests, Tom Macaulay's abolitionism kept him in favor with his father at a time when Tom was drifting away from Evangelical orthodoxy. In the 1820s antislavery served a similar legitimizing function in British politics, as the banner passed from the Tories to Brougham and even to the great Catholic leader, Daniel O'Connell. Clive's analysis of Tom Macaulay's emerging social philosophy illuminates the meaning of class hegemony in the 1820s: "The important thing was that those who were going forward should feel that they were doing so as part of a general movement that embraced all classes. Since it was plainly impossible to unteach the poor, it was essential to teach those who could by comparison, be called the rich, that is, the middle class." For Macaulay, who wished above all to avoid

Such continuities do not imply that antislavery was a cloak for selfish interests. No doubt the movement unconsciously reflected the interests and aspirations of the English middle class. More important, however, it helped to crystallize an awareness of those interests and to identify them with those of the nation. An end to economic protectionism could thus be styled as the ultimate "emancipation." This conclusion is not weakened by the fact that the free-trade issue divided both the abolitionists and the middle class. Most abolitionists were far less concerned with extending the potential impact of their ideology than with the need to prevent a direct challenge to property rights in human beings from undermining the sanctions for property rights in general. The question of middle-class ideology does not involve individual motives but rather the ways in which antislavery precedents were actually used. Antislavery was a transitional social movement that served to mediate values and to prepare the way for the largely unforeseen things to come.

In some respects, the movement also fits Oliver MacDonagh's abstract "model" for later British reforms, although MacDonagh has specifically excluded antislavery as an appropriate example. The model can be summarized, with some oversimplification, as follows: a sudden and sensational exposé of a social evil is followed by a popular outcry, by a reaction from endangered interests, and by legislation that falls short of original reform objectives; soon it is discovered that the original evils still exist, and the precedent of the first law opens the way for further legislation and stricter rules of enforcement; a need for supervision and regulation replaces the earlier demands for abolition, and investigative commissions give way to more permanent bureaucratic agencies.[21] For our purposes the mechanisms of a "revolution in government" are less significant than a point which MacDonagh does not develop. The interaction between middle-class reformers and government provides an outlet for noisy and indignant agitation and gives a sanctioned recognition of limited conflict. Yet it also ensures some kind of compromise and the illusion of an ultimate harmony of interests. England was not governed by a slaveholding class, though the ruling elites

---

democracy or revolution and to link the general progress of society with social stability, the middle class was " 'not likely to carry its zeal for reform to lengths inconsistent with the security of property and the maintenance of social order' " (Clive, *Macaulay*, 58–60, 70, 103, 112).

21. Oliver MacDonagh, "The Nineteenth-Century Revolution in Government: A Reappraisal," *Historical Journal*, 1 (1958): 52–67; MacDonagh, *A Pattern of Government Growth, 1800–1860* (London, 1961). Brian Harrison has shown that the British temperance movement fails to fit MacDonagh's model (*Drink and the Victorians: The Temperance Question in England, 1815–1827* [Pittsburgh, Pa., 1971], 28–29).

had included and tolerated a few slaveholders. An attack on the slave system could thus become a permissible means of responding to change without a weakening or discrediting of class hegemony.

On another level, antislavery provided a new channel for political action. The year 1787 marked the transformation of the Quaker anti-slave-trade committee into a secular pressure group that soon began collecting evidence and petitions for Wilberforce's great parliamentary campaign, a campaign initially proposed by Pitt and later endorsed enthusiastically by such rival leaders as Fox and Burke. Seven years earlier the so-called Gordon Riots, which had convulsed London in a week of pillage climaxing in an attack on the Bank of England, had shown how popular agitation could unleash diverse grievances. By 1780, mainly as a result of the American war, it was also clear that large segments of the middle class would continue to demand some form of extraparliamentary political activity, and that such activity could prove exceedingly useful to strong factions, like the Rockingham Whigs, when they were out of power. From 1779 to 1785 the Yorkshire-based movement for parliamentary reform provided a safe channel for controlled agitation. The "Association" movement served a multitude of purposes: it allowed the "out" factions to embarrass the "in" factions so long as the latter did not appropriate the reform cause; it enhanced the popular reputation of aspiring leaders like Fox and Pitt; it enabled a practical-minded organizer, the Reverend Christopher Wyvill, to neutralize the more radical demands of metropolitan supporters; above all, it tested the amount of popular participation the system was willing to allow. But in 1783, with the achievement of peace, the reform movement suffered serious division and disillusionment when Fox sacrificed his principles and entered the "infamous coalition" with Lord North in the Portland ministry. By 1786, after Pitt as prime minister had been defeated in his third and last attempt at moderate parliamentary reform, there appeared to be no further hope. As Ian Christie has pointed out, the American crisis had raised the specter of a court conspiracy undermining the liberties of the ancient constitution; but the period of fear and agitation barely survived the war.[22]

Meanwhile, Wyvill had swung his Yorkshire Association behind Pitt, who had acquired the popular image as a champion of liberal causes. Wyvill's political protegé, William Wilberforce, was also an intimate friend of

22. George Rudé, *Wilkes and Liberty: A Social Study of 1763–1774* (Oxford, 1962), 135–48; Ian R. Christie, *Wilkes, Wyvill and Reform: The Parliamentary Reform Movement in British Politics, 1760–1785* (London, 1962), 70–81, 110–32, 146–66, 202–23; Eugene Charlton Black, *The Association: British Extraparliamentary Political Organization, 1769–1793* (Cambridge, Mass., 1963), 14, 31–33, 60–66, 87, 99–105, 111–21, 132, 201–4.

Pitt. By 1788, Wilberforce was writing Wyvill that "our little kingdom" of Yorkshire should not be backward in organizing district meetings to petition Parliament against the slave trade (adding, *"entre nous,"* that Wyvill would be delighted to hear Pitt talk on the slave question). Veteran organizers of Wyvill's Yorkshire Association were soon at work collecting petition signatures. Eugene Charlton Black is perhaps too harsh when he writes that "Wilberforce learned his techniques for antislavery agitation in the Yorkshire Association school, and, intriguingly enough, Pitt used Wilberforce much the same way that he had previously used Wyvill."[23] On the other hand, if we suspend questions of personal motive and deliberate strategy (and there can be no doubt that both Pitt and Wilberforce found the slave trade morally repugnant), confining our view to the history of extra-parliamentary association, it seems apparent that antislavery petitioning revived enthusiasm among a constituency that had become bored or disillusioned over the futile struggle to "purify" Parliament. Indeed, the slave-trade issue gave Parliament a chance to vindicate its own moral purity and to prove its responsiveness to "respectable" petitioning. And the new movement provided the public with a safe distraction—or to put it more charitably, with a mode of political participation which did not directly threaten the sources or structure of political power.

As Pitt was quick to perceive, extraparliamentary groups could be as useful to the government as to factions aspiring to power, although he personally detested the word "association." During the early years of the French Revolution, his own administration gave support and encouragement to vigilante societies such as the Association for the Preservation of Liberty and Property, which helped to terrorize the advocates of liberal reform. Abolitionist agitation was still on the rise when loyalist mobs were attacking the premises of men like Joseph Priestley and Thomas Walker, and when other dissidents were being tried for treason and sedition. The key question, then, is whether antislavery would be perceived as potentially subversive or as a force that helped to preserve "liberty and property."

The second part of this question will require extensive development [ . . . ], but I shall touch on the first part now. Until 1792 there were still ideological ties between the antislavery movement and the constitutional societies that were beginning to distribute Painite literature to the working class. It was to be expected that English radicals like Thomas Paine and

23. Wilberforce to Wyvill, 25 January 1788, Wilberforce papers, in possession of C. E. Wrangham, Esq. (hereafter CEW), to whom I am much indebted for allowing me to consult this collection; E. M. Hunt, "The North of England Agitation for the Abolition of the Slave Trade, 1780–1800" (M.A. thesis, University of Manchester, 1959), 252–53; Black, *The Association*, 124.

Thomas Hardy, who embraced the ideals of the American and French Revolutions, should include antislavery among the political causes they espoused. When Thomas Cooper combined anti-slave-trade agitation with more radical activities in the north of England, a hysterical pamphlet accused Cooper, Paine, Clarkson, and Wilberforce of being "the JACOBINS OF ENGLAND." Wilberforce himself, who saw that it was only "natural" that Jacobins should be friendly to abolitionism, sent word to Clarkson that any further talk of the French Revolution "will be ruin to our cause." In some of the provincial centers, middle-class abolitionists complained that no one except "Republicans" would sign petitions against the slave trade.[24]

Consequently, the more frightened and conservative members of the antislavery committees tended to withdraw from the cause at the very time when radicals were becoming wholly absorbed with the struggle against domestic suppression. By the summer of 1792, Thomas Hardy of the London Corresponding Society was not alone in fearing that abolitionism might divert attention from more pressing and critical issues. The Manchester Abolition Committee, which contained a growing preponderance of radicals, held its last meeting on 17 April 1792; eleven days later the radical *Manchester Herald* delivered what E. M. Hunt has termed "the last blast of the campaign in Manchester," announcing "with grief" that the House of Commons had decided to sanction the slave trade for seven more years: "She weeps, indignant, whilst she announces to the world the tardiness of the REPRESENTATIVES of the people of BRITAIN to do JUSTICE." Yet the movement as a whole survived both the suppression of radical dissent and the growing disillusion of radical reformers. It also survived middle-class defections from more dangerous causes. The London Abolition Committee continued to meet, though with growing infrequency, until 1797. And if the tides of reaction finally made it prudent to suspend further public agitation, antislavery remained popular in the House of Commons, which as late as 1796 rejected Wilberforce's immediate abolition bill by the narrow margin of seventy-four to seventy votes. British antislavery suffered for a while from the taint of Jacobinism, but it largely purged itself of the embarrassing association.[25]

---

24. Austin Mitchell, "The Association Movement of 1792–1793," *Historical Journal*, 4 (1961): 56–77; Maurice J. Quinlan, *Victorian Prelude: A History of English Manners, 1700–1830* (London, 1965), 73–86; James Walvin, "How Popular Was Abolition? Popular Dissent and the Negro Question, 1787–1833" (MS); Black, *The Association*, 223–67; *A Very New Pamphlet Indeed! Being the Truth . . .* (London, 1792), 3–5; Robert Isaac Wilberforce and Samuel Wilberforce, *The Life of William Wilberforce* (London, 1838), 1: 343.
25. Hunt, "North of England Agitation," 57–58, 105–13; Walvin, "How Popular Was Abolition?" The Abolition Committee met three times in 1796, once in 1797,

I have already noted the apparent discrepancy between the political economists' sympathy for the slave and their hostility toward the "false charity" that had kept the English poor in a state of moral bondage. The contemporary interpretations of that discrepancy require a third level of analysis: the use of antislavery literature as a means of resolving conflicts in value.

Much as white Americans had learned to deny or rationalize the worst evils of Negro slavery, so had middle-class Englishmen learned to screen out most of the oppression and suffering in their midst. If the cult of sensibility encouraged sympathy for individual misfortune, the cult of utility gave  grounds for believing that such misfortune was a necessary part of the general good. It is true that the mechanisms of denial were becoming increasingly sensitive, especially after the French Revolution evoked a consciousness of peril. Yet a half-century later, as E. P. Thompson observes, "when the girls were brought half-naked out of the pits, the local luminaries seem to have been genuinely astonished." Thompson adds: "We forget how long abuses can continue 'unknown' until they are articulated: how people can look at misery and not notice it, until misery itself rebels."[26] Although the various religious and benevolent societies helped to foster an awareness of domestic suffering, it was blunted by the fear of revolution and by the reigning attitudes toward property and responsibility. Yet the misgivings of men of goodwill, arising from the "inconsistency" between liberal profession and daily practice, could be psychologically displaced in a concern for "the unfortunate slave."

This is a difficult thesis to substantiate. At best it can illuminate no more than one aspect of an enormously complex movement. The central questions do not concern conscious intent but rather selectivity, context, and emphasis.

For our first illustration, let us return to James Stephen's musings, early in 1807, on the reasons for God's vengeance against England. It should be noted in passing that Stephen was perhaps the most powerful intellect of the British abolition movement, and that for some thirty years he had a decisive influence on the movement's policy. His indictment of the inconsistency of English practice is also a panegyric of English society:

---

and then suspended meetings until 23 May 1804. It is significant that when Clarkson was contemplating retirement, for personal reasons in August 1793, he gave a candid prediction to Wilberforce, William Smith, Josiah Wedgwood, and Matthew Montagu that it would be "two or three years" before the cause succeeded (Clarkson to Matthew Montagu, 28 August 1793, Clarkson papers, HEH).

26. E. P. Thompson, *The Making of the English Working Class* (New York, 1963), 342.

Who are the people that have provoked God thus heinously, but the same who are among all the nations of the earth, the most emi-nently indebted to his bounty. He has given to us an unexampled portion of civil liberty; and we in return drag his rational creatures into a most severe and perpetual bondage. Social happiness has been showered upon us with singular profusion; and we tear from op-pressed millions every social, nay, almost every human com-fort. . . . For our plenty we give them want; for our ease, intolerable toil; for our wealth, privation of the right of property; for our equal laws, unbridled violence and wrong. Science shines upon us, with her meridian beams; yet we keep these degraded fel-low-creatures in the deepest shades of ignorance and barbarity. Morals and manners, have happily distinguished us from the other nations of Europe; yet we create and cherish in two other quarters of the globe [Africa and the West Indies], an unexampled depravity of both.[27]

This was hardly the England perceived by the London Corresponding So-ciety, by Francis Place or William Cobbett, by John Thelwall, Henry Hunt, or "General Ludd." Yet for Stephen an attack on the slave system provided the occasion for an explicit vindication of the English social order. What could account, he asked, for the divine vengeance that had heaped so many calamities upon England? According to Scripture, the causes most fre-quently assigned for the chastisement of sinful nations were "the sins of oppression, injustice, and violence towards the poor and helpless; and the shedding of innocent blood." To English radicals these words might have re-called the domestic oppression of the 1790s, the Irish bloodbath of 1798, or Cobbett's charge, made in 1806, that England was "daily advancing to the state in which there are but two classes of men, *masters*, and abject *depen-dents*."[28] Stephen's own view is important enough to quote at some length:

If we cast our eyes around us in this happy island, there is still less matter of charge against the national conscience on the score of vio-lence and oppression. In no other part of the globe, are the poor and helpless so well protected by the laws, or so humanely used by their superiors. Nor are the laws chargeable with injustice towards the less fortunate peasantry of our sister island; though here perhaps, there is much that ought to be reformed. If the legislature be now culpable in regard to Ireland, it is for omission and neglect, rather than for positive wrong; nor does the fault arise from any of those unrighteous principles, or from that oppressive use of power, which

27. James Stephen, *The Dangers of the Country* (Philadelphia, 1807; originally printed London, 1807), 121.
28. *Ibid.*, 112; Raymond Williams, *Culture and Society* (New York, 1958), 14–15.

are so peculiarly offensive to heaven. If therefore we are suffering for such offences as have usually provoked the scourge of the Most High, if it be as the protector of the poor and destitute, that God has entered into judgment with us, we must, I repeat, look to Africa, and to the West Indies, for the causes of his wrath.[29]

It should be stressed that Stephen, a deeply religious man, was obsessed by fears of collective guilt and retribution. Unlike his brother-in-law, Wilberforce, he personally knew the meaning of oppression and poverty. His father, a tempestuous Scot who had admired the French *philosophes* and who had sent young James to the school of Peter Annet, the notorious Deist, had not been "well protected by the laws" or "humanely used" by his superiors. As a result of bankruptcy he had, in fact, been thrown into King's Bench Prison and then transferred to a more secure jail after leading an attempted breakout to protest the illegality of imprisonment for debt. Along with his destitute mother, James had lived for a time in the squalid jail, surrounded by spectacles of drunkenness and despair.[30] England had been for him anything but a "happy island" until he returned, as a young lawyer, from the West Indies and won acceptance in the Clapham Sect. Apart from his own experience with poverty, he was clearly aware of England's conduct in India (which he goes on to defend), as well as of the torture, arbitrary imprisonment, and massacre that had marked the suppression of Irish dissent (Henry Grattan had proclaimed that "the Irish Protestant can never be free until the Irish Catholic has ceased to be a slave"). And yet the meaning of Stephen's language is quite explicit. Interpreting God's justice to his countrymen, he made an attack on Negro slavery serve as an all-redeeming atonement.[31]

But the ideological functions of antislavery literature were still more

29. Stephen, *Dangers of the Country*, 115–16.
30. James Stephen, MS Memoirs "written by himself for the use of his children," British Museum Add. MSS 46443–44. Stephen was the father of Sir James Stephen and the grandfather of Leslie and Sir James Fitzjames Stephen.
31. Henry Grattan is quoted in J. Steven Watson, *The Reign of George III, 1760–1815* (Oxford, 1960), 392. Stephen's theme also appeared in parliamentary speeches and, more significantly, in handbills like *The Contrast; or, the African Slave, and the English Labourer* (c. 1805?), which announced that the English worker was blessed with a twelve-hour day, that he had wages with which to buy food, that "he is as independent as his employer," and that he "would be ready to strike his master to the ground if he saw him degrade a woman" by flogging her on the naked breasts. James Walvin has pointed out that English radicals like John Thelwall employed antislavery rhetoric to dramatize the similar plight of English workers and West Indian bondsmen. Although more research is needed on the subject, I suspect that Walvin exaggerates the continuing appeal of antislavery to working-class leaders (for later proslavery feeling among English radical leaders, see Mary Ellison, *Support for Secession: Lancashire and the American Civil War* [Chicago, 1972]).

complex. The wider connotations of Negro slavery appear in a portion of William Cowper's "Charity," a long sermon in verse which had immense and continuing appeal to abolitionists and which is virtually a paradigm of early British antislavery thought.[32] Writing five years after the publication of *The Wealth of Nations*, Cowper sings the praises of Captain Cook and of international trade, which is providentially designed "To give the pole the produce of the sun, / And Knit the unsocial climates into one." Commerce is the great engine of human progress; it "Spreads foreign wonders in his country's sight, / Imports what others have invented well / And stirs his own to match them or excel."

But this happy lesson in political economy brings us to the slave merchant, who grows "rich in cargoes of despair." Clearly the expansion of Europe has not been a universal blessing to mankind. The name Cortez is "odious for a world enslaved!" Catholic Iberia has suffered divine vengeance for centuries of greed and plunder. The lesson should not be lost on traders who "buy the muscles and the bones of man." Cowper pictures the conventional sable warrior, "frantic with regret / Of her he loves, and never can forget." Slavery is the "most degrading of all ills": "Yes, to deep sadness sullenly resigned, / He feels his body's bondage in his mind; / Puts off his generous nature; and, to suit / His manners with his fate, puts on the brute." Cowper boldly advises the slave to "Wait for the dawning of a brighter day, / And snap the chain the moment when you may." This leads the poet to a lyrical passage on natural liberty, which moves from an external command to exuberant release, subsiding into pastoral contentment:

> Nature imprints upon whate'er we see
> That has a heart and life in it, "Be free!"
> The beasts are chartered—neither age nor force
> Can quell the love of freedom in a horse:

32. William Cowper, "Charity," in *The Poems of William Cowper*, J. C. Bailey, ed. (London, 1905), 165–78. In the spring of 1788, Lady Hesketh suggested that Cowper write some songs on the slave trade "as the surest way of reaching the public ear." Cowper was at first reluctant; he had "already borne my testimony in favour of my black brethren [in "Charity"] and . . . was one of the earliest, if not the first, of those who have in the present day expressed their detestation of the diabolical traffic." After writing five ballads, including "The Negro's Complaint" and "Pity for Poor Africans," he wrote Lady Hesketh: "I shall now probably cease to sing of tortured negroes—a theme which never pleased me, but which, in the hope of doing them some little service, I was not unwilling to handle." These poems were immensely popular on both sides of the Atlantic and were read by many who would never have opened an antislavery pamphlet. See Thomas Wright, *The Life of William Cowper* (London, 1892), 471–72; Gilbert Thomas, *William Cowper and the Eighteenth Century*, 2d edn. (London, 1948), 28–29; Lodwick Hartley, *William Cowper: The Continuing Revaluation* (Chapel Hill, N.C., 1960), 8–9.

He breaks the cord that held him at the rack;
And, conscious of an unencumbered back,
Snuffs up the morning air, forgets the rein;
Loose fly his forelock and his ample mane;
Responsive to the distant neigh, he neighs;
Nor stops till, overleaping all delays
He finds the pasture where his fellows graze.

This is an artful blend of British primitivism and natural rights philosophy, appealing to our impulsive yearnings to throw off the restraints and encumbrances of society, to be as free as a prancing horse. Yet there are striking ambiguities even in Cowper's image of spontaneous natural liberty. As an active force, nature "imprints" upon passive life its command of freedom. The beasts are "chartered" with an irrepressible desire to break all cords of bondage, to forget the rein. But charters restrict and prescribe, as well as protect. In effect, Cowper defines our love of freedom in words that suggest passivity and bondage. Liberation ends, finally, in a complacent grazing with "fellows."

After this pastoral excursion, Cowper returns to human slavery:

Canst thou, and honoured with a Christian name,
Buy what is woman-born, and feel no shame?
Trade in the blood of innocence, and plead
Expedience as a warrant for the deed?

Expediency, he reminds us, is the excuse for all crime and aggression:

So may the wolf, whom famine has made bold
To quit the forest and invade the fold;
So may the ruffian, who with ghostly glide,
Dagger in hand, steals close to your bedside;
Not he, but his emergence forced the door,
He found it inconvenient to be poor.

Thus far Cowper has used the slavery issue as a medium for expressing fairly radical but ambiguous attitudes toward liberty and authority. He equates liberty with the unrestrained release of natural instincts, which are nevertheless externally prescribed and which lead the horse to a peaceful and uncoerced sociability with his "fellows." Significantly, the idyll of pasture and sheepfold is threatened by the wolf, whose boldness has apparently been "chartered" by the famine and brutality of the wilderness; and, analogously, by the criminal, who voluntarily places self-interest and expediency above natural justice. Later in the poem Cowper insists that "the foe of virtue" has no claim on charity: "Let just restraint, for public peace de-

signed, / Chain up the wolves and tigers of mankind." In line with
conventional imagery, the native African is associated with pastoral innocence and natural liberty. His European abductor is linked with the wolf
who invades the fold and with the ruffian who finds it "inconvenient to be
poor." Neither famine nor poverty justifies violent resistance. But presumably the slave has a perfect right to break the cord that holds him at the rack,
and we should feel the same empathy toward the fugitive slave that we feel
toward the escaped horse "overleaping all delays."

But Cowper was an Evangelical and a devoted admirer of John Newton
and Henry Thornton. It was one thing to experiment with imagery of natural freedom and quite another to suggest that all men should snuff up the
morning air and forget the reins of society.[33] Cowper's nostalgic yearning
for rustic innocence is always balanced by his conviction that man, the
"progeny and heir of sin," can never learn his duty from reason and nature
alone. It is precisely the tension between these values which gives force to
Cowper's concept of charity and which gives him a solution to the moral
problem of European expansion.

Cowper cannot believe that New World slavery is part of God's design
for human progress. Surely God has not "Built a brave world, which cannot
yet subsist, / Unless His right to rule it be dismissed?" And even if one
grants the plea of economic necessity, there is still room for charity. Souls
have no "discriminating hue." Christ's love paid one price for all men. And
on this proselytizing note, Cowper shifts key and begins discussing spiritual slavery, by which he means ignorance of Christ's saving truth. Any
nominal Christian who scorns the "godlike privilege" of saving others is
"himself a slave." This brings us to the consummate image of "charity"—
a Negro slave kneeling before his evangelical liberator:

> And slaves, by truth enlarged, are doubly freed.
> Then would he say, submissive at thy feet,
> While gratitude and love made service sweet,
> "My dear deliverer out of a hopeless night,
> Whose bounty bought me but to give me light,
> I was a bondman on my native plain,
> Sin forged, and ignorance made fast, the chain;
> Thy lips have shed instruction as the dew,

---

33. Though Cowper was much distressed by the plight of the Olney poor, he was
even more distressed by the failure of the poor to embrace serious Christianity. In
1782 he expressed typical doubts about the value of "charity": "The profane are so
profane, so drunken, dissolute, and in every respect worthless, that to make them
partakers of his bounty would be to abuse it" (Wright, *Life of Cowper*, 319). For
Cowper's alarm over the Gordon Riots and the state of English society, see Maurice
J. Quinlan, *William Cowper: A Critical Life* (Minneapolis, 1953), 108–9.

Taught me what path to shun, and what pursue;
Farewell my former joys! I sigh no more
For Africa's once loved, benighted shore;
Serving a benefactor I am free;
At my best home, if not exiled from thee."

Our picture of freedom has swung abruptly away from the polarity of natural innocence. Note that the slave was a bondman on his "native plain," which is now a "benighted shore." He was not enslaved by a rapacious European but by sin and ignorance. Unlike the liberated horse, the black learns to "sigh no more / For Africa's once loved, benighted shore" (the horse, we should recall, neighs in response to the distant neigh, "nor stops till, overleaping all delays, / He finds the pasture where his fellows graze"). The black's liberator has taught him "what path to shun, and what pursue." His freedom lies in a conversion from unwilling to willing servitude. "Gratitude and love" enable him to internalize his new master's commands. His submission is legitimized by his sense of obligation.

For Cowper, as for many of his contemporaries, the image of Negro slavery evoked a contrary image of release, liberation, and natural freedom. Since slavery required physical coercion, its implied antithesis was a perfect freedom of will, instinct, and physical movement, or in other words, a state of self-sovereignty. This concept of freedom had considerable appeal, on levels of theory and emotion, to men of the late eighteenth century. It can be found in primitivistic fantasies, in portraits of the American as a New Adam, and in highly qualified form, in the Wesleyan ideal of the sanctified Christian.

But natural self-sovereignty threatened traditional Christian values as well as secular ideologies that justified social rank and social control. Had nature imprinted the mandate, "Be free!" upon the hearts of common laborers as well as upon horses? (And of course no one who took vicarious delight in a horse's freedom advocated the burning of saddles.) Was every man who wielded power in the name of expediency to be likened to a thief who finds it "inconvenient to be poor"? Cowper did not have to fret over such questions. The subjects of slavery and emancipation provided him with a medium for bridging two worlds of contradictory value. The remote institution of Negro slavery represented an idealized model of physical oppression which allowed both a paean to natural liberty and the rejection of expediency as an excuse for injustice. The fantasy of emancipation and conversion, with the grateful servant submissive at his benefactor's feet, gave sanction to dependence and authority by redefining the relationship—in contrast to physical slavery—as one of natural freedom. Charity redeemed the fruits of trade as well as the existing social order. "Some men," Cowper assures us, "make gain a fountain, whence proceeds / A stream of liberal and heroic deeds." In a leap of psychological imperialism, Cowper exorcized the guilt of commercial exploitation—first, by associating slavery with the loss of primitive liberty; then, by picturing emancipation as a conversion to voluntary servitude. In so doing, he helped define the identity of the evangelical deliverer.

## Antislavery as Reinforcement of Legitimate Authority

For a time it was at least conceivable that British antislavery might become part of a wider challenge to traditional authorities. During the mid-eighteenth century the most outspoken protests against Negro slavery had come from anonymous revolutionaries like "Philmore" or from egalitarian theorists like George Wallace.[34] By 1780 opposition to the American war, coupled with alarm over ministerial corruption, brought Granville Sharp, Thomas Day, and Richard Price, all noted opponents of slavery, together with metropolitan reformers like John Jebb, Capel Lofft, and Major John Cartwright. The methods and goals of their Society for Promoting Constitutional Information (S.C.I.) were far more radical than those of Wyvill's Yorkshire Association. And in 1783 the Society endorsed the Quaker petition to Parliament against the slave trade, a remonstrance which at least raised the question whether the "benevolent purposes" of government had been perverted, "that its terrors have fallen on the innocent, while evil doers, and oppressors, have been openly encouraged?" There is some truth to Eugene Black's argument that antislavery served as one of the distractions that diluted the effectiveness of the S.C.I. Yet in the provincial cities like Manchester, antislavery retained a radical flavor into the 1790s, and was frequently associated with bolder programs for political and economic reform. E. M. Hunt has pointed to the ties between antislavery and the Dissenters' campaign to repeal the Test and Corporation Acts. And according to Hunt, the anti-slave-trade cause gave Manchester radicals like Thomas Walker and Thomas Cooper their first experience in national agitation. In 1790, Walker linked antislavery with the "general principles of universal Liberty (unconfined to Colour or to Clime) . . . so recently and so widely adopted on the

34. In 1787, Major Cartwright sent Granville Sharp a subscription "towards the Emancipation of the Negroes" from the Reverend John Charlesworth, who had also loaned Cartwright Philmore's radical pamphlet, *Two Dialogues on the Man-Trade,* which Cartwright thought had been published forty or fifty years before (John Cartwright to Granville Sharp, 15 October 1787, Clarkson papers, HEH). Though Benezet had quoted from the pamphlet in 1762, two years after its actual publication, I have encountered no other references to it.

European continent." A few years later Walker stood trial for high treason after defending his premises against a drunken loyalist mob.[35]

The resistant power of traditionalism can be seen in Dr. Daniel Burton's serene reply, in 1768, to a letter from Anthony Benezet. Burton, who had been chancellor of the diocese of Oxford, was then secretary of the Society for the Propagation of the Gospel (S.P.G.), which Benezet had attacked for oppressing slaves on the Society's Barbadian plantations. Burton expressed a patronizing "esteem" for the Quaker's feelings of tenderness and humanity toward Negroes. He assured Benezet (quite without foundation) that members of the S.P.G. paid strict attention to the welfare and Christian instruction of their slaves: "But they *cannot condemn* the *Practice* of *keeping Slaves* as unlawful, finding the contrary very plainly implied in the precepts given by the Apostles, both to Masters & Servants, which last were for the most part Slaves." In other words, the doctrine that slave-keeping was unlawful might undermine the authority of Scripture. Furthermore, the dissemination of such a doctrine would tempt slaves to rebel and would make masters "more suspicious & cruel, & much more unwilling to let their Slaves learn Christianity." The S.P.G. advised the deluded but well-intentioned Quaker "not to go further in publishing your Notions, but rather to retract them, if you shall see cause, which they hope you may on further consideration."[36]

It was Granville Sharp, the grandson of an Anglican archbishop and a complex figure, in many ways atypical of English antislavery leaders, who

35. London Yearly Meeting and London Meeting for Sufferings, *The Case of Our Fellow-Creatures, the Oppressed Africans, Respectfully Recommended to the Serious Consideration of the Legislature of Great Britain, by the People Called Quakers* (London, 1783), 3–4; Black, *The Association*, 84, 177–78, 200–204; Hunt, "North of England Agitation," 12–14, 22–23, 33, 58–69, 99–115; Thomas Walker, printed sheet, 1790, William Smith papers, Duke University Library (hereafter DUL); Thomas Cooper, *Letters on the Slave Trade: First Published in "Wheeler's Manchester Chronicle"* (Manchester, 1787), *passim*; "Junius," "An Expostulatory Address to the *People* of *England* on the Late Memorable Decision Against the Abolition of the Slave Trade," *Gentleman's Magazine*, 61 (June 1791): 537–38; Thompson, *Making of the English Working Class*, 11–12, 120. Walker affirmed that since Britons had been "the *foremost* to propagate" such principles of liberty, they should not be the last to practice them. The principle of universalism, which Thompson finds in the London Corresponding Society, was also endorsed by the Manchester radicals, who called for the total abolition of *slavery* throughout the world (Hunt, 113). Walker, a wealthy textile manufacturer, frequently attended meetings of the London Abolition Committee, and continued to send the Committee money and petitions as late as March 1792 (Abolition Committee Minutes, 3: 42). That summer he was close to Thomas Paine, and in December he defended his premises against the loyalist mob.
36. Quoted in George S. Brookes, *Friend Anthony Benezet* (Philadelphia, 1937), 417–18.

countered this strategy by converting antislavery into a defense of traditional authority.[37] By 1767, Sharp had developed the following line of argument: no one could claim a Negro as private property, in the manner of
a horse or dog, unless he could prove that Negroes were not human beings
and thus *subjects* of the king; all men, women, and children including aliens
and strangers, were in a relative sense the "property" of the king; as subjects, they were bound by the king's laws and were entitled to the king's protection; the latter included the Habeas Corpus Act of 1679, which protected
subjects from arbitrary imprisonment or from being involuntarily shipped
out of the realm; the importation or exportation of slaves was thus an innovation, unjustified by either law or precedent; a master's rights could
derive only from contract, and any contract would be nullified if it perma-
nently deprived a servant of his corporal liberty. Indeed, Sharp assumed the
position of a discoverer and vindicator of the true law of England. In 1769,
he could write the Lord High Chancellor, protesting that a public advertise-
ment for the sale of a black girl was a breach not only of the laws of nature,
humanity, and equity, but of "the established law, custom, and constitution
of England." Three years later he won international fame when, in the case
of James Somerset, the Court of King's Bench appeared to say that he was
right.[38]

[ . . . ] The point to be stressed here is that Sharp drove a wedge between the defense of slavery and the defense of traditional privilege. His
more knowledgeable opponents, like Samuel Estwick, the assistant colonial
agent for Barbados, conceded that Negro slavery was an innovation unknown to common law and "totally different" from ancient villeinage. In
his commentary on the Somerset case, Estwick fell back upon the argument
that where there was no law, there could be no remedy. If slavery was in-
compatible with the maxims of common law, so were other practices, such

37. Sharp was in fact much upset by Burton's letter, and sent a private complaint to
the bishop of Llandaff (25 July 1774, Sharp papers, British and Foreign Bible Society). He declined, however, Benezet's request for public support. "I had too much
veneration for the Society," he later wrote the archbishop of Canterbury, "to permit
their opinion to be called publickly in question." Sharp did answer the S.P.G.'s
"missionary," the Reverend Thomas Thompson, who had gone further than Burton
by trying to vindicate the slave trade; and Burton's position led Sharp into scriptural
studies designed to remove the "stigma" Burton had thrown on "our Holy Religion" (Sharp to the archbishop of Canterbury, 1 August 1786, John A. Woods's
transcripts of Sharp papers [hereafter JAW]; also printed in Prince Hoare, *Memoirs
of Granville Sharp, Esq. Composed from His Own Manuscripts . . .* [London,
1820], 262).
38. Granville Sharp, *A Representation of the Injustice and Dangerous Tendency of
Tolerating Slavery; or of Admitting the Least Claim of Private Property in the Persons of Men, in England* (London, 1769), 10–41; Hoare, *Memoirs of Granville
Sharp,* 44–45, 49.

as the impressment of seamen, which were justified by special circumstances. And though Parliament had not specifically enacted a slave code, it had authorized the slave trade and had thus recognized legal claims to property in men. Estwick tried to avoid discussing servitude and dominion, claiming that the question must be confined to the ownership of legitimate articles of commerce. He admitted, however, that Parliament had the right to remedy any defects in the law. And by focusing on the bare "facts" of property rights and parliamentary sanction, he helped to sever the authority of slaveholders from more traditional forms of dominion.[39]

Antislavery ideology is usually considered as part of a wider egalitarian and liberalizing movement. Most of the arguments used against human bondage could have been turned against the forms of religious and hereditary privilege which dominated eighteenth-century England. Yet on the eve of the American Revolution, Granville Sharp's legal triumph helped to frame the boundaries of future controversy. The Somerset decision—which would be looked upon as the opening act of the antislavery drama—was interpreted as a vindication of law and tradition. It defined slavery as essentially "un-British," as an alien intrusion which could be tolerated, at best, as an unfortunate part of the commercial and colonial "other-world." A denunciation of colonial slavery therefore implied no taste for a freer or more equal society.

On the contrary, much of the early British antislavery writing reveals an almost obsessive concern with idealizing hierarchical order. The Reverend James Ramsay begins his highly praised *Essay on the Treatment and Conversion of African Slaves* (1784) by stating that "there is a natural inequality, or diversity, which prevails among men that fits them for society." When founded upon nature or revelation, such inequalities serve the best interests of both superiors and inferiors: "Each man takes that station for which nature intended him; and his rights are fenced around, and his claims restrained, by laws prescribed by the Author of nature."[40]

Ramsay praises the "voluntary" relationships between servant and master, blending a traditional ideal of organic interdependence with a Whiggish emphasis on implicit contract. Thus he finds that the entrepreneur's "superiority," derived from the ownership of material, is balanced by the workman's "liberty" to accept or refuse employment. Yet law and mutual

39. Samuel Estwick, *Considerations on the Negro Cause Commonly So Called, Addressed to the Right Honourable Lord Mansfield, Lord Chief Justice of the Court of King's Bench* . . . , 2d edn. (London, 1773), xiii, 21, 25–26, 31, 38–39.
40. James Ramsay, *An Essay on the Treatment and Conversion of African Slaves in the British Sugar Colonies* (London, 1784), 1–2. A naval surgeon before he took holy orders, Ramsay had spent some twenty years in the West Indies.

interest must be reinforced by religion—meaning the established church—
which inculcates obedience to legitimate authority. Such arguments seem
closer to those of Daniel Burton than to the equalitarian rhetoric of the
more radical American and French abolitionists. Indeed, Ramsay makes no
attempt to disguise his admiration for the discipline of the sugar plantation.
Drawing on his own experience in St. Kitts, he speaks glowingly of a system
which ensures that every hour will have its employment and every piece of
work its overseer: "Nor are any families among us so well regulated as
those connected with plantations, where method in correction and work
makes some amends for the want of principle in our manner of managing
slaves."[41]

Nevertheless, this "want of principle" means that slavery is the very
"negation of law":

> Opposed to this law of nature, and of God, that gives and secures to
> every man the rights adapted to his particular station in society,
> stands the artificial, or unnatural relation of master and slave;
> where power constitutes right; where, according to the degree of his
> capacity of coercion, every man becomes his own legislator, and
> erects his interest, or his caprice, into a law for regulating his con-
> duct to his neighbor.[42]

Slavery, then, is an evil not because of its inherent injustice, its inequality, or its permanent subordination of one class of men. It is an "artificial" and "unnatural" relation which lacks the legitimacy of tradition and
which removes both master and slave from the restraints that should control
all men. The institution presupposes that superior and inferior "are natural
enemies to each other," that there should be "tyranny on one side, treach-
ery and cunning on the other." And what clearly disturbs Ramsay the most
is the lack of sufficient control over the moral conduct of the slaves. His solution, as one might expect, is to replace physical terror with internalized
controls. He offers us images of young Negro children repeating moral precepts as they pick grass for the cattle; of "religious examinations" of families marshaled for review; of "merrymaking" under the strict direction of
slaves noted for sobriety; and of rare corporal punishments "inflicted with
solemnity, in presence of the gang, accompanied with some short explanation of the crime, and an exhortation from the chaplain, to abstain from it."
Such were the mechanisms for creating a society of free and willing laborers.[43]

41. *Ibid.*, 9–11, 172–73.
42. *Ibid.*, 3, 18.
43. *Ibid.*, 107–8, 173–75, 184–88.

If Ramsay's respect for discipline was a bit excessive, he was by no means unusual in his respect for traditional order. The year 1788, marking the centennial of the Glorious Revolution, gave a brief impetus to domestic reform, but also provided opportunities for converting antislavery into a vehicle for  social control. In the preface to a sermon preached at Cambridge University, Peter Peckard, the vice-chancellor and master of Magdalen College, supported the abolition of both slavery and the slave trade as part of a wider reformation of manners. He noted that a century had passed since Providence had blessed England with a free constitution. Let this year be a Jubilee of Commemoration, he pleaded, a time not for riot and drunkenness, but for the extension of the blessings of all Englishmen to the suffering Negro slaves. It was a time for "breaking every yoke, and setting the poor Captive free." Peckard hoped that by infusing into students a loyalty to the king, an obedience to magistrates, and a reverence for the constitution, a firm foundation could be built for the abolition cause. Thus, he coupled the emancipation of slaves with a call for domestic obedience and loyalty, and with an affirmation that the Glorious Revolution had defined the boundaries of legitimate freedom.[44]

In 1788, Edward White went even further in equating antislavery with a respect for governmental power. Though he disclaimed any intent of praising absolutist government, White suggested that a free people might find something worthy of imitation in the despotic regime of France. "That arbitrary power should ever be a friend to liberty," he wrote, "or to the alleviation of slavery, may appear a thing too opposite to its very nature to be admitted. But so it is." White had hit upon a profound point, one which Adam Smith had already underscored in *The Wealth of Nations*. He went on to argue that the French slaveholder could never dare be tyrannical: "He is kept in awe by a higher and stronger hand, that would instantly crush him, should avaricious views of private emolument tempt him to dishonour or endammage the community." The worst abuses of the British slave system were thus the product of too much freedom.[45]

Even after the St. Domingue insurrection had cast doubts on one part of White's thesis, English writers continued to link slaveholding with an im-

44. Peter Peckard, *Justice and Mercy Recommended, Particularly with Reference to the Slave Trade* . . . (Cambridge, 1788), viii–x. In his sermon, however, Peckard expressed a warm belief in moral progress. In 1788 the *Annual Register* hailed the slave-trade debates as proof that "liberty, humanity and science are daily extending, and bid fair to render despotism, cruelty and ignorance subjects of historical memory, not of actual observation" (quoted in Anstey, "A Re-interpretation of the Abolition of the British Slave Trade," 311).
45. [Edward White], *Hints for a Specific Plan for an Abolition of the Slave Trade, and for Relief of the Negroes in the British West Indies* (London, 1788), 18–19.

munity from authority, and emancipation with an extension of governmental power. By 1792, British abolitionists were alarmed and divided by the revolutionary events in France and St. Domingue. At the outset, in 1789, they had generally rejoiced at the news of "a most extraordinary & wonderful Revolution," as Granville Sharp put it, which they interpreted as a restoration of government by law. Even skeptics, like James Beattie, who feared that the French and North Americans understood liberty to mean the privilege of being subject to no laws but those of one's own making, expressed hope that the Revolution would benefit the "poor Negroes."[46] After the conservative reaction had begun to grow, abolitionists were increasingly embarrassed by accusations of Jacobinism, by Thomas Clarkson's continuing support for the Revolution, and by Anglican suspicions that the anti-slave-trade cause was linked to the radical plots of Dissenters. In time, the fear of Jacobinism would become the official rationalization for Parliament's refusal to end the slave trade: it was not that the crown and House of Lords were deficient in a sense of justice; they were simply swayed by an understandable, if irrelevant, dread of Jacobin principles. There was one point, however, on which all antislavery men could agree, whatever their differences in timing in disavowing the French Revolution: the St. Domingue insurrection was not the result of protests against the slave trade or of the activities of the Amis des noirs. Rather, the savage violence of the blacks was a direct response to the brutal tyranny of their masters. The revolt should demonstrate to England, wrote William Roscoe, "that the preservation of our own islands from similar disasters, depends on the early adoption of measures which, whilst they are vigorous and decisive, are just, conciliatory, and humane."[47]

In 1794, William Fox, an unusually radical abolitionist, used similar arguments to defend the French decree of emancipation. It was altogether wrong, he argued, to interpret this measure as a step toward anarchy. For the first time, French Negroes had been brought under the *subjection* as well as the protection of the law. Slaveholders had never cared whether their

46. Granville Sharp to John Sharp, 6 July 1789, JAW; William Forbes, *An Account of the Life and Writings of James Beattie* (Edinburgh, 1807), 3: 66–67.
47. Samuel Hoare, Jr., to William Wilberforce, 20 February 1792, *The Correspondence of William Wilberforce*, Robert Isaac Wilberforce, and Samuel Wilberforce, eds. (London, 1840), 1: 89–90; Thomas Clarkson, *The History of the Rise, Progress and Accomplishment of the Abolition of the African Slave-Trade by the British Parliament* (London, 1808), 2: 208–12; *Parliamentary History of England*, 31: 467–70; [William Roscoe], *An Inquiry into the Causes of the Insurrection of the Negroes in the Island of St. Domingo* . . . (London, 1792), 1–3, 10, 18–26; *The Life of William Roscoe*, Henry Roscoe, ed. (Boston, 1833), 1: 67–71; Samuel Romilly to Mme. G., 6 December 1791, *Memoirs of the Life of Sir Samuel Romilly*, ed. by his sons (London, 1840), 1: 455.

slaves practiced personal vices unacceptable to any genuine society. Paradoxically, slaves had been "free" to commit the worst sins. As a result of emancipation, however, French blacks would presumably be subject to the full powers of civil government. Even infants and idiots, Fox pointed out, were never given over to the arbitrary will of an individual. If Negroes were deficient in any human capacities—and Fox suspected they were superior in character to the English lower classes—this was all the more reason for bringing them under the protection and control of government. By 1802, James Stephen could find merit even in the brutal military regime that Victor Hugues had established in Guadaloupe. For the private authority of masters, Hugues had substituted the public authority of municipal law and military policy. If English governors had issued similar proclamations for ensuring industry by means other than "a mere physical effect to be excited by the application of the lash," every English planter would have considered it an impertinent interference with the "interior discipline of his plantation."[48]

These arguments carry implications that I have touched upon before but may now develop somewhat further. British antislavery writers expressed particular indignation over the arbitrary authority of West Indian slave masters, whom they portrayed, essentially, as the modern and anachronistic counterparts of feudal lords and barons. The abolitionists demanded that bonds of personal dependence give way, however gradually, to uniform and impersonal standards. And in their preference for objective, bureaucratic authority, they appeared to look forward to a future when all workers would be citizens, subject to the same laws and to the same forces of the market. From our point of view, one could justify exploitation only by making it impersonal. According to Thomas Clarkson, there was nothing inequitable about slavery when considered merely as a form of labor. Any state, for example, might legitimately use convicts to clear rivers, repair roads, or work in mines. Granville Sharp suggested that "Negroes that are not capable of managing and shifting for themselves, nor are fit to be trusted, all at once, with liberty, might be delivered over to the care and protection of a *County Committee* (in order to avoid the baneful effects of *private property in Men*)." The committee could then hire out such servants, "the *Hire* to be paid (*also in produce*) towards the discharge of the *Registered Debt* for each Man's original price." Nor did Sharp object to the purchase of slaves by a corporate entity, such as an African colonizing company, so long as the pur-

48. William Fox, *A Defence of the Decree of the National Convention of France for Emancipating the Slaves* (London, 1794), 12–16; [James Stephen], *The Crisis of the Sugar Colonies; or, an Enquiry into the Objects and Probable Effects of the French Expedition to the West Indies* . . . (London, 1802), 17–25.

chase price was considered a "mere pecuniary debt" that the slave could redeem by working for the company.[49] What Sharp and Clarkson did object to were claims of personal proprietorship which gave a master exclusive control over the body and produce of a dependent, and which deprived the dependent of selling his labor in a reasonably free market. And it followed, in accordance with this outlook, that the master-slave relationship epitomized those artificial restraints, including monopoly and guaranteed subsistence, that prevented self-interest from being harnessed to the general good. Gilbert Francklyn, a Tobago planter and propagandist for the West India Committee, reported a credible story about Sharp which would hardly have shocked the new disciples of laissez faire. As a promoter of Sierra Leone colonization, Sharp was distressed to find many of London's Negroes unwilling to embark for Africa, despite their current misery and destitution. According to Francklyn, Sharp then distributed handbills around the city, requesting gentlemen not to relieve blacks in distress, since charity would blind them to their own best interest.[50]

On the other hand, Wilberforce and other antislavery writers clung to the paternalistic ideals of the past and expressed considerable ambivalence toward Adam Smith's exaltation of self-interest and market relations. Even the classical economists, it should be stressed, approved acts of private benevolence which did not stifle individual initiative. Wilberforce (like Sharp)

49. Thomas Clarkson, *An Essay on the Slavery and Commerce of the Human Species, Particularly the African . . .* (Philadelphia, 1786; originally printed London, 1786), 75–76; Granville Sharp to Benjamin Rush, 18 July 1775; 1 August 1783, Rush papers, Historical Society of Pennsylvania (hereafter HSP); Sharp to the archbishop of Canterbury, 9 October 1788, JAW.
50. Francklyn, *Observations*, xii–xiii. Christopher Fyfe, in his masterly *A History of Sierra Leone* (Oxford, 1962), 14–19, touches on the difficulty of persuading London blacks to embark for Sierra Leone. James Walvin's *Black and White: The Negro and English Society, 1555–1945* (London, 1973), provides a more detailed account of the plight of London's blacks, many of whom had joined the king's armed forces during the American Revolution. Although Sharp helped to organize relief for this destitute population, he was convinced that African colonization afforded the only permanent solution. In 1786 the Committee for the Black Poor acknowledged that, "considering the disposition of the Blacks and their want of discipline," it would be difficult to fill the three Royal Navy ships scheduled to embark for Sierra Leone. The government tried to increase incentive by stopping daily welfare payments of 6d per person. Early in 1788, when Sharp heard the news of the disastrous mortality of the first expedition, he assured his brother that "I cannot find that the Climate has been at all to blame; nothing but the intemperance of the people, and their enervating indolence in consequence of it" (quoted in *Black and White*, 147). In a letter of 13 October 1788, to Dr. John Coakley Lettsom (Huntington Library), Sharp admitted that over fifty blacks had died soon after the ships had left the Thames, and that by September 1787 only 276 were still alive in Sierra Leone, out of the 439 to 441 who had embarked. Again, he blamed intemperance.

devoted much of his personal income to private charity; in 1800, when he was alarmed by the plight of starving workers in the West Riding, he attacked the callousness of those who "servilely" accepted Smith's principles without allowance for the thousand circumstances which might qualify a general principle. Later, when the same region was threatened with rebellion, he associated the insubordination of the lower orders with

> the modern system of making expediency the basis of morals and
> the spring of action, instead of the domestic and social affections and
> the relations of life and the duties arising out of them. Not that the
> lower orders understand this generalizing abstract way of thinking
> and feeling; but the opinions and emotions which are taught and
> imbibed in this school, receiving their stamp in the mint of the
> higher orders . . . obtain a currency throughout the inferior classes
> of society.[51]

The early industrial revolution coincided with defensive attempts to rehabilitate the values of the old social order. The 1780s and 1790s produced a considerable literature that outlined the duties of the higher ranks and that eulogized the deference and loyalty of the poor. The two classes were united, in the idealized view, by an invisible "chain" or "bond."[52] Abolitionists never tired of contrasting the impersonality of slavery to the benevolent paternalism that most English workers supposedly still enjoyed. As we have seen, Cowper's emancipated slave is not abandoned to the cold winds of the marketplace. Submissive at his liberator's feet, he vows: "Serving a benefactor I am free; / At my best home, if not exiled from thee." The reformers' alternative to slavery was not the modern factory but a master-servant relationship based on mutual respect, obligation, and above all, belief in the legitimacy of each man's station. Moreover, it was absenteeism, in the eyes of abolitionists, that accounted for many of the worst evils of the plantation system. The Negro slave, from the time of his sale on the West African coast, could appeal to no responsible authority. Neither the slave-ship captain nor the agent who managed a plantation had any interest beyond "private emolument." Obviously this "artificial" way of delegating authority and manipulating a labor force was not a vestige from the archaic past. It was a mark of the emerging capitalist order.

There were, to be sure, contradictory tendencies within colonial slavery

51. Wilberforce, *Life of William Wilberforce*, 2: 163–64, 387–88; 4: 28–29. Of course abolitionists also delighted in quoting Adam Smith to the effect that a slave's only "interests" could be to eat much and labor little. See, e.g., [Thomas Burgess], *Considerations on the Abolition of Slavery and the Slave Trade, upon Grounds of Natural, Religious, and Political Duty* (Oxford, 1789), 154, 158.
52. Briggs, "Language of 'Class,' " 43–54.

itself. In some respects, plantation slavery prefigured the salient features of the factory system; yet it also retained the characteristics of preindustrial labor discipline.[53] The institution's mixed character helps to explain why the British abolitionists' critique could be significantly selective. It was neither a traditionalist attack on a capitalistic innovation, nor a capitalist attack on an archaic form of authority. In some ways it was a combination of both.

*Summary* British antislavery helped to ensure stability while accommodating society to political and economic change; it merged Utilitarianism with an ethic of benevolence, reinforcing faith that a progressive policy of laissez faire would reveal men's natural identity of interests. It opened new sources of moral prestige for the dominant social class, helped to define a participatory role for middle-class activism, and looked forward to the universal goal of compliant, loyal, and self-disciplined workers. The abolitionists' ideal of the plantation's future was thus a strange hybrid: a kindly, paternalistic master ministering to his grateful Negro "yeomen," both subject to the administrative agents of the king and both dedicated to the commercial prosperity of the empire! And the realization of this dream was supposed to have profound reverberating effects. The abolition of the slave trade would not only reform the motives and character of planters, but would lead to the more important goal of Christianizing and civilizing Africa. In Ramsay's vision, "this measure promises to realize the fabulous golden age, when mutual wants and mutual good, will & shall bind all mankind in one common interest."[54]

53. Eugene D. Genovese has given this point theoretical elaboration in *The Political Economy of Slavery: Studies in the Economy and Society of the Slave South* (New York, 1965) and in *The World the Slaveholders Made: Two Essays in Interpretation* (New York, 1969), 3–113. I have particularly profited, however, from reading chapters of Genovese's *Roll, Jordan, Roll* (New York, 1974), a profound study of the accommodations and contradictions of New World slavery.
54. James Ramsay, MS volume, fols. 71, 95, Phillipps MS 17780, Rhodes House, Oxford. For the influence of the anti-slave-trade movement on later imperialist ideology, see Ralph A. Austen and Woodruff D. Smith, "Images of Africa and British Slave-Trade Abolition: The Transition to an Imperialist Ideology, 1787–1807," *African Historical Studies*, 2 (1969): 69–83. It is perhaps symbolic that in 1834, the year of West Indian emancipation, Thomas Babington Macaulay sailed to India for precisely the same motive that had earlier led would-be planters to the Caribbean: he was almost penniless and aspired to become financially independent. He returned to England in three and a half years, wealthy enough to avoid any future financial worries. But whereas the Caribbean planters had been unconcerned with transforming Caribbean culture, Macaulay, as a member of the law-making Council of India, had helped to lay the groundwork for momentous change. He had seen India as a testing ground for his ideology of progress—for the formation, as phrased in his influential "Minute on Indian Education," of "a class who may be interpreters between us and the millions whom we govern; a class of persons, Indian in blood and colour, but English in taste, in morals, and in intellect." Macaulay's struggles for a

free press, for a humane penal code, and for the teaching of English language and literature were essentially struggles for cultural hegemony, as distinct from dominion by physical force. Significantly, he argued that a free press could not endanger British rule, since India lacked any class "analogous to that vast body of English labourers and artisans whose minds are rendered irritable by frequent distress and privation, and on whom, therefore, the sophistry and rhetoric of bad men often produce a tremendous effect" (Clive, *Macaulay*, 330–31, and *passim*; *Macaulay*; *Prose and Poetry*, selected by G. M. Young [London, 1952], 722, 729).

# Part 2

## THE *AHR* DEBATE

Chapter 4

# Capitalism and the Origins of the Humanitarian Sensibility, Part 1

*Thomas L. Haskell*

An unprecedented wave of humanitarian reform sentiment swept through the societies of Western Europe, England, and North America in the hundred years following 1750. Among the movements spawned by this new sensibility, the most spectacular was that to abolish slavery. Although its morality was often questioned before 1750, slavery was routinely defended and hardly ever condemned outright, even by the most scrupulous moralists. About the time that slavery was being transformed from a problematical but readily defensible institution into a self-evidently evil and abominable one, new attitudes began to appear on how to deter criminals, relieve the poor, cure the insane, school the young, and deal with primitive peoples.[1] The resulting reforms were, by almost any reasonable standard, an improvement over old practices that were often barbarous. Even so,

So many people have given me advice about an earlier and briefer version of this essay that I can scarcely call it my own, except insofar as it errs or offends. My principal debt is to David Brion Davis, whose extraordinarily generous and thoughtful correspondence saved me from many errors of fact, taste, and judgment. The essay was first presented to the Social Science Seminar of the Institute for Advanced Study, Princeton, N.J., in April 1979. Since then I have also benefited from discussions with members of the Social Science Seminar at Rice University and the Department of History and Philosophy, Carnegie-Mellon University. For especially thorough and helpful comments, I am grateful to Seymour Drescher, Stanley Engerman, Ira Gruber, Albert Hirschman, Jay Hook, Jackson Lears, Elizabeth Long, George Marcus, Lewis Perry, Andrew Scull, Quentin Skinner, Peter Stearns, Richard Teichgraeber, Larry Temkin, Mark Warren, Roger Wertheimer, Morton White, and Bertram Wyatt-Brown. Martin Wiener's encouragement and advice have been especially valuable. The work was made possible by leaves funded by the Institute for Advanced Study, the Rockefeller Foundation, and the Dean of Humanities, Rice University. It is part of a larger study in the history of moral responsibility in Anglo-American culture after 1750.
1. David Brion Davis, *The Problem of Slavery in Western Culture* (Ithaca, 1966).

twentieth-century historians have not been satisfied to attribute those reforms either to an advance in man's moral sense or, simply, to a random outburst of altruism. In explaining the new humanitarianism, historians have repeatedly pointed to changes in what Marxists generally call the economic base or substructure of society, that is, the growth of capitalism and beginnings of industrialization. Tracing links between humanitarianism and capitalism has been a major preoccupation of historians, and the enterprise has succeeded, I believe, in greatly extending our understanding of the new sensibility. We know now that the reformers were motivated by far more than an unselfish desire to help the downtrodden, and we see more clearly now why their reforms went no farther and took the particular form they did.[2] Historians are never again likely to believe, as did W. E. H. Lecky in 1876, that Britain's campaign against slavery was "among the three or four perfectly virtuous acts recorded in the history of nations."[3]

But these advances in understanding have been achieved only at the expense of a growing ambivalence as we try to acknowledge two things at once: that humanitarian reform not only took courage and brought commendable changes but also served the interests of the reformers and was part of that vast bourgeois project that Max Weber called rationalization. This ambivalence reached painful heights in Michel Foucault's *Discipline and Punish*, in which he questioned whether there really was a new humanitarian sensibility and argued that, though a new sensitivity to suffering did exist, its aim in prison reform was not humane. Its real aim, Foucault concluded, was "not to punish less, but to punish better; to punish with an attenuated severity perhaps, but in order to punish with more universality and necessity; to insert the power to punish more deeply into the social body."[4] Foucault's position contains much truth, yet in contemplating it we must not lose sight of another truth, namely, that to put a thief in jail

---

2. For the touchstone of what has become a large body of literature, see Eric Williams, *Capitalism and Slavery* (Chapel Hill, 1944). Also see C. L. R. James, *The Black Jacobins: Toussaint L'Ouverture and the San Domingo Revolution* (New York, 1963); Roger Anstey, "Capitalism and Slavery: A Critique," *Economic History Review*, 2d ser., 21 (1968): 307–20; Eugene Genovese, "Materialism and Idealism in the History of Negro Slavery in the Americas," in Laura Foner and Eugene Genovese, eds., *Slavery in the New World: A Reader in Comparative History* (Englewood Cliffs, N.J., 1969), 238–55; Christine Bolt and Seymour Drescher, eds., *Anti-Slavery, Religion, and Reform: Essays in Memory of Roger Anstey* (Hamden, Conn., 1980); and James Walvin, ed., *Slavery and British Society, 1776–1846* (Baton Rouge, La., 1982). Additional major contributions to the controversy by Anstey, Davis, Drescher, and Temperley are cited below.
3. Lecky, as quoted in David Brion Davis, *The Problem of Slavery in the Age of Revolution, 1770–1823* (Ithaca, 1975), 353.
4. Foucault, *Discipline and Punish: The Birth of the Prison*, trans. Alan Sheridan (New York, 1977), 82.

is more humane than to burn him, hang him, maim him, or dismember him.

The inadequacy of prevailing modes of explanation tempts scholars to migrate toward two extremes: either to abandon the very idea of humanitarianism lest it veil the play of domination or to reassert the classical liberal view that humanitarian ideas belong to a transcendant realm of moral choice, which no inquiry into social or economic circumstances can hope to illuminate. The latter strategy, essentially one of compartmentalization, finds considerable support in Roger Anstey's sophisticated effort to refurbish the traditional image of British abolitionists as moral giants. Even more decisive encouragement comes from Seymour Drescher's *Econocide*, which seeks to show, contrary to the thesis of Eric Williams, that slavery was a profitable and important part of the British economy and that the decision to abolish it ran directly counter to Britain's economic interest.[5]

The present historiographical dilemma has been aptly described by Howard Temperley. To argue that "abolition had nothing to do with economics except insofar as economic interest was a factor to be overcome," he observed, leads to conclusions that are, "to put it mildly, a little odd."

> Here we have a system—a highly successful system—of large-scale capitalist agriculture, mass producing raw materials for sale in distant markets, growing up at a time when most production was still small-scale and designed to meet the needs of local consumers. But precisely at a time when capitalist ideas were in the ascendant, and large-scale production of all kinds of goods was beginning, we find this system being dismantled. How could this happen unless "capitalism" had something to do with it? If our reasoning leads to the conclusion that "capitalism" had nothing to do with it, the chances are that there is something wrong with our reasoning.[6]

5. Anstey, *The Atlantic Slave Trade and British Abolition, 1760–1810* (Atlantic Highlands, N.J., 1975); and Drescher, *Econocide: British Slavery in the Era of Abolition* (Pittsburgh, 1977).
6. Temperley, "Capitalism, Slavery, and Ideology," *Past and Present*, 75 (1977): 105. I wrote the first draft of this essay before reading Temperley's article, but his aim in many ways parallels my own. And I certainly share Temperley's view that the question to answer is "how could a philosophy which extolled the pursuit of individual self-interest have contributed, in the absence of any expectation of economic gain, to the achievement of so praiseworthy an object as the abolition of slavery." *Ibid.*, 117. I am not convinced, however, that a full answer to this question can be gotten by examining capitalism as an ideology. Also see Temperley, "Anti-Slavery as a Form of Cultural Imperialism," in Bolt and Drescher, *Anti-Slavery, Religion, and Reform*, 335–50. In his later article, Temperley stressed the convergence of nationalism, an accelerating pace of economic growth, and notions of naturally or divinely ordained progress, factors that mesh closely with the somewhat more abstract argument to be presented here.

I believe that a real change in sensibility occurred, and that it was associated with the rise of capitalism. The way out of the current historiographical impasse is to find a way to establish the connection without reducing humane values and acts to epiphenomena in the process. To do this we must begin by reexamining the ways in which substructural developments like the rise of capitalism might have influenced superstructural developments like humanitarianism. There is more than one way in which these phenomena might be linked, and the purpose of this essay is to bring into focus a kind of linkage that historians have sometimes tacitly assumed but never explored in a deliberate and systematic way.

Today the most popular way to formulate the linkage between capitalism and the humanitarian sensibility goes under the banner of "social control" or "class hegemony." Reduced to its basic outlines, this scheme of explanation rests on two assumptions. The first concerns what we really have in mind when we use the umbrella phrase "rise of capitalism," which, after all, covers a large cluster of quite diverse concrete developments, any one of which we might think more important than others. When social control theorists use this phrase, they usually mean only one of the elements hidden under the umbrella—the ascendancy of a new, entrepreneurial class, the bourgeoisie. This new class is understood to have distinctive interests deriving from its control over the society's predominant means of production. Those interests are understood to be such that the class will favor any measure that ensures the docility of the less advantaged sectors of the population, that enhances the discipline and productivity of the work force on which the economy depends, that strengthens its own morale or weakens that of other groups, or that contributes in any other way to the maintenance of its own supremacy.

The second assumption basic to the social control interpretation flows naturally from the first: class interest is the medium—and presumably the *only* important medium—through which substructural change influences developments in the superstructure. Given these assumptions and the bourgeois origins of almost all humanitarian reformers of the late eighteenth and early nineteenth centuries, the strategy of explanation becomes obvious: the way for the social control historian to explain humanitarianism is to show how supposedly disinterested reforms actually functioned to advance bourgeois interests. To state the explanatory schema so baldly makes it sound simpler and more vulnerable than it really is. The social control thesis, like any other, is capable of sophisticated as well as crude applications, as the following discussion of a very refined application of the thesis should make clear. But however indirectly and subtly reform may be said to have served class interest, the historian employing the social control schema is strongly predisposed to look to class interest alone for the connecting link between capitalism and humanitarianism, base and superstructure.

The alternative interpretation that I shall present rejects both assumptions of the social control thesis. Without questioning the great importance of self-interest and class interest in human affairs, and while fully recognizing that interests exert an important influence on belief through what Weber called "elective affinity," I shall argue that in this particular inquiry the concept of class interest has obscured almost as much as it has revealed.[7] Stated plainly, my thesis is this: Whatever influence the rise of capitalism may have had generally on ideas and values through the medium of class interest, it had a more telling influence on the origins of humanitarianism through changes the market wrought in *perception* or *cognitive style*. And it was primarily a change in cognitive style—specifically a change in the perception of causal connection and consequently a shift in the conventions of moral responsibility—that underlay the new constellation of attitudes and activities that we call humanitarianism. What altered cognitive style in a "humanitarian" direction was not in the first instance the ascendancy of a new class, or the assertion by that class of a new configuration of interests, but rather the expansion of the market, the intensification of market discipline, and the penetration of that discipline into spheres of life previously untouched by it. To explain humanitarianism, then, what matters in the capitalist substructure is not a new class so much as the market, and what links the capitalist market to a new sensibility is not class interest so much as the power of market discipline to inculcate altered perceptions of causation in human affairs.

This approach has certain advantages. Instead of prompting the historian to unmask the interestedness of ostensibly disinterested reforms, the explanatory approach advocated here would lead the historian to demonstrate the "naturalness" of these reforms, given the historical development of certain cognitive structures that were formed in the crucible of market transactions. Because these cognitive structures underlay *both* the reformers' novel sense of responsibility for others and their definition of their own interests, there is indeed a certain congruence between the reforms they car-

---

7. Although Weber's treatment of the relationship between ideas and interest in *The Protestant Ethic and the Spirit of Capitalism* seems to me the best model we have, Weber used the concept of elective affinities in very diverse ways. See Weber, *The Protestant Ethic and the Spirit of Capitalism*, trans. Talcott Parsons (New York, 1958, 1976); and Richard Herbert Howe, "Max Weber's Elective Affinities: Sociology within the Bounds of Pure Reason," *American Journal of Sociology*, 84 (1978): 366–85. Also see Weber, "Religious Ethics and the World," in Guenther Roth and Claus Wittich, eds., *Economy and Society: An Outline of Interpretive Sociology*, trans. Ephraim Fischoff et al., 2 (New York, 1968): 577.

ried out and the needs of their class. The social control argument errs not in stressing the existence of this congruence but in the account given of its origins. The approach recommended here does not aim to turn the social control argument on its head, retaining its opposition of ideas and interests while reversing their causal relationship; instead, the purpose is to overcome this dualism altogether by acknowledging that ideas and interests are interwoven at every level and in fact arise from the same source—a certain way of perceiving human relations fostered by the forms of life the market encouraged.

In another respect, however, the reader will note that my argument does reverse what is commonly thought to be the proper order of things. The pervasive, if diffuse, influence of the neo-Freudian tradition has prepared us to accept without much question the idea that feelings influence perception, that our emotional needs shape the way we see and experience the world around us. Although I do not doubt in the least that emotion has the power to influence perception, and often does, the present study shows, I believe, that the reverse can also be true. The rise of antislavery sentiment was, among other things, an upwelling of powerful feelings of sympathy, guilt, and anger, but these emotions would not have emerged when they did, taken the form they did, or produced the same results if they had not been called into being by a prior change in the perception of causal relations.

The order of argument is roughly as follows. In order to specify more exactly the dilemmas inherent in the social control interpretation, I will examine the most penetrating and sophisticated example of that approach—David Brion Davis's *The Problem of Slavery in the Age of Revolution.* My aim is to show that, although this book's sophistication has many sources, one is the tendency to play down class interest (even while finally embracing it) by stressing the concept of self-deception; that, in trying to avoid making class interest the exclusive or overpowering link between substructural and superstructural change, Davis naturally moved in the direction of cognitive style; and that, by going one step further in the same direction, some residual ambiguities in his analysis can be clarified. Once the need has been established, a new formulation can be attempted.

Davis moved so far beyond the ordinary limitations of the social control thesis that one is tempted to credit him with having superseded it. Certainly much of the alternative approach that I wish to recommend is implicit in Davis's analysis. He never denied the authenticity of the reformers' good intentions and never claimed that their "actual" aim was to achieve social control. He was, however, content to depict the antislavery movement as peculiarly susceptible to efforts to convert it into a "vehicle for social control," and, even after all of his many qualifications are taken into account, class interest is the only link between base and superstructure that he specifically recognized.[8] For Davis, "the key questions concern the relationship between antislavery and the social system as a whole."

> Why did a seemingly liberal movement emerge and continue to win support from major government leaders in the period from 1790 to 1832, a period characterized by both political reaction and industrial revolution? How could such a movement be embraced by aristocratic statesmen and yet serve eventually as a vehicle for the triumphant middle class, who regarded West Indian emancipation as the confirmation of the Reform Bill of 1832, and who used antislavery rhetoric and strategy as models for their assault upon the Corn Laws? How could antislavery help ensure stability while also accommodating society to political and economic change? Antonio Gramsci defined "hegemony," in the words of his biographer, as "the predominance, obtained by consent rather than force, of one class or group over other classes"; or more precisely, "the 'spontaneous' loyalty that any dominant social group obtains from the masses by virtue of its social and intellectual prestige and its supposedly superior function in the world of production." The paramount question, which subsumes the others, is how antislavery reinforced or legitimized such hegemony.[9]

Unlike Foucault, Davis was confident that humanitarianism, or at any rate its antislavery component, represents an authentic and "remarkable shift in moral consciousness . . . a momentous turning point in the evolution of man's moral perception and thus in man's image of himself." Like Foucault, however, Davis insisted that the new sensibility "did not spring from transcendant sources." Rather its origin, he said, lies in "the ideological needs of various groups and classes."[10] Davis achieved a highly nuanced view of the reformers' motivation by creating in the reader's mind a tense double image in which reformers appear not only as free moral actors, moved by ethical considerations of which they are fully conscious, but also as unwitting agents of class interest, moved by social needs that worked "over their heads" and were scarcely (if at all) accessible to consciousness. As long as one assumes, as Davis apparently did, that class interest is the only important link between base and superstructure, this juxtaposition of contradictory images is perhaps the only way to ward off reductionism and to do justice to the insolubility of the old problem of free will and determinism.

8. Davis, *The Problem of Slavery in the Age of Revolution*, 379.
9. Davis quoted John M. Cammet; *ibid.*, 348–49.
10. *Ibid.*, 41–42.

In an earlier book, *The Problem of Slavery in Western Culture*, Davis identified four major intellectual transformations that set the stage for an antislavery movement. Primitivist currents of thought permitted at least a momentary ambivalence about the superiority of European civilization. The evangelical movement in Protestantism dramatized the dangers of moral complacency even as the latitudinarian reaction against Hobbesian and Calvinistic views of man popularized an ethic of benevolence. Secular social philosophers from Hobbes to Montesquieu stripped away many of the previous sanctions for slavery and moved closer to a rejection of the institution, though Bodin was the only one who actually condemned it. These developments came to a practical focus in the affairs of the Quakers, the only perfectionist sect spawned by the revolutionary turmoil of seventeenth-century England that found a way to compromise and thus to survive and prosper. By the mid-eighteenth century, the Quakers were both representatives of the most radical strand of the Protestant tradition and figures in the vanguard of the development of capitalism and industrial society. The Quakers supplied a natural pivot for Davis's analysis as he turned in his second book away from the history of ideas to "more material considerations which helped both to shape the new moral consciousness and to define its historical effects."[11]

Here in the material substructure Davis found the two principal threads of argument that he followed throughout his second volume. First, he explored "the ideological functions and implications of attacking this symbol of the most extreme subordination, exploitation, and dehumanization, at a  time when various enlightened elites were experimenting with internalized moral and cultural controls to establish or preserve their own hegemony."[12] The second theme, less relevant to the purposes of this essay, traced the geopolitical and international economic considerations that led Great Britain to tolerate the annihilation of a species of property within its imperial borders and to exert military force against the slave trade, whether conducted by foreign nationals or its own citizens.

Davis turned away from the history of ideas in his second volume and opened the door to a much less voluntaristic and rationalistic mode of explanation than that tradition has thought acceptable. Yet his conversion was incomplete and uncertain. Characteristically, his strongest assertions explaining superstructural developments by reference to substructural ones are immediately followed by reservations that accumulate nearly to the point of contradiction. For example, Davis attributed receptivity to anti-

11. *Ibid.*, 48.
12. *Ibid.*, 49.

run down of argument

slavery ideology to "profound social changes" connected with "the rise of new classes and new economic interests." But in the following sentence he declared that "this ideology emerged from a convergence of complex religious, intellectual and literary trends—trends which are by no means reducible to the economic interests of particular classes, but which must be understood as part of a larger transformation of attitudes toward labor, property and individual responsibility."[13] Davis came closer in this passage than anywhere else to a recognition of the role played by cognitive style, yet, having almost said that class interest cannot be the exclusive link between humanitarianism and capitalism, he named no alternative link.

Davis's interpretation is not reductionist. He forthrightly rejected the argument that "Quaker abolitionists were governed by 'economic interest' in the sense that they stood to profit from the destruction of the slave trade or a weakening of the plantation system."[14] Instead of direct profit, the relevant interests were those of an entrepreneurial class preoccupied with problems of unemployment and labor discipline. And Davis was acutely aware that even this argument "must be developed with considerable care to avoid the simplistic impression that 'industrialists' promoted abolitionist doctrine as a means of distracting attention from their own form of exploitation."[15]

Although Davis denied the existence of any crude cause-and-effect relationship between the needs of capitalists and the attack on slavery, he assigned great importance to a more subtle linkage based solidly on class interest. The heart of his analysis lies in the claim that, "as a social force, antislavery was a highly selective response to labor exploitation. It provided an outlet for demonstrating Christian concern for human suffering and injustice, and yet thereby gave a certain moral insulation to economic activities less visibly dependent on human suffering and injustice."[16] Elsewhere, speaking of long-range consequences rather than immediate intentions, he concluded that the abolitionist movement helped "clear an ideological path for British industrialists" and noted that, by exaggerating the harshness of slavery, abolitionists "gave sanction to less barbarous modes of social discipline." In the same breath Davis credited the abolitionist movement with breeding "a new sensitivity to social oppression" and providing a "model for the systematic indictment of social crime."[17]

The tendency of protests against chattel slavery to overshadow the evils of "wage slavery" had special significance for Davis because of the extraor-

13. *Ibid.*, 82.
14. *Ibid.*, 251.
15. *Ibid.*, 455.
16. *Ibid.*, 251.
17. *Ibid.*, 466–68.

dinary role that Quakers played in the early antislavery movement. The Quaker reformers who were so prominent in antislavery and every other humanitarian endeavor of the age were often fabulously successful businessmen who epitomized the Protestant ethic and the capitalist mentality. Either directly or through close family connections they were deeply involved in industry, shipping, banking, and commerce; they knew firsthand the task of devising new modes of labor discipline to replace older methods of social control. As members of an entrepreneurial class confronted by an "unruly labor force" prone to "uninhibited violence" and not yet "disciplined to the factory system," late eighteenth-century reformers had strong incentives to formulate an ideology that would "isolate specific forms of human misery, allowing issues of freedom and discipline to be faced in a relatively simplified model."[18]

As these statements illustrate, Davis relied heavily on the explanatory power of class interest as the driving force behind ostensibly disinterested reforms. Apart from explicit denials of reductionism, what prevents his account from reducing the humanitarian sensibility to a reflexive instrument of the class struggle is his often-repeated conviction that the reformers were generally unaware of the interested character of their ideology and unable to see that it played a role in furthering the hegemony of their own class. The reformers, wrote Davis, "*unwittingly* drew distinctions and boundaries which opened the way, under a guise of moral rectitude, for unprecedented forms of oppression." He said of David Barclay and other Quakers that it was "*inconceivable*" to them "that English servants were in any sense unfree," and it was "*unthinkable* that an attack on a specific system of labor  and domination might also validate other forms of oppression."[19] In Davis's opinion, the formalistic conception of human freedom that enabled people militantly opposed to slavery to ignore the plight of the impoverished factory laborer and to turn their back on the ex-slave once he was legally free was powerful enough to constrain the vision even of the more radical abolitionists. "At issue, then," Davis concluded, "are not conscious intentions, but the social functions of ideology."[20]

By insisting that the reformers were unaware of the hegemonic function served by their ideology, Davis opened a crucially important space between their intentions and the long-term consequences of their ideas and activities. It is mainly this zone of indeterminacy and free play that keeps his account clear of the reductionist and conspiratorial overtones that have so often plagued the social control argument. Yet it is also indispensable to Davis's

18. *Ibid.*, 241, 252, 254.
19. *Ibid.*, 253, 350. My emphasis.
20. *Ibid.*, 266 n., 350.

purpose that the gap between intentions and consequences not grow too wide, for, if the aid and comfort that abolitionism gave to capitalist hegemony was utterly unrelated to the intentions of the reformers, or if it was related only in an incidental or accidental way, Davis would have to abandon his conclusion.[21] In order to conclude (as he did) that the attack on slavery was crucially shaped by the needs and interests of the rising class to which the reformers belonged, capitalist hegemony cannot be merely one among the many unintended consequences of reform. The category of unintended consequences is too loose to supply either the ethical or the causal quality that his explanation requires. After all, when Hank Aaron hit a home run, one of the consequences of the act was to put a new baseball into the hands of some lucky spectator. But this was not what Aaron intended by swinging at the ball, and we do not credit him with generosity because of the "gift" he bestowed on the spectators (nor would we have blamed him if the ball had struck one of them on the head). If the aim of furthering capitalist hegemony entered into the intentions of the abolitionists no more significantly than the aim of gift giving figured in Aaron's mind as he swung at the ball, we would not feel that humanitarianism had anything important to do with the rise of capitalism—not, at least, as long as we assume that class interest is the only way to link the two. To say that a person is moved by class interest is to say that he *intends* to further the interests of his class, or it is to say nothing at all.[22]

21. *Ibid.*, 350: "The antislavery movement, like [Adam] Smith's political economy, reflected the needs and values of the emerging capitalist order. Smith provided theoretical justification for the belief that all classes and segments of society share a natural identity of interest. The antislavery movement, while absorbing the ambivalent emotions of the age, was essentially dedicated to a practical demonstration of the same reassuring message."
22. Although in my opinion he finally skirted its inescapably reductive implications, Raymond Williams fully concurred that the social control explanation cannot do without intention; Williams, "Base and Superstructure in Marxist Cultural Theory," *New Left Review*, 82 (1973): 3–16. Speaking of formulations like Georg Lukacs's that stress the "totality" of social practices rather than a layered image of base and superstructure, Williams said, "It is very easy for the notion of totality to empty of its essential content the original Marxist proposition." The danger, wrote Williams, is that of "withdrawing from the claim that there is any process of determination. And this I, for one, would be very unwilling to do. Indeed, the key question to ask about any notion of totality in cultural theory is this: whether the notion of totality includes the notion of intention. . . . Intention, the notion of intention, restores the key question, or rather the key emphasis." In order for an interpretation to be called "Marxist," Williams believed it should at least depict the "organization and structure [of society] . . . as directly related to certain social intentions, intentions by which we define the society, intentions which in all our experience have been the rule of a particular class"; *ibid.*, 7. My complaint, of course, is not that Davis, by relying on a soft form of intention, has veered too far from any

The intention need not be simple, of course. What is wanted, as Davis himself put it, is a way to show that the reformer's thinking was "rooted . . . in the needs of a social group" yet not "reducible" to them.[23] The problem (faced by Davis and anyone else striving to formulate a non-reductive explanation based on class interest) is that interest explains the conduct of reformers only by reducing it, revealing beneath the pretty surface of laudable intentions another layer that better accounts for their reforms. Interest explains much, but it explains by reduction. To shy away from the reductive step is to sacrifice explanatory force. No amount of cautious language can overcome the trade-off built into the logic of this kind of explanation.

Unwilling to give up the explanatory force of class interest, yet uncomfortable with its tendency to undercut the authenticity of stated intentions, Davis, like many other recent scholars, resorted to the "soft" form of intentionality embodied in the notion of self-deception. By so doing he adopted a concept that bids fair to become the keystone of an imposing historiography constructed by Raymond Williams, E. P. Thompson, Eugene Genovese, and many other scholars who have drawn theoretical inspiration from the work of Gramsci. The notion of self-deception or some close equivalent of it has played an important role in the efforts of the "cultural school" to escape the criticism that doomed an earlier and more "positivist" tradition in Marxian historiography. The question I wish to raise is whether this conception can bear the explanatory weight thus thrust upon it.[24]

Davis observed that "ideological hegemony is not the product of conscious choice and seldom involves insincerity or deliberate deception." He then quoted the sociologist Peter Berger, who said that "deliberate deception requires a degree of psychological self-control that few people are capable

---

"original proposition" but that he has clung to a greater degree of intention than he seems comfortable with, and a greater degree than the evidence can substantiate. The rival scheme of explanation I advocate retains the claim that there is a "process of determination" but deliberately abandons the claim of intentionality.

23. Davis, *The Problem of Slavery in the Age of Revolution*, 349.

24. On the two traditions in Marxist historiography, see Richard Johnson, "Edward Thompson, Eugene Genovese, and Socialist-Humanist History," *History Workshop*, 6 (1978): 79–100. On Gramsci, see Walter L. Adamson, *Hegemony and Revolution: A Study of Antonio Gramsci's Political and Cultural Theory* (Berkeley and Los Angeles, 1980), chap. 6; James Joll, *Antonio Gramsci* (New York, 1977), chap. 9; Thomas R. Bates, "Gramsci and the Theory of Hegemony," *Journal of the History of Ideas*, 36 (1975): 351–66; and Antonio Gramsci, *Selections from the Prison Notebooks of Antonio Gramsci*, ed. Quintin Hoare and Geoffrey Nowell Smith (New York, 1972).

of. . . . It is much easier to deceive oneself."[25] In a passage that Davis did not quote but that would have suited his purposes equally well, the Marxist art critic Arnold Hauser made a similar point:

> What most sharply distinguishes a propagandistic from an ideological presentation and interpretation of the facts is . . . that its falsification and manipulation of the truth is always conscious and intentional. Ideology, on the other hand, is mere deception—in essence self-deception—never simply lies and deceit. It obscures truth in order not so much to mislead others as to maintain and increase the self-confidence of those who express and benefit from such deception.[26]

Unquestionably the concept of self-deception represents a major advance over the mechanistic formulations for which it substitutes. It virtually banishes the implication of conspiracy that so marred the work of Eric Williams, for example, and, if it does not grapple with the problem of free will at a very deep level, the concept at least does not pretend to have solved that problem by the discovery of an all-encompassing theory of determinism. In short, self-deception has the distinct merit of occupying the space between intention and consequence, precluding any rigid coupling of the two while maintaining a connection between them. The notion is, however, very slippery and, in spite of all its virtues, is not the best way to formulate the relationship between the abolitionists' intentions and the hegemonic consequences of their actions.

The problem with self-deception is not that it is a rare mental state or overly technical term. All of us can recall episodes in our lives when we ignored or denied what now seems the plain and reprehensible meaning of our actions—moments when, to paraphrase what Sigmund Freud said about dreams, we knew what the consequences of our actions would be but did not know that we knew.[27] But the usefulness of the concept of self-deception to the historian is limited by two considerations. The first has to do with the ambiguous ethical import of acts committed by a person said to be deceiving

25. Davis, *The Problem of Slavery in the Age of Revolution*, 349.
26. Hauser, as quoted in William A. Muraskin, "The Social Control Theory in American History: A Critique," *Journal of Social History*, 9 (1976): 566.
27. "For I can assure you that it is quite possible, and highly probable indeed, that the dreamer *does* know what his dream means: *only he does not know that he knows it and for that reason thinks he does not know it*"; Freud, *Introductory Lectures on Psychoanalysis*, trans. James Strachey (New York, 1977), 101. Freud likened the hidden knowledge to a person's name that we know but cannot recall. His proof of the existence of such knowledge was, of course, hypnosis, and free association was the means of bringing it to light. Also see *ibid.*, 103, 110, 113.

himself; the second concerns the difficulty of distinguishing between cases
of true self-deception and cases in which a person simply is either ignorant
of some of the consequences of his actions or convinced that those consequences are incidental to his aim. Let us examine each problem in turn.

The ambiguity inherent in the idea of self-deception appears immediately when we ask what degree of ethical responsibility a person bears for
acts the consequences of which he has deceptively concealed from himself.
If we construe the term in a Freudian manner, knowledge of the unpalatable
consequences is presumably hidden in the unconscious. Can a person will
that what is unconscious become conscious? If not, he cannot be held responsible for acting on knowledge he does not know he possesses. Although
a moralist in many ways, Freud had no patience with the idea that psychic
events were undetermined or with the glib confidence that reason could
master the unconscious. Making the unconscious conscious was for him the
world-historical task of psychoanalysis, not the personal responsibility of
ordinary individuals, unaided by therapeutic intervention.[28]

But we also use the term self-deception to describe situations that are
blameworthy. When we decide that an episode in our own past was a case
of self-deception, we are embarrassed and feel regretful about it. The implication of our embarrassment is that we suspect we could have done other
than we did, that by trying harder we could have become cognizant of the
self-concealed consequences of our action and changed course accordingly.
And of course the blame we attach to our own actions in such cases applies
with at least equal force to the self-deceptions we think we see others commit.

What does it mean, then, to say that the abolitionists deceived themselves? That they could and should have overcome their self-imposed blindness? Or that they did all that could be expected, given the limitations of
the only perspective available to them? The concept of self-deception is ambiguous enough to sustain either reading. More specifically, was Davis saying that chattel slavery and "wage slavery" were so similar that anyone
opposing one ought to have opposed the other, that the formalism confining
prevalent nineteenth-century definitions of freedom (among abolitionists
and many others) to the mere absence of physical or legal constraint was so
transparent that anyone who tried could have seen through it? This seems
to be the clear implication of Davis's contention that abolitionism was a
"highly selective response to labor exploitation." Yet as we have seen, Davis
was not at all comfortable with this implication; he also said that the re-

28. *Ibid.*, 106, 273–85.

formers contributed to capitalist hegemony only "unwittingly" and that it would have been "unthinkable" and "inconceivable" for them to adopt less formalistic conceptions of liberty. These are strong words, and they play an important role in Davis's account. They imply a far less voluntaristic image of the reformers, one that holds them essentially blameless for the limitations of their ideology—even though those limitations are said to have been self-imposed.[29] Without pursuing these conundrums any further, we can see that self-deception is an exceedingly spacious concept. I suspect that some readers welcome Davis's use of the term precisely because it seems to insist on a fairly high degree of intentionality and responsibility, while others welcome it because it seems to let the abolitionists entirely off the hook. Life has irreducible ambiguities, but this is a case in which there may be greater ambiguity in the terms of representation than in the reality we seek to represent.

29. Davis's claim that abolitionism was a "selective response to labor exploitation" is, of course, an echo of the criticism that radical labor leaders, such as William Cobbett, Richard Oastler, and Bronterre O'Brien, leveled against the abolitionists in their own time. What remains unclear, in spite of much recent discussion of the relation between abolitionism and the labor movement, is the exact basis of the labor critique. Did labor leaders work from a more advanced humanitarian perspective that really assigned equal importance to all varieties of exploitation, whether of slave or free labor (as Davis himself did)? Or did they simply assign a higher priority to the problems of wage laborers (nearby and racially similar) than to those of enslaved laborers (far away and racially different)? To what extent was the workingman's criticism of abolitionism a pragmatic tactic for drawing attention to his own cause rather than a considered judgment of the equivalence of exploitation in the two cases? These are not easy questions to answer for the period before the 1840s, and they become easy then only in the case of a few extreme figures, like Marx and Engels, whose perspective clearly embraced (albeit abstractly) a wider world of suffering than did that of the abolitionists. Moreover, as we shall see in the first of two hypothetical exercises, even if we conclude that labor spokesmen really did "transcend" the limiting conventions of the day, this would not justify us in thinking that it would have been easy for their contemporaries to follow suit, or that their contemporaries would have done so but for self-deception. On labor and abolition, see Patricia Hollis, "Anti-Slavery and British Working-Class Radicalism in the Years of Reform," in Bolt and Drescher, *Anti-Slavery, Religion, and Reform*, 295–315; Eric Foner, "Abolitionism and the Labor Movement in Antebellum America," in *ibid.*, 254–71; Jonathan A. Glickstein, " 'Poverty is not Slavery': American Abolitionists and the Competitive Labor Market," in Lewis Perry and Michael Fellman, eds., *Antislavery Reconsidered: New Perspectives on the Abolitionists* (Baton Rouge, 1979), 195–218; Marcus Cunliffe, *Chattel Slavery and Wage Slavery: The Anglo-American Context, 1830–1860* (Athens, Ga., 1979); and Betty Fladeland, " 'Our Cause Being One and the Same': Abolitionists and Chartism," in Walvin, *Slavery and British Society*. In *Slavery and British Society*, see the essays by Drescher and Walvin that stress the great popularity of the abolitionist cause in England, even outside middle-class ranks.

Now let us turn to the second and more serious limitation on the usefulness of the concept of self-deception. Although the ethical import of self-deception is ambiguous, the intentionality of it is not. Self-deception implies intention, although not of the conscious variety. If it did not imply intention, it would not have served Davis's purpose, which was to treat humanitarianism as a product in part of a specific kind of intention—advancing the interests of one's own class.[30] The intentions implied by self-deception presumably operate unconsciously, and, as we have seen, this complicates their ethical significance but does not turn them into something other than intentions. Freudian theory is quite clear on this point: what resides in the unconscious are intentions (relegated to that nether region precisely because of their ugly character) that compete with and sometimes overwhelm the conscious intentions of the actor.[31] One might argue that there are degrees of intentionality and that the self-deceiver's is less than the deliberate actor's, but in the last analysis the person deceiving himself must be said to know basically what the outcome of his action will be and to desire it (even though he may not be aware that he knows and desires it). Otherwise, the person who deceives himself would be no different from the person who through incomplete knowledge simply fails to anticipate all the consequences of his acts. That would make the term utterly vaporous. The person who deceives himself about the consequences of his actions knows a great deal more about them than the person who is ignorant of them.

Underlying any explanation built on the notion of self-deception, then, is an implicit claim to have successfully reconstructed the historical actor's unconscious intention. The claim is a bold one. Even conscious intentions are notoriously difficult to nail down in the absence of explicit statements of purpose (or even in their presence, for that matter), and unconscious intentions are much more problematical. By definition, they leave no direct empirical trace. One can only hypothesize their existence from the "goodness of fit" between the actor's interests (as reconstructed by the analyst) and certain consequences that follow from his actions. The reasoning process behind such hypothesizing is treacherous. After all, every act (or failure to act) has consequences both proximate and remote that are potentially infinite in number and extension. This is the stuff of which debates about the influence of horseshoe nails and Cleopatra's nose are made. It is altogether too easy to pluck from the ever-widening stream of consequences some that fit our reconstruction of the actor's interests and repackage these as his unconscious intention. Even if we assume that we know his interests,

30. Raymond Williams's comments on intentionality, quoted in footnote 22, above, are pertinent here as well.
31. Freud, *Introductory Lectures on Psychoanalysis,* 40–41, 61.

a question remains: what empirical evidence could, even in principle, confirm that the observed "goodness of fit" is more than coincidental?[32]

The impossibility of confirming our hunches about the existence of unconscious intentions is only an aspect of a larger problem: the absence, even in principle, of any empirical evidence that would permit us to distinguish between the *unconsciously intended consequences* that the self-deception explanation requires and the *unintended consequences* that make up so much of what happens in human affairs. To return to an earlier analogy, when Hank Aaron hit a home run, we felt confident that the spectator's acquisition of a baseball was not Aaron's intention, even though it was unquestionably a consequence of his action. Our confidence might have yielded to confusion, however, if we had grounds for believing that Aaron had an incentive for currying the favor of fans by giving them gifts in this manner. In that unlikely circumstance, we might suspect, but could never confirm, that gift giving was a significant, even though unconscious, part of his intention. Even if we could be sure that he was aware of the gift-giving consequences of his home run (say, by having called it to his attention as he strode to the plate), we could not confirm our suspicion, for all of us are always aware (or can easily be made aware) of consequences of our actions that fall outside intention in spite of our awareness of them. Knowing that a certain consequence will follow from one's actions does not necessarily make the production of that consequence part of one's intentions. The immense category of unintended consequences includes not only events of which the actor is completely ignorant but also events of which the actor may be aware but which social convention nonetheless classifies as uninten-

---

32. I pass hastily over a deep abyss—the glib assumption so characteristic of modern scholarship that a person's "interests" are readily identifiable and constitute a complete explanation of his conduct. In fact, the term is utterly elastic. There is no human choice that cannot be construed as self-interested. As a limiting case, consider a situation in which persons A and B happen on a burning house; person A dives into the flames to save the screaming occupants, while B refuses to endanger himself. B's selfishness is plain to see, but A's conduct can also be understood to reflect "enlightened" self-interest. The difference, one can argue, is simply that in A's subjective scheme of valuation, physical safety counts for less than social approbation. So he, like B, pursues what interests him most. (There is even a perspective from which one might prefer B's plainly selfish act to A's, on the grounds that B at least did not strive for the potentially "hegemonic" pleasure of achieving moral supremacy over another.) Needless to add, I am deeply troubled by any perspective on human affairs that obscures the radical moral superiority of A's choice over B's. The breath-taking scope of the metatheoretical issues at stake here is evident in the pivotal role that debates over the very possibility of altruistic action in a Darwinian universe have had in recent discussions of evolutionary theory and sociobiology. See Arthur L. Caplan, ed., *The Sociobiology Debate: Readings on Ethical and Scientific Issues* (New York, 1978), 213–26, 254, 308.

tional—as incidental concomitants of his action (like Aaron's "gift" to the spectator) rather than the aim of it. Given the immensity of this category of events, and the absence of any empirical means by which unintended consequences can be distinguished from unconsciously intended consequences, one may well doubt that the social control argument gains anything of substance by relying on the notion of self-deception.

Among all these liabilities, the really fatal flaw of the self-deception argument is its obliviousness to the paramount role played by convention in all judgments of moral responsibility. Once we understand the inescapable part that conventions play in channeling and limiting responsibility, it becomes apparent that imputations of unconscious intention (empirically unverifiable anyway) are gratuitous in the case of the abolitionists. What I aim to show in the next section of the essay is that abolitionists did not need to hide anything from themselves. All of us, no matter how humane, disown responsibility every day for known consequences of our own acts (and omissions) that are far more horrifying than those the abolitionists disowned when they chose to help slaves rather than wage workers. Keeping a clear conscience in spite of being causally involved in the suffering of others does not require self-deception. There was nothing distinctively selective about the abolitionists' preoccupation with chattel slavery: all humane action entails "selectivity." What enables us all—the abolitionists in their day and you and me in ours—to maintain a good conscience, in spite of doing nothing concretely about most of the world's suffering, is not self-deception but the ethical shelter afforded to us by our society's conventions of moral responsibility. These conventions allow us to confine our humane acts to a fraction of suffering humanity without feeling that we have thereby *intended*, in any way, or *caused*, in any morally significant way, the evils that we leave unrelieved.

The reader may well suspect sleight-of-hand at this stage of my argument. Are not these social conventions merely collective forms of self-deception? And might they not conceal widely held unconscious intentions of the sort that Davis and many other historians have postulated? I think even a skeptical reader will be persuaded by the following arguments that the burden of proof rests heavily on anyone who makes these claims. The conventions I have in mind are always open to criticism from the vantage point of rival conventions (we certainly need not admire those of any earlier generation), but they are not the transient reflexes of any social interest, and not even the most extraordinary feats of moral gymnastics would permit a person to transcend the limits of all such conventions, thereby becoming perfectly humane and invulnerable to the charge of "selectivity."

To show that this is so I ask the reader to participate in two mental exercises, which have a twofold purpose. First, they explore the problem of "selectivity" and highlight the role that conventions play in judgments of moral responsibility, thus wrapping up my criticisms of the self-deception argument and the social control thesis that it supports. Second, the longer of the two exercises, the "case of the starving stranger," brings into view the crucial anatomical features of the historical process that I believe gave rise to the modern humanitarian conscience and, therefore, paves the way for an alternative to the social control explanation, one that does not rely on class interest as the connecting link but nevertheless firmly connects capitalism with the emergence of the humanitarian sensibility.

First, we can illuminate the charge of "selectivity" and self-deception by imagining ourselves to be in a situation analogous to that of the abolitionists, men and women living in the midst of a great change in moral sensibility. The crux of the analogy addresses the intriguing problem to which Davis returned again and again: why were the abolitionists so slow, at best, to concern themselves with the misery of free workers. That they *could* have been quicker to see through the formalism so characteristic of nineteenth-century liberalism and *could* have acknowledged the similarity of chattel slavery to wage slavery is sufficiently demonstrated by those contemporary reformers, such as Owen, Fourier, Marx, and Engels, who actually did so. But the fact that abolitionists could have been more concerned with the plight of the free laborer does not justify the speculation that they really knew they should be and only failed to be because they deceived themselves.

Imagine that fifty or a hundred years from now the world is swept by another great shift in moral sensibility—this time a wave of revulsion against man's carnivorous way of life. The possibility is not, after all, so farfetched: philosophers have long debated what duties man owes to other sentient beings; antivivisection is an issue that has moved many; hard-boiled legislators pass statutes protecting endangered species; prominent publications like the *New York Review of Books* occasionally run articles on the problematical ethics of eating flesh. Dietary regulations occupy an important place in many religions, and whole Asian cultures have for extended periods regarded vegetarianism as a prerequisite to the ethical life. Moreover, we have in our midst many people who practice vegetarianism, providing a living model to those of us (including myself) who continue to eat meat.

If vegetarianism should someday become the mainstream point of view, how would the historians among our vegetarian descendants view us, their carnivorous ancestors? I suppose they would ask much the same questions about us that Davis asked about the abolitionists. How can we draw such an arbitrary line between human misery and the misery of nonhuman, but certainly sentient, creatures? Is not our comparatively intense concern for oppressed human beings a highly selective response to the general problem of predation, one that provides an outlet for demonstrating concern for suffering yet thereby gives a certain moral insulation to even more ruthless predatory practices in our society? Surely it would be tempting from the vegetarian point of view to say that all our busy efforts to alleviate human misery serve to isolate specific forms of suffering, thereby allowing issues of moral responsibility to be faced in a relatively simplified model. And they might even say that exaggeration of the harsh consequences of poverty, the pain of discrimination, the penalties of class, and the horrors of human warfare allows our most dedicated reformers to give tacit sanction to the systematic slaughter of nonhumans.

Readers who refrain from eating meat on ethical grounds may wish to endorse this interpretation insofar as it is an embodiment of their own anti-carnivorous values. But I think even they would agree that the vegetarian historian's interpretation is flatly wrong on two counts. First, it errs in tacitly assuming that, because some twentieth-century people are ethically opposed to eating meat, others must know in their hearts that it is wrong and can only maintain a clear conscience by deceiving themselves. It is conceivable to me that I may someday become convinced that eating meat is wrong, but by no stretch of the imagination can I persuade myself that in some way I already know that it is wrong. I continue eating meat not because I am deceiving myself but because whatever suffering my dietary preference causes falls outside the conventions of responsibility by which I presently live.[33] Second, the vegetarian historian would err even more egregiously if he supposed that we carnivores, in order to sustain our self-deceptions, busy ourselves with projects to alleviate human suffering as a means (conscious or not) of putting animal suffering out of mind. My indifference to animal suffering may depend on seeing only the end product of the butcher's work, but it does not depend on my all-too-infrequent efforts to alleviate human suffering. The vegetarian historian's error in imputing self-deception to us, his humane but unrepentantly carnivorous ancestors, is duplicated when we impute self-deception to the abolitionists on account of their failure to extend help to wage slaves.

Now let us proceed to a more elaborate exercise designed to show how

---

33. A defender of the self-deception argument might ask how I can claim to know whether I am deceiving myself or not, to which the appropriate reply is that, in the absence of any possibility of empirical demonstration, my claim, based on introspection, has at least as much merit as any opposing claim.

inescapable conventions are in the allocation of moral responsibility, and how the conventions themselves change in time. Let us call this the "case of the starving stranger." As I sit at my desk writing this essay, and as you, the reader, now sit reading it, both of us are aware that some people in Phnom Penh, Bombay, Rangoon, the Sahel, and elsewhere will die next week of starvation. They are strangers; all we know about them is that they will die. We also know that it would be possible for any one of us to sell a car or a house, buy an airline ticket, fly to Bombay or wherever, seek out at least one of those starving strangers, and save his life, or at the very least extend it. We could be there tomorrow, and we really could save him. Now to admit that we have it in our power to prevent this person's death by starvation is to admit that our inaction—our preference for sitting here, reading and writing about moral responsibility, going on with our daily routine— is a necessary condition for the stranger's death. But for our refusal to go to his aid, he would live.

This means that we are causally involved in his death. Our refusal to give aid is one of the many conditions that, all together, make up what John Stuart Mill called the cause "philosophically speaking" of this evil event. Now to say that we are causally involved is, of course, not to say that our failure to act is "the cause" of his death: it is only one among many conditions, and not every condition is properly regarded as "the cause." But the troubling fact remains that *but for* our inaction this evil event would not occur.[34]

Why do we not go to his aid? It is not for lack of ethical maxims teaching us that it is good to help strangers. Presumably we all subscribe to the Golden Rule, and certainly if we were starving we would hope that some stranger would care enough to drop his daily routine and come to our aid. Yet we sit here. We do not do for him what we would have him do for us. Are we hypocrites? Are we engaged in self-deception? Do we in any sense *intend* his death?

I think not—unless, of course, we wish to stretch the meaning of intention way beyond customary usage, so that it indiscriminately lumps to-

34. Mill, as quoted in H. L. A. Hart and A. M. Honoré, *Causation in the Law* (London, 1959), 16. Hart's analysis is the foundation of much of what I say here, though I am strongly attracted to Joel Feinberg's amendments to Hart's excessively voluntarist perspective. See Feinberg, "Causing Voluntary Actions," in Feinberg, *Doing and Deserving: Essays in the Theory of Responsibility* (Princeton, 1970), 152–86. It is noteworthy that much of Hart's magisterial volume is an inquiry into "the principles governing the selection we apparently make of one of a complex set of conditions as the cause" and that when he inaugurated that inquiry it was "a problem scarcely mentioned before in the history of philosophy"; Hart and Honoré, *Causation in the Law*, 16.

gether premeditated murder with a failure to avail ourselves of an opportunity to do good. There is much more to say about the way we arrive at judgments of both causation and intention, but for my purposes it is enough to observe that the limits of moral responsibility have to be drawn somewhere and that the "somewhere" will always fall far short of much pain and suffering that we could do something to alleviate. What is crucially important to see is that we never include within our circle of responsibility all those events in which we are causally involved. We always set limits that fall short of our power to intervene. Whatever limits we do set can therefore always be challenged and made to look arbitrary or "selective" by insistent questioning—for they are finally nothing more than conventions. Good reasons can be given for preferring some conventions to others, but there is no escaping convention itself and even a degree of arbitrariness in our choice of which to accept. The necessity for being selective is built into the nature of the problem. Even the person who tries to extend his limits to encompass all those events in which he is causally involved will, in his futile efforts to save all the starving strangers in the world, have to choose whether to go first to Bombay or Calcutta and whether to begin with person X or person Y. These choices will appear no less arbitrary (at least to the stranger not chosen) than the convention that permits you and me to exclude this predictable consequence of our inaction from the category of intention, and to sit here with only a pinprick of guilt as we contemplate our involvement in the stranger's death.[35]

Curiously, our feeling of responsibility for the stranger's plight, though nowhere near strong enough to move us to action, is probably stronger today than it would have been before the airplane. If William Wilberforce had faced this question in 1800, he at least could have begged off on the grounds that the sea voyage to India was long and costly and he might die enroute. This suggests that new technology—using that word broadly to refer to all means of accomplishing our ends, including new institutions and political organizations that enable us to attain ends otherwise out of reach—can change the moral universe in which we live. Technological innovation can

---

35. Among these sheltering conventions are those that permit us to feel that we have done our part by making donations to charitable organizations, or by committing ourselves to a political movement that, if it should triumph, would, we trust, alleviate the suffering in question. The latter route to a good conscience is especially vulnerable to the charge of self-delusion, and neither of these routes can seem anything but arbitrary and "selective" from the standpoint of the stranger who starves next week. Yet these are the best choices available to us. Surely it *is* better to send an annual check to CARE, or even merely to adopt a political rhetoric that condemns maldistribution of wealth, than to do nothing at all. How much better remains far more open to question than any of us like to think.

perform this startling feat, because it supplies us with new ways of acting at a distance and new ways of influencing future events and thereby imposes on us new occasions for the attribution of responsibility and guilt. In short, new techniques, or ways of intervening in the course of events, can change the conventional limits within which we feel responsible enough to act. Imagine that we have at our disposal an as yet uninvented technology, far more advanced than the airplane, that will enable us to save the starving stranger with minimal expenditure of time and energy, no disruption of our ordinary routine. If we could save him by just reaching out to press a button, then a failure to act would become indefensible. What convention previously enabled us to regard as an acceptably incidental concomitant of our inaction would then be transformed into heinous neglect or even—arguably—an intention to do harm. No convention could save us from responsibility then. And notice that this drastic change in our operative sense of responsibility could be brought about without any change at all in our ethical convictions. All of our ideas, every abstract formulation of moral obligation could remain the same; the only change needed to get us over the threshold of action is an expansion of the range of opportunities available to us for shaping the future and intervening in other lives. The latter point constitutes an especially telling objection to those who believe that humanitarianism can be explained merely by pointing to the proliferation of sermons and other texts on the importance of love and benevolence.

These "ways of intervening in the course of events" and "opportunities for shaping the future" play such an important role in the history of moral responsibility and will occupy such a prominent place in my analysis that they deserve a distinctive label. The word "technique" carries misleading connotations—of superficialities of style, on the one hand, and of highly organized bodies of scientific knowledge, on the other. What we need is a word that suggests the full range of practical know-how about cause-and-effect connections, from that required to put a man on the moon, at the upper end of the scale, to that needed to get in a harvest on time or mobilize the manpower and material needed to run a blacksmith's shop, at the lower and much more important end of the scale.

The philosopher Douglas Gasking not only suggested a suitably homely name in his essay "Causation and Recipes" but also explained why this category of practical formulas for getting things done is so important. The very idea of causation, in its most fundamental or primitive sense, is, according to Gasking, "essentially connected with our manipulative techniques for producing results." Not science but plain *recipe* knowledge, or technique in its most inclusive sense, is the wellspring of causal thinking. "A statement about the cause of something," wrote Gasking, "is very closely connected with a recipe for producing it or for preventing it."[36] Although one can think of science as an elaboration of recipe knowledge, resulting from the substitution of open-ended inference-licenses for recipes, it is what Gasking called the "producing-by-means-of relation" that underlies causal thinking, and this relation emerges from man's most basic efforts to sustain life.

> Men discovered that whenever they manipulated certain things in
> certain ways in certain conditions certain things happened. When
> you hold a stone in your hand and make certain complex movements
> of arm and fingers the stone sails through the air approximately in a
> parabola. When you manipulate two bits of wood and some dry
> grass for a long time in a certain way the grass catches fire. When
> you squeeze an egg, it breaks. When you put a stone in the fire it
> gets hot. Thus men found out how to produce certain effects by ma-
> nipulating things in certain ways: how to make an egg break, how
> to make a stone hot, how to make dry grass catch fire, and so on.[37]

What makes recipe knowledge important for the historian trying to understand the rise of humanitarianism is that neither causal perception nor feelings of moral responsibility can exist in the absence of appropriate recipes. One simply cannot see a human act (or omission) "A" as the cause of event "E" unless one possesses a recipe for producing events *like* "E" by means of acts (or omissions) *like* "A." And where the very possibility of causal perception is lacking, there can be no feelings of moral responsibility. By the same token, other things remaining equal, an enhancement of causal perception by the introduction of new or more far-reaching recipes can extend moral responsibility beyond its former limits.

Armed with this understanding of the dependence of moral conventions on recipe knowledge and causal perception, we can find in the case of the starving stranger many clues and research suggestions for the historian who wants to explain the origins of humanitarian sensibility. Although the clues point strongly in the direction of capitalism, they do not point toward class interest. To extract these clues it will be helpful to formalize the case of the starving stranger, recasting it as a set of preconditions that must exist before people will go to the aid of strangers.

There are four preconditions to the emergence of humanitarianism as a historical phenomenon. First and most obvious, we must adhere to ethical maxims that make helping strangers the right thing to do before we can feel

36. Gasking, "Causation and Recipes," *Mind*, 64 (1955): 483. Also see Hart and Honoré, *Causation in the Law*, 26, 29, 69.
37. Gasking, "Causation and Recipes," 486, 482.

obliged to aid them. If our ethical convictions permit us to ignore the suffering of people outside our own family or clan, then there can be no basis whatever for the emergence of those activities and attitudes that we call humanitarian. Although adherence to appropriate maxims is indispensable, the case of the starving stranger shows that it is not enough by itself to provoke humane behavior. The Golden Rule alone provides a sufficient ethical basis for our deciding right now to get up and go to Ethiopia, yet we remain seated.

A second precondition, also illustrated in the case of the starving stranger, is that we must perceive ourselves to be causally involved in the evil event. Once again, being causally involved does not mean that we regard ourselves as "the cause" but only that we recognize our refusal to act as a necessary condition without which the evil event would not occur. Along with this prerequisite goes the third. We cannot regard ourselves as causally involved in another's suffering unless we see a way to stop it. We must perceive a causal connection, a chain made up of cause-and-effect links, that begins with some act of ours as cause and ends with the alleviation of the stranger's suffering as effect. We must, in short, have a technique, or *recipe*, for intervening—a specific sequence of steps that we know we can take to alter the ordinary course of events. As long as we truly perceive an evil as inaccessible to manipulation—as an unavoidable or "necessary" evil—our feelings of sympathy, no matter how great, will not produce the sense of operative responsibility that leads to action aimed at avoiding or alleviating the evil in question.

Although the possession of such recipes sets the stage for going to the stranger's aid, even this is not enough. Today you and I have a recipe for getting to Ethiopia and preventing starvation, we admit that our failure to go is a necessary condition for the stranger's death, and we all subscribe to the Golden Rule. Yet here we sit.

The fourth precondition, the one that finally gets us into a psychological frame of mind in which *some* of us will feel compelled to act, is this: the recipes for intervention available to us must be ones of sufficient ordinariness, familiarity, certainty of effect, and ease of operation that our failure to use them would constitute a suspension of routine, an out-of-the-ordinary event, possibly even an intentional act in itself.[38] Only then will we begin to feel that our inaction is not merely one among many conditions

38. The fourth precondition is not that we must have an ordinary, familiar, and certain recipe specifically tailored to the specific task at hand but that our ordinary, familiar, and certain recipe must be sufficiently *like* what is needed to inspire confidence that the task can be accomplished with only moderate adjustments of the available and proven means.

necessary for the occurrence or continuation of the evil event but instead a significant contributory *cause*.

To say that our refusal to aid the stranger only assumes causal status when it appears extraordinary against a background of ordinary recipe usage is to base ourselves securely in the existing literature on the philosophy and psychology of causal attribution, for that literature continually reaffirms that abnormality is the principal criterion that prompts us to single out certain events, acts, or conditions as causal.[39] The main reason you and I can go about our daily routine and not be overwhelmed with guilt about the stranger's plight is that the only recipe we have for going to his aid is far more exotic and more difficult to implement than the recipes we customarily use in everyday life. It involves a causal connection between his life and ours that is much more indirect, remote, and tenuous than the ones we habitually employ, so we do not regard our failure to act on the recipe as abnormal. None of us habitually liquidates major assets and departs on a moment's notice for the remotest parts of the globe in the pursuit even of selfish ends. If in our everyday routines we normally employed recipes as exotic as this one, then our failure to use it would begin to look extraordinary, and would therefore begin to assume causal status. And, once we begin to perceive our inaction as a cause of the stranger's suffering, then the psychological pressure to do something in his behalf can grow irresistible.[40]

*Compelled* [handwritten margin note]

39. "The notion, that a cause is essentially something which interferes with or intervenes in the course of events which would ordinarily take place, is central to the common-sense concept of cause, and at least as essential as the notions of invariable or constant sequence so much stressed by Mill and Hume"; Hart and Honoré, *Causation in the Law*, 27. Hart also assigned a special place to voluntary acts, but Feinberg argued that these are so often perceived as causal only because of their "abnormality." "*The more expectable human behavior is, whether voluntary or not, the less likely it is to 'negative causal connection'* [that is, to be seen as a cause rather than as the effect of some more remote cause]"; Feinberg, "Causing Voluntary Actions," 165. Also see N. R. Hanson, "Causal Chains," *Mind*, 64 (1955): 309: "We tend to be very selective about the sorts of things of which we ask, 'What is its cause?' This question is usually asked only when we are confronted with a *breach* of routine."

40. Recipe knowledge stems from many sources. Because my aim in this essay is to link humanitarianism to the market, the recipe knowledge of immediate interest is that which originated in market transactions. But no recipe knowledge was more critical in the origins of humanitarianism and antislavery than that which originated in the special religious and political experience of the Quakers. Howard Temperley noted that, in the course of their struggles against tithe bills and other injurious legislation, Quakers by the 1730s had already mobilized quarterly, monthly, and local meetings into "a political machine of remarkable strength and sophistication . . . [combining] central direction with constituency action. Long before anyone else, Quakers had become adept at using a broad range of techniques designed to exert extraparliamentary pressure, including mass petitioning, lobbying, drawing up voting lists, and obtaining pledges"; Temperley, "Anti-Slavery," in Patricia Hol-

These preconditions drawn from the case of the starving stranger help clarify both the way in which revolutions in moral sensibility ought to be conceived and the way in which they are to be explained. First, we ought to construe major alterations of sensibility such as the rise of abolitionism as the result of shifts in the conventional boundaries of moral responsibility. Thus, what emerged in the century after 1750 was not, in the first instance at least, either a new configuration of class interests or a novel set of values geared to the hegemony of a rising class. Instead, the principal novelty was an expansion of the conventional limits of moral responsibility that prompted people whose values may have remained as traditional (and as unrelated to class) as the Golden Rule to behave in ways that were unprecedented and not necessarily well suited to their material interests. What happened was that the conventional limits of moral responsibility observed by an influential minority in society expanded to encompass evils that previously had fallen outside anyone's operative sphere of responsibility. The evils in question are of course the miseries of the slave, which had always been recognized but which before the eighteenth century had possessed the same cognitive and moral status that the misery of the starving stranger in Ethiopia has for us today.[41]

The question historians need to answer is why events such as the death of the starving stranger sometimes move out of the morally indifferent category of "unintended consequences," for which no one feels any operative sense of responsibility, and become matters for which certain people feel acutely responsible. Here lies the second lesson to be drawn from our list of prerequisites: once revolutions in moral sensibility are understood to result from shifts in the conventional boundaries of moral responsibility, the task of explanation can be seen to consist in finding the historical developments that exerted an outward, expansionary pressure on those conventional limits. Our set of preconditions also suggests what successful

lis, ed., *Pressure from Without: In Early Victorian England* (London, 1974), 31. Quakers were not only adept at manipulating public opinion and Parliament but also knew more than anyone else about shaping the traits of individual character, a kind of recipe knowledge that was presupposed by the penitentiary and the "moral treatment" of the insane. See Richard T. Vann, *The Social Development of English Quakerism, 1655–1755* (Cambridge, Mass., 1969), chap. 1, and pp. 167–79, 204–8.

41. A section of *Las Siete Partidas*, thirteenth-century legal guidelines that influenced later legislation in Spain and Spanish America (both of which accepted the institution of slavery), declared that "slavery is the most evil and the most despicable thing which can be found among men, because man, who is the most noble and free creature, among all the creatures that God made, is placed in the power of another"; Herbert S. Klein, "Anglicanism, Catholicism, and the Negro Slave," in Ann J. Lane, ed., *The Debate over Slavery: Stanley Elkins and His Critics* (Urbana, 1971), 142.

explanations might look like by alerting us to the intimate relationship between feelings of responsibility and perceptions of causal involvement. It suggests that the limiting conventions by which people live are a function of the range of events in which they perceive themselves to be causally involved, either by commission or omission and, further, that the range of events in which they perceive themselves to be involved is shaped by the number and the "power" or "reach" of the recipes for intervention that they and the people around them habitually use. What expands a person's horizons of causal involvement, and hence potentially expands also his limits of moral responsibility, is the routine employment of recipes of great complexity or temporal extension. So what the historian needs to look for are historical factors that give people heightened confidence in recipes they already have or encourage them to develop new recipes, or more complex recipes, or recipes that reach farther into the future. Every new recipe, or increase in the "reach" or complexity of recipes, extends the horizons of causal perception and thereby broadens the sphere within which a person may *potentially* feel himself to be the cause of an evil.

The word "potentially" requires special attention. We are not concerned with individual episodes of human kindness and decency—which I assume can occur anywhere, anytime—but with a sustained, collective pattern of behavior in which substantial numbers of people regularly act to alleviate the suffering of strangers. That, I take it, is what we mean by the emergence of a new humanitarian sensibility in the eighteenth century. Our aim, then, is to specify the minimum conditions that must be satisfied before this collective phenomenon can begin. Not all people who experience these conditions will become humanitarian reformers. In fact, most will not, and to account for those few who do we would have to look beyond the limits of this explanatory scheme to conventional biographical and historical details about the teachings to which they were exposed, their personal temperaments, the depth of their religious faith, their courage, and so on.

Although the form of explanation suggested here does not pretend to explain why certain individuals become humanitarian reformers and others do not, it does alert us to the distinctiveness of the moral experience of people who are equipped with a large repertoire of far-reaching recipes. Because such people feel comparatively confident of their ability to intervene in the course of events and to shape the future at will, they are the prime candidates for the first historical appearance of that heightened feeling of causal involvement that is a prerequisite for humanitarianism. With the capacity to intervene goes the possibility of feeling obliged to take responsibility—but only the possibility. Many people, whose large endowment of recipe knowledge gives them the capacity to intervene, will not do so, or will do so only for the sake of self-aggrandizement, but some unusually sensitive individuals will be "trapped," as it were, by their broadened horizons of causal involvement and feel compelled to go to the aid of strangers for whose misery they would previously have felt no more than passive sympathy. The explanatory approach recommended here does not pretend to plumb the mysteries of individual sensitivity or compassion. It does, however, offer a way to understand why even the most scrupulous and compassionate men and women did not feel obliged to go to the aid of suffering slaves before the middle of the eighteenth century.[42]

Far from transforming acts of conscience into subtle reflexes of more fundamental drives, this explanatory approach permits us to give the humanitarian reformers full credit for their moral insight, their courage in the face of adversity, and their tenacity in uprooting entrenched institutions. They were consummate interpreters of a new moral universe. Yet it also enables us to see that their new interpretation was called forth by changes in the social and economic conditions of life and that, once the stage was set, similar measures almost certainly would have been carried out by other individuals if not by Wilberforce, Garrison, Phillips, and all the other formidable men and women who actually did the job. One need not pretend that human beings are uncaused causes in order to admire them.

42. In fact, this mode of explanation is perfectly compatible with the assumption that such individual personality traits as compassion and scrupulosity were as evident before 1750 as after. If being "good" consists—as I think it must, for the most part—of scrupulous adherence to the ethical maxims of one's culture (such as the Golden Rule), within the operational limits prescribed by convention and the availability of techniques for intervention, then it makes perfectly good sense to say that people did not become "better" after 1750; they just adapted their conduct to a new set of conventions and capabilities. The argument thus does not rest on any assumption of moral progress, as that term is ordinarily understood, though it does assume that post-1750 conventions of responsibility embrace a wider range of suffering humanity and are in that sense superior to earlier ones.

*Chapter 5*

# Capitalism and the Origins of the Humanitarian Sensibility, Part 2

*Thomas L. Haskell*

Having set forth the limitations of the social control thesis and explored the implications of the case of the starving stranger, we can now proceed to the third and final stage of the argument, a brief sketch—no more—of an alternative way to formulate the relationship between capitalism and the origins of the humanitarian sensibility. As the reader will recall, the thesis to be maintained here is that the crucial links between capitalism and humanitarianism stem not from the rise of the bourgeoisie per se but from its most characteristic institution, the market, and they are bonds created not by class interest but by the subtle isomorphisms and homologies that arise from a cognitive style common to economic affairs, judgments of moral responsibility, and much else.

This is not to deny that some effects of the attack on slavery furthered bourgeois interests. The consequences of the antislavery movement that Davis called "hegemonic" are real enough, but we have not been given any adequate reason to think they were produced by class interest, by a desire for hegemony, or by any other form of intention, conscious or unconscious. They belong mainly to the category of unintended consequences. "Hegemonic" exaggerates their purposefulness, and the term "self-deception" is not capable of clarifying their status.

None of these conclusions require us to give up the most important contribution of Marxian historiography: the suggestion that the humanitarian impulse emerged when and where it did because of its kinship with those social and economic changes that we customarily denominate as "the rise of capitalism." The task now is to specify the nature and extent of that kinship.

One could argue in the spirit of Norbert Elias that the kinship is very strong indeed, that the practices we label "capitalistic" and the acts we identify as "humanitarian" are simply different manifestations of a single cultural complex, or "form of life." Elias's brilliant account of the shifting "thresholds of embarrassment" and "standards of affective control" that have regulated manners during European man's long ascent up the ladder of the "civilizing process" provides immensely suggestive insights into the present subject.[1] One cannot help being amused by Elias's description of the gradual elaboration of rules and taboos affecting the polite way to spit, expel gas, blow one's nose, defecate, and lift morsels of food into one's mouth. But the boundaries between polite and impolite, permissible and impermissible, that operate in these comparatively trivial matters are not unlike the conventions that determine whether knowledge of a starving stranger will produce only passive sympathy or a flood of emotion and expressive action. Indeed, Elias devoted a chapter to the shift of boundaries that made brutality, one of the uncomplicated "pleasures of life" in the medieval period, deeply horrifying (though still titillating) to more modern sensibilities.[2] Incongruous though the thought may seem, the boundaries we observe today between good and bad manners could prove to be seamlessly interwoven both with the "capitalist" conventions that authorize the individual to adopt a comparatively high level of aggressiveness in economic affairs and with the "humanitarian" conventions that inhibit us from taking pleasure in (or even remaining indifferent to) the agony of others. Perhaps, as Elias said, "The question why men's behavior and emotions change is really the same as the question why their forms of life change."[3]

Although the explanatory approach recommended here converges with that of Elias, it is less holistic and more concerned with identifying specific mechanisms of change. It does not treat capitalism and humanitarianism as two expressions of a single form of life but does argue that the emergence of a market-oriented form of life gave rise to new habits of causal attribution that set the stage for humanitarianism. Before proceeding with the development of this form of explanation, however, we must pause to consider a possibility at the opposite end of the spectrum from Elias's holism—the possibility that there is no kinship at all between capitalism and humanitarianism. The idea that humanitarianism arose from or depended in any way on the marketplace, with its notoriously lax ethical standards, will seem perversely counterintuitive to many readers, and for good reason. The face of the market that we all know best, regardless of our political preferences, is the grim visage that warns "Caveat emptor!" Buyer beware! How,

1. Elias, *The Civilizing Process: The History of Manners*, trans. Edmund Jephcott (New York, 1978).
2. *Ibid.*, chap. 10.
3. *Ibid.*, 205.

the skeptic may ask, can an institution that explicitly foreshortens or confines within narrow, formal limits the responsibility of each person for his
fellow man be said to have extended anyone's sense of moral responsibility?
That the market has faces other than this most familiar one is the principal
argumentative burden of the following pages. Let us begin, however, by
conceding the full force of the classical indictment.

Consider the rules of the marketplace as they were embodied in the Anglo-American law of contract at its zenith in the nineteenth century. The
rules assume that everyone will put his own interests first and withhold
even customary or neighborly levels of concern for everyone else. The seller
charges what the market will bear, not what the buyer can afford to pay. In
negotiating a contract, the parties deal at what the law calls "arm's length,"
each relying on his own skill and judgment, neither owing any fiduciary duties to the other. As they maneuver for advantage and work out the terms
on which their carefully limited cooperation will proceed, the parties are
neither obliged to volunteer relevant information nor entitled to expect others to do so. The deal is sealed by agreement. Differences of bargaining
power, mistakes, pressures of time, ignorance of pertinent facts, subjective
intentions are all beside the point, for these pressures are deemed to be a
normal part of life in the marketplace. Unless the voluntariness of the
agreement can be undercut by demonstrating force, threat, or fraud, each
party can be compelled by law to carry out its part of the bargain, no matter
how unjust the agreed-upon exchange of goods and services may appear to
be.[4] In all of this there is undeniably a license for callousness, for the implicit assumption is that the individual is not only the sole proper judge of
his own needs and interests but also their sole proper guarantor.

The most rigorous students of the market in its early years, the political
economists, by no means conceded that it was exclusively a force for moral
indifference, but both friends and foes of capitalism often read into technical
analyses of wage and price movements a very simple message: since the
laws of supply and demand automatically transmute each individual's self-
interest into the greater good of the greater number, no one need be concerned with the public interest. Once this lesson with its time bomb of
antitraditional implications was incorporated into common sense, the very
possibility of moral obligation was put in doubt; the burden of proof henceforth rested on those who wished to deny that "everything is permitted."
If we couple this familiar line of argument with the rich nineteenth-century
folklore about avaricious landlords and piratical factory owners, and then
add to that combination the metahistorical imagery of a class of me-first
bourgeois individualists displacing a feudal aristocracy still enmeshed in a

4. P. S. Atiyah, *The Rise and Fall of Freedom of Contract* (London, 1979), 402–4.

traditional web of clientage and patronage relations, we will indeed scarcely see how the coming of capitalism could have expanded the conventional boundaries of moral responsibility. And yet it did.

After nearly two centuries of criticism of market society, it is easy to forget how brutal life could be before the profit motive ruled supreme and how moderate, in the long perspective of human history, the capitalist's license for aggression really is. The paternalist code that required the lord to care for his dependents provided no basis whatsoever for systematically going out of one's way to aid strangers, and, even in the eighteenth century, Elias's "civilizing process" had made so little headway that most people could, like their medieval ancestors, still ignore a cry of "Help! Help!" without any feeling of distress.[5] As for the fabled greed of the capitalist, one can only say again what has been said so many times: although plentiful in the marketplace, greed is not the distinguishing feature of the capitalist. As Max Weber put it:

> The impulse to acquisition, pursuit of gain, of money, of the greatest possible amount of money, has in itself nothing to do with capitalism. This impulse exists and has existed among waiters, physicians, coachmen, artists, prostitutes, dishonest officials, soldiers, nobles, crusaders, gamblers, and beggars. One may say that it has been common to all sorts and conditions of men at all times and in all countries of the earth, wherever the objective possibility of it is or has been given. It should be taught in the kindergarten of cultural history that this naive idea of capitalism must be given up once and for all. Unlimited greed for gain is not in the least identical with capitalism, and is still less its spirit. Capitalism *may* even be identical with the restraint, or at least a rational tempering, of this irrational impulse.[6]

5. The minstrel Bertran de Born sang joyfully of hearing the cry "Help! Help!" and seeing "the dead pierced by the wood of the lances decked with banners." As late as the sixteenth century the king and queen of France celebrated Midsummer Day in Paris by joining a festive throng to burn alive one or two dozen cats; Elias, *Civilizing Process*, 193, 203. The gruesome agonies inflicted on the regicide Damiens in 1757 supply the opening scene for Michel Foucault's work; Foucault, *Discipline and Punish: The Birth of the Prison*, trans. Alan Sheridan (New York, 1977), 3–6. Trial by ordeal was not abolished until the Fourth Lateran Council met in 1215, and the use of judicial torture as a means of eliciting confessions in cases of serious crime continued on the Continent (though seldom in England) from the thirteenth century until the last half of the eighteenth. In Central Europe it lingered on even into the nineteenth century. See John H. Langbein, *Torture and the Law of Proof: Europe and England in the Ancien Régime* (Chicago, 1977).
6. Weber, *The Protestant Ethic and the Spirit of Capitalism*, trans. Talcott Parsons (New York, 1958), 17; E. P. Thompson, "The Transforming Power of the Cross," in *The Making of the English Working Class* (New York, 1966); Bernard Semmel, *The*

The capitalist marketplace is a scene of perpetual struggle, and its tendency to inject calculations of least cost into every sphere of life can, indeed, stunt the human spirit. But contrary to romantic folklore, the marketplace is not a Hobbesian war of all against all. Many holds are barred. Success ordinarily requires not only pugnacity and shrewdness but also restraint.

The market presents another face—perhaps equally unsmiling but suggesting quite different conclusions—as soon as we think of it as the abolitionists and their generation often did: as an agency of social discipline or of education and character modification. Adam Smith's "invisible hand" was, after all, not merely an economic mechanism but also a sweeping new mode of social discipline that displaced older, more overt forms of control precisely because of its welcome impersonality and the efficiency with which it allocated goods and resources. The spread of competitive relationships not only channeled behavior directly, encouraging people through  shifting wage and price levels to engage in some activities and disengage from others, but also provided an immensely powerful educational force, capable of reaching into the depths of personal psychology. The market altered character by heaping tangible rewards on people who displayed a certain calculating, moderately assertive style of conduct, while humbling others whose manner was more unbuttoned or who pitched their affairs at a level of aggressiveness either higher or lower than the prevailing standard.

The autonomous power of the market to shape character is often underestimated because of the stress Weber and more recent scholars have placed on the reverse of this phenomenon: the inability of the market to flourish where it lacks an ample supply of self-disciplined individuals, already made alert to the promptings of the invisible hand by inward-turning, self-monitoring habits like those taught by the Protestant sects. But on this point Weber was explicit: capitalism in Europe needed the personality-transforming power and sweeping recruitment capacity of religion only in order to breach the walls of traditionalism and gain a dominant position. Once the market has a secure foothold, said Weber, it no longer needs the support of religious doctrine because it independently "educates and selects the economic subjects it needs through a process of economic survival of the fittest."[7] Weber

*Methodist Revolution* (New York, 1973); and Paul E. Johnson, *A Shopkeeper's Millennium: Society and Revivals in Rochester, N.Y., 1815–1837* (New York, 1978).
7. Weber, *Protestant Ethic*, 55. For the history of the expectation, widespread from the sixteenth to the eighteenth century, that capitalism would bring political harmony by taming the passions and infusing a wholesome discipline into the population, see Albert O. Hirschman, *The Passions and the Interests: Political Arguments for Capitalism before Its Triumph* (Princeton, N.J., 1977).

recognized an obvious and nonvicious circularity in the relationship between institutions and individual character: the institution of the market could not sustain itself without large numbers of "economic men," and, in turn, the proportion of these men to the population and the esteem in which they were held depended largely on the framework of opportunity and affirmation that the market established.

The form of life that the market both presupposed and encouraged is, of course, too complex to be adequately described in this essay, but at the expense of some oversimplification one can think of the process in terms of two "lessons" taught (and simultaneously presupposed) by the market. The lessons were closely interwoven: the first taught people to keep their promises; the second taught them to attend to the remote consequences of their actions. Those who learned these lessons well and who could take for granted the existence of many others imbued with the same lessons were the first to cross the threshold into a new moral universe, one in which the horizons of causal perception were sufficiently wide, and the techniques routinely employed in everyday tasks sufficiently complex and future oriented, that failing to go to the aid of a suffering stranger might become an unconscionable act.[8]

Consider first the lesson of promise keeping. In the long history of human morality there is no landmark more significant than the appearance of the man who can be trusted to keep his promises. The norm of promise keeping (observed often in the breach, as all norms are) is so basic to the form of life that prevails today that we take it for granted, forgetting how recently it came into being and at what cost, in terms of instinctual renunciation, this stage of the "civilizing process" was attained. Ironically, it was Friedrich Nietzsche—whom no one will accuse of being a friend of capitalism (or, for that matter, of humanitarianism or anything else requiring instinctual renunciation)—who gave the most eloquent testimony to the importance of this historical moment. He began the second essay of *The Genealogy of Morals* with these words: "To breed an animal *with the right to make promises*—is this not the paradoxical task that nature has set itself in the case of man? Is it not the real problem regarding man?" Keeping promises can only occur to a human animal who has developed the capacity to remember what he once willed, and memory, argued Nietzsche, is diametrically opposed to animal good health. Forgetfulness, he contended (in passages strongly suggestive of Freud on repression), is "a form of *robust*

---

8. On my use of the term "techniques" and the preconditions for the appearance of the humanitarian sensibility, see the "case of the starving stranger" in my "Capitalism and the Origins of the Humanitarian Sensibility, Part 1," *AHR*, 90 (1985): 354–59.

On promise Keeping

health," without which man can experience "no happiness, no cheerful-ness, no hope, no pride, no *present*."[9]

That, in spite of this, man has to a great extent become an animal with the right to make promises seemed to Nietzsche a "remarkable" achieve-ment, a "tremendous labor" of self-overcoming, in view of the strength of the forces opposing such a development. Promise keeping requires

> a desire for the continuance of something desired once, a real *memory of the will*: so that between the original "I will," "I shall do this" and the actual discharge of the will, its *act*, a world of strange new things, circumstances, even acts of will may be inter-posed without breaking this long chain of will. But how many things this presupposes! To ordain the future in advance in this way, man must first have learned to distinguish necessary events from chance ones, to think causally, to see and anticipate distant eventu-alities as if they belonged to the present, to decide with certainty what is the goal and what [are] the means to it, and in general be able to calculate and compute. Man himself must first of all have become *calculable, regular, necessary*, even in his own image of himself, if he is to be able to stand security for *his own future*, which is what one who promises does![10]

Contemptuous though he was of asceticism, "bad conscience," and all the other signs of "morbid softening and moralization through which the ani-mal 'man' finally learns to be ashamed of all his instincts," Nietzsche's at-titude toward this basic phase of renunciation was decidedly respectful. In fact, the "ripest fruit" of this tremendous cultural process is what he called the "sovereign individual," who, precisely because he has earned the right to make promises, cannot help but be aware of his "mastery over circum-stances, over nature, and over all more short-willed and unreliable crea-tures."[11]

> The proud awareness of the extraordinary privilege of *responsi-bility*, the consciousness of this rare freedom, this power over one-

9. Nietzsche, *On the Genealogy of Morals and Ecce Homo*, trans. Walter Kauffman and R. J. Hollingdale (New York, 1969), 57–58.
10. *Ibid.*, 57–59.
11. *Ibid.*, 67, 59–60. Nietzsche's admiration is sincere: "The existence on earth of an animal soul turned against itself, taking sides against itself, was something so new, profound, unheard of, enigmatic, contradictory, *and pregnant with a future* that the aspect of the earth was essentially altered. Indeed, divine spectators were needed to do justice to the spectacle that thus began and the end of which is not yet in sight"; *ibid.*, 85. Now that the ladder of renunciation had been arduously climbed, of course, Nietzsche was inexplicably confident that his new model man could kick it away and simply levitate.

self and over fate, has in his case penetrated to the profoundest
depths and become instinct, the dominating instinct. What will he
call this dominating instinct, supposing he feels the need to give it a
name? The answer is beyond doubt: this sovereign man calls it his
*conscience*.[12]

Set aside for a moment the surprising resemblance between the abolitionists
and Nietzsche's "sovereign individual," with his terrific conscience and extraordinarily extended sense of responsibility; let us dwell, instead, on the
relationship between more ordinary levels of self-overcoming and the rise
of capitalism. Here Nietzsche allows us to make a crucial point. Historically
speaking, capitalism requires conscience and can even be said to be identical
with the ascendancy of conscience. This "tremendous labor" of instinctual
renunciation on which promise keeping rests—a labor that even Nietzsche,
a reckless critic of renunciation, felt obliged to endorse and make the starting point for his "sovereign individual" (one whose freedom would continue
to be conditioned by his promises)—is an absolute prerequisite for the
emergence of possessive individualism and market society. The individual
cannot be said to possess his capacity to perform labor at some future time,
or to be free to dispose of his labor to others for due compensation, until he
is "self-possessed"—until, in other words, he can overcome his "healthy"
forgetfulness and feel obliged to act on long chains of will.[13] And, in the reciprocal manner that always holds between institutions and character, the
practices and traits of personality that the market presupposes as a condition
of its existence, it also induces and perpetually reinforces.

Conscience and promise keeping emerged in human history, of course,
long before capitalism. Moreover, promise keeping is not merely a free-
standing psychological trait but a cultural practice, deeply imbedded in a
fabric of social relationships and dependent in part on an effectively institutionalized threat of force in the event of noncompliance. But it was not
until the eighteenth century, in Western Europe, England, and North
America, that societies first appeared whose economic systems depended on
the expectation that most people, most of the time, were sufficiently conscience-ridden (and certain of retribution) that they could be trusted to keep
their promises. In other words, only then did promise keeping become so
widespread that it could be elevated into a general social norm. Only to the

12. *Ibid.*, 60.
13. C. B. Macpherson, *The Political Theory of Possessive Individualism: Hobbes to Locke* (London, 1962), 48: "If a single criterion of the possessive market society is wanted it is that man's labour is a commodity, i.e. that a man's energy and skill are his own, yet are regarded not as integral parts of his personality, but as posses- sions, the use and disposal of which he is free to hand over to others for a price."

extent that such a norm prevails can economic affairs be based on nothing
more authoritative than the obligations arising out of promises. And a
growing reliance on mutual promises, or contractual relations, in lieu of relations based on status, custom, or traditional authority comes very close to
the heart of what we mean by "the rise of capitalism."

Both the growing force of the norm of promise keeping and its synchro-
nization with the spread of market relations are clearly inscribed in the history of the law of contract. A contract is, of course, an exchange of promises,
and as such the law of contract provides us with a direct measure of the centrality of promise keeping in society. But the significance of the rising tra-
jectory that we can trace in the history of Anglo-American contract law is
not limited to this, for, in addition to being an exchange of promises, every
contract is also an ensemble of mutually contingent recipes.[14] When people
enter into contractual relations with one another, each commits himself to
bring to pass some designated future event, usually without bothering to
spell out the intricate but taken-for-granted sequence of mundane cause-
and-effect connections that he plans to rely on. Although the documents
supporting contractual agreements ordinarily specify little more than the
desired outcome, the very fact that the parties have contracted together sig-
nifies two things: a tacit claim by each promisor that he possesses the recipe
knowledge necessary for producing the desired outcome and a tacit expression of faith by each promisee that the promisor's recipes do exist and can
be expected to work. Contract law, therefore, supplies not only evidence of
the growing force of conscience in market society but also evidence about
the growing fund of recipe knowledge on which perceptions of causal involvement and moral responsibility necessarily rest.

The historical record shows that the norm of promise keeping attained
only recently the ascendancy we take for granted. In England before the
twelfth century, promises exchanged by private individuals were generally
beneath the notice of the king's courts. In that century and the next, a few
contractual relationships gained legal sanction through writs of covenant,
debt, and detinue. The rigidity and limited scope of these forms of pleading
led to their growing circumvention by actions of trespass, or what today
would be called torts or wrongs, and by the early seventeenth century a sub-
species of trespass, the action of assumpsit (meaning "undertaking," or assumption of responsibility for bringing an event to pass), had developed into

14. For my use of the term "recipe" and the role that recipe knowledge plays in establishing the background against which causal attribution and judgments of moral
responsibility are made, see "Capitalism and the Origins of the Humanitarian Sensibility, Part 1," 356–57.

a general remedy for breaches of contract.[15] Extensive though the early development of contract law was, it pales in comparison with what happened in the last decades of the eighteenth century, when the hitherto gradual reorientation of English life to the market accelerated dramatically. So great was the corresponding leap of the law that as late as 1765, when Blackstone published his *Commentaries*, contract law played (by comparison to its later role) a " very small part in the legal scheme," amounting to little more than "an appendage to the law of property."[16]

In the decades following 1770, as contract law disentangled itself from property law and grew explosively, swiftly subsuming property law and much else within its widening province, a subtle shift occurred in the grounds of promissory liability, one that gave still greater impetus to the prodigious enlargement in the sphere of legally enforceable promises then underway. Traditionally, liability had rested on a combination of promise and consideration. Promise alone, the mere fact of a voluntary and deliberate declaration of intent to do something, was not enough. What made a promise binding was consideration, proof that there had been "adequate motivating circumstances"—such as a fee or other concrete benefit—to induce the promisor to give his promise. Since judge and jury determined the adequacy of consideration, this doctrine left an opening for judicial discretion and for communal standards of "just price" and fairness that imposed severe constraints on the kinds of contractual relations individuals were able to form.[17]

In decline, yet still surprisingly vigorous in Blackstone's day, these constraints gave way completely in the last decades of the eighteenth century and early decades of the nineteenth (the entire process in America lagging a couple of decades behind England). As Anglo-American law entered the "Age of Contract," it simultaneously shifted toward a pure "will" or "consensus theory" of liability according to which obligation arose less from consideration than from the naked will of the contracting parties—the very

15. A. W. B. Simpson, *A History of the Common Law of Contract: The Rise of the Action of Assumpsit* (London, 1975), 4, 199, 215–18, 281–316.
16. Atiyah, *Rise and Fall of Freedom of Contract*, 102. On parallel developments in America, see Morton J. Horwitz, *The Transformation of American Law, 1780–1860* (Cambridge, Mass., 1977), chap. 6. Also see Grant Gilmore, *The Death of Contract* (Columbus, Ohio, 1974). Although Horwitz's book is extremely valuable, it falls victim (as Atiyah's does not) to the usual weaknesses of the social control mode of explanation: an exaggeration of the role played by class interest, based on the assumption that only interest can link base with superstructure.
17. Simpson, *History of the Common Law of Contract*, 323; and Atiyah, *Rise and Fall of Freedom of Contract*, 139–49.

*nuda voluntas* that traditional law had rejected. Originating as a kind of tort, contract now took on its modern status as the antithesis of tort: obligations created not by law but by private agreement. Traditionally, the courts had been willing to enforce a promise only when the circumstances inducing the defendant to give it (the consideration) were so strong that he was in a sense obliged to perform the act in question whether or not he had promised to do so. A much wider range of promises became binding, as the courts abandoned any attempt to evaluate the circumstances underlying an uncoerced declaration of intention. Now that intent was a sufficient ground of obligation, a promisor could be made to perform, or pay damages in lieu of performance, even if he backed out of his contract before the promisee had relied, to his detriment, on the promise given. Even if the promisor had not yet received any of the benefits that the contract called for, he could be held liable. For the first time the law strained to make promisors generally liable for whatever expectations their promises created. Never before had promises counted for so much in human affairs, and never before had the penalties for being short-willed and unreliable been so severe.[18]

It is not merely coincidental that humanitarianism burst into bloom in the late eighteenth century just as the norm of promise keeping was being elevated to a supreme moral and legal imperative. At the most obvious level, the new stress on promise keeping contributed to the emergence of the humanitarian sensibility by encouraging new levels of scrupulosity in the fulfillment of ethical maxims. If one's customers and trading partners were increasingly conceded the right and actual power to invoke legal penalties for one's failure to live up to one's promises, what of the obligations created by one's covenant with God? The Golden Rule took on a new operational significance for pious men like John Woolman not simply because of an upwelling of piety but also because the spread of market transactions changed the backdrop against which scrupulosity was measured by imposing on everyday affairs an unprecedentedly high standard of conscientious performance.[19]

What of caveat emptor? We have seen that the code of the marketplace encouraged contracting parties to treat each other in an unneighborly way, coldly and suspiciously—as strangers, in fact—and it is well known how devastating the consequences of this market-induced callousness could be, especially in relations between employers and employees. But even as the market shrank the conventional limits of moral responsibility in this respect, it was expanding them in others. For in the Age of Contract those

18. Atiyah, *Rise and Fall of Freedom of Contract*, 139–49, 194–205, 208, 212–16; and Horwitz, *Transformation of American Law*, 160, 174, 180–86, 200–201.
19. I discuss Woolman more fully in the closing pages of this essay.

who engaged in market transactions *were*, more often, strangers, people who shared no tie of blood, faith, or community. Such people would not have dared to do business with one another but for the growing assurances provided them by the law and other market-oriented institutions that promises would be kept—even promises made to a stranger. For example, the dominance in the transatlantic trade that Jewish and Quaker merchants of New York and Newport enjoyed because of their ability to trust fellow believers in faraway ports broke down in the 1750s precisely because the norm of promise keeping had by then gained such force that the "arm's length" variety of trust needed to do overseas business was no longer confined to fellow members of persecuted sects.[20]

Nor was the extension of trust to strangers the only way in which a promise-keeping form of life raised standards of scrupulosity. As Lord Kames, Scottish moral-sense philosopher and sessions judge, observed in his *Principles of Equity* (1767), "Contracts and promises are not confined to commercial dealings: they serve also to make benevolence a duty, independent of any pecuniary interest. . . . For it is remarkable in human nature, that though we always sympathize with our relations, and with those under our eye, the distress of persons remote and unknown affects us very little."[21] What made the customary level of indifference for the fate of strangers seem "remarkable" to Kames was the routinization of the norm of promise keeping in everyday affairs. And, of course, once indifference had become remarkable, it had potentially become unconscionable as well.

But scrupulosity is not enough. The case of the starving stranger shows us that even scrupulous adherence to ethical maxims need not lead to humane action. No matter how hard people strive to live up to moral codes, they have no occasion for feeling causally implicated in the sufferings of a stranger until they possess techniques capable of affecting his condition. Even then their response is not likely to go beyond passive sympathy unless the relevant techniques are so familiar that not to use them would stand out as an abnormality, a suspension of expected levels of carefulness. So in order to link capitalism with humanitarianism we need to show not only that the market induced a higher level of conscientiousness but also that it ex-

---

20. Daniel Snydacker, "Traders in Exile: Quakers and Jews of New York and Newport in the New World Economy, 1650–1776" (Ph.D. dissertation, Johns Hopkins University, 1982).
21. Henry Home, Lord Kames, *Principles of Equity* (2d edn., Edinburgh, 1767), 16–17. These words appear in Kames's "Preliminary Discourse: Being an Investigation of the Moral Laws of Society," which was not included in any other edition of *Principles of Equity*.

panded the range of causal perception and inspired people's confidence in their power to intervene in the course of events. Here lies the significance of the fact that contracts are both promises and mutually contingent recipes, for, as we saw in our hypothetical case, new ways of acting on the world, new recipes for producing desired events, are what push people over the threshold separating passive sympathy from humane action.

The explosive growth of contract law in the century following 1770 gives us a useful measure of the increasing frequency of recipe usage and the burgeoning fund of recipe knowledge available to the merchants, manufacturers, artisans, and improving farmers of England and America in these years. Not only was the fund of knowledge growing but recipes of increasing complexity and unprecedented temporal extension were being employed. In the early development of English law, suits for breach of contract typically involved simple undertakings like the conveyance of a cow across a river or the construction of a cottage, but by the end of the eighteenth century we find extremely complex transactions, often requiring the coordination of an intricate sequence of activities by people far removed from one another in space and time.[22] The variety of goals that private citizens pursued and the range of means available for pursuing them were clearly on the rise. In view of what we have learned from the case of the starving stranger, this is exactly the sort of development that we would expect to give some people such a strong conviction of their ability to intervene at will in the course of events that passivity would, for them, begin to appear abnormal and, hence, blameworthy. By the middle of the nineteenth century this conviction was strong enough in the mind of an abolitionist like O. B. Frothingham that, although the evils of pauperism still struck him as "providential," something growing "out of the inevitable condition of things," the miseries of the slave no longer seemed beyond the reach of reform. Slavery, he wrote, is "an institution which the conscious will of man has built up, and which the same will, faithfully exerted, might . . . abolish in a year, a month, a week, a day. . . . Pauperism, from its nature involves no direct Guilt. Slavery is essential Guilt."[23]

22. Simpson, *History of the Common Law of Contract*, 204, 249; and Atiyah, *Rise and Fall of Freedom of Contract*, 219–26.
23. Frothingham, as quoted in Jonathan A. Glickstein, " 'Poverty is not Slavery': American Abolitionists and the Competitive Labor Market," in Lewis Perry and Michael Fellman, eds., *Antislavery Reconsidered: New Perspectives on the Abolitionists* (Baton Rouge, La., 1979), 199. Frothingham also predicted that pauperism, "in all its dismal shapes, with all its terrible sorrows, . . . will be outgrown as man becomes more wise and powerful"; *ibid.* Yet another outward shift in the horizon of causal involvement not unlike what Frothingham predicted can perhaps be observed in Wendell Phillips's change of opinion on wage labor. Before the Civil War he dismissed the term "wage slavery" as "utterly unintelligible" but by 1871 had declared

The breath-taking confidence of the Age of Enlightenment is too well known to need any review here. Countercurrents of doubt and skepticism notwithstanding, doctrines of automatic progress enjoyed greatest currency during the century following 1750. Neither before nor since has European man felt so sure that merely by daring to use his own reason he might make himself master of both nature and fate. The supreme sense of individual and collective potency that prevailed in these decades made all existing institutional constraints seem malleable and contributed powerfully to the creation of a situation in which slavery could be challenged and other humanitarian reforms set in motion. To trace all the sources of this outburst of exaggerated pride in man's role as a causal agent, capable of shaping the future to his own will, would lead us far afield, for example, into the history of science and mechanical invention. But one important source lies close at hand in the market and in the impetus it gave to the accumulation and elaboration of manipulative techniques for the conduct of everyday affairs. It was not only the exotic achievements of Newtonian science or dramatic labor-saving devices like the steam engine that underwrote Enlightenment optimism but also the buoyancy supplied by a surge of homely recipes for getting things done.

By its very nature the market encouraged the production of recipe knowledge. As the prime mover of a promise-keeping form of life, the market established a domain within which human behavior was cut loose from the anchor of tradition and yet simultaneously rendered as stable and predictable as "long chains of will" could make it. The combination of change-ability and foreseeability created powerful incentives for the development of a manipulative, problem-solving sort of intelligence. As early as 1697 Daniel Defoe gave the name "projectors" to the distinctively future-oriented and knowledge-possessing men whose form of life was most closely attuned to the dynamics of market competition.

> If industry be in any business rewarded with success, 'tis in the merchandizing part of the world, who indeed may be more truly said to live by their wits than any [other] people whatsoever. All foreign negoce [sic], tho' to some 'tis a plain road by the help of custom, yet it is in its beginning all project, contrivance, and invention. Every new voyage the merchant contrives is a project, and ships are sent from port to port, as markets and merchandizes differ, by the help of strange and universal intelligence; wherein some are so exquisite, so swift, and so exact, that a merchant sitting at home in his counting-house, at once converses with all parts of the known

---

his opposition to the entire wage system. Phillips, as quoted in Daniel Rodgers, *The Work Ethic in Industrial America* (Chicago, 1978), 32.

world. This, and travel, makes a true-bred merchant the most intel-
ligent man in the world, and consequently the most capable, when
urg'd by necessity, to contrive new ways to live.[24]

Himself an exemplar of "the Projecting Humour that now reigns," Defoe
devoted most of his *Essay Upon Projects* to no fewer than thirteen elaborate and ambitious plans for the improvement of national life, including a
modernization of the banking system, construction of a national system of
paved highways, establishment of nationwide pension and casualty insurance plans, a military academy, a college for women, and a "Fool's House"
where the mentally incompetent would be sheltered from ridicule and exploitation.[25] As a recent student of economic thought and ideology in seventeenth-century England observed, "The extension of the market through
individual initiative also worked to activate the participants' imaginative
powers." Once the market had become a crucial regulator of human activity,
dispensing rewards and providing valuable information, it could not help
but encourage "long-range planning through rational calculations."[26]

Not only raw intelligence—a *capacity* for envisioning the future and
solving the problems it presented—but also solutions themselves took on
added value under the market's aegis. Being imitative creatures, we humans
solve most of our problems by adapting the techniques that have worked in
the past to the different, yet partly similar, circumstances we now face. So
the market's thirst for foresight and mental resourcefulness could not have
been slaked without a quantum leap in the production, proliferation, cir-
culation, and preservation of recipe knowledge. The extent and almost infinite variety of this homely sort of knowledge defies description, yet its
importance can hardly be exaggerated. This expanding fund of ever more
complex and powerful recipes for the conduct of daily affairs is what satisfied the critical preconditions for the emergence of the humanitarian sensibility.

24. Defoe, *An Essay Upon Projects* (Menston, Eng., 1969), 7–8. The earliest entry
in the Oxford English Dictionary for "project" in the sense of "a plan, scheme, purpose," something proposed for execution, is dated 1601.
25. *Ibid.*, 24.
26. Joyce Oldham Appleby, *Economic Thought and Ideology in Seventeenth-Century England* (Princeton, N.J., 1978), 246, 84. Also see her comments on the importance of calculating equivalencies and on the power of abstraction; *ibid.*, 245,
247, 93. She noted that Defoe's demarcation of the period after 1680 as a "projecting
age" is justified by the rapid economic growth and great surge of inventions that
took place in these years; *ibid.*, 164–65. Seymour Drescher observed that the abolitionists "represented that portion of European society most completely mobilized
for living with the sense of individual power, responsibility, and insecurity that
flowed from the market"; Drescher, *Econocide: British Slavery in the Era of Abolition* (Pittsburgh, Penn., 1977), 183.

The growing preoccupation of English and American courts with contractual litigation after 1770 mirrors the increasing density of recipe usage in the society outside the courtroom and thus reveals the power of the market to push outward the limits of causal perception and involvement. But contracts not only mirror recipe usage, they are themselves a singularly important kind of recipe for the mobilization of manpower and knowledge. When contracting parties commit themselves to bring certain designated events to pass, they fix the future with regard to those events, thereby providing each other with a significantly stabilized environment in which to operate. By making its own behavior predictable, each party to a contract enables the others to depend on it, and to incorporate its promised future performance into their own recipes as one ingredient. The result is a magnification of personal power, a way of doing collaboratively what no individual could do alone. Once the norm of promise keeping gained the legal sanction and the position of cultural ascendancy implied by the "will theory" of liability, the recipe of "contracting together" could become a powerful tool for shaping the future.

Among all the new techniques that flourished under the encouragement of the market, none did more to stretch people's sense of personal power—and therefore to extend their sense of causal involvement in other lives—than contractualism itself. And among all the sources of the humanitarian sensibility, none was more important than the contribution made by a promise-keeping form of life: a heightened sense of personal effectiveness created by the possession and use of powerful recipes—recipes made powerful in part by the growing calculability of a market society that tethered each ego to its own past intentions with "long chains of will," even as this society liberated each ego from traditional constraints on personal ambition. Nietzsche got the paradox right: by becoming sufficiently "calculable," "regular," and "necessary" to stand security for his own future, European man extended his sovereignty over nature and fate. And with every outward shift of the perimeter of sovereignty, the sphere within which conscience and responsibility potentially operated had to expand as well.

The promise-keeping aspect of the form of life spawned by the market did a great deal to satisfy the critical preconditions for the emergence of humanitarianism. But this was not the only contribution that the market made to the humanitarian sensibility. In fact, promise keeping can be regarded as only one particular manifestation of a still more fundamental lesson the market taught: to attend to the remote consequences of one's acts. The two lessons were so closely entangled that in discussing the first we have already touched on the second, but the second was taught in every phase of market life—not just in the making of contracts.

The force of the market's second lesson is evident in the special place assigned to the idea of principle during the entrepreneurial phase of capitalism. As the legal scholar P. S. Atiyah observed, the "Age of Contract" was also an "Age of Principle."[27] Since the term could refer to rules of moral conduct as well as to law-like uniformities of nature, it bridged the widening chasm between nature and morality. "There were principles of political economy, principles of ethics and morality, principles of jurisprudence, principles of political behaviour, principles of commercial behaviour; there were also Men of Principle; and there was the contrast between Principle and Expediency."[28] No doubt Atiyah was correct to argue that the search for principles was sparked by the decay of traditional authority and the need for an alternative foundation flexible enough for a society of self-governing individuals. But more to the present point, the person who firmly grasped correct principles was one fit to prosper in a market society.

The defining characteristic of the "man of principle," the moral paragon of a promise-keeping, market-centered form of life, was his willingness to act on principle no matter how inconvenient it might be. Comparatively speaking, he cared little for the short-term consequences of his actions and was firmly convinced that in the long run adherence to the highly generalized maxims of conduct that he called principles would produce the most desirable outcomes. His was a calculus of utility that assigned such low weight to immediate consequences and such high value to remote ones that he could seem at times to be above utilitarian considerations altogether. What gave him the assurance to do this was, initially, his faith in the principle he adhered to—a recipe, let us note, of a very general and overarching character, such as "time is money" or "never go back on your word." Armed with his principles, gaze fixed on the remote good they assured him he would receive, the man (or woman) of principle was a formidable character in history, if also a rigid and uncompromising one. The abolitionists were notoriously men and women of principle, and, as we noted earlier, they bear more than a passing resemblance in this regard to Nietzsche's "sovereign individual." Once again Nietzsche saw exactly what was required. In order to preserve the connection between an original "I will" and the actual "discharge of the will" at a later time, the man of principle must, like the sovereign individual, "see and anticipate distant eventualities as if they were present."[29] He must, in other words, devote such close attention to the

27. Atiyah, *Rise and Fall of Freedom of Contract*, 345.
28. *Ibid.*, 345–46.
29. Nietzsche, *On the Genealogy of Morals*, 60, 58.

remote consequences of the various choices before him that he lives partly in the future.

In order to satisfy this *cognitive* precondition for the moral stature that goes with conscience and the right to make promises, one thing further is required: that man learn, as Nietzsche said, to "think causally."[30] Since thinking causally consists of linking present choices to consequences more or less remote in time by the use of recipes that map a route from one to the other, what crucially distinguishes the man of principle from all "more short-willed and unreliable creatures" is a preoccupation with the remote consequences of his actions—a preoccupation made possible by his possession of far-reaching recipes and "principles" and a form of life that validates his trust in them.

Earnest people with a bent toward self-control have existed in all human societies, and their personality traits have often enjoyed the endorsement of religion. But through most of recorded history people imbued with these traits could not be at all certain that their earthly rewards would be measurably superior to the rewards accruing to less disciplined personality types. Scrupulous attention to remote consequences brings little advantage when life is either fixed by tradition or so lacking in fixity that it defies prediction. With the advent of the market came a sweeping endorsement of self-control and all the traits that accompany it, in the form of palpable benefits that no one could ignore. Although the growth of political stability and economic abundance played an important part, it was mainly the disciplinary force of the market that provided the intricate blend of ceaseless change, on the one hand, and predictability, on the other, in which a preoccupation with remote consequences paid off most handsomely. Every recipe postulates a causal regularity, and the farther a recipe reaches into the future, or the more complex the qualitative transformations it calls for, the greater the risk that it will fail. The man of principle, who tries to live by recipes of the most extended and risky sort, can thrive only under conditions like those that prevailed in the early entrepreneurial phase of capitalism, when the future was at once open enough to the individual to be manipulable and yet closed enough to be foreseeable.

The premium the market paid for accurate forecasts was readily visible to anyone routinely involved in market transactions. Where direct experience with the market was lacking, the same lesson, suitably draped in a moral and religious vocabulary, was driven home by numerous Victorian moralists. Anticipating the remote consequences of one's actions was thought to require not only concentrated attention but also self-restraint

30. *Ibid.*, 58.

and a capacity to delay gratification that the middle class found lamentably lacking in criminals, paupers, madmen, children—not excepting their own—and others who became objects of humanitarian concern. "Want of Reflection," declared John Burt, a typical prison reformer, "is preeminently the characteristic of the criminal. The habit is always wanting, often the capacity for it defective."[31]

The missionary zeal of the middle class to disseminate to each rising generation and to all "dependent classes" its own habit of deferring immediate gratification for the sake of remote and principled rewards is well known. Teaching people the virtues of reflection and close attention to the distant consequences of their actions came to be regarded as a universal key to social progress, whether in the education of children, the "moral treatment" of the insane, the cultivation of self-reliance in paupers (through plans like those of Samuel Gridley Howe), or the widely imitated incentive schemes of Alexander Maconochie, which were intended to produce the same effect among prisoners.[32] Early nineteenth-century moral reformers felt that their crusade was succeeding, and, though they may have claimed credit for lessons that the market found its own ways to teach, there seems little reason to doubt that the character traits of the English and American populations did shift in these years. John Stuart Mill spoke as if the crucial battles

31. Burt, as quoted in George Combe, *Remarks on the Principles of Criminal Legislation and the Practice of Prison Discipline* (London, 1864), 64 [italics deleted].
32. Michael Katz, writing of school reformers, said "the control of the passions coincided with another goal, especially necessary for social mobility but usually expressed in rather different terms: the ability to plan for the future. 'Forming plans for a distant future,' individuals 'rise nearer and nearer to a spiritual existence.' Ideally the parents and, if not, the school had to teach this lesson: substitute future for immediate gratification. . . . Restraint it was that separated the child from the adult. Men, claimed one writer, 'act from principle . . . the restraints of society are felt. They can see remote consequences. But children act from the impulses of their natures quickened by the objects around them.' Thus restraint was the personality characteristic central to education"; Katz, *The Irony of Early School Reform: Educational Innovations in Mid-Nineteenth-Century Massachusetts* (Cambridge, Mass., 1968), 121. Also see Brian Harrison, *Drink and the Victorians: The Temperance Question in England, 1815–1872* (Pittsburgh, Penn., 1971); Blake McKelvey, *American Prisons: A History of Good Intentions* (Montclair, N.J., 1977), 36–38; David J. Rothman, *The Discovery of the Asylum: Social Order and Disorder in the American Republic* (Boston, 1971); Michael Ignatieff, *A Just Measure of Pain: The Penitentiary and the Industrial Revolution* (New York, 1978); Andrew Scull, *Museums of Madness: The Social Organization of Insanity in Nineteenth-Century England* (New York, 1979); "Moral Treatment Reconsidered: Some Sociological Comments on an Episode in the History of British Psychiatry," *Psychological Medicine*, 9 (1979): 421–28; Martin Wiener, ed., *Humanitarianism or Control? A Symposium on Aspects of Nineteenth-Century Social Reform in Britain and America: Rice University Studies*, 67 (1981); and Harold Schwartz, *Samuel Gridley Howe: Social Reformer, 1801–1876* (Cambridge, Mass., 1956), chap. 6.

had already been won when he claimed in 1835 that "the commonest person lives according to maxims of prudence founded on foresight of consequences. . . . The whole course of human life is founded upon the fact" that many consequences can be foreseen.[33] Although Herbert Spencer thought a severe regimen of prison discipline was appropriate for people "who dwell only in the present, the special, the concrete [and] who do not recognize the contingencies of the future," he favored comparatively mild treatment for the prison inmates of England, where liberal political institutions presupposed a population already habituated to "weighing distant results and being chiefly guided by them."[34]

It is obvious today that Spencer and the Victorian middle class for whom he spoke greatly overestimated the universality of the values that a newly emergent form of life made supreme and underestimated the resistance to those values that would soon come not only from other classes but also from the sons and daughters of the middle class. But it should be equally obvious that the very possibility of feeling obliged to go to the aid of a suffering stranger—whether his suffering was that occasioned by chattel slavery or by what the observer interpreted as slavery to sin—was enormously heightened by the emergence of a form of life that made attention to the remote consequences of one's acts (or omissions) an emblem of civilization itself. On this issue Spencer and Nietzsche agreed: people who "dwell only in the present" live in a world that cannot sustain "bad consciences" or acute sensations of moral responsibility. To acknowledge this is not to say that all those who learned to dwell partly in the future became abolitionists. Clearly, most people equipped with the wide causal horizons that go with powerful recipes either devoted themselves to the new opportunities for self-aggrandizement that the market also opened up or, at best, tended their own gardens, abiding by traditional conventions of moral responsibility. But some of these long-willed people were bound to discover that traditional conventions were no longer compatible with the extended causal recipes they and their neighbors increasingly took for granted. Attributing to themselves far-reaching powers of intervention, they also found themselves exposed to sensations of guilt and responsibility that their predecessors, no matter how conscientious, had not experienced.

What, then, did capitalism contribute to the freeing of the slaves? Only a *precondition*, albeit a vital one: a proliferation of recipe knowledge and consequent expansion of the conventional limits of causal perception and moral responsibility that compelled some exceptionally scrupulous indi-

33. Mill, as quoted in Atiyah, *Rise and Fall of Freedom of Contract*, 432.
34. Spencer, "Prison Ethics," in *Essays Moral, Political, and Aesthetic* (New York, 1888), 216–17.

viduals to attack slavery and prepared others to listen and comprehend. The precondition could have been satisfied by other means, yet during the period in question no other force pressed outward on the limits of moral responsibility with the strength of the market. Since capitalism supplied only a precondition, no one need be surprised that the subsequent history of capitalist societies has not been greatly distinguished by humanitarian achievements. The argument presented here is not that markets breed humane action but that in the particular historical circumstances of late eighteenth-century Anglo-American culture the market happens to have been the force that pushed causal perception across the threshold that had hitherto made the slaves' misery (and much other human suffering) seem a necessary evil. One would no more expect markets continually to elevate the morality of the population than one would expect oxygen—in the absence of which ignition cannot occur—always to produce fire. Then, too, there is reason to fear that still another face of the market has prevailed in the later stages of capitalism, one far less supportive of the humanitarian sensibility.[35]

The early Quaker abolitionist John Woolman supplies a fittingly concrete concluding illustration of the process we have been discussing. Familiar with the extensive libraries and busy counting-houses of family friends in nearby Philadelphia, Woolman, at age twenty-one, left his father's farm to keep books and tend store. Soon he opened his own retail store, learned the tailor's trade, and supplemented his earnings by keeping an orchard, teaching, drafting wills and legal documents, and conducting land surveys. "The increase of business became my burden," he later said, "for though my natural inclination was toward merchandise, yet I believed Truth required me to live more free from outward cumbers."[36] Giving up his store at age thirty-six, Woolman spent the rest of his life traveling widely as an itinerant Quaker minister, displaying everywhere a remarkable gift for challenging the morality of slaveholding without offending slaveholders.

The order of Woolman's thoughts in his classic 1746 essay, "Some Considerations on the Keeping of Negroes," corresponds closely with the stages I contend anyone would have had to undergo as he moved intellectually from a world in which slave misery provoked only the passive sympathy we feel

---

35. Here I have in mind Philip Rieff's *The Triumph of the Therapeutic: The Uses of Faith after Freud* (New York, 1966) and T. J. Jackson Lears's *No Place of Grace: Antimodernism and the Transformation of American Culture, 1880–1920* (New York, 1981).
36. Woolman, *The Journal and Major Essays of John Woolman*, ed. Phillips P. Moulton (New York, 1971), 53.

today for starving strangers to a world in which remaining passive in the face of such misery seemed unconscionable. Woolman began with convention. Although the "customs" governing the extent of our duty to care for our fellow men seem as deeply fixed in the nature of things as "the natural produce of a soil," said Woolman, the highest wisdom requires us to "forego" these customs and adhere to God's "infallible standard: Truth." Conceding that God may have favored "us" over Negroes, Woolman insisted that it was not with any design that we exploit them or be indifferent to their fate. God's love is universal, and ours should imitate His. The "natural affection" that we tend to confine to our own immediate family is only a "branch of self-love," and it neither distinguishes us from inferior creatures nor satisfies our Savior's injunction to love all of mankind. The criterion by which we should test our conduct is known to us all: "How should I approve of this conduct were I in their circumstance and they in mine?"[37]

Then Woolman addressed two anticipated objections. The first was that the Golden Rule does not really require care for strangers. This he countered with a passage from Leviticus: "The stranger that dwelleth with you shall be as one born amongst you, and thou shalt love him as thyself." The second was the slaveowner's plea that, having made an investment and undertaken risk, he was now entitled to the slave's labor. Here Woolman responded that the master's property in the slave is "wrong from the beginning. . . . if I purchase a man who hath never forfeited his liberty, the natural right of freedom is in him."[38]

Having called existing conventions of moral responsibility into question and pointed to an accepted ethical maxim that, if acted upon, would require radical changes of conduct, Woolman then graciously conceded the fallibility of human understanding and even a kind of limited relativity of values. This concession is extremely revealing within the framework of explanation developed here, because it is based on his clear recognition that many people in his society were virtually incapable of perceiving their acts or omissions as significant contributory causes of the slave's plight.

---

37. *Ibid.*, 198–203. The Golden Rule first appears in the sixth paragraph of Woolman's essay; this version, later in the book, is in a passage that Woolman drew from the works of a London Quaker, Alexander Arscott. Sydney James observed that for Quakers "even launching a business without adequate training and credit was a case of failure to do 'unto all men, as we would they should do unto us' "; James, *A People Among Peoples: Quaker Benevolence in Eighteenth-Century America* (Cambridge, Mass., 1963), 32.

38. Woolman, *Journal and Major Essays*, 203, 204. Woolman's inclusion of the proviso that the slave never forfeited his liberty indicates that he was familiar with the work of the natural rights philosophers. See Richard Tuck, *Natural Rights Theories: Their Origin and Development* (New York, 1979).

While we have no right to keep men as servants for term of life but that of superior power, to do this with design by their labour to profit ourselves and our families I believe is wrong. But I do not believe that all who have kept slaves have therefore been chargeable with guilt. If their motives thereto were free from selfishness and their slaves content, they were a sort of freemen, which I believe hath sometimes been the case.

Whatever a man does in the spirit of charity, to him it is not sin; and while he lives and acts in this spirit, he learns all things essential to his happiness as an individual. *And if he doth not see that any injury or injustice to any other person is necessarily promoted by any part of his form of government, I believe the merciful Judge will not lay iniquity to his charge. Yet others who live in the same spirit of charity from a clear convincement may see the relation of one thing to another and the necessary tendency of each; and hence it may be absolutely binding on them to desist from some parts of conduct which some good men have been in.*[39]

From Woolman's perspective, the slaveholder's conduct was not immoral as long as he failed to see "the relation of one thing to another and the necessary tendency of each." To persist after being convinced of these causal connections was another matter, and, of course, convincing slaveholders that their conduct had more distant consequences than they recognized was Woolman's lifework. If the points he addressed in his essay are any reflection of the arguments he heard as he traveled around the country meeting with slaveholders, the slaveholders' principal defense against Woolman's gentle prodding was the remoteness of their responsibility, as mere owners of slaves, for the undoubted misery inflicted on the slave by the person who enslaved him. Historians have treated this defense as a cynical dodge, but Woolman took it very seriously. The geographical remoteness of the scene of initial enslavement, argued Woolman, was no defense: "Great distance makes nothing in our favour. To willingly join with unrighteousness to the injury of men who live some thousands of miles off is the same in substance as joining with it to the injury of our neighbours." Nor was temporal remoteness any defense: "Can it be possible for an honest man to think that with view to self-interest we may continue slavery to the offspring of these unhappy sufferers, merely because they are the children of slaves—and not have a share of this guilt?"[40]

It was, however, not only spatial and temporal remoteness with which Woolman had to contend. The misery of slaves seemed remote to his lis-

39. Woolman, *Journal and Major Essays*, 211. My emphasis.
40. *Ibid.*, 233, 235.

teners in a more fundamental way. The crucial novelty of Woolman's own perspective—the element of his thinking that set him far apart from most of his audience in the 1740s but that, when more widely shared a century later, helped swell antislavery ranks—was his recognition of the causal relationship that exists in market societies between supply and demand.

> Whatever nicety of distinction there may be betwixt going in person on expeditions to catch slaves, and buying those with a view to self-interest which others have taken, it is clear and plain to an upright mind that such distinction is in words, not in substance; for the parties are concerned in the same work and have a necessary connection with and dependence on each other. *For were there none to purchase slaves, they who live by stealing and selling them would of consequence do less at it.*[41]

How natural that a man who was both a devout Quaker, vigorously striving for a clear conscience in worldly affairs, and a skillful "projector," attentive to the remote consequences of his acts and familiar with the intricate web of mutual dependencies that the market establishes between buyers and sellers, should be among the first to see the seemingly civilized and law-abiding slaveowner as engaged in essentially "the same work" as the barbaric slave stealer. Woolman, writing thirty years before Adam Smith's *Wealth of Nations* put talk of supply and demand on everybody's lips, was ahead of his time and knew better than to be angry when his contemporaries failed to perceive the "dependence" and "necessary connection" that seemed so obvious to him. The idea that by owning a slave (or even a product of slave labor) one helped constitute the demand without which suppliers of slave labor could not stay in business gained plausibility in the decades ahead, as more and more people came to share in the form of life Woolman and other Quakers adopted so early.[42]

41. *Ibid.*, 234. My emphasis.
42. In his journal Woolman recorded his anxiety about accepting hospitality from slaveholders, because it enabled him to save his own money and thereby made him a party to their oppression of slaves. He cleared his conscience by carrying small silver coins with him that he paid to the slaves of the household, either directly or through their masters; *ibid.*, 59–61. Although recipe knowledge and an awareness of the "necessary connection" between prerequisites is a precondition for the emergence of the humanitarian sensibility, these things are by no means sufficient in themselves to produce that sensibility. Daniel Defoe, a disappointed investor in the Royal African Company, is a case in point. Like Woolman, he conceived of the slave trade as part of a network of cause-and-effect relationships. But from this he drew in 1713 the conclusion that the slave trade was indispensable to England's prosperity: "The case is as plain as cause and consequence: Mark the climax. No African trade, no negroes; no negroes no sugars, gingers, indicoes [sic] etc; no sugars etc no island; no islands no continent; no continent no trade." Defoe, as quoted in Peter

Within little more than one long lifetime after Woolman wrote, slavery, an ancient institution from which millions of people profited, directly or indirectly, was completely overthrown in North America and the British empire. In spite of the enormous interests at stake, the rarity, even among abolitionists, of notions of racial equality, and the availability in England and America of a political-legal culture strongly oriented to the defense of property rights, surprisingly few people were willing to defend those who owned property in slaves. Thus, an institution, which, had it been evaluated in purely technical terms, might have represented a solution to the problems of labor discipline that modernizers everywhere confronted, was abruptly abandoned.[43] This astounding reversal of fortunes does not testify to the importance of "interests," which could as easily be said to have favored the opposite outcome, or to the autonomous power of high ideals, which are, in themselves, compatible with many levels of passivity and activism. What it shows instead is the force of the conventions that govern causal perception and moral responsibility, without which we would not know what our interests are or what it means to be responsible.

---

Earle, *The World of Defoe* (London, 1976), 131. Defoe's involvement with the slave trade was brought to my attention by Seymour Drescher.
43. Stanley Engerman brought this possibility to my attention.

Chapter 6

# Reflections on Abolitionism and Ideological Hegemony

*David Brion Davis*

Attention is turning once again to the almost simultaneous appearance of industrial capitalism and antislavery sentiment in Great Britain. Since the publication of Eric Williams's *Capitalism and Slavery* more than a generation ago, the relation between these two broad forces has provoked considerable debate. Historians have discredited Williams's argument that Britain's antislavery measures were economically determined acts of national self-interest, cynically disguised as humanitarian triumphs.[1] But it has been difficult to find a middle ground that rejects Williams's cynical reductionism while also taking account of the realities of class power. In 1975, in *The Problem of Slavery in the Age of Revolution, 1770–1823*, I suggested that British abolitionism served conflicting ideological functions but that it helped reinforce, in this initial period, the hegemony of capitalist values. This view has recently evoked fruitful criticism, especially a two-part theoretical essay by Thomas L. Haskell in *The American Historical Review*.[2] Be-

1. See especially Roger Anstey, *The Atlantic Slave Trade and British Abolition, 1760–1810* (London, 1975); Stanley L. Engerman, "The Slave Trade and British Capital Formation in the Eighteenth Century: A Comment on the Williams Thesis," *Business History Review*, 46 (Winter 1972): 430–43; Howard Temperley, "Capitalism, Slavery, and Ideology," *Past and Present*, 75 (1977): 94–118; Seymour Drescher, *Econocide: British Slavery in the Era of Abolition* (Pittsburgh, Pa., 1977); Seymour Drescher, "Cart Whip and Billy Roller: Antislavery and Reform Symbolism in Industrializing Britain," *Journal of Social History*, 15 (September 1981): 3–24; Seymour Drescher, *Capitalism and Antislavery: British Mobilization in Comparative Perspective* (New York, 1987); *British Capitalism and Caribbean Slavery*, Barbara Solow and Stanley L. Engerman, eds. (New York, 1987); and David Eltis, *Economic Growth and the Ending of the Transatlantic Slave Trade* (New York, 1987).
2. Thomas L. Haskell, "Capitalism and the Origins of the Humanitarian Sensibility, Part 1," *AHR*, 90 (April 1985): 339–61; Part 2, *AHR*, 90 (June 1985): 547–566. See also the relevant article by T. J. Jackson Lears, "The Concept of Cultural He-

cause I bear some responsibility for the misinterpretations that have been given to my "thesis," I would like to take this opportunity to restate and clarify my argument and to assess some of the criticisms.

I should first point out that my hegemonic argument fills only a few pages in a 570-page volume and that it applies only to British history in a limited period from the 1790s to 1823, with some brief speculations reaching ahead to the 1830s. I did not extend the concept of hegemony to America or France, where abolition movements emerged in wholly different contexts. Certainly, I advanced no general theory of abolitionism *per se* as an instrument of hegemonic control (although I would claim it was always related to the need to legitimate free wage labor). I have never meant to suggest that abolitionism can best be understood as a device for deflecting white working-class discontent or that it was not part of the wider egalitarian and liberalizing movement I described in *The Problem of Slavery in Western Culture* (1966).

It is important to distinguish the *origins* of antislavery sentiment, a subject I discussed at length in the first volume, from the *conditions* that favored the acceptance of antislavery ideology among various governing elites. This is a distinction that Haskell continually blurs. In all my work, I have taken pains to emphasize the importance of religious sources of antislavery thought and the religious transformations that made slave emancipation a symbolic test of the efficacy of Christian faith. In *The Problem of Slavery in the Age of Revolution*, I did not say, and here Haskell misquoted me, that the "origin" of the new humanitarian sensibility lay in "the ideological needs of various groups and classes."[3] I did maintain that "the continuing evolution" of antislavery opinion "reflected the ideological needs of various groups and classes."[4] I had in mind the ideological needs generated by the French Revolution and the early Industrial Revolution, by war, nationalism, and religious revivalism. At issue are the uses made of antislavery doctrine and rhetoric as the movement pulled away from the Painite

gemony: Problems and Possibilities," in *AHR*, 90 (June 1985): 567–93. Although my response to Haskell meets some of the criticisms advanced by Betty Fladeland and Seymour Drescher, I have tried to deal with their substantive arguments, many of which are compatible with my own views, in a different version of this article, "Capitalism, Abolitionism, and Hegemony," in Solow and Engerman, eds. *British Capitalism and Caribbean Slavery*, 209–27. See Betty Fladeland, *Abolitionists and Working-Class Problems in the Age of Industrialization* (Baton Rouge, La., 1984); Drescher, "Cart Whip and Billy Roller," 3–24; and Drescher, *Capitalism and Antislavery*.

3. Haskell, "Capitalism and the Origins of the Humanitarian Sensibility, Part 1," 344.

4. David Brion Davis, *The Problem of Slavery in the Age of Revolution, 1770–1823* (Ithaca, N.Y., 1975), 42.

radicals of the early 1790s, won legitimacy from government ministries in 1806–7, was appropriated by the aristocratic African Institution, and was then reshaped by wealthy merchant philanthropists.

In *The Problem of Slavery in the Age of Revolution*, I dealt with Britain in the period from 1793 to 1823, decades of reactionary politics and domestic repression that should not be confused with the era of social ferment and reform that accompanied West Indian slave emancipation and the abolition of apprenticeship. The crucial question, therefore, was not why groups of enlightened British, French, and Americans attacked slavery from the 1760s to the 1780s but why this single reform cause, which attracted significant radical support in the early 1790s and which some conservatives denounced as a Jacobin front, won growing acceptance in the early nineteenth century from British political and social elites otherwise obsessed with the fear that social reform would open the gates to revolution.

During the long period from the late 1790s to 1823, the British public showed little interest in the slavery issue except at the end of the Napoleonic wars. In 1814, an eruption of petitions expressed outrage at the prospect that the government would allow France to resume the Atlantic slave trade, which Britain had earlier renounced on moral grounds. This brief popular outburst drew on nationalistic pride and was orchestrated by abolitionist leaders who were eager to demonstrate to the courts of Europe that "with a single voice" the English people demanded international suppression of the slave trade. The cause served the purposes of Wellington and Castlereagh, who actively cooperated with the abolitionists. But the crucial antislavery measures from 1800 to 1823 were not the result of public pressure. Leaders of government and a few influential abolitionists were responsible for the decisions to curtail and then stop the flow of African slaves to Guiana and other foreign colonies conquered by Britain and later to prohibit the British slave trade to all foreign nations and colonies. The successful abolition bill of 1807 originated in the House of Lords; the prevailing public apathy and ignorance of the question prompted William Wilberforce to publish and widely circulate *A Letter on the Abolition of the Slave Trade; Addressed to the Freeholders and Other Inhabitants of Yorkshire*. The subsequent campaign to establish a central registry of all colonial slaves aroused little public interest, although it was seen as an essential preparatory step toward amelioration and gradual emancipation. Even in 1823 and 1824, when an organized emancipation movement got underway, the abolitionists who solicited petitions and organized auxiliary societies were surprised by the general public ignorance concerning West Indian slavery. Yet the governing elites, while still divided on the issue, had become increasingly committed to colonial labor reform. By 1833, even the Tory opposition in the House of

Commons failed to rally behind the West Indian interests.[5] In pursuing the question of why colonial slavery seemed so repugnant to such groups, I should have made it clearer that by "ideology" I did not mean a fixed set of ideas and doctrines used to promote concrete class interests. When referring to an ideology as a "mode of consciousness," I was thinking of a perceptual lens, a way of viewing social reality that helps to define as well as legitimate class, gender, or other collective interests. Keeping this definition in mind, it is important to draw a distinction between the motives of individual reformers and the ideological context that gave hegemonic meaning to their rhetoric and influence.

When, in 1786, Thomas Clarkson published his prizewinning Cambridge University essay on the horrors of the African slave trade, he clearly had no intention of condoning British child labor in factories and mines. But Clarkson's proslavery opponents, such as Gilbert Francklyn and Jesse Foot, immediately contrasted the alleged comfort and security of West Indian slaves with the oppression of English workers and the plight of English children exposed to the "pestilential vapour" of factories. Francklyn pointedly asked why the universities did not offer prizes "for the best dissertation on the evil effects which the manufactures of Birmingham, Manchester, and other great Manufacturing towns, produce on the health and the lives of the poor people employed therein?" He proceeded to show how Clarkson's rhetorical techniques could be applied to the specific consequences of the early Industrial Revolution. Francklyn was probably not surprised when Lancashire manufacturers took the lead in 1787 in initiating the great petition campaign to abolish the African slave trade.[6] Antiabolitionist counteroffensives such as these had appeared even earlier, and they became a dominant theme of British and, later, American proslavery writing. Similar points were made by representatives of radical labor who were in principle opposed to all forms of economic and political bondage. Given the venom of the debate, no abolitionist could plead ignorance of the charge that moral outrage was being directed against oppression overseas while similar or worse oppression was complacently tolerated at home. In 1818, for example, Francis Burdett asked why Wilberforce could be shocked by the enslavement of

5. Eltis, *Economic Growth*, chap. 2. Eltis argued that abolishing the slave trade and emancipating colonial slaves were contrary to Britain's economic interests but were the result of a free-labor and free-market ideology that led to the New Poor Law of 1834 and to concerted efforts to increase the productivity of labor.
6. Cited in Davis, *Problem of Slavery in the Age of Revolution*, 462–63. Because I am responding to misreadings of this book, I will take most of my examples from it. Seymour Drescher has recently drawn attention to the crucial role of Lancashire industrialists in initiating the antislave trade campaign (*Capitalism and Antislavery*, 67–88).

Africans and yet support in Parliament a seditious meetings bill and the suspension of *habeas corpus*, measures that allowed the English to be seized and treated like African slaves.

In theory, abolitionists faced by these challenges could condemn all forms of social oppression and simply give priority to the slave trade or chattel slavery as the most flagrant and remediable crime against humanity. Such a course would entail a disavowal of the claims of proslavery writers and at least a private expression of regret over the unintended consequences of extolling free wage labor. As a second alternative, exemplified by some of the radical Garrisonians and labor reformers, the abolitionists could assert that both distant and nearby evils arose from a common cause. As a third choice, they could deny any comparability between black slaves who were subjected to constant physical coercion and English workers who faced merely the threat of starvation, which was termed a "liberal motive" and a "rational predicament" by the reformer who drafted the slave emancipation act of 1833.[7]

In response to both proslavery and radical indictments of the wage-labor system, most abolitionists accentuated the moral contrast between what they conceived of as the free and slave worlds. Their greatest hope, after all, was to end the involuntary shipment of Africans to the New World and to transform black slaves into cheerful, obedient, and grateful laborers whose wants could be satisfied only by working voluntarily for wages. This hope rested on the assumption that the British system of labor had achieved a reasonable balance between freedom and order and could serve as a norm against which harsher regimes should be measured. I am not suggesting that early abolitionists were mostly conservatives who accepted the status quo and opposed domestic reforms, although some of them fit this description. But the sharp contrast they drew between British and colonial society had ideological meaning, especially at a time when there was a growing need to valorize wage labor as a universal norm, when the Industrial Revolution was introducing new forms of exploitation and suffering, and when it was by no means clear that the British working class was less victimized than were West Indian slaves.

For example, early in 1807, at a depressing stage in Britain's war against Napoleon, James Stephen the elder, who was the master strategist for the abolitionists, singled out British depravity in Africa and the West Indies as the cause for God's vengeance. Stephen specifically excluded domestic sins and proceeded to marvel over the "social happiness [that] has been showered upon us with singular profusion." "In no other part of the globe, are

7. David Brion Davis, *Slavery and Human Progress* (New York, 1984), 218.

the poor and helpless so well protected by the laws, or so humanely used by their superiors. . . . If it be as the protector of the poor and destitute, that God has entered into judgment with us, we must, I repeat, look to Africa, and to the West Indies, for the causes of his wrath."[8] Stephen was a deeply religious man who was genuinely concerned with collective guilt and retribution. We can be almost certain that he did not consciously intend to use his abhorrence of slavery and the slave trade, which he had observed first-hand in the West Indies, as a means of diverting attention from domestic suffering. Although as a boy he and his mother had lived in debtors' prison, he honestly believed, at least after marrying into the Wilberforce family and allying himself with paternalistic Tories, that Britain's treatment of its poor could not be a cause for divine displeasure. Later in 1807, Stephen played an important role in securing the abolition of the British slave trade, in a law hailed by political leaders as the most altruistic act since Christ's crucifixion and as proof that Britain waged war for human brotherhood. National pride is especially dangerous and deceptive, as Reinhold Niebuhr reminds us, when it is based on the highest achievements of human history.[9]

Haskell has argued that it is difficult if not impossible to reconstruct a historical actor's unconscious intention or to distinguish between consequences that are unconsciously intended and consequences that are unintended and even random. This difficulty, in his view, invalidates any historical explanation based on the concept of self-deception. I would reply that the concept of self-deception is so central to any quest for self-understanding or social analysis that it cannot be discredited by a kind of positivistic behaviorism. In everyday life, people continually recognize self-deception without resorting to depth psychology or finding the source of unconscious intention. To cite one obvious example, advertising agencies know they can rely on self-deception when they link cigarette smoking or the consumption of "lite" alcoholic drinks with health, slim figures, and vitality. Because the actual effects of smoking cigarettes and consuming alcoholic beverages are well known to the public, the success of the advertisements cannot be attributed simply to ignorance or gullibility.

A subtle complicity often exists between self-deception and externally imposed deception that produces what some historians would call "false consciousness." That term carries unfortunate connotations that lead to

---

8. Quoted in Davis, *Problem of Slavery in the Age of Revolution*, 366–67. Wilberforce also warned in 1807 that Britain's afflictions might be a prelude to much worse divine punishment if the nation persisted in the criminal slave trade (*Letter on the Abolition of the Slave Trade* [London, 1807], 4–6).
9. Richard Wightman Fox, *Reinhold Niebuhr: A Biography* (New York, 1985), 181.

unnecessary controversy. But, as historians, we do need to recognize the reality of deceptive or biased consciousness—of collective rationalizations, sometimes consciously crafted, that serve identifiable interests and help convince individuals of their own innocence and virtue. Biased consciousness, which Haskell tried to subsume under the morally neutral term "convention," also shields individuals from any sense of complicity in social injustice and oppression. The abolitionists dramatized the personal guilt entailed by one form of biased and deceptive consciousness. Modern history, from the Holocaust and Vietnam War to the peril of Star Wars and nuclear annihilation, teems with examples of individual and collective self-deception. Although biased consciousness can result from ignorance as well as individual self-deception, historians should by now be skeptical of the excuse that "we never knew." Self-deception usually involves choices to screen out or discount disagreeable truths. Human beings are not passive automata wholly programmed by "society."

But Haskell ignored or dismissed a vast body of knowledge that reveals the ways in which class, gender, and social circumstances tend to guide our selective attention, control our mechanisms of avoidance, displacement, and projection, and shape the very cognitive style to which Haskell gives center stage. Sexism provides a telling example, since many American men are just beginning to realize the ways in which their language, culture, and daily conventions reinforce sexual inequalities. Sexism is seldom the result of conscious intent, but individual males benefit from the assumption that female disabilities are part of the natural order of things. Male hegemony has usually been accepted by women, who have redefined it in their own way but have found it difficult to create an alternative world. Class and racial hegemony can have similar effects, although Haskell's emphasis on conscious intention can blind us to the psychological realities we confront every day.

Historians' assumptions about human behavior are necessarily drawn from personal experience or from reading about the experiences of others. Most of us are probably aware of the complexity and ambiguity of our own intentions and may recall making choices that led to supposedly unintended consequences that we may still have intuited or dimly foreseen. Fiction offers endless variations on the themes of contradictory impulses, inner division, and the need for self-justification. Historians must engage in a dialectical process in which we strive to discover the "otherness" of the past while also making sense of past events from a present-day perspective. If we have empirical evidence that a group of historical actors believed they were advancing the interests of all humanity when they were actually promoting the interests of a special class, we can justifiably speak of self-deception. But my central concern in *The Problem of Slavery in the Age of Revolution* was not the conscious or unconscious motives of individuals but rather the social meanings and consequences of certain moral perceptions.

From the time of the Mosaic Exodus, slavery and redemption have been extremely powerful paradigms involving the ultimate questions for both individual and collective life: the passage from present misery and degradation to a land of Canaan. Apart from their religious meanings, these paradigms are capable of being extended to a wide range of social experiences with oppression and liberation or of being confined to the historical sufferings of a specific people. According to Rousseau, "man is born free— and everywhere he is in chains." But since Rousseau, at least, there has always been a tension between such generalizing proclamations and attempts to dramatize the horrors of a special instance of human bondage.

For James Stephen, William Wilberforce, and the government leaders who deplored the African slave trade and who moved toward gradualist antislavery policies, it was essential to maintain a sharp distinction between the evils of the colonial slave world and the ostensibly free institutions that had been imperiled both by French tyranny and English Jacobinism. The constant comparisons in abolitionist literature between the agony of black slaves and the smiling, contented life of English husbandmen was not fortuitous. Abolitionists repeatedly reminded Britons that the Somerset decision of 1772 had outlawed slavery in England. At a time when many of the peoples of Europe were said to be "enslaved" by French despotism, it was crucial to define England as a "free" nation—both in the sense of having no slaves and of having successfully resisted foreign domination. With the growth of nationalism in the Napoleonic era, "freedom" increasingly signified membership in a nation that had resisted or thrown off foreign tyranny. When national leaders were perceived as the protectors of liberty in this collective sense, it was more difficult to accuse them of fostering various forms of domestic oppression.

If the existence of the slave colonies allowed England to define itself as free soil—much as communist countries enable the United States to define itself as the leader of the free world—they also helped specify the nature of freedom. The African slave trade defined, by negative polarity, the conditions necessary for consensual and acceptable labor transport. On the one hand, it was unacceptable for an employer to claim ownership of the person of an employee, to sell husbands apart from their wives, or children apart from their parents. But it was acceptable, on the other hand, to buy the labor of adults or children under conditions that led to the separation of families and that made a mockery of the worker's supposed consent. Labor

conditions could be seen as the effects of market forces, not human intentionality.

In discussing intentionality, Haskell pointed to the absurdity of blaming
Hank Aaron, when he hits a home run, for allowing the ball to strike a spectator on the head. The gap between Aaron's intention of hitting the ball and
the consequence of injuring a spectator is too wide to be of any significance.
Haskell was primarily concerned with the virtue or blameworthiness of individual moral choice. But, if the rules of a game were constructed in a way
that ensured that many spectators would be hit on the head during every
inning, and if it were assumed that this was simply one of the costs of the
sport, we would consider the consequences culturally significant regardless
of the conscious intentions of the players.

Haskell also argued that selectivity is inevitable, that limits of moral responsibility have to be drawn somewhere, and that it is therefore unfair to
blame abolitionists for not attacking forms of exploitation closer to home. I
should emphasize that I am not interested in blame but rather in understanding the moral ambiguities of history. But Haskell's argument reminds
me of similar reasoning advanced by Serafim Leite, the historian of the Jesuits in Brazil. In praising Manuel da Nóbrega and other sixteenth-century
Jesuits for protecting the Brazilian Indians from enslavement and mistreatment, Leite is forced to deal with the unfortunate fact that Nóbrega openly
defended and encouraged the African slave trade. But, according to Leite, to
accuse the Jesuits of injustice for favoring Indians is like condemning a person for founding a hospital for tuberculosis while ignoring the victims of
leprosy. One has to draw the line somewhere. Yet selection is seldom neutral, either culturally or psychologically, as we can see in Leite's own illus-
trative choices of tuberculosis and leprosy. Indians were conventionally
pictured as the victims of consumptive physical or social diseases introduced
by whites; the African's dark skin and physiognomy were sometimes seen
as a kind of leprosy, or as the result of a leprous disease for which the European bore no responsibility. Leite accepts the traditional distinction between the freeborn Indian and the enslaved African, who was accustomed
to bondage and whose labor was essential for successful colonization.[10]

British selectivity, as I suggested in *The Problem of Slavery in the Age of
Revolution*, must be understood in terms of historical context. The government's first interventions in the colonial labor system coincided with an ur-

10. Serafim Leite, *História da Companhia de Jesus no Brasil*, 10 vols. (Rio de Ja-
neiro and Lisbon, 1938–50), 2: 227, 246–47; 6: 350–51.

gent domestic problem of labor discipline and labor management—not yet the problem of an industrial proletariat but of an immense rural labor force that had been released from traditional restraints and controls but not deprived of the independence of preindustrial village culture. Many Britons, including abolitionists, felt ambivalent about the changes accompanying early industrialization. Tensions mounted between the advocates of hardheaded utilitarianism and the defenders of traditional paternalism or evangelical benevolence. The issue of slavery provided a meeting ground for these diverse groups and for members of different propertied classes who longed to ensure stability while benefiting from the economic changes underway.

"Because the slave system was both distinctive and remote," I wrote, "it could become a subject for experimental fantasies that assimilated traditional values to new economic needs. An attack on the African slave trade could absorb some of the traditionalist's anxieties over the physical uprooting and dislocation of labor. . . . By picturing the slave plantation as totally dependent upon physical torture, abolitionist writers gave sanction to less barbarous modes of social discipline. For reformers, the plantation offered the prospect of combining the virtues of the old agrarian order with the new ideals of uplift and engineered incentive. Abolitionists could contemplate a revolutionary change in status precisely because they were not considering the upward mobility of workers, but rather the rise of distant Negroes to the level of humanity. . . . British antislavery provided a bridge between preindustrial and industrial values; by combining the ideal of emancipation with an insistence on duty and subordination, it helped to smooth the way to the future."[11] I have quoted at length from this passage because I have sometimes been interpreted as arguing that British abolitionism was a "screening device" designed to distract attention from metropolitan exploitation.[12] In actuality, I was trying to suggest a far more complex model in which the colonial plantation system served as a projective screen or experimental theater for testing the ideas of liberation, paternalism, and controlled social change that were prompted in part by domestic anxieties. As one might expect in a society as deeply divided as early industrial Britain, different audiences drew contradictory conclusions from the experiments in overseas reform. But it is difficult to deny that the abolition cause offered both national and local ruling elites an increasingly attractive opportunity to demonstrate their commitment to decency and justice.

In the passage quoted above, I was also concerned with the implications

11. Davis, *Problem of Slavery in the Age of Revolution*, 466–67.
12. See especially Drescher, "Cart Whip and Billy Roller," 4.

of sharply separating slavery from other kinds of coerced labor and social domination. It is noteworthy that even Thomas Clarkson, who retained much of the liberal spirit of the late 1780s and early 1790s, found nothing inequitable about coerced labor. Any state, he said, could legitimately use convicts to work in mines or clear rivers. What outraged Clarkson and other early abolitionists was the claim of personal proprietorship that justified arbitrary and unlimited authority. The slaveowner's claims contrasted sharply with those of the idealized British squire, whose authority was constrained by law and custom, and with the rights of the rising capitalist, who was content to purchase labor in the market like any other commodity.

Above all, the slave system came to epitomize an inherent and inescapable conflict of interest, a kind of warfare sublimated or suspended from the time the original captive was subdued. For a while, the more moderate abolitionists searched for means to ameliorate this conflict, hoping that an end to further slave imports, for example, would persuade masters to promote their slaves' welfare as part of their own long-term self-interest. But the continuing negative growth rate of the West Indian slave population seemed to show that the system itself was unreformable and would lead to eventual genocide. This impression was reinforced by the slaveholders' truculent resistance to missionaries, moral uplift, the abolition of Sunday markets, restrictions on the flogging of women, and other benevolent measures. The major goal of the British antislavery movement by the early 1820s was to create a natural harmony of interests between planters and black workers, a relation similar to the assumed mutuality between British landlords and tenants.

In arguing that the antislavery movement mirrored the needs and tensions of a society increasingly absorbed with problems of labor discipline, I was not saying that such needs and tensions are sufficient to explain the emergence and ultimate direction of antislavery thought. While emphasizing the importance of class and social context, I specifically warned against "the simplistic impression that 'industrialists' promoted abolitionist doctrine as a means of distracting attention from their own forms of exploitation."[13] My main theme was that opposition to slavery cannot be divorced from the vast economic changes that were intensifying social conflicts and heightening class consciousness; in Britain, it was part of a larger ideology that ensured stability while acclimating society to political and social change.

Even in Britain, where the cause won significant support from the governing elites, abolitionist thought had both conservative and radical aspects.

13. Davis, *Problem of Slavery in the Age of Revolution*, 455.

Some readers have focused exclusively on the first part of my argument, in which I claimed that the acts of selectivity by abolitionists "helped to strengthen the invisible chains being forged at home." But I also emphasized that abolitionism "bred a new sensitivity to social oppression," "that it provided a model for the systematic indictment of social crime," and that it "ultimately taught many Englishmen to recognize forms of systematic oppression that were closer to home."[14] To illustrate the radical potentialities of antislavery thought, I quoted from Friedrich Engels precisely because he showed how abolitionist perceptions and locutions had become universalized by the 1840s: even a resident alien, with no roots in the abolitionist movement, appropriated the language and perspective of Anglo-American abolitionists when he exposed the "slavery" of Manchester's working class. As early as 1817, when Wilberforce and his friends in Lord Liverpool's cabinet feared that England was on the verge of revolution, another radical alien pointed to the connections between the oppression of West Indian slaves and the oppression of England's poor. Iain McCalman has recently discovered that Robert Wedderburn, a Jamaican mulatto whose slave mother was born in Africa, edited a London periodical, *Axe Laid to the Root*, that called for a simultaneous revolution of West Indian chattel slaves and English wage slaves. Working with Thomas Spence, Thomas Evans, and other London radicals, Wedderburn popularized a plebeian antislavery rhetoric in the taverns and hayloft chapels of London's underworld.[15]

Reform causes often serve opposing or contradictory functions as innovative doctrine is co-opted by different social groups. As I have already indicated, slavery and emancipation have long been extraordinarily complex

14. Davis, *Problem of Slavery in the Age of Revolution*, 455, 467–68. Drescher has greatly amplified these themes, which do not contradict my position, as he seems to think. No doubt I should have cited more varied examples of the linkage between denunciations of colonial slavery and wage slavery, and I was unaware of the language in petitions that Drescher has discovered. It is my intention to explore this subject in a succeeding volume on the "Age of Emancipation." Drescher does not seem to deny that Wilberforce, Stephen, Macaulay, Clarkson, Cropper, Buxton, and the other national leaders of the early period were unsympathetic to the wage-slavery argument, which they associated with their enemies.
15. Iain McCalman, "Anti-Slavery and Ultra-Radicalism in Early Nineteenth-Century England: The Case of Robert Wedderburn," *Slavery and Abolition*, 7 (September 1986): 99–117. Although Wedderburn dedicated his autobiography to Wilberforce, it is clear that Wilberforce abhorred the ideology and culture that Wedderburn represented. Nevertheless, disguised as a "stranger" and equipped with a Bible, Wilberforce visited Richard Carlile in prison and attempted to convert him to Christianity; Carlile reported that Wilberforce also talked to the imprisoned Wedderburn and declared the black to be an "honest and conscientious man"; John Pollock, *Wilberforce* (New York, 1977), 258; McCalman, "Anti-Slavery and Ultra-Radicalism," 113.

paradigms capable of almost infinite extension to both material and spiritual states. Even in the 1820s, antislavery agitation led American radicals like Langton Byllesby and Thomas Skidmore to the conclusion that black slavery was not only the quintessential American crime but that it revealed deep structural flaws allowing a fortunate few to live off the labor of the so-called free majority.[16] Yet, when radical American reformers later contended that the wage system was slavery, that conventional marriage was slavery, and that submission to any government using coercion was slavery, their rhetoric surely diluted the charge that Negro slavery in the South was a system of exceptional and intolerable oppression. Frederick Douglass was outraged in 1843 when his white abolitionist colleague John Collins asserted that antislavery was "a mere dabbling with effects" and that tolerating private ownership of land was worse than enslaving human beings. As Christopher Lasch has observed with respect to our own time, the language of radical protest was impoverished when it was appropriated by fat people, short people, old people, and other such groups who claimed that they were as much oppressed as racial minorities: "Since interest-group politics invites competitive claims to the privileged status of victimization, the rhetoric of moral outrage becomes routine, loses its critical edge, and contributes to the general debasement of political speech."[17] Likewise, an indispensable term such as "holocaust" becomes trivialized when it is extended metaphorically to every atrocity or instance of ethnic oppression.

The concept of hegemony is easily discredited by misconstruction or misunderstanding—by attacking the argument, for example, that a discrete capitalist class imposed a form of false consciousness on a passive populace, duping people with antislavery propaganda designed to divert attention from the women and children in the mills and mines. It is now clear that, by the early 1830s in both England and the United States, the abolitionist movement had attracted significant support from artisans and other skilled workers; that in England the "pressure from without" ran ahead of the elite antislavery leadership, embarrassing Thomas Fowell Buxton in his negotiations with government ministers; and that a few reformers moved from an apprenticeship in the abolitionist campaign to more radical activism as Chartists or labor reformers.[18]

16. Sean Wilentz, *Chants Democratic: New York City and the Rise of the American Working Class, 1788–1850* (New York, 1984), 164–67, 183–90.
17. Waldo E. Martin, Jr., *The Mind of Frederick Douglass* (Chapel Hill, N.C., 1984), 28; Christopher Lasch, "The Great American Variety Show," *New York Review of Books*, 2 February 1984, 36.
18. For a discussion of the pressure exerted on Buxton and the parliamentary abolitionists, see Davis, *Slavery and Human Progress*, 195–202. Drescher's *Capitalism and Antislavery* emphasizes the broad-based, popular character of the antislavery

But these facts in no way invalidate the hegemonic argument when it is properly understood. Hegemony, as Eugene D. Genovese has written, implies no more than the ability of a particular class to contain class antagonisms "on a terrain in which its legitimacy is not dangerously questioned."[19] Ideological hegemony is a process that is never complete or total; it can be understood in different ways by opposing groups or classes as long as it limits the terms of debate, heads off more fundamental challenges, and serves to reinforce the legitimacy of the ruling groups and existing order. Seymour Drescher, who scornfully rejects the hegemonic thesis, lends it invaluable support in his description of the mass political mobilization by abolitionists that was "virtually unopposed in most areas." A perfect example of ideological hegemony can be seen in Drescher's claim that "Parliament's assessment of property claims in persons residing in the metropolis appears to have been congruent with that of the Irish chimney sweep." In France, in sharp contrast, "antislavery was clearly distinguished by an inability to combine a stable élite leadership with a mass appeal."[20] Obviously, British antislavery agitation had different meanings in 1814, 1833, and 1838, and a detailed analysis would be required to show the degree to which abolitionism stabilized or destabilized Britain's social and political order at a particular time. But a few preliminary points can be made in response to the common view of an expansive, one-directional surge of democratic consciousness.

No doubt many British workers empathized with colonial slaves and understood abolitionist principles in ways that would have deeply troubled Wilberforce, Buxton, and Zachary Macaulay. But rank-and-file abolitionists could not escape the fact that the governing classes succeeded in appropriating the cause and defining the terms of the debate. Britain's landlords, merchants, and manufacturers showed by their behavior that there were varieties of exploitation that would no longer be tolerated in England or on the high seas, and that there were forms of labor, even in the distant colonies, that would have to be brought more in line with metropolitan standards. This affirmation of moral standards helped legitimate both the existing system of class power and the emerging concept of free labor as an impersonal, marketable commodity. The emancipation act of 1833 gave assurance to Britons of various classes that there were limits to the rapid socioeconomic changes taking place: workers could not literally be reduced to chattel slav-

movement. For abolitionist Chartists, see Betty Fladeland, " 'Our Cause Being One and the Same': Abolitionists and Chartism," in *Slavery and British Society, 1776–1846*, James Walvin, ed. (Baton Rouge, La., 1982), 69–99.
19. *Roll, Jordan, Roll: The World the Slaves Made* (New York, 1974), 26.
20. Drescher, *Capitalism and Antislavery*, 46–47, 53, 75.

ery; owners of even the most questionable form of private property could not be deprived of their capital without generous compensation.

Although the politics of slave emancipation were extremely complex, the act of 1833 fostered the illusion that the newly reformed Parliament had become an almost democratic assembly that would respond to the voice of a moral majority. The succession of antislavery victories and official commitments, beginning with the order-in-council of 1805 restricting the slave trade to conquered colonies, vindicated trust in the government's basic sense of justice. It is no wonder that, when various British groups wanted to dramatize their own oppression or lack of freedom, they complained that their condition was at least as bad as that of West Indian slaves. Defenders of colonial slavery had opened this door, and their argument implied two propositions: first, to receive attention, one had to meet the "slavery test" by enumerating horrors equivalent to those in abolitionist literature; second, because Parliament and the middle-class public were attuned to this language, the same techniques that had persuaded Parliament to bestow liberty on West Indian slaves would also bring freedom and justice at home.

In effect, the antislavery radicals were addressing the governing classes as follows: wage labor under present conditions leads to even worse misery than chattel slavery; because you responded to moral arguments in abolishing the slave trade and in freeing the colonial slaves, you should now relieve the distress of England's poor. But this reinforcement of ruling-class standards is precisely what is meant by "ideological hegemony." Denunciations of "wage slavery" were a way of expressing outrage and resentment over working conditions in industrial Britain and America. But as Christopher Lowe pointed out, there could be no lower standard than to ask that free laborers be treated better than slaves.[21] Everyone knew that white workers were not really slaves. The analogy, whatever its emotive power, invited a rhetorical response celebrating the benefits of the market and the inestimable privilege of being free to change employments. The dichotomous terms of this debate forced radicals to prove that, in some fundamental respects, wage earners were no freer or better off than slaves.

There can be no doubt that abolitionism contributed to more radical kinds of social criticism. Especially in the United States, where slavery was abolished in a cataclysm of violence, radical labor leaders and socialists found that parallels between black and white slavery retained their resonance well into the twentieth century.[22] But analogies with chattel slavery

---

21. Christopher Lowe, "Ideology, Hegemony and Class Rule" (Yale Graduate School seminar paper, 1985).
22. Barry Herbert Goldberg, "Beyond Free Labor: Labor, Socialism and the Idea of Wage Slavery, 1890–1920" (Ph.D. dissertation, Columbia University, 1979).

may also have retarded the development of a vocabulary that could depict more subtle forms of coercion, oppression, and class rule. To be a free worker was to be as unlike a Negro slave as possible. Most opponents of slavery equated unjust domination with a legalistic concept of property rights in human beings. This absolutist approach often made it difficult to distinguish the forms of domination concealed by voluntary contracts and the "bundle of powers" that could be exercised over nominally free workers.

Haskell seemed primarily concerned with the *moral* status of individual acts of benevolence and charity, such as our going to the aid of a starving stranger. He evidently feared that any links with class interest would inevitably tarnish the virtue of humanitarian acts by reducing them to lowly motives. His thesis allowed a place for class interest but minimized its importance when compared with his own alternative explanation: "Whatever influence the rise of capitalism may have had generally on ideas and values through the medium of class interest, it had a more telling influence on the origins of humanitarianism through changes the market wrought in *perception* or *cognitive style*."[23] Aside from the point that changes in perception and cognitive style are often closely associated with changing class interests, I fail to see why aiding a starving stranger is more praiseworthy when it is the psychological by-product of market forces that may also encourage moral callousness and bring starvation to the unemployed. Indeed, one can argue that we have even less reason to admire Haskell's humanitarians, since their altered perceptions seem to be the mechanistic and behavioristic result of what he himself terms "market discipline."[24]

I see no need, however, to fall into this trap of reductionism and counter-reductionism. Few historians would maintain today that abolitionists were hypocrites who consciously exploited humanitarian sentiments for ulterior aims. Few historians would argue that abolitionism was simply a spontaneous eruption of virtue, wholly unrelated to the rise of modern capitalism and the concomitant redefinition of property, labor, and contractual responsibilities. The abolitionists were neither otherworldly saints nor the agents of a capitalist conspiracy. Whatever their virtues or shortcomings, they have been vindicated by history: morally, they were right. But, like their opponents, their private moral and personal needs had public consequences that reinforced or altered relationships of power. Haskell confused the issue

23. Haskell, "Capitalism and the Origins of the Humanitarian Sensibility, Part 1," 342.
24. Haskell, "Capitalism and the Origins of the Humanitarian Sensibility, Part 1," 342.

by conflating the hegemonic argument with the origins of the antislavery movement. The movement had various origins and was supported by different groups for different reasons. Only gradually did the British movement become hegemonic in the sense of promoting an alliance of various religious, social, and political blocs that succeeded in overriding the interests of West Indian merchants, landowners, and their conservative allies. It was precisely because the antislavery alliance could convincingly present itself as disinterested and high-minded that it bestowed moral legitimacy on the reformed Parliament, British society, and the British character.

Haskell recognized a connection between British capitalism and antislavery thought, but he posited an original and ingenious theory about the effects of the market on the understanding of causation, promise-keeping, foresight, and the conventions defining personal responsibility. Haskell's reasoning deserves more careful consideration than I can give here, but I will offer a few preliminary observations.

It should be noted that Haskell applied extremely rigorous standards to the hegemonic theory, demanding that it explain, in class terms, the origin and rise of British abolitionism. In other words, Haskell seemed to be looking for a strong causal link between some element of capitalism and the appearance of abolitionism. Any link based on class, he argued, must ultimately rely on intentionality, for which there is no empirical justification. When Haskell turned to his own alternative thesis, however, he retreated from the demand for a strong causal link. His market mechanisms and recipe knowledge supply only one of various unnamed preconditions for the humanitarian sensibility and, more specifically, for the rise of abolitionism. This weak connection has no predictive power—that is, Haskell did not suggest that merchants involved in a world market were more likely to become abolitionists than were merchants confined to a traditional village clientele. But this very softness shields Haskell from serious empirical attack. For example, there can be no doubt that the market tended to teach people to keep their promises and attend to the remote consequences of their acts. But such lessons were especially useful for slavetraders, who were in the vanguard of long-distance commerce and who had to calculate costs and risks against long-delayed payment. The British slave trade flourished and indeed rose to its peak during the very period when Haskell's capitalist market was becoming triumphant. It is clear that a market mentality enabled many merchants to scorn older, paternalistic notions of responsibility and to justify virtually any practice that was good for business. Indeed, one can argue that market values tended to shrink the scope of effective human agency, as economists ascribed the misery of the poor to the effects of immutable economic laws and as people became aware of the interconnections of a global economy that fractionalized individual responsibility beyond measure. The knowledge that our economic acts are related in some way to most of the world's crime and oppression can blunt any sense of complicity. Even so, Haskell can claim that nothing is proved by the failure of slave-traders to become humanitarians. The market did not breed humanitarians but was a precondition that enabled certain kinds of people to become humanitarians.

The same reply can be given, though with much less force, to certain counterexamples. Antislavery opinion emerged in various societies including those of Virginia and North Carolina, France and Brazil. These societies were involved in international markets that required a degree of rational calculation and long-range planning. But only in industrializing Britain did this opinion crystallize into a national consensus that received official sanction. If the British pattern had appeared in market-oriented nations that had not yet shifted to a wage-labor economy, Haskell's thesis would appear more plausible. Given Haskell's criteria, a strong antislavery movement should have emerged in Holland, which was certainly involved in mercantile capitalism, in long-distance commerce, in world markets, and in complex banking and credit. Surely, the Dutch learned to attend to the remote consequences of their actions, and there must have been as many potential humanitarians per capita in the Dutch population as in Britain or the United States. Yet, despite repeated prodding from British abolitionists, the Dutch remained stolidly indifferent to the whole abolitionist campaign. Antislavery ideas excited virtually no popular interest. Before 1840, only twelve pamphlets were published in Holland on the issue of slave emancipation. It was not until 1853 that Dutch liberals succeeded in founding an antislavery society, but, according to Peter Emmer, the minutes of the annual meetings "show a complete lack of enthusiasm among its members: only seventeen to twenty of them attended." In 1863, long after slavery had been abolished in the British, French, and Danish colonies, the Dutch government emancipated Holland's colonial slaves in an almost perfunctory gesture.[25]

The market theory also fails to account for the large number of women who were involved in the abolitionist campaigns of Britain and America. Clearly, women as a group were relatively removed from the kind of liberating capitalist market Haskell had in mind; married women were not even permitted to make contracts in their own name. They were not subject to a market discipline that rewarded "impersonality" and "efficiency," to use Haskell's terms, or that "taught them to attend to the remote conse-

25. P. C. Emmer, "Anti-Slavery and the Dutch: Abolition without Reform," in *Anti-Slavery, Religion, and Reform: Essays in Memory of Roger Anstey*, Christine Bolt and Seymour Drescher, eds. (Folkestone, Kent, 1980), 80–94.

quences of their actions."[26] Yet women were strongly represented among the petition-gatherers, the local organizers, and the writers and distributors of antislavery literature. Haskell ignored the whole pre-Romantic and Romantic cults of sensibility and domesticity that were pitted against the brutality and insensitivity of the marketplace but that gave a powerful impetus to the abolitionist crusade. One can argue that the cultivation of empathy, which was obviously central to all humanitarian reform, arose in large part as a reaction to what Haskell termed the "nineteenth-century folklore about avaricious landlords and piratical factory owners . . . the metahistorical imagery of a class of me-first bourgeois individualists."[27]

Haskell made some extremely interesting points about the effects of the market on cognitive style and recipes for action. But I would shift attention from the origins of individual humanitarian sensibility to the way that market values highlighted the evils of Negro slavery. Haskell failed to see that thinking causally, keeping promises, learning to calculate and compute, and taking responsibility for the remote consequences of one's actions is precisely the kind of behavior that slavery proscribed. How could a slave be expected to keep all promises or make responsible choices? Slavery stood in direct opposition to the virtues inculcated by the market, the virtues that English employers and ratepayers wished to instill in the English working class. This line of reasoning brings me back to class interests and hegemony—not to any rigid or mechanical notion of social control but to the broad moral, political, and cultural transformations that accompanied the triumph of capitalism.

26. Haskell, "Capitalism and the Origins of the Humanitarian Sensibility, Part 2," 550, 551.
27. Haskell, "Capitalism and the Origins of the Humanitarian Sensibility, Part 2," 549.

# Chapter 7

# The Relationship between Capitalism and Humanitarianism

*John Ashworth*

Since an obvious temporal correspondence exists between the development of capitalism and the rise of humanitarianism, historians are understandably reluctant to believe that there is no causal connection. The problem, however, is to explain, indeed to theorize, this connection. The two-part article recently published in this journal by Thomas L. Haskell is an attempt to do just that.[1] One can hardly fail to be impressed by the authority that Haskell brings to the subject. The wide-ranging knowledge, the variety of sources consulted, and the rigor of the theoretical analysis make his article a landmark in the historiography of antislavery. I have reason, nevertheless, to be skeptical about the interpretation he offers and, perhaps more important, reason to question the sociological assumptions on which it rests.

It may be helpful to begin with a brief review of the historiography or at least parts of it. First, there was the Whig view of the abolitionists. It was probably not very different from the abolitionists' view of the abolitionists. The emphasis was on progress; waves of humanitarian sentiment came lapping onto the shores of Britain and then the United States as part of the divinely ordained scheme of things. Quaint though some of their notions may seem today, Whig historians did recognize that morality and values were subject to change over time. At this point, enter Eric Williams with his attack on the abolitionists and his reduction of humanitarianism to a simple reflex of self-interest. This view has been effectively demolished by, among

For their assistance in the production of this article, I should like to thank my colleagues Richard Crockatt, Geoffrey Searle, and especially Howard Temperley, my friends Greg and Christy Ludlow, and also my father, Eric Ashworth. I should also like to thank the anonymous reviewers of an earlier version, whose comments I found extremely valuable, and the editorial staff of the *AHR*.
1. Thomas L. Haskell, "Capitalism and the Origins of the Humanitarian Sensibility," 2 parts, *AHR*, 90 (April 1985): 339–61; (June 1985): 547–66.

others, Howard Temperley and Seymour Drescher, who have shown that good cause exists for doubting whether abolition promoted Britain's economic interest. But, as Temperley has pointed out, the Williams view does at least have the merit of connecting the rise of capitalism to the emergence of the humanitarian movement. His view also explains the contrast between the abolitionists' condemnation of slavery and their tolerance of, or even enthusiasm for, the system of wage labor then emerging. It seems to be difficult, if not impossible, however, to demonstrate the existence of a direct economic interest in the abolition of slavery.[2] But David Brion Davis, against whose work much of Haskell's article is directed, has concluded that capitalism brought to prominence a bourgeois class whose interest it was to attack slavery. This was not a simple financial interest that can be calculated in pounds, shillings, and pence but a much broader one, involving ideas about labor discipline and unemployment. With this more subtle notion of self-interest, Davis was able to explain, without resort to crude charges of hypocrisy, what he took to be the abolitionists' lack of concern with, for example, factory conditions. The abolitionists were responding to their own class needs. Davis also argued that they were not generally conscious of these limitations on their world view: they believed their ideals were universal rather than partial.[3]

This interpretation allowed Davis, like Williams, to recognize that values and morality are subject to change. It also maintained the spotlight on the limitations of the abolitionists, their special concern with slavery. In other respects, Davis has advanced beyond Williams, and Haskell justly praised him for not charging those who opposed slavery with conscious deception. Yet, according to Haskell, Davis has fallen into a different trap. Haskell's principal criticism of Davis maintains that he was wrong to try to connect abolitionism and capitalism via class interest.

This criticism raises an important theoretical point. Haskell's argument,

2. Thomas Clarkson, *A History of the Rise, Progress and Accomplishment of the Abolition of the African Slave Trade*, 2 vols. (London, 1808); W. P. Garrison and F. J. Garrison, *William Lloyd Garrison, 1805–1879*, 4 vols. (New York, 1885–89); Eric Williams, *Capitalism and Slavery* (Chapel Hill, N.C., 1944); Seymour Drescher, *Econocide: British Slavery in the Era of Abolition* (Pittsburgh, Pa., 1977); Howard Temperley, "Capitalism, Slavery and Ideology," *Past and Present*, 75 (May 1977): 94–118; Howard Temperley, "The Ideology of Antislavery," in *The Abolition of the Atlantic Slave Trade: Origins and Effects in Europe, Africa and the Americas*, David Eltis and James Walvin, eds. (Madison, Wis., 1981), 21–35; Howard Temperley, "Eric Williams and the Abolitionists: The Birth of a New Orthodoxy," in *British Capitalism and Caribbean Slavery*, Stanley Engerman and Barbara Solow, eds. (Cambridge, 1987).
3. David Brion Davis, *The Problem of Slavery in the Age of Revolution, 1770–1823* (Ithaca, N.Y., 1975).

I believe, is misdirected. Scholars now agree that it is a mistake to charge the abolitionists with conscious deception or hypocrisy. And Haskell has spent a considerable amount of time showing that it is impossible to claim that unconscious intention was present, either. For how can historians establish an unconscious intention? If an intention is unconscious, the individual is presumably not aware of its existence. How can the historian ever hope to demonstrate self-deception and unconscious intention? Showing conscious intention is difficult enough. Davis's argument is in fact incoherent. Haskell concluded, "To say that a person is moved by class interest is to say that he *intends* to further the interests of his class, or it is to say nothing at all."[4]

Although Haskell's conclusion sounds plausible enough, it must be resisted. Davis has only himself to blame for talking about self-deception and thus opening himself to Haskell's criticism. Davis ought to have focused on "false consciousness," the notion that the awareness of historical actors is incomplete, with the result that they misperceive the world around them. Historians are often, understandably, reluctant to employ this concept, perhaps because it smacks of condescension toward the past, perhaps because the word "false" is insufficiently nuanced. Yet, it seems to me, we cannot do without the concept. Otherwise, we are limited to the understanding of events that contemporaries possessed. The most important factors to them will have to be the most important for us; what they are unaware of, we will be unable to discuss. But Haskell's objection to the idea of self-deception is quite justified. The way out of this impasse lies, quite simply, in a recognition that society rather than the individual generates false consciousness. In the words of one Marxist theorist, "it is not the subject that deceives himself, but reality which deceives him." When Marie Antoinette told the peasants of Paris (never mind that the story is probably apocryphal) to eat cake when there was no bread, she was not deceiving herself in thinking that they could afford it. Rather, the nature of her involvement in society obscured from her the realization that peasants could not in fact afford cake. False consciousness, which human beings all possess to a greater or lesser degree, is not a matter of self-deception.[5]

4. Haskell, "Capitalism and the Origins of the Humanitarian Sensibility, Part 1," 347.
5. M. Godelier, "System, Structure and Contradiction in Capital," quoted in Nicholas Abercrombie, *Class, Structure and Knowledge* (Oxford, 1980), 77. It is evident that no individual can ever attain an entirely "true" consciousness, just as the person burdened with a consciousness that is utterly "false" would be incapable of any rational behavior or thought. In other words, we are dealing with a continuum rather than the dichotomy that is perhaps implicit in the term "false."

One can say that a person is moved by certain ideals that have grown out of class interest. This knowledge may or may not be reflexive; the individual may or may not be aware of the relationship between ideals and self-interest. History often illustrates the proposition that actors are not always conscious of the forces that operate on them. It is clearly quite possible to argue that an individual is moved by class interest without showing that the individual intends to further those interests either consciously or unconsciously.

I do agree with Haskell that current interpretations that point to class interest as the major causal factor are open to serious criticism.[6] Haskell of course answered his main question, the relationship between capitalism and humanitarianism, by reference to the market and its multifarious effects. Before considering this view, let us first note that, in what it seeks to do, Haskell's argument marks a retreat from certain issues. Davis's view, despite its limitations, did tackle this crucial point about the selectivity of the abolitionists, their concern with chattel slavery rather than, as some contemporaries put it, "wage slavery." Haskell has nothing to say on this selectivity except for his demonstration that there was no conscious hypocrisy on the part of the abolitionists and his (powerful) argument against the notion of self-deception. Granting that neither conscious hypocrisy nor self-deception was present makes the question of the abolitionists' selectivity of concern more, not less, urgent. Haskell introduced an interesting analogy here. If, in a hundred years' time, everyone were a vegetarian, would the many twentieth-century reformers who ignore this question today be deceiving themselves? Indeed, they would not, but the analogy is perhaps better than Haskell realized. If that moment were ever to arrive, a vital question for historians studying the twentieth century would be why its peoples were selective in their concerns. In other words, the historians of the future would want to know why so many of us, unlike their own contemporaries, were indifferent to this reform. Does Haskell assume that he is not entitled to go beyond the actors' own understanding of their ideas? Certainly, when he finds abolitionists who speak of what he regards as the

6. The major problem arises not from the concept of intentionality but from that of interest. On this subject, Haskell's words seem to me important enough to bear repeating. He referred to "the glib assumption so characteristic of modern scholarship that a person's 'interests' are readily identifiable and constitute a complete explanation of his conduct." The problem is that "the term is utterly elastic" so that "there is no human choice that cannot be construed as self-interested." To this, I would add only that this is an especially severe problem for scholars of a Marxist persuasion. Haskell, "Capitalism and the Origins of the Humanitarian Sensibility, Part 1," 351.

crucial factor (the market), he seems to think these statements are especially significant.[7] Yet, if one had asked abolitionists why they were abolitionists, they would have talked a good deal about God and righteousness, a good deal about the evil effects of slavery, and very little about the spread of the market. In short, something very like the Whig view.

It is important theoretically to decide whether the abolitionists' understanding of their own ideas is definitive or not. If it is, historians must speedily resurrect the Whig view. But if it is not, we are entitled to ask Davis's question again: why were abolitionists selective in their concerns? Search Haskell's article as we may, we will find nothing that helps answer this question. All the links postulated between capitalism and humanitarianism via the market might just as easily have operated to make the conscientious reformer hostile to wage labor, too. In this connection, we can also note that abolitionists in the United States and Britain tended to be involved in many other reform causes. Why did they accept wage labor? Haskell quoted an abolitionist, O. B. Frothingham, saying that slavery, unlike poverty, was susceptible to human control. We need neither doubt Frothingham's sincerity nor accuse him of self-deception to ask why it was that he and others reasoned in this way. Haskell, far from answering this question, seems to doubt whether it should even be posed.[8]

Haskell presented his explanation with admirable lucidity in one of his concluding paragraphs: "What, then, did capitalism contribute to the freeing of the slaves? Only a *precondition*, albeit a vital one: a proliferation of recipe knowledge and consequent expansion of the conventional limits of causal

7. Haskell, "Capitalism and the Origins of the Humanitarian Sensibility, Part 2," 564.

8. Haskell, "Capitalism and the Origins of the Humanitarian Sensibility, Part 2," 557. Historians have recently revised the assumption that abolitionists were uninterested in reforming institutions and practices that were closer to home. Many maintained an interest in a wide range of issues, and some were concerned with the conditions of the laboring poor in their own societies. Nonetheless, for all but a small minority, there was a characteristic belief that the relation between capitalist and worker either was, or could be made, harmonious; by contrast, the relation between slave and slaveholder by contrast, could not. See Betty Fladeland, *Abolitionists and Working-Class Problems in the Age of Industrialization* (London, 1984); Jonathan A. Glickstein, " 'Poverty Is Not Slavery': American Abolitionists and the Competitive Labor Market," in *Antislavery Reconsidered: New Perspectives on the Abolitionists*, Lewis Perry and Michael Fellman, eds. (Baton Rouge, La., 1979). There are many comments by American abolitionists on the virtues of wage labor. See, for example, *Liberator*, 1 January 1831, 24 December 1841, 19 and 26 March 1847, 9 July 1847, 1 October 1847; *The Letters of William Lloyd Garrison*, 4 vols., Walter M. Merrill, ed. (Cambridge, Mass., 1971), 2: 167; *Emancipator*, 10 October 1839, 31 December 1840; Theodore Parker, *The Slave Power* (1916; rpt. edn., New York, 1969), 63, 116.

perception and moral responsibility that compelled some exceptionally scrupulous individuals to attack slavery and prepared others to listen and comprehend. The precondition could have been satisfied by other means, yet during the period in question no other force pressed outward on the limits of moral responsibility with the strength of the market."[9] That is, the market enhanced causal understanding, deepened the sense of responsibility, and thus spurred the reformer into action.

Of course, Haskell was aware of the other effects of capitalism. The market could also encourage the atavistic pursuit of self-interest. As he himself commented, "both friends and foes of capitalism often read into technical analyses of wage and price movements a very simple message: since the laws of supply and demand automatically transmute each individual's self-interest into the greater good of the greater number, no one need be concerned with the public interest."[10] This message was undoubtedly received loud and clear by many nineteenth-century Europeans and Americans. The market in this case had contradictory effects. Surely, to substantiate his argument, Haskell must show that the effects he wants to emphasize were actually greater than the opposite ones. If one demonstrates that factor $f$ tends both to produce and to prevent result $r$, then to make $f$ a significant cause of $r$, one must show that the productive effects are greater than the preventive ones. Nowhere did Haskell do this. He did not even acknowledge the difficulty. Yet it may be that he sensed the problem. Certainly, he was at pains to emphasize the positive effects of the market. The language he used to refer to the negative ones is revealing. He refers to "the rich nineteenth-century *folklore* about avaricious landlords and piratical factory owners" and to "the *metahistorical* imagery of a class of me-first bourgeois individualists displacing a feudal aristocracy" (emphasis added). More explicit is the remark that "it is easy to forget . . . how moderate, in the long perspective of human history, the capitalist's license for aggression really is."[11] Whether one agrees or disagrees with this statement, it hints at a major problem in Haskell's argument, a problem that was not adequately identified, let alone resolved.

Let us for the moment concede that Haskell was correct in emphasizing

9. Haskell, "Capitalism and the Origins of the Humanitarian Sensibility, Part 2," 563.
10. Haskell, "Capitalism and the Origins of the Humanitarian Sensibility, Part 2," 549.
11. Haskell, "Capitalism and the Origins of the Humanitarian Sensibility, Part 2," 549. It is perhaps necessary to add that this is separate from the (important) question of who the reformers actually were. Haskell quite legitimately disclaimed any intention of answering this question. I too am concerned with the overall societal effect.

these positive effects of the market. Suppose that more individuals do become aware of the importance of their actions and the consequences that will flow from them. Will this be conducive to reform movements such as abolitionism? Haskell cited the case of John Woolman, the early Quaker abolitionist. In an essay in 1746, "Some Considerations on the Keeping of Negroes," Woolman suggested that custom might have to be breached and people treat Negroes as they would themselves wish to be treated. He made it his responsibility to point out to his readers the extent to which they were implicated in slavery and the slave trade. Woolman argued that both geographical and temporal remoteness were irrelevant. Woolman recognized (as few did until the nineteenth century) "the causal relationship that exists in market societies between supply and demand." Haskell quoted Woolman at some length: " 'Whatever nicety of distinction there may be betwixt going in person on expeditions to catch slaves, and buying those with a view to self-interest which others have taken, it is clear and plain to an upright mind that such distinction is in words, not in substance; for the parties are concerned in the same work and have a necessary connection with and dependence on each other. *For were there none to purchase slaves, they who live by stealing and selling them would of consequence do less at it'* " (emphasis in original).[12] Haskell concluded that a man "attentive to the remote consequences of his acts in business and familiar with the intricate web of mutual dependencies that the market establishes between buyers and sellers" was naturally "among the first to see the seemingly civilized and law-abiding slaveowner as engaged in essentially 'the same work' as the barbaric slave stealer."[13] Woolman provides good evidence for Haskell. Unfortunately, it is negated by the case of Daniel Defoe, whom Haskell also cited but without seeing the damage it did to his thesis. Although Defoe "conceived of the slave trade as part of a network of cause-and-effect relationships, he drew from this in 1713 the conclusion that the slave trade was indispensable to England's prosperity." Defoe represents one who appreciated the role of the market in producing intricate patterns of interdependence but who, instead of arguing for abolition, drew the opposite conclusion: one must not tamper with its workings. This stance was anything but rare. In the United States, for example, it was adopted time and time again. To blunt the force of the abolitionist attack on slavery, proslavery advocates pointed to "the intricate web of mutual dependencies" established by the market between buyers and sellers. Too many people, too

12. Haskell, "Capitalism and the Origins of the Humanitarian Sensibility, Part 2," 565.
13. Haskell, "Capitalism and the Origins of the Humanitarian Sensibility, Part 2," 566.

many interests, it was said, were dependent on slavery. So the complexity produced by the market could have a paralyzing effect. Once again, the consequences are contradictory; once again, Haskell supplied no reason for believing the tendencies that he emphasized were not offset by the opposite ones.[14]

In common with many other writers on the subject, Haskell seemed to define capitalism very much in terms of the market. Let us consider for a moment the South. According to Haskell, the market promoted new levels of scrupulous attention to ethics. An unprecedentedly high standard of conscientious performance was encouraged. The South had always been connected very firmly with the international market. From 1820 onward, Southerners were major suppliers of raw cotton to Europe and particularly to Britain. They were involved in the market and, at the same time, required by Southern honor to maintain high "levels of scrupulosity in fulfilling ethical maxims."[15] Yet no powerful humanitarian movement took place in the South. Not only antislavery but all the other reform movements that flourished in the North and in Britain were much weaker there. Why was this? It is not easy to see how Haskell's thesis can explain this anomaly.[16]

Finally, an even greater difficulty confronts his argument. Whatever the deficiencies of the Whig view of history, which saw the abolitionists as representatives of a new and superior moral order, it did at least have the merit of recognizing that morality itself, the notion of what is right and wrong, has not been a constant in human history. Changes in morality are not the same as a judgment whether an evil is or is not bearable; I am concerned here with the prior question of whether a practice is an evil at all. This distinction is important in the case of slavery. At times, Haskell assumed that the problem of slavery is analogous to that of the starving stranger today: we all know the situation is bad, but we lack a feeling of responsibility for it and a recipe to end it. Thus he referred to "the miseries of the slave, which had always been recognized but which before the eighteenth century had possessed the same cognitive and moral status that the misery of the starving stranger in Ethiopia has for us today."[17] But is this correct? Did people always recognize that slavery was an evil? There is every reason to doubt it. Davis's earlier volume, *The Problem of Slavery in Western Culture*,

14. Haskell, "Capitalism and the Origins of the Humanitarian Sensibility, Part 2," 564–66.
15. Haskell, "Capitalism and the Origins of the Humanitarian Sensibility, Part 2," 555.
16. On Southern honor, see Bertram Wyatt Brown, *Southern Honor: Ethics and Behavior in the Old South* (New York, 1983).
17. Haskell, "Capitalism and the Origins of the Humanitarian Sensibility, Part 1," 359.

clearly demonstrates that many defenses of slavery were offered and that, while some individuals and groups were convinced that the enslavement of human beings was an evil, others held the opposite view, and a third group had an ambivalent attitude. Davis concluded an excellent analysis of antiquity's view of slavery with the words: "For some two thousand years men thought of sin as a form of slavery. One day they would come to think of slavery as sin."[18]

It would be wrong to imply that Haskell was unaware of the evidence for changing morality. As he himself observed, "Although its morality was often questioned before 1750, slavery was routinely defended and hardly ever condemned outright, even by the most scrupulous moralists."[19] This statement sits rather awkwardly with the analogy of the starving stranger. Is poverty in the third world "routinely defended and hardly ever condemned outright"? The core of the problem is an ambiguity in Haskell's argument. Was he arguing that a change in values occurred so that what was once believed acceptable ceased to appear so? When he discussed earlier attitudes to slavery, that was the impression we were given. Or was he instead emphasizing a continuity of values but a discontinuity of technique and cognitive style? That was the impression offered when the starving stranger was being considered. A possible way out of this impasse would be to argue that a change in technique can generate a change in values, so that, having found a recipe or perceived a causal connection, human beings then find intolerable an evil they had previously been prepared to tolerate. Although this may seem the most sophisticated position to adopt, it tends toward reductionism. For it is clear that the relationship can easily be reversed. Having come to find an old practice intolerable, people look for a recipe to end it or discover the extent of their complicity in it. To the extent that he assumed that the process is one-way, Haskell reduced values to technique and recipe knowledge. Again using "technology" in the broadest sense, so that it includes cognitive style, recipe knowledge, and technique, Haskell offered us an analysis that comes perilously close to technological determinism.

So, there are many reasons why historians should be reluctant to accept Haskell's thesis. First, the market has contradictory effects on a sense of re-

18. David Brion Davis, *The Problem of Slavery in Western Culture* (London, 1966), 90. Of course, there were good reasons why people were slow to condemn slavery. As Davis noted, "if slavery were an evil and performed no divinely appointed function, then why had God authorized it in Scripture and permitted it to exist in nearly every nation?"; Davis, *ibid.*, 91–92.
19. Haskell, "Capitalism and the Origins of the Humanitarian Sensibility, Part 1," 339.

sponsibility, and, while Haskell realized this, he did not justify his own emphasis on its positive ones. Second, even if the market makes individuals conscious of causal processes in a new way, this consciousness may serve to deter rather than encourage reform. Third, even if the reformer were encouraged by the market, we would be no nearer an answer to the question Eric Williams posed: why the selectivity of concern; why some reforms rather than others? Why reject slavery but tolerate wage labor? Fourth, no conceptual space is allotted to the possibility that changes in values may precede and even cause the changes in cognitive style and technique that Haskell outlines. Fifth, difficulties occur with certain geographical regions such as the South. This is not to deny that a market was one of the necessary conditions for the rise of humanitarianism; capitalism cannot exist without markets, and it would not be surprising if there were some connection between markets and humanitarianism. But I shall argue that the connection is utterly different from the one Haskell suggested.

At one point in his article, Haskell introduced an analogy of oxygen and fire: "Since capitalism [for this, read "markets," since for him they are the same thing] supplied only a precondition, no one need be surprised that the subsequent history of capitalist societies has not been greatly distinguished by humanitarian achievements. The argument presented here is not that markets breed humane action but that in the particular historical circumstances of late eighteenth-century Anglo-American culture the market happens to have been the force that pushed causal perception across the threshold that had hitherto made the slaves' misery (and much other human suffering) seem a necessary evil. One would no more expect markets continually to elevate the morality of the population than one would expect oxygen—in the absence of which ignition cannot occur—always to produce fire. Then, too, there is reason to fear that still another face of the market has prevailed in the later stages of capitalism, one far less supportive of the humanitarian sensibility."[20] This passage is highly problematic. First, Haskell recognized that the market does not necessarily and indeed has not since the mid-nineteenth century operated in this way. Yet we are not really told why. What crucial change occurred? Or rather, what was present before the change? The analogy with oxygen is incomplete. While a fire cannot burn without oxygen, oxygen only rarely and in special circumstances produces a fire. What are these special circumstances?

20. Haskell, "Capitalism and the Origins of the Humanitarian Sensibility, Part 2," 563.

The root of Haskell's problem, it seems to me, lies in his definition of capitalism. If we move beyond the assumption that capitalism is merely production for the market and for profit, we may be able to understand its relationship with humanitarianism more easily. It is surely preferable to define capitalism as generalized commodity production. Among these commodities is labor power. Capitalism involves not only markets but wage labor, a class of wage-laborers, in fact, selling their labor power. Markets, after all, have existed for millennia, but capitalism, according to this definition, is a more specific occurrence. In order to explain the rise of humanitarianism in general and antislavery in particular, we need to focus on the relationship between capitalist and wage-laborer.[21]

For most of human history, the status of the wage-laborer has been exceptionally low. At least some wage-laborers have been present in most pre-modern societies, and they have been a despised and hated lot. Aristotle believed that to be a wage-laborer was to be virtually a slave, and this attitude seems to have been prevalent in Europe (and perhaps elsewhere) for two thousand years after him. Christopher Hill has shown how the wage-laborer was viewed in seventeenth-century England, and it is apparent that the English, perhaps without knowing it, were good Aristotelians in this respect. It is also easy to show that early American democrats, as late as the Jacksonian era, had much the same attitude. The problem was dependence. Wage-laborers were dependent on those who paid their wages, and the word frequently used to describe the dependence was "slavish." So, when we study the rise of antislavery, it is even more striking that abolitionists should have attacked chattel slavery while defending wage labor. Why the break with the past?[22]

Whereas some historians may be tempted to make light of the growth of wage labor, its impact was actually enormous. The vast increases in material production recorded in the last two centuries have occurred in societies that have been capitalist in this sense. Apart from those that achieved industrialization at the point of the gun, no nation has modernized without wage labor on a large scale. This alone suggests that the relationship between capitalist and laborer is likely to have a profound structural effect on a society. In the nineteenth century, the effects were indeed profound. The home and family ceased to be the center of production they had traditionally been. Similarly, notions of individualism, long potent in England and the

21. I am, of course, following Marx's definition of capitalism.
22. G. E. M. de Ste. Croix, *The Class Struggle in the Ancient Greek World* (London, 1983), 179–204; Christopher Hill, "Pottage for Freeborn Englishmen: Attitudes to Wage Labour," in Hill, *Change and Continuity in Seventeenth-Century England* (London, 1974), 219–38.

United States, came to be modified in many subtle ways. These were some of the processes by which capitalism fostered humanitarianism.[23]

I can perhaps best present my argument by comparing abolitionist thinking with that of classical republicanism.[24] Among the key questions for all political and social theorists are these: what is the foundation of individual morality? How is social stability to be achieved? How is loyalty to the state to be secured? The classical republican tradition could not conceive of a stable society unless the vast majority of the citizenry owned their own means of production, either tools and shops if they were to be artisans or, more typically, land if they were farmers. Classical republicans wanted the informed and politically active citizen to be able to place the common good ahead of private and personal gain. The egotistical pursuit of self-interest, it was believed, would plunge a republic into anarchy. Wage-laborers lacked the independence to be able to consider the common good.[25]

Yet wage labor did emerge and on an ever-increasing scale. Not surprisingly, the rise of wage labor called into question many traditional assumptions. In societies that were changing in this way, people altered their attitudes and practices in an attempt to bring them into line with the new realities. They looked for, and found, new supports for individual morality and the social order. Among these were the family, the home, and the individual conscience. None had been previously ignored but all came to be redefined. In societies that had redefined them or were in the process of redefining them, slavery came to appear as a greater and greater evil. Thus a small but growing number of influential individuals were sensitized to the evils of slavery. As they viewed their own society differently, these individuals initiated a new hostility to slavery (and other evils, too) and led the humanitarian movement.[26]

23. At one point, Haskell did refer to C. B. Macpherson's notion of possessive individualism, which accords easily with the Marxist definition of capitalism, but he did not follow up the point. Haskell, "Capitalism and the Origins of the Humanitarian Sensibility, Part 2," 553; C. B. Macpherson, *The Political Theory of Possessive Individualism: Hobbes to Locke* (London, 1962).
24. The interpretation I am offering is in a highly abbreviated form. I am seeking to provide evidence sufficient to demonstrate its plausibility rather than firmly establish the case. Nor have I considered temporal or geographical differences in antislavery opinion. For additional evidence of some of the attitudes I am describing, see Ronald G. Walters, *The Antislavery Appeal: American Abolitionism after 1830* (Baltimore, Md., 1976).
25. J. G. A. Pocock, *The Machiavellian Moment: Florentine Political Thought and the Atlantic Republican Tradition* (Princeton, N.J., 1975).
26. It is not necessary to claim that the abolitionists were aware of the social origin of their beliefs. Indeed, the very fervor of abolitionism and of humanitarian reform generally came from the conviction that the ideals espoused were timeless and unconnected with any specific social formation. Although historians should take this

The spread of the market meant that a growing part of human life was subject to the force of individual self-interest. But a society in which the pursuit of self-interest is universal is a society that is about to collapse. The pursuit of self-interest threatens to subvert the rules by which the game is played. Why should self-interested individuals not seek to buy the law? Why should they not sell out the nation for gain? Why should they not rob, kill, or maim their competitors? It might well be in their interest to put an end to the system by which everyone else's interest can be pursued. This, of course, is the paradox of freedom. If all are free, will not some use their freedom to end the freedom of others? A society based on the pursuit of self-interest needs certain institutions, certain practices that must remain outside the area in which self-interest can operate. This requirement perhaps explains why right-wing groups that have sought the free play of market forces in the economy have, in a search for transcendental values, often emphasized the nation, the family, the race, and the soil. In order for self-interest to operate, there must be a sphere from which self-interest is barred.

Without ever expressing this notion in these terms, nineteenth-century Americans were fully aware of the need for a sphere in which self-interest did not operate. Behind most of the political controversies of the antebellum period lay an implicit understanding of this most fundamental problem. The tariff controversy concerned the propriety of selling labor power in factories; temperance disputed the right to sell liquor on the market. Slavery raised the question of the sale of human beings. Generally speaking, those who were willing to sell humans were reluctant to see labor power being bought and sold while those most keen to see the spread of wage labor tended to be antislavery.[27] To allow the sale of labor power was to consent to the most dramatic and far-reaching spread of market relations in society and create a need both for an area from which the market would be barred and for a morality to support the new society. The abolitionist argued that the market must be barred from dealing in human beings so that man himself, with his conscience and his "soul immortal," could become the prop for the new social order. Although these new attitudes are clearly expressed in much of the humanitarian writing of the eighteenth and nineteenth centuries, I shall confine myself to American abolitionists in the last thirty years of American slavery.

---

belief seriously enough to seek to explain its origin, we need not assume that it is correct.

27. Thus with some exceptions the Democratic party, even in the North, was more tolerant of slavery than the Whig, the party of the tariff and the factory system. See John Ashworth, *"Agrarians" and "Aristocrats": Party Political Ideology in the United States, 1837–1846* (London, 1983).

"The whole question of the duty of opposition to slavery," declared the American and Foreign Anti-Slavery Society, "rests on the sinfulness of reducing innocent men and women, and their children after them, to articles of merchandise." The use of the word "innocent" implies an optimistic view of humanity. More explicitly, the society condemned the practice of converting "into articles of merchandise . . . beings charged with no crime, made a little lower than the angels, and redeemed by His own blood." Abolitionists frequently referred to man's "immortality" and displayed their contempt for those who blasphemously assigned to it a mere commercial value. Thus Gerrit Smith, in an open letter to Henry Clay, referred to "the abhorrent calculation of the worth in dollars and cents of immortal man," and George Bourne asserted that "to traffic in flesh and blood animated by the reasoning capacities is the greatest practical indignity which can be offered to men as immortals."[28] Abolitionists deliberately juxtaposed references to humanity's higher qualities with the language of trade and commerce in order to emphasize their utter incommensurability. This was the strategy that Theodore Dwight Weld employed in order to direct his readers' attention to the enormity of the slaveholder's sin: "ENSLAVING MEN IS REDUCING THEM TO ARTICLES OF PROPERTY—making free agents, chattels—converting *persons* into *things*—sinking immortality into *merchandize* . . . MEN, bartered, leased, mortgaged, invoiced, shipped in cargoes, stored as goods, taken on executions, and knocked off at a public outcry. Their *rights*, another's convenience, their interests, wares on sale, their happiness a household utensil; their personal inalienable ownership, a serviceable article or a plaything, as best suits the humour of the hour, their deathless nature, conscience, social affections, sympathies, hopes, marketable commodities."[29] Often, abolitionists emphasized that it was above all the human soul that must be placed beyond earthly or worldly considerations. "How can there be room for further wrong," William Alger asked, "when a soul is made a thing?" Eliza Lee Follen told her readers that "he who pretends to own a soul usurps the prerogative of the Almighty," and George Bourne argued that "as no person can possibly offer an equivalent for a human soul, no purchase could ever be honestly made of a rational being." But it was perhaps Harriet Beecher Stowe in *Uncle Tom's Cabin*, surely the most influential antislavery work ever written, who gave fullest vent to the abolitionist's sense of outrage at the attempt to make the human soul a commodity. One of the most powerful passages in the book comes

28. *An Address to the Anti-Slavery Christians of the United States* (New York, 1852), 3, 2; *Letter of Gerrit Smith to the Hon. Henry Clay* (New York, 1839), 22; [George Bourne], *A Picture of Slavery in the United States of America* (Middletown, Conn., 1834), 35.
29. [Theodore Dwight Weld], *The Bible against Slavery* (New York, 1838), 8.

when the narrator describes a slave warehouse in New Orleans. She tells the reader to expect that "you shall be courteously entreated to call and examine, and shall find an abundance of husbands, wives, brothers, sisters, fathers, mothers, and young children, to be 'sold separately, or in lots to suit the convenience of the purchaser'; and that soul immortal, once bought with blood and anguish by the Son of God, when the earth shook, and the rocks rent, and the graves were opened, can be sold, leased, mortgaged, exchanged for groceries or dry goods, to suit the phases of trade, or the fancy of the purchaser."[30] There had to be a rigid separation between those areas of life where the market could rule and those where it was forbidden.

In place of tradition, in place of the stability offered by ownership of one's farm or workshop, the reformer offered the individual conscience. It was an unfailing guide to action. It could not be repressed. Its dictates could not be reasoned away. Referring to a slavetrader, "Uncle" Tom says: "I'm sure I'd rather be sold, ten thousand times over, than to have all that ar poor crittur's got to answer for." Another virtuous character in the novel remarks, "What we are conscience bound to do; we can do no other way." Hence the sinner, as Stowe explains, turned to drink to drown out reflection and the voice of the soul.[31]

Abolitionists generally agreed on the conscience as the underpinning for society. As one of them put it, "our strength all lies in a single force—the conscience of the nation." Even though "all else" was "on the side of the oppressor," this difficulty need not provoke despair, since conscience, "that force of forces when properly instructed, is all, and always, on our side." Wendell Phillips, in the aftermath of John Brown's raid on Harpers Ferry, declared that it was not the old "gray-headed man" himself that made "Virginia tremble." Instead, Virginia "trembled at a John Brown in every man's conscience." In Theodore Parker's view, conscience was "relatively perfect" and "the last standard of appeal." Gilbert Haven believed that conscience was "employed by our Creator as His representative in the soul."[32] From this premise, it followed that people must obey their consciences. "Let every one settle it as a principle," William Lloyd Garrison exhorted his read-

30. William Alger, *The Historic Purchase of Freedom, An Oration Delivered in . . . Boston, December 22, 1859 . . .* (Boston, 1859), 8; Eliza Lee Cabot Follen, *To Mothers in the Free States* (n.p., n.d), 2; [Bourne], *Picture of Slavery*, 37; Harriet Beecher Stowe, *Uncle Tom's Cabin: Or, Life among the Lowly* (1852; rpt. edn., London, 1981), chap. 30, p. 467.
31. Stowe, *Uncle Tom's Cabin*, chap. 7, p. 111; chap. 17, p. 289.
32. *Revolution the Only Remedy for Slavery* (New York, 1855), 16; Wendell Phillips, *Speeches, Lectures, and Letters*, 1st series (Boston, 1863), 273; Parker, *Slave Power*, 292; Gilbert Haven, *National Sermons, Speeches and Letters on Slavery and Its War . . .* (Boston, 1869), 9.

ers, "that his conscience, and not his lay or spiritual leaders, must be his commander." The conscience must "govern the movements of soul and body." To Parker, it was imperative that, having learned from his conscience "the moral law of God," man must obey it. Indeed "nothing can absolve men from this duty."[33]

These beliefs promoted abolitionism in two ways. First, they made it appear abhorrent to trade in, and assign commercial value to, the human conscience. Second, they ensured that antislavery would be pursued in an uncompromising manner and with all the righteousness of a holy crusade. Northerners were in general opposed to slavery, but those who shared this moral absolutism became its severest critics. The conscience would thus be one barrier against the destructive force of self-interest. A second was the home and the family. The nineteenth-century family as described in the novels of Charles Dickens, for example, was preeminently a refuge, a haven from the tumultuous world outside. This was the abolitionist view, too. Without the family, "the world would be nothing better than one scene of pollution and wo." It would be "a wilderness." The family brought to a man "the comfort and solace of wife and children, whatever may betide him in this rugged world." The family home was "the place where we must cultivate all the narrow virtues which cannot bear the cold atmosphere of the outside world"; it was "a sanctum wherein the world has no right to intrude, where the heart may freely expand in every possible manifestation to which Nature prompts."[34]

Abolitionists believed that the family was an essential counterweight to the spirit of selfish acquisitiveness that an increasingly commercial society promoted. At home, a man "forgets this strife, and all the hardness which the world demands of him, living quietly once more." "The effect of common toil, of intercourse with the business of men, as both are now managed," Parker noted, "tends often to harden the man and make him selfish." Yet "the sweet influence of home" was, fortunately, "just the reverse." "The sphere of a man's daily business" made few demands "on his affections, on the loftier and better sentiments of his nature," since those "he finds not necessary to attain his private ends." Home was the "school for

---

33. *Liberator*, 26 January 1833; Henry C. Wright, *Marriage and Parentage: Or, the Reproductive Element in Man, as a Means to His Elevation and Happiness* (Boston, 1855), 249–50; Parker, *Slave Power*, 292–93.

34. "Letter of Gerrit Smith to Rev. James Smylie," in *Anti-Slavery Examiner*, 1 (1837); *Mr. Allen's Report of a Declaration of Sentiment on Slavery, Dec. 5, 1837* (Worcester, Mass., 1838), 7; [George Allen], *A Report on American Slavery Read to the Worcester Central Association March 2, 1847* (Boston, 1847), 13; Theodore Parker, *Lessons from the World of Matter and the World of Man* (Boston, 1873), 197; Wright, *Marriage and Parentage*, 308.

affection and kindly sympathy." It was in the home that "we learn the great lesson of affection, gentleness, tenderness," it was there that "a man learns to trust another, without fear," and in the home, "qualities which our daily calling does not exercise" would experience "a serious and healthful growth."[35]

Abolitionist writers portrayed the family as a potent force for good in the world. The law of conjugal loyalty was "inscribed deep in the nature of man." According to Stephen S. Foster, "the conjugal relation has its foundation deeply laid in man's nature, and its strict observance is essential to his happiness." One anonymous writer declared that marriage was "the most intimate, endearing, and sacred union, that can be formed on earth" so that "a strict and high regard for its sacredness must lie at the foundation of a well ordered and virtuous state of society." Henry C. Wright even went so far as to assert that "in their power over the organization, character and destiny of human beings, the Church is nothing, the State is nothing; religion, government, priests and politicians are nothing, compared to marriage and parentage, to the husband and wife, the father and mother." Wright believed that it was "only in a true home" that "the soul" could "attain its full development in all directions" and there "alone" that "the conscience" could "become a universe of light to guide the soul onward and upward." Theodore Parker reasoned that since "its roots" were "in the primeval instincts of the human race," "the family will last forever."[36]

Abolitionists gave close attention to the relationship between parents and children. They did not simply claim that it was the duty of parents to instill correct moral values into children but expressed a faith in the redemptive powers of children themselves. In an extraordinary passage, Henry Ward Beecher explained the process: "When your own child comes in from the street, and has learned to swear from the bad boys congregated there, it is a very different thing to you from what it was when you heard the profanity of those boys as you passed them. Now it takes hold of you, and makes you feel that you are a stockholder in the public morality. Children make men better citizens. Of what use would an engine be to a ship, if it were lying loose in the hull? It must be fastened to it with bolts and screws, before it can propel the vessel. Now a childless man is just like a loose engine. A man must be bolted and screwed to the community before he can begin to work

35. Theodore Parker, *Sins and Safeguards of Society* (Boston, n.d.), 209, 211–13; 36. *Mr. Allen's Report*, 7; Stephen S. Foster, *The Brotherhood of Thieves; Or, a True Picture of the American Church and Clergy* (Concord, Mass., 1886), 11; "A Native of the South-West," *The Family and Slavery*, tract no. 37, American Reform Tract and Book Society (n.p., n.d.), 5; Wright, *Marriage and Parentage*, 276, 291; Parker, *Lessons*, 187.

for its advancement; and there are no such screws and bolts as children."[37] Beecher employed the language of commerce ("a stockholder in the public morality") as well as an extended metaphor that reflected the importance of technology to the age in which he lived. But it was apparent that the process he described depended on the inviolability of the family and required that both home and family be kept strictly separate from the pervasive values of commerce and finance.

In this light, slavery presented a spectacle that was profoundly shocking. "The worst abuse of the system of slavery," according to Harriet Beecher Stowe, "is its outrage upon the family." Since the master could buy and sell slaves at will and since slaves could not legally marry, slavery "breaks into the sanctuary of the home." The power the master had over his female slaves meant that the sanctity of his own family was in constant danger. Gerrit Smith claimed that slavery was "essentially and inevitably at war with the family state." Charles Beecher argued that slavery "nullifies the family" and was, as a consequence, "in direct and flagrant opposition to the law of God." He added that it "must excite his deepest displeasure." Another abolitionist declared that "the Family is the head, the heart, the fountain of society and it has not a privilege that slavery does not nullify, a right that it does not violate, a single facility for improvement it does not counteract, nor a hope that it does not put out in darkness." This writer also pointed out that "those who impose and those who suffer the bondage, alike suffer."[38]

Since the abolitionists had rejected many of the institutions of their nation, they necessarily placed a heavy burden on those that they wished to sustain. The family was preeminent among them. Abolitionists believed that the family was redemptive, a means of supplying the altruism that was threatened by the dissolvent force of self-interest. In *Uncle Tom's Cabin*, the head of one (virtuous) family spells out this function: " 'Thee uses thyself only to learn how to love thy neighbor, Ruth,' said Simeon, looking, with a beaming face on Ruth. 'To be sure. Isn't it what we are made for? If I didn't love John and the baby, I should not know how to feel for [Eliza].' " By contrast, a vicious individual like Simon Legree, we are told, rejects both conscience and mother. Indeed, had Legree not rejected his mother, he would have been saved from sin.[39] Even as the family was losing its economic im-

37. Beecher quoted in *Atlantic Monthly*, 1 (May 1858): 866.
38. Harriet Beecher Stowe, *The Key to Uncle Tom's Cabin* (Boston, 1853), 257; "Letter of Gerrit Smith to Smylie," 41; Charles Beecher, *The God of the Bible against Slavery* (New York, 1855), 3; "A Native of the South-West," *Family and Slavery*, 23.
39. Stowe, *Uncle Tom's Cabin*, chap. 19, p. 331; chap. 13, p. 220. It is tempting to speculate that a shift was occurring at this time in the locus of moral values, a dis-

portance, it was being asked to assume this other role. Traditionally, writers had been inclined to view society, or at least the local community, as the family writ large. That is, rather than see the family as a refuge from society, ruled by different conventions and norms, they had often viewed society as a family. The family was society in microcosm. As these attitudes came to be revised, the humanitarian crusades of the eighteenth and nineteenth centuries gathered momentum. The heightened concern for the soul and the individual conscience, nourished within the family circle, necessarily intensified the concern for slavery, which disrupted family ties and offered many temptations and opportunities for the slaveholder to sin. (It is interesting to note that drink was also condemned for undermining the family and for silencing the conscience.) In other words, one route from capitalism to humanitarianism was via an altered understanding of home, family, and conscience. Since it was also possible to claim that slavery slowed the pace of economic advance, it is not surprising that to more people than ever before it seemed an unmitigated evil.[40]

For several reasons, an interpretation that emphasizes wage labor has more explanatory power than one that focuses on the market. First, as I have indicated, Haskell's view makes a bit of a mystery of the abolitionists' selectivity of concern. On the hypothesis I am proposing, it ceases to be a surprise that the abolitionists accepted wage labor at the same time as they attacked slavery. Indeed, it was precisely because of the spread of wage labor that they attacked slavery in the way they did. Haskell needs to show why a set of attitudes generated by the market made the idea of a market in human beings especially unattractive. The market produced attacks on the market. But to accord causal primacy to wage labor leaves no corresponding difficulty. Second, we are now more easily able to explain a change in values. It is not necessary to claim either that slavery was always regarded as evil (as implied in the starving stranger analogy) or to assume that there is a one-way, causal relationship between changes in recipe knowledge and

placement away from the traditional community, in toward the family and the individual conscience and out toward the nation.
40. It was possible to condemn slavery on either moral or economic grounds, and some individuals pressed one set of criticisms to the exclusion of the other. It was more common, however, for humanitarians to employ the economic arguments, too. A complete explanation of the relationship between capitalism and antislavery must, of course, take account of this. See the works by Howard Temperley cited in note 2.
    One group closely involved in wage labor that nevertheless remained indifferent or even hostile to the antislavery crusade was the factory owners of the North who depended for their livelihood on the supply of cotton from the South, a clear case of direct economic interest obstructing the process by which broader economic developments generate ideas.

changes in values. Third, the problem of the South can now be seen not to be a problem at all. A lower level of humanitarian sentiment is precisely what one would expect in a society based on slavery rather than wage labor. Finally, the diverse and contradictory effects of markets in both strengthening and weakening the sense of responsibility cease to present a problem. As Haskell suggested, the market supplied the oxygen. But wage labor was the explosive. While both are necessary, it is an odd explanation of a fire that emphasizes the oxygen rather than the explosive. Indeed, it is the explosive that historians need to handle with care and attention.

Chapter 8

# Convention and Hegemonic Interest in the Debate over Antislavery
## A Reply to Davis and Ashworth
*Thomas L. Haskell*

I am deeply indebted to both David Brion Davis and John Ashworth for reading my essay with such care and responding to it so intelligently and cre-
atively. It is rare to have such acute critics and rarer still to have civil ones.
My sense of gratitude to Davis is especially strong because of the obvious
dependence of my work on his. But for his research into the problem of slavery in Western culture, the question that my article addressed could not
have been formulated. Indeed, because my principal concerns have to do
with changing concepts of personal agency and moral responsibility, rather
than with the history of the movement to abolish slavery, I am in the position of a rude stowaway in Davis's finely crafted historiographical vessel:
not only did I come aboard uninvited, I have even challenged the master's
authority by proposing a change of course. For the captain to react to this
impertinence by accusing me of sins no worse than "misinterpretation,"
"reductionism," and "positivistic behaviorism" is, I suppose, better treatment than a stowaway has any right to expect.

Cogent though my critics have been, no one will be surprised to hear that
there are aspects of my argument that I think they have overlooked or misunderstood, as well as some that my original essay did not develop adequately. Because Ashworth is something of a stowaway himself (and since
he seems little more content with the vessel's present heading than I am) I
will examine the differences between Davis and myself before turning to
Ashworth's proposal for still another change of course.

Davis's response takes the form of a rousing reaffirmation of faith in the
hegemonic mode of explanation, including especially the self-deception argument that both Ashworth and I find unpersuasive. But, even as Davis re-

A critical reading of an earlier version of this article by Martin Wiener led to important improvements, for which I am most grateful. All responsibility remains
mine.

affirms the hegemonic mode, he severely narrows its scope to a single nation, a limited period, and a certain phase of the antislavery movement, its "acceptance" rather than its "origin." The effect of this shift of emphasis is to render the argument less vulnerable to objections but also far less ambitious than I and many other readers have assumed that it was originally meant to be.

In most respects, Davis seems little concerned whether we take his current remarks to be a restatement of his original position, a needed clarification of it, or a revision, a redeployment on more defensible terrain. This is as it should be, for Davis's volumes on slavery constitute one of the towering achievements of historical scholarship in our generation, and the author of a continuing project of this magnitude and high level of distinction need not apologize to anyone for changing his mind. But, on one point, Davis's unconcern gives way to a different tone: in regard to a distinction he is now eager to make between the origins of the antislavery movement and its acceptance, he says that I seriously misrepresented his original views—"here Haskell misquoted me."[1] Davis knows better than anyone else what he intended to say, but I did not misquote him. Nor can I even agree that I was mistaken about the spirit of what he actually wrote. To show that this is true and to clear the way once again for the alternative to the hegemonic argument that I am recommending, I must begin by examining the differences between Davis's original position and the one he now occupies.

The hegemonic argument, Davis now says, "fills only a few pages" of a long book and was meant to apply "only to British history in a limited period from the 1790s to 1823, with some brief speculations reaching ahead to the 1830s. I did not extend the concept of hegemony to America or France, where abolition movements emerged in wholly different contexts. Certainly, I advanced no general theory of abolitionism *per se* as an instrument of hegemonic control (although I would claim it was always related to the need to legitimate free wage labor)."[2] This is a puzzling statement. The last sentence, with its highly elastic parenthetical proviso, is its most problematical part, but the first sentence is also surprising. Far from devoting only a "few pages" of *The Problem of Slavery in the Age of Revolution* to the hegemony argument, Davis organized much of the book around it. In his own words, "much of this book will be concerned with the ideological functions and implications of attacking this symbol of the most extreme subordination, exploitation, and dehumanization, at a time when various enlightened elites were experimenting with internalized moral and cultural

1. David Brion Davis, "Reflections on Abolitionism and Ideological Hegemony," *AHR*, 92 (October 1987): 798.
2. Davis, "Reflections on Abolitionism," 798.

controls to establish or preserve their own hegemony."[3] In contrast to his original stress on the hegemonic implications of the movement, Davis now minimizes those implications, in form if not in substance, by drawing a sharp distinction between saying that abolitionism was an instrument of hegemonic control and saying that it was "related to the need to legitimate free wage labor." But what substantive difference stands behind this formal distinction? To say that abolitionism is in some degree explicable in terms of the need to legitimate wage labor is to say that it is, in that same degree, hegemonic. Everything therefore depends on what Davis means by "related." If abolitionism is strongly related to the need to legitimate free labor, the parenthetical proviso counts for nothing, and we are right back where we began, with the claim that abolitionism is largely to be understood as an instrument of hegemonic control. If the relation is weak, then abolitionism's hegemonic implications fade in significance, possibly to the vanishing point. Where on this wide spectrum of possibilities does Davis mean to stand?

In the present article, Davis attaches great significance to a distinction between the *origins* of the antislavery movement and its *acceptance* by governing elites. The story of its origins, he says, is the one he told in the first of the three volumes he has published on slavery; it is a tale of the seventeenth and eighteenth centuries, and it concerns authentic religious impulses and radical popular initiatives. None of this, Davis now seems to believe, is much illuminated by the hegemonic argument. Antislavery took on a hegemonic character, according to his current view, only in the 1790s and the early decades of the nineteenth century, when it was appropriated by the aristocratic African Institution, reshaped by wealthy merchant philanthropists, and translated into state policy by conservative governing elites otherwise hostile to social change.[4]

Hegemony was not originally confined to this modest and unobjectionable explanatory role. Consider the following two paragraphs from *The Problem of Slavery in the Age of Revolution*. They present an arresting vision of a dynamic transformation in moral sensibility that defies any neat division into "origin" and "acceptance." Material interests are invoked to illuminate the entire transformation, not a phase of it. It is in connection with these paragraphs that Davis states that he was misquoted.

> The diversities of New World slavery should not blind us to the central point. In the 1760s there was nothing unprecedented about

3. David Brion Davis, *The Problem of Slavery in the Age of Revolution, 1770–1823* (Ithaca, N.Y., 1975), 48, 49.
4. Davis, "Reflections on Abolitionism," 798–99.

chattel slavery, even the slavery of one ethnic group to another. *What was unprecedented by the 1760s and early 1770s was the emergence of a widespread conviction that New World slavery symbolized all the forces that threatened the true destiny of man. How does one explain this remarkable shift in moral consciousness, if it was not a direct response to an innovation of unparalleled iniquity?* Presumably men of the eighteenth century were no more virtuous than men of earlier times, although something might have altered their perception of virtue. No doubt the new antislavery opinion drew on the misgivings and anxieties which slavery had always engendered, but which had been checked by desire for independence and wealth. Yet the slave systems of the New World, far from being in decay, had never appeared so prosperous, so secure, or so full of promise.

*The emergence of an international antislavery opinion represented a momentous turning point in the evolution of man's moral perception, and thus in man's image of himself. The continuing "evolution" did not spring from transcendent sources: as a historical artifact, it reflected the ideological needs of various groups and classes* [my emphasis].[5]

My summary of these words read as follows: "Like Foucault . . . Davis insisted that the new sensibility 'did not spring from transcendent sources.' Rather, its origin, he said, lies in 'the ideological needs of various groups and classes.' "[6] The words I had enclosed in quotation marks accurately reproduce Davis's language. It is evidently my use of the word "origin" in place of "continuing 'evolution' " that he objects to, yet in his own text, the latter term presumably refers back to the previous sentence in which he spoke of the "emergence" of international antislavery opinion and the evolution of "man's" moral perception. How different is "origin" from "emergence?" How can "man's" moral perception be understood to refer exclusively to the perceptions of a British elite between 1790 and 1823? Is not a "source" from which attitudes "spring" an origin? Nothing in the original text suggests that Davis thought that the "origin" of antislavery opinion and its "acceptance" (or "continuing evolution") were distinct chronological phases centered on the 1790s or that they posed crucially different problems of explanation. Davis described, in the two paragraphs quoted above and in the adjacent pages, the emergence in many minds of an unprecedented conviction that slavery constituted an intolerable evil. That conviction, he specifically said, was already "widespread" by the 1760s. He called it a

5. Davis, *Problem of Slavery in the Age of Revolution*, 41–42.
6. Thomas L. Haskell, "Capitalism and the Origins of the Humanitarian Sensibility, Part 1," *AHR*, 90 (April 1985): 344.

"momentous turning point in the evolution of man's moral perception" and a "remarkable shift in moral consciousness," and he took pains to insist that it did not spring from transcendent sources.

He originally invoked "ideological needs" to explain not just the "acceptance" of the movement by conservative governing elites after the 1790s but the entire process by which a deep repugnance for the principle of slavery spread beyond the handful of sectarians and eccentrics who first expressed it and gradually gained strength in ever wider and more influential circles. It was, in Davis's view, ideological needs that prepared a receptive audience, and this effect was being felt before the nineteenth century. "By the eighteenth century," Davis wrote, " . . . profound social changes, particularly those connected with the rise of new classes and new economic interests in Britain and America, created an audience hospitable to antislavery ideology." Although he was always extremely careful to avoid any simple reduction of antislavery opinion to class interest, Davis clearly believed that material interest affected not only the political repercussions of the new sensibility but also the emergence of the sensibility itself: in his own words, "material considerations . . . helped *both* to shape the new moral consciousness and to define its historical effects" (my emphasis).[7]

Any attempt to exempt religion from the hegemonic mode of explanation, or to confine hegemonic considerations to the period after the 1790s or to governing elites, would make a shambles of the interpretation Davis presented in the pivotal chapter of his book, "The Quaker Ethic and the Antislavery International." In that chapter, he ranged brilliantly across the entire last half of the eighteenth century and traced a multitude of interconnections between Quaker organizational skills, religious principles, and concerns about labor discipline. The fabric he wove displays no seam between "origins" and "acceptance." Eighteenth-century Quakers in both England and America, not a nineteenth-century British governing elite, first demonstrated that "testimony against slavery could be a social correlative of inner purity which seemed to pose no threat to the social order—at least to that capitalist order in which the Quakers had won so enviable a 'stake.' " It was also the transatlantic community of Quakers about which Davis was speaking when he formulated the keystone of his entire interpretation, the idea that "as a social force, antislavery was a highly selective response to labor exploitation" and one that "gave a certain moral insulation to economic activities less visibly dependent on human suffering and injustice."[8] If this is not the hegemonic argument, I am at a loss to know what would be.

7. Davis, *Problem of Slavery in the Age of Revolution,* 82, 48.
8. Davis, *Problem of Slavery in the Age of Revolution,* 251.

Ambiguous though his present position is, Davis has obviously abandoned much of the territory he once claimed under the banner of hegemony. In spite of his rousing reaffirmation, a considerable disenchantment with the hegemonic mode of explanation is plainly evident in his attempts to confine it (formally, at least) to a narrower range of events. Although I am a critic of the hegemony argument and believe that some sort of retreat from exposed terrain was in order, I am not convinced that this particular move was the right one to make. The sponsors of the African Institution certainly make a more likely target for hegemonic explanation than do the Quakers, and living in Reagan's America gives us ample demonstration that clamorous attacks on distant evils can function effectively to obscure problems uncomfortably close at hand. But, by confining hegemonic considerations so narrowly, Davis threatens to tear apart the rich and subtle network of connections between consciousness and society that make *The Problem of Slavery in the Age of Revolution* a historiographical landmark.

Discovering non-reductionist ways of relating consciousness to social structure and change is, in my view, the most pressing historiographical issue before us today. And, for all its many drawbacks, the hegemony schema—self-deception and all—did enable Davis to bring the economic developments that we associate with the rise of capitalism into extremely close explanatory conjunction with the new humanitarian sensibility (especially in the lives of the Quakers) without falling victim to either of the excesses that usually spoil efforts to relate consciousness to social structure: he neither disregarded the stated intentions of the reformers nor projected into their activities any implication of conspiracy. So successfully did he navigate the treacherous divide between consciousness and society, in fact, that in spite of my reservations about hegemony, if forced to choose between Davis's original position and the present one, I might well prefer the former. It at least acknowledged the existence of pervasive links between consciousness and society in all phases of the antislavery movement and did not imply that authentic moral innovators—the "originators" of antislavery as opposed to those who merely "accepted" it—must be seen as uncaused causes. I would rather cling to the frail reed of hegemony than accept the claim that shifts of moral sensibility spring from transcendent causes, beyond the power of any social or economic analysis to illuminate, and then become tainted by material concerns only when they spread to the upper classes.

This is not to say, however, that I find the hegemony model adequate. It grapples with the problem of relating consciousness to society but does not carry us very far toward a satisfying formulation. In logic, if not in fact, its principal appeal ought to be to people who once construed the relation between consciousness and society in classic Marxian terms (and thus were confronted with an anomaly in the failure of conflicting class interests to generate a rising curve of working-class radicalism) but who have come to regard the classic formulation as excessively reductionistic and need an alternative that does not carry them beyond the Marxian pale altogether. Because the Gramscian alchemy acknowledges the existence of pluralism and consensus, even as it transmutes them into proof of domination, it serves—paraphrasing what Erasmus Darwin said about the relation of Unitarianism to Christianity—as a feather pillow, perfect for catching falling Marxists.[9] The fact that people other than falling Marxists, including myself, occasionally find it comforting is attributable less to its intrinsic merits than to the dearth of alternative ways of formulating the relationship between consciousness and society.

The difficulties of the hegemonic mode of explanation are notorious and need no extensive rehearsal here. Its most sophisticated defenders strive to make it more flexible, allowing that there can be "open" as well as "closed" hegemonies and that hegemony need not imply control from the top down but can "bubble up from below." When Jackson Lears writes that "even the most successful hegemonic culture creates a situation in which the dominant mode of discourse—and each visual or verbal text within it—becomes a field of contention where many-sided struggles over meaning are constantly fought out," he succeeds in accommodating the schema to the diversity and complexity of modern society but only at the expense of tacitly acknowledging that hegemonic and pluralistic societies are almost impossible to tell apart.[10]

This mode of explanation is already much too flexible. There seems to be no concrete situation around which it cannot be wrapped. No doubt the upper classes exert a disproportionate influence in cultural matters, but it is specific instances that we need to be able to identify as hegemonic or not, and the question of whether a particular social consensus is "spontaneous" or the product of ruling-class influence, conscious or otherwise, is scarcely ever open to empirical resolution. Even to hope for empirical testability is thought a gauche display of positivism in some circles, but many scholars, including some who have impeccable antipositivist credentials and are eager to see the Gramscian schema work, have acknowledged that the problem is a grave one.[11]

9. Gertrude Himmelfarb, *Darwin and the Darwinian Revolution* (New York, 1968), 15.
10. T. J. Jackson Lears, "The Concept of Cultural Hegemony: Problems and Possibilities," *AHR*, 90 (June 1985): 587, 591.
11. Lears, "Concept of Cultural Hegemony," 579; Robert W. Westbrook, "Goodbye to All That: Aileen Kraditor and Radical History," *Radical History Review*, 28–30 (1984): 69–89; E. P. Thompson, *The Poverty of Theory* (New York, 1978), 37–50.

To adopt Davis's practice, which identifies as hegemonic any measure that reinforces ruling-class standards or otherwise stabilizes a regime, would be to make all societies always hegemonic, for any measure short of handing over the reins of power to a new ruling class can—by virtue of the more extreme concessions it forestalls—be said to stabilize and reinforce the status quo.[12] It seems unlikely that rulers ever knowingly destabilize their regimes except for the sake of what they perceive as a higher stability, and even the most dramatic concessions to radical critics can always be construed as co-optation from a standpoint still more radical. Hegemony, by this standard, becomes indistinguishable from governance. I would not claim that this unwanted flexibility renders the concept entirely unusable for explanation, but it does make it highly volatile. Like dry ice, hegemony always tends toward sublimation, becoming merely a diffuse aspect of the human condition rather than a distinct feature of particular societies that one could ever point to in explanation of specific events and actions.

Davis's reply provides a striking illustration of the tendency of arguments in the hegemonic mode to float off in directions that have little to do with historical explanation. He gives as an example of hegemony—indeed, an illustration of "precisely what is meant by 'ideological hegemony' "—the "reinforcement of ruling-class standards" that occurred when radicals were "forced" by the dichotomous terms of the antislavery debate to argue that "in some fundamental respects wage earners were no freer or better off than were slaves." After all, he observes, "there could be no lower standard."[13] Problems abound in this statement. To begin with, I doubt that "forced" is the right word here, either for the degree of restraint felt by radicals or the degree of control over discourse exercised by the rulers. Also, there is room to doubt that people who liken their condition to that of slaves thereby accept a low standard—on the contrary, by rhetorically equating one's own possibly bold demands with the slave's humble plea for liberty, one may be setting a very high standard. Consider the hyperbolic efforts by Thomas Jefferson and other patriots on the eve of the Revolution to characterize British policy as a "deliberate, systematical plan of reducing us to slavery"; surely, this rhetoric did not imply the acceptance of a low standard and neither was it evidence of George III's secure hegemony.[14]

It is in his next paragraph that Davis leaves behind historical explanation

12. Davis, "Reflections on Abolitionism," 809, 808. It should also be noted that if, as Davis now says, "reinforcement of ruling-class standards is precisely what is meant by 'ideological hegemony,' " it becomes very difficult to see how hegemonic considerations can be confined to one country or period. This raises the question of just how far Davis means to go in abandoning hegemony.
13. Davis, "Reflections on Abolitionism," 809.
14. Jefferson quoted in Gordon S. Wood, *The Creation of the American Republic, 1776–1787* (Chapel Hill, N.C., 1969), 39.

altogether and enters a dimension of abstract meanings that is quite detached from any judgment scholars might want to make about how things happened or who was responsible for them. After conceding that abolitionism served in some instances to stimulate radical protest against other forms of oppression, Davis argues that the movement also produced effects that worked in the opposite direction: "analogies with chattel slavery may also have retarded the development of a vocabulary that could depict more subtle forms of coercion, oppression, and class rule."[15] Obviously, if anything had the retarding effect Davis describes, it was slavery itself, not the attack on it. If the reformers had withheld their attack, prolonging the life of the institution, a vocabulary suited to more subtle forms of oppression would presumably have been even slower to develop. So Davis cannot mean that in the absence of antislavery rhetoric a refined vocabulary would have developed earlier. Instead, his point, valid and unobjectionable in itself, is simply that as long as people were preoccupied by the stark oppressiveness of chattel slavery, milder forms of oppression seemed minor by contrast, and this condition, which was utterly beyond the control of the reformers, helped discourage other kinds of challenges to the status quo. This tells us nothing about why people attacked slavery, why the movement grew, or even how abolition *per se* contributed to hegemony; Davis is not in this passage trying to give a causal explanation of anything, he is merely savoring an irony, a "moral ambiguity" that inescapably attended the existence and overthrow of slavery. Such ambiguities are well worth noting as long as they are not mistaken for explanatory assertions. The danger is that some readers (all but the most careful, I suspect) are likely to come away with the preposterous impression that this supposed effect is one more of the hegemonic consequences that abolitionists unconsciously intended—that antislavery flourished partly *because* its rhetoric retarded the development of a more extensive vocabulary of oppression.

But the frailties of the hegemonic mode and the degree of Davis's ambivalence about it are of only passing interest. At the heart of the disagreement between Davis and myself is a different way of formulating the relationship of consciousness and society. That there is a relationship—that consciousness is shaped to a great extent by the social situation of the thinker—both of us take for granted. Davis construes the relationship mainly in terms of class interest and relies on self-deception to introduce a saving element of indeterminacy into the linkage between humane intentions and hegemonic consequences. My formulation, while acknowledging the reality of self-deception and not denying that interest plays an utterly

15. Davis, "Reflections on Abolitionism," 809.

indispensable role in the explanation of human affairs, directs attention instead to another factor that is generally ignored: the role played by social conventions, especially those governing causal attribution and thereby establishing the outer limits of moral responsibility. The stress on conventions and skepticism about the explanatory value of self-deception are the two aspects of my thesis that Davis finds most objectionable. Indeed, apart from his claim that I exaggerated his reliance on the hegemonic argument and his empirical complaints that my thesis cannot account for the existence of women abolitionists or the weakness of antislavery in Holland (points to which I will return), his reply consists largely of an impassioned reaffirmation of the reality of self-deception, coupled with warnings about the moral dangers of convention as an analytical category.

Although Davis misunderstands my views on self-deception, he is correct that we are at loggerheads over the issue of convention. I believe that the unprecedented surge of humanitarian activity in the century following 1750 can be traced to a shift in the network of conventions that govern the attribution of moral responsibility and personal agency. In my view, such conventions exist in all societies, and they are no cause for dismay: without them, no one could possibly know how to apply abstract moral prescriptions such as the Golden Rule in concrete cases. From Davis's perspective, convention and morality tend to be mutually exclusive, and all talk of convention merely shrouds in an unwholesome neutrality the evils associated with "biased consciousness"—self-deception, selective attention, rationalization, mechanisms of avoidance, displacement, projection, and so on. He seems sincerely to believe that my preoccupation with convention can only shelter evildoers from the blame they deserve and sap our will to resist palpable evils such as the Holocaust and the growing threat of nuclear annihilation.[16] These fears are misdirected.

I have never doubted either the reality of self-deception or its ubiquity. "The problem with self-deception," I originally wrote, "is not that it is a rare mental state or overly technical term. All of us can recall episodes in our lives when we ignored or denied what now seems the plain and reprehensible meaning of our actions—moments when, to paraphrase what Sigmund Freud said about dreams, we knew what the consequences of our action would be but did not know that we knew."[17] I argued not that self-deception does not exist but that it must be distinguished from other deceptively similar states of mind. Although the *unconsciously intended* con-

16. Davis, "Reflections on Abolitionism," 802.
17. Haskell, "Capitalism and the Origins of the Humanitarian Sensibility, Part 1," 348–49.

210 / *Thomas L. Haskell*

sequences that self-deception implies are very different in moral tone and
explanatory significance from the *unintended* consequences that make up
much of what happens in human affairs, the two are not readily distin-
guishable empirically. Because every event or condition generates a potential infinity of unintended consequences (think of Cleopatra's nose or the
two-penny nail for want of which the battle was lost), it is very difficult to
show that a specific consequence belongs not in this immense category but
rather in the special and much smaller category of consequences that are
unconsciously intended. I said that this difficulty "limited" the utility of
the concept for historians, not, in Davis's words, that it "invalidates any historical explanation based on the concept of self-deception."[18]

Davis and I do not disagree about the reality of self-deception but about
the sort of warrant a historian needs in order to establish the existence of
self-deception in particular cases. Granting, as I always have, that one of the
many and often contradictory effects of the attack on slavery was to cast the
wage-labor system in a comparatively favorable light, I do not find either in
Davis's book or in his reply to my previous article any adequate warrant for
his claim that this effect was unconsciously intended by substantial numbers of reformers.[19] Davis still contends that it was and offers as example the
case of abolitionist James Stephen, whose blend of sincere humanitarianism
and chauvinistic patriotism does not seem to me to cast any light on the
question.[20]

Davis also cites as an "obvious example" of self-deception people who
respond favorably to advertisements for "lite" beer and cigarettes. "Because the actual effects of smoking cigarettes and consuming alcoholic beverages are well known to the public, the success of the advertisements

18. Haskell, "Capitalism and the Origins of the Humanitarian Sensibility, Part 1,"
349; Davis, "Reflections on Abolitionism," 801.
19. Davis suggests in his reply that his principal concern is not with individual motivation but with "social meanings." This is very hard to reconcile with his ardent
defense of the analytical value of the category of self-deception. Self-deception is a
vital element of his interpretation precisely because of what it says about the unconscious motivation of individuals. Moreover, meaning resides nowhere but in individual minds: we can speak of meaning as perceived by actors, as perceived by
their various contemporaries, and as perceived by us, looking back retrospectively
on events—all these discriminations are well worth making, and perhaps these are
what Davis has in mind when he speaks of "social meanings." But there is no meaning that resides in society itself. See Davis, "Reflections on Abolitionism," 799, 802.
20. Davis, "Reflections on Abolitionism," 801. A much harsher side of Stephen
emerges in his plans to bring West Indian freedmen under the sway of "the rational
predicament"—work or starve—but the harshness of the plan does not in itself tell
us anything about unconscious motives. See David Brion Davis, *Slavery and Human Progress* (New York, 1984), 218–19.

cannot be attributed simply to ignorance or gullibility," he writes.[21] No doubt self-deception accounts for some of the sales of these products, but would we really want to say that it accounted for all or most of their success? Surely, the ignorance and gullibility that Davis mentions explain a large share, and different attitudes toward prudence and risk aversion—which he does not mention—explain still more. The health risks of smoking pale beside those associated with skydiving, spelunking, rock-climbing, and automobile racing, yet these activities do not necessarily entail self-deception. Even daredevils need not deceive themselves; they need only define interest and acceptable risk in eccentric ways. Much less does it require self-deception to smoke cigarettes or drink "lite" beer. Human perceptions vary: some people prize forethought, others value spontaneity; some get their kicks hang gliding, others refuse to fly even in airplanes. Only at the far end of this spectrum, as we approach behavior that is plainly suicidal, do we find a boundary between realistic and unrealistic perceptions of risk that is independent of the perspective of the observer. Only there, it seems to me, can we confidently say that risk-takers deceive themselves. Human interest is less a matter of objective fact and more a matter of subjective interpretation than Davis allows.

A similar overestimation of the accessibility of objective knowledge is built into much of what Davis says about self-deception. For example, in summing up his discussion of the subject, he says that we can justifiably speak of self-deception whenever a group of historical actors "believed they were advancing the interests of all humanity when they were actually promoting the interests of a special class."[22] This is not a workable test of self-deception. It ignores the problem of distinguishing between consequences that are brought into being by the actors' unconscious intentions and consequences that are wholly unintended but that happen, in retrospect, to serve the interests of the actors (or fit some interpretation of those interests). The word "actually" also implies in this context the existence of a perspectiveless knowledge that we rarely possess in moral matters. Morally interesting acts ordinarily are susceptible to more than one empirically accurate description, and their moral quality varies with the description given. Davis's statement tacitly assumes that all morally competent people perceive the same objective good and therefore arrive at the same description—unless they deceive themselves. To those of us who are less optimistic than Davis about the availability of objective knowledge, it is virtually a de-

21. Davis, "Reflections on Abolitionism," 801.
22. Davis, "Reflections on Abolitionism," 802.

fining feature of the human condition that there is no course of action so pure that its disinterestedness and universality cannot be challenged from some plausible point of view—after all, if liberating slaves does not qualify as disinterested, what would? If no course of action is proof against the charges of interestedness, then, by Davis's test, all moral choices become self-deceptive in some degree or from some point of view. Defined this loosely, the category possesses little discriminatory power.

Davis employs an even looser test of self-deception when he speaks of the sixteenth-century Jesuits in Brazil, who strove to protect Indians from enslavement and mistreatment even while encouraging the slave trade. The historian of the Jesuits, Serafim Leite, argued that, although this choice seems oddly "selective" from our standpoint, it would be wrong to call it unjust, just as it would be wrong to complain that a person who founded a hospital for tuberculosis thereby committed an injustice against the victims of leprosy. Davis disclaims any interest in mere "blame," as opposed to the "moral ambiguities of history," but he makes much of the fact that Leite chose to mention leprosy, a disease historically associated with white prejudice against blacks, and he clearly feels that Leite's judgment on this issue is morally flawed. Presumably thinking in terms of self-deception rather than conscious bias, Davis concludes ominously that Leite "accepts" a traditional distinction that prejudicially singles out blacks as suitable for enslavement.[23]

To see how loose a standard of self-deception Davis is applying here (both to Leite and to the Jesuits), we need only turn the tables. How would we respond if a historian who had devoted his career to the history of slavery (David Davis himself, let us say) was accused on that account of unjustly and prejudicially neglecting the history of the whites' oppression of Indians? Historians' career choices, too, are selective, and certainly one predictable consequence of devoting one's career to the history of slavery is to pass up the opportunity of drawing public attention to the plight of Native Americans.[24] Unconscious intention or prejudice could account for such a choice, and no doubt a speaker for Native American interests, justifiably eager to attract attention to the cause, might feel some temptation to adopt such an interpretation, at least for polemical purposes. "If you are not for us, you are against us" is a familiar refrain among activists competing for

23. Davis, "Reflections on Abolitionism," 804.
24. The list of opportunities omitted stretches potentially to infinity, as does the stream of unintended consequences that may be said to stem from any act or omission; so the historian in question might equally well be accused of neglecting the Holocaust, nuclear annihilation, environmental catastrophe, and so on.

public support. But it is a fallacy, and, in the absence of other evidence tending to show prejudice, we would, I think, decide that it was not only invalid but frivolous to take the historian's choice of slavery as a sign of prejudice toward Native Americans. The world is overflowing with suffering strangers; choosing to help one does not signify an intention to prolong the suffering of the others. It plainly will not do to claim that people must intend, either consciously or unconsciously, all the consequences that predictably follow from their choices. Some predictable consequences are intended, some are not; the difference, though by no means entirely arbitrary or irrational, is inescapably a matter of convention and cannot be ascertained without close attention to the norms of the relevant community—without attending, in other words, to the range of meanings that a certain culture makes available to its members.

Davis's strongest evidence for thinking that the abolitionists deceived themselves about the hegemonic consequences of their attack on slavery is that some of their contemporaries accused them of exaggerating the suffering of distant slaves while neglecting that of nearby wage-laborers. Davis assumes that, even if the reformers were initially unaware that one consequence of their attack on slavery would be to cast the wage-labor system in a comparatively favorable light, these contemporary critics—proslavery writers on the one hand and radical labor leaders on the other—brought it to their attention. Once they had been made aware of it, Davis assumes that it became part of their intention, unless they specifically disavowed it. In his present article, Davis concedes that, in the face of this criticism, an abolitionist who was genuinely opposed to all forms of oppression might nonetheless have chosen to give priority to the struggle against slavery on the grounds that it was the most "flagrant and remediable" form of oppression, but Davis assumes that "such a course would entail a disavowal of the claims of proslavery writers and at least a private expression of regret over the unintended consequence of extolling free wage labor."[25] Finding in the archives no expressions of regret and taking into account the rapturous extremes to which abolitionists sometimes went in contrasting free labor with slave labor, Davis concludes that the hegemonic implications of antislavery were indeed intended, though only unconsciously.

Why should we find Davis's imputation of hostile (though unconscious) intention any more persuasive than that of the hypothetical Native American advocate above, who sought to advance a worthy cause by accusing anyone who did not embrace it of deliberately opposing it? Is that not what

25. Davis, "Reflections on Abolitionism," 800.

labor leaders like William Cobbett were doing when they lambasted the abolitionists as "the hypocritical sect of negro-loving philanthropists"?[26] Or when they complained, as the *Poor Man's Guardian* reported in 1833, that the slave worked "only 55 hours and had everything provided for his comfort" while "the mechanic of England procured a bare subsistence by 84 hours hard work"?[27] Was anything weightier than this at stake in the accusations of selectivity hurled by the defenders of slavery? Proslavery writers certainly needed no deep insight into the fundamental continuities between free and coerced modes of labor discipline to see that it was to their advantage to accuse their antagonists of hypocrisy and to set the various components of metropolitan opinion against one another by complaining that the self-appointed protectors of the Caribbean slave cared nothing for the suffering of their neighbors. English labor leaders could not fail to see that one way of hitching their own cause to the immensely popular and remarkably successful campaign for abolition was to equate the misery of free workers with that of slaves and to pound away on the selectivity of the reformers.[28] "If you are not for us, you are against us" is a fallacy, but it is a useful one for activists competing for scarce resources.

By accepting the claims of the abolitionists' critics at face value, Davis construes as a dispassionate and objectively true report what may more fruitfully be understood as a familiar rhetorical tactic to change behavior. It is certainly true that when we disapprove of people's behavior and wish to alter it, we often can do so by disregarding their actual intentions and treating them as if the behavior in question could only signify some sort of reprehensible intention. Thus inattentive spouses are routinely accused of spurning their mates; whether the imputed intention is accurate or not is irrelevant to its tactical efficacy. The leverage this tactic is capable of producing one-to-one can be immensely magnified when large numbers of people threaten the same deliberate misinterpretation. This is what happens, for instance, when university trustees are put on notice that the small measure of stability that they have unintentionally supplied to an oppressive regime (South Africa or Russia) by investing in stocks of companies doing business there will henceforth be interpreted as an intended endorsement of that regime and all its worst practices. Deliberately misinterpreting another person's intentions is a shabby way of treating them, but this process of "creative misinterpretation," as it might be called, is no trivial cha-

26. Cobbett quoted by Seymour Drescher, *Capitalism and Antislavery: British Mobilization in Comparative Perspective* (New York, 1987), 252 n.41.
27. Drescher, *Capitalism and Antislavery*, 149–50.
28. The wide popularity of the movement has been stressed by Drescher, *Capitalism and Antislavery*.

rade, and any movement or political persuasion that abstained from the use of this manipulative strategy would be paying a high price for purity. Cultures can be transformed in this way, and, once the network of conventional meanings available in a culture has been rewoven, by this or other means, the rules for imputing intentionality will have truly been changed, so that what was once an unintended consequence or meaning will conventionally be construed as intentional.

But this change is not accomplished overnight—or in a year or a decade. Culture always remains an arena of contested meanings. More "misinterpretive" projects are always underway than can succeed, and few bring about the permanent transformation they aim at. Until such a project achieves a very substantial degree of success, the instrumentally skewed accounts its supporters give of their opponents' motivation remain just that— skewed accounts or misinterpretations—no matter how good the cause. To mistake them all for innocent reports of the truth would inundate historians with a flood of seemingly malicious intentions and render us incapable of understanding what is going on.

Davis's evidence for thinking that the abolitionists unconsciously intended to legitimate free labor by confining their attack to slavery consists essentially of two classes of facts: the first showing that critics advanced this interpretation (or something close enough to it to lend it credibility), and the second that the abolitionists did not take the trouble to disavow in writing the intention to legitimate free labor. Would we accept similar evidence as a basis for judgments about the unconscious intentions of political activists in our own day? Would we agree, for example, that twentieth-century liberals are guilty of an unconscious desire to foster "welfare dependency"—unless they publicly disavow it? If we accept Davis's evidence, it would seem that we should, for dependency is one predictable consequence of welfare programs, and conservatives have not been shy about alerting the public to it. Of course, conservatives, by the same measure, become guilty not only of indifference but of harboring a deliberate intention to inflict hunger and malnutrition on the poor, for these are predictable consequences of cutting back on welfare. Likewise, by Davis's criteria, feminists favoring abortion rights would stand convicted of unconsciously intending the destruction of thousands of fetuses a year, and right-to-life advocates of wanting to repress women and confine them to traditional roles. College trustees who oppose divestment would be guilty of endorsing apartheid and those who march in protest against them of seeking "easy grace." All of us who read and write about slavery, instead of marching against nuclear weapons, would manifest a latent death wish. The list could go on and on, but the drift toward absurdity is clear enough. If we demand no more evidence than

Davis provides, no person or group is free of self-deception and malicious intention. Not that all of these imputations of unconscious intention are flatly false; some may be accurate accounts of the motivation of some individuals. Nor am I saying that historians should never adopt the motivational interpretations set forth by one party to a dispute. Instead, if we want the idea of self-deception to carry any analytical weight, historians need stricter criteria. We cannot make sense of human affairs if we treat all predictable consequences of human choice as intentional. Many predictable consequences are neither consciously nor unconsciously intended, and, since culture cannot be transformed overnight, many remain unintentional even when a vocal interest group is hard at work to intentionalize them.

I am wary of self-deception for much the same reason Davis is wary of convention: each of us fears that the other's approach is self-indulgent. Indignation is a powerful appetite, and nothing satisfies it so abundantly as the idea that our opponents are deceiving themselves—that, in their heart of hearts, they perceive moral issues just as we do, and know that we are right to condemn them. By imputing self-deception to those we criticize, we affirm the universality of the standards by which we judge them and set aside the disturbing possibility that the world is one in which equally competent moral reasoners can arrive at conflicting interpretations of right and wrong.

Davis's argument presupposes that conscience dictated a single path of moral duty in the era of abolition: opposition to all forms of labor exploitation, whether slave or free. Observing that most abolitionists confined their protest to chattel slavery, Davis wonders (in spite of his admission that slavery was the most "flagrant and remediable" form of exploitation) why they strayed from the path of objective duty. Self-deception is his answer. The question is made necessary by the presupposition that morality is in the fullest sense objective; once we give up the idea that conscience has a single message, we will no longer be puzzled by the abolitionists' failure to take on a larger task than they did, and we will feel little incentive to resort to the idea of self-deception. I will have more to say about selectivity at the end of this article, when I respond to Ashworth's criticism, but for now it is enough to observe that Davis's pivotal question—why were the abolitionists selective in their response to labor exploitation?—is prompted in large part by his apparent conviction that morality is a matter of objective fact rather than interpretation.

When Davis wrote *The Problem of Slavery in the Age of Revolution*, he was more appreciative of the importance of convention than he seems to be now. In spite of the prominence he assigned to self-deception, much of what he originally wrote implied, logically, not that the reformers deceived themselves but rather that their vision was confined within certain conventional limits. For example, when Davis spoke of the reformers furthering the interests of their class only "unwittingly" and said that it would have been "unthinkable" and "inconceivable" for them to recognize the hegemonic implications of antislavery, he gave us a glimpse of a kind of explanation that would not depend on self-deception or unconscious intention and would not necessarily point toward hegemonic interests.[29] "Unthinkability" does not denote self-deception but a meaning that is genuinely unavailable to the actor and is therefore not a part of intention, conscious or otherwise. Similarly, Davis's remark that "prior to the Revolution, few colonists were capable of the imaginative leap of placing themselves in their slave's position" and his observation that "neither Luther nor Calvin . . . had any notion that Christian liberty could alter the fact that some men are born free and others slaves" also acknowledge in convention a constraining power over moral judgment that Davis now seems to find worrisome.[30]

The question of whether morality can be authoritative when it is admitted to have no firmer or deeper base than social convention is, of course, a problem of immense philosophical importance. Neither Davis nor I mean to set up shop as philosophers, but in this regard we unavoidably take well-worn positions in an ancient controversy. I am not sure to what extent Davis would be prepared to treat moral obligation as an objective fact, inherent in the very nature of mankind and the world, timeless in character and therefore not dependent on human consciousness or social convention. But he is certainly closer to that honorable tradition of moral philosophy, often identified with Plato and Aristotle, than I am. Although I am not at all in sympathy with the reckless, Derridean assault on "foundationalism" that is fashionable in some literary and philosophical circles, I am enough of a historicist, in the contemporary sense of that term, to believe that human morality is neither natural nor divine but a historical product, and it therefore has an inescapably conventional component.[31]

Temperamentally, Davis and I are not far apart. I lament, as I believe he

29. Davis, *Problem of Slavery in the Age of Revolution*, 253, 350.
30. Davis, *Problem of Slavery in the Age of Revolution*, 279, 44.
31. A list of books relevant to this wide-ranging debate that began in literary studies a decade or more ago, and about which historians cannot much longer remain innocent, would be impossibly long. Some exceptionally lucid works are: Jonathan Culler, *On Deconstruction* (Ithaca, N.Y., 1982); Allen Megill, *Prophets of Extremity: Nietzsche, Heidegger, Foucault, Derrida* (Berkeley, Calif., 1985); Gerald Graff, *Literature against Itself: Literary Ideas in Modern Society* (Chicago, 1979); Richard Rorty, *Philosophy and the Mirror of Nature* (Princeton, N.J., 1979); Frederick Crews, "The House of Grand Theory," *New York Review of Books*, 33 (29 May 1986): 36–42; and David Hollinger, "The Knower and the Artificer," *American Quarterly*, 39 (Spring 1987): 37–55.

does, the evasiveness of our current "emotivist" or "therapeutic" culture, in which the word "moralist" has become an epithet, and all talk about moral obligation is liable to be taken as a mask for personal preference. We agree, I believe, that a culture that acknowledges no difference between the statements "I *ought* to do this," and "I *want* to do this"—the former an invocation of objective obligation, the latter a report of merely subjective desire—is in deep trouble.[32] But there is, in my view, no help to be had outside the sphere of history and convention. Notwithstanding the persistent and sometimes eloquent protests of Leo Strauss and others, it is widely acknowledged among philosophers that three centuries of inquiry into the basis of moral judgment have shown that ultimate foundations are not to be found, in nature or anywhere else. Instead, our best hope is to demonstrate that treating morality as conventional rather than natural does not mean we are setting it adrift and leaving it at the mercy of every ripple of fashion and stray breeze of personal whimsy. Convention need not be the same as fashion, and the place of convention in moral judgment can be acknowledged without capitulating to subjectivism. Morality can, I believe, possess a constraining and even objective (at least, non-subjective) quality, even though it is conventional.[33] In one of the most widely influential books of our time, Thomas Kuhn has demonstrated that, when scholars give up the idea that scientific thinking aims at correspondence with an objective reality, timeless and independent of human consciousness, the authority of scientific knowledge is not diminished, the familiar practices of rational debate and justification among scientists are not discredited, and science remains as real, as rational, and as relevant to the conduct of life as ever.[34] I am confident that much the same can be said about moral thinking when we give up the contention that it aims at correspondence with truths that are immune to time and have origins somewhere outside human society.[35]

32. Alasdair MacIntyre, *After Virtue: A Study in Moral Theory*, 2d edn. (Notre Dame, Ind., 1984); Philip Reiff, *The Triumph of the Therapeutic: The Uses of Faith after Freud* (New York, 1966).
33. I have argued this point at greater length in "The Curious Persistence of Rights Talk in the 'Age of Interpretation,'" *Journal of American History*, 74 (Dec. 1987): 984–1012.
34. Thomas S. Kuhn, *The Structure of Scientific Revolutions*, 2d edn. (Chicago, 1970).
35. The preeminent work in recent moral philosophy is that of John Rawls, who specifically rejects "rational intuitionism" and identifies his own position in conventionalist terms: "What justifies a conception of justice is not its being true to an order antecedent to and given to us, but its congruence with our deeper understanding of ourselves and our aspirations, and our realization that, given our history and the traditions imbedded in our public life, it is the most reasonable doctrine for us. We can find no better charter for our social world. Kantian constructivism holds that moral objectivity is to be understood in terms of a suitably constructed social point of view that all can accept"; John Rawls, "Kantian Constructivism in Moral

To demonstrate the large and vital role that convention necessarily plays in our moral thinking, my original article set forth a hypothetical exercise, the "case of the starving stranger," to which Davis and Ashworth give little attention.[36] This exercise embodies the crucial anatomical features of the process that I believe gave rise to the humanitarian sensibility, and anyone wishing to challenge my thesis will find their target here. In particular, I should think that anyone who is disturbed, as Davis is, by the large role I assign to convention, would want to grapple with this exercise and try to explain what it is, if not convention, that allows us to feel that we have lived up to the Golden Rule, even though we render aid to only a minuscule fraction of those in need. This is one of the more elementary lessons taught by the case of the starving stranger: that selectivity is an utterly inescapable feature of humane action in a world that overflows with suffering. All of us, no matter how humane, confine our operative sense of responsibility within limits that fall far short of what we could do to alleviate human misery, and it would make a mockery of the idea of intentionality to say that we "intend," consciously or not, all the suffering we leave unrelieved. An immense gap exists between what a literal interpretation of the Golden Rule would seem to require and what even the best of us actually do and consider sufficient, indeed, admirable. What bridges this gap if not convention? Instead of confronting the problem, Davis brushes it aside, insisting that "selection is seldom neutral" and archly advising us to "be skeptical of the excuse that 'we never knew.' "[37]

We would all prefer to believe that our own moral judgments are a pure exercise of reason, shaped only by the immutable nature of mankind and the world and shared by all whose moral judgment is worthy of respect. It is disconcerting to acknowledge that convention, which is liable to vary incommensurably from one cultural and historical situation to another, sets the stage for judgment, establishes its limits, and channels its direction. Yet this is the implication not only of the case of the starving stranger but also of a familiar truism of moral philosophy, "Ought implies can."

To say that "ought implies can" is, obviously, to say that we do not hold people responsible for doing what they cannot do. Less obviously, the truism also means that our sense of what people are responsible for extends no further than our causal perception. At most, we feel responsible only for evils over which we believe we have causal influence (ones about which we

Theory," *Journal of Philosophy*, 77 (September 1980): 519; *A Theory of Justice* (Cambridge, Mass., 1971)

36. Haskell, "Capitalism and the Origins of the Humanitarian Sensibility, Part 1," 353–59.

37. Davis, "Reflections on Abolitionism," 804, 802.

"can" do something), and even this is an outer limit, for there are many evils that we obviously could do something to alleviate for which we do not hold ourselves or anyone else responsible. Because convention enters crucially into what we think we "can" do, the dependence of "ought" on "can" carries with it the further implication that convention plays a large role in moral judgment. Cause-and-effect relations pervade our thinking at every level, from high theory to the most mundane affairs of everyday life. They constitute, as one philosopher said, "the cement of the universe."[38] We do not fry an egg, drive to work, or please a lover without drawing on our fund of knowledge about the relation of present acts to future states of the world. But the fund is distinctly cultural. Cause-and-effect relations are not given in raw experience, and what we think we "can" do is very much a matter of interpretation and social convention. Indeed, it is doubly a matter of convention, for convention not only shapes our understanding of cause-and-effect relations (and thus helps define the farthest horizon of our moral vision), it also maps the entire moral landscape within that distant perimeter, specifying which of the many things that we know we could do to relieve suffering we must actually do in order to feel that our lives accord tolerably well with the moral prescriptions of our society. These are what I call our causal horizons.

Let us imagine, for example, that a great earthquake has just occurred, such as that which struck Mexico City in 1985. In a strictly physical sense, I "can" stop writing this essay, fly to Mexico City, and help save at least one endangered stranger's life by lifting debris and performing other emergency tasks. If I took literally the moral rule, "Do unto others what you would have them do unto you," this would seem to be the only acceptable thing to do, for if I were pinned beneath a collapsed building, I would certainly want others to drop their daily routines and come to my aid. Yet I continue working instead of going to the aid of the stranger, and no one accuses me of violating the Golden Rule. Why not? Because, by the prevailing conventions of my time and place, this "can" is not real, not operative. Mexico City is "too far away"; it would disrupt my life "too much." Too far and too much by what measure? Convention supplies the measure. Convention authorizes me to say that I "cannot" help the stranger, at least not in this direct way, even though, in a purely physical sense, I certainly possess the power to do so. This shared, tacit understanding that converts the "can" of physical ability into the "cannot" or "need not" of acceptable moral practice, is a large part of what we mean by convention.[39]

38. J. L. Mackie, *The Cement of the Universe: A Study of Causation* (Oxford, 1974).
39. One's first instinct is to think that anything that eases our conscience about the

If ought implies can, and "can" is conventional in this sense, it follows inexorably that our concepts of moral responsibility—of what we "ought" to do—are deeply imbedded in social practice and are influenced at least in broad outline by the material circumstances, historical experiences, and technological capabilities of the society in which we live. As our collective circumstances, experiences, and capabilities change, we should expect the limits of moral responsibility to change as well, though not in any simple or automatic manner. The easiest way to illustrate the point is to imagine a radical change in what we "can" do. Obviously, the invention of technology that would enable us to travel to and from Mexico City, or any other scene of disaster, instantaneously and at trivial expense would be very likely to alter the conventions governing moral responsibility in our society, making the passivity that convention now authorizes quite unacceptable, at least in some circles. If we could save someone's life by merely reaching out to press a button, we would be monsters not to do so. A more familiar example of an innovation in institutional "technology" that induces people to make a (nominally) humane gesture they would not otherwise have made is the "Live Aid" rock concert; another, of a much more substantial sort, is the creation of an organization such as Amnesty International that collects funds, publicizes abuses, and provides a new means of exerting influence. Projects of "creative misinterpretation" by large groups of people can have the same effect. Any change in the practices of our society that stretches our causal horizons and expands the sphere within which we feel we "can" act, has the potential to transform what we hitherto perceived as "necessary evils" into remediable ones, thereby exposing us to feelings of guilt and responsibility for suffering that previously aroused only passive sympathy— like the sympathy we feel today for distant earthquake victims who are "too far away" to help. This is the sort of change that I believe accounts for the emergence of the humanitarian sensibility in the eighteenth century.

Because Davis and Ashworth have rival claims of their own to advance about the determining influence that material interest exerts on moral judgment, it is amusing that each wraps himself in the tattered mantle of vol-

---

suffering of others must be a bad thing and that the path to a better world must lead away from such conventions altogether. But a little thought will show that conventions limiting responsibility in this fashion are utterly indispensable; a world without them is quite impossible to conceive. Even the perfect altruist who devotes his or her life to helping others must choose which victims to help first, and, from the vantage point of the victims not helped, the choice will appear "selective." Some sort of limiting convention is inescapable, but of course that does not prevent us from preferring a more inclusive set of limits than now prevails. A valuable exploration of this and related problems is James S. Fishkin, *The Limits of Obligation* (New Haven, Conn., 1982).

untarism to complain that my mode of explanation is deterministic. Davis throws in for good measure the all-purpose academic pejorative of our era, "positivistic"—in spite of crediting mankind with much fuller access to positive moral knowledge than I do.[40] I plead guilty to a few overzealous rhetorical flourishes in my original essay that may have exaggerated the explanatory completeness of my scheme, but the scheme itself is not deterministic.[41] The three propositions that "ought" depends on "can," that "can" is largely defined by convention, and that convention is deeply imbedded in social practice—thus making "ought" indirectly contingent to some degree on changing social practices—will no doubt be unsettling to anyone who assumes that moral judgment is an unconditioned exercise of reason aiming at the apprehension of timeless absolutes or Platonic essences. But acknowledging these things does not subvert consciousness or reduce moral choice to a phenomenon of a lower order.

My scheme of explanation requires only that we admit that moral thinking, like all thinking, is carried on within a mutable framework of assumptions about what the world is and how we relate to it. The scheme is probabalistic rather than mechanistic, and it applies in the first instance to collectivities rather than to individuals. Good Samaritans go back as far as our records go, and I stipulated from the outset that I was not trying to explain their existence. "We are not concerned," I wrote, "with individual episodes of human kindness and decency—which I assume can occur anywhere, anytime—but with a sustained, collective pattern of behavior in which substantial numbers of people regularly act to alleviate the suffering of strangers. That, I take it, is what we mean by the emergence of a new humanitarian sensibility in the eighteenth century."[42] And that is what I set out to explain. Far from denying the authenticity of the reformers' moral outrage or rendering epiphenomenal their choices or values, my purpose has been to protest the transmogrification of all these lively and productive states of mind into monotonous shades of class interest.

If my aim had been to present a full descriptive account of the emergence of antislavery, I would of course have had to write a book instead of an ar-

40. John Ashworth, "The Relationship between Capitalism and Humanitarianism," *AHR*, 92 (October 1987): 820; Davis, "Reflections on Abolitionism," 801, 802, 809–10.
41. I do not share the curious confidence widespread among historians today that "deterministic" accounts of human affairs must be wrong and "voluntaristic" ones right, as if the question of free will and determinism had been solved once and for all. If my account were deterministic, I would defend it as such. But it is not.
42. Haskell, "Capitalism and the Origins of the Humanitarian Sensibility, Part 1," 360.

ticle and devote much more space than I did to Evangelical piety, Quaker earnestness, the ambitions of artisans for independence, and many other subjects. My aim instead has only been to suggest a better way to conceptualize the rich body of evidence and interpretation that Davis and other specialists have already assembled and which I take as the descriptive foundation for my argument.

I have tried to identify a threshold in the perception of personal agency and responsibility, one that helps us make sense of the most striking finding of Davis's first volume on slavery: namely, that before the eighteenth century practically no one, no matter how compassionate or scrupulous, regarded slavery as an intolerable evil. To see the significance of this threshold, it is important to be clear about what was novel in the eighteenth century. The novelty was active opposition to the institution of slavery, based on the conviction that it was an intolerable evil, not recognition that the slave's lot was a bitter one. The suffering of slaves had long been recognized. John Locke, father of liberalism, who invested in the Royal African company and wrote slavery into the Fundamental Constitutions of Carolina, was perfectly aware that it was a "vile and miserable" state of being. As early as the thirteenth century, the authors of *Las Siete Partidas*, a model legal code that specifically authorized slavery and influenced later legislation in the slaveholding societies of Spain and Spanish America, acknowledged that "slavery is the most despicable thing which can be found among men, because man, who is the most noble and free creature . . . is placed in the power of another."[43] The myth of the contented slave of course propped up many a slaveholder's conscience, but in every slave regime some people were morally perceptive enough to recognize that slaves suffered— not only when their masters violated local standards of decency but always, even under the best of material conditions, simply because they were "in the power of another." This moral perspective, which recognized that slaves suffered and acknowledged that it was bad for people to suffer and yet tolerated slavery, seems alien to us. Why, in a culture that had long identified humanity with spiritual autonomy, and ethical conduct with reciprocity, did practically no one before the eighteenth century interpret the Golden Rule to require active opposition to the very institution of slavery? Or, to put it

43. Herbert S. Klein, "Anglicanism, Catholicism, and the Negro Slave," in *The Debate over Slavery: Stanley Elkins and His Critics*, Ann J. Lane, ed. (Urbana, Ill., 1971), 142. Theoretical considerations aside, the document also contains the observation that the actual condition of Moorish slaves in Spain was "the most miserable that men could have in this world"; David Brion Davis, *The Problem of Slavery in Western Culture* (Ithaca, N.Y., 1966), 103, 118.

another way, why, in a culture that has long honored the Golden Rule, does recognition that slaves suffer have such a long history and opposition to slavery such a short one?

The answer was once sought in the idea of progress, the happy faith that civilization has its own inner dynamic, carrying mankind to ever-higher plateaus of moral knowledge and ability. We have, for good reasons that need no rehearsal here, grown skeptical of the cozy assumption that we moderns abolished slavery because of our superior insight into the requirements of morality. A second possibility lies at the level of explicit appeals, sermons, and speeches. But the answer cannot be found exclusively or even mainly here. There were many such appeals, of course, and they played an indispensable part in mobilizing opposition to slavery. Any fully descriptive account of the history of the antislavery movement would necessarily allot much space to them. Had no one ever preached that slavery was evil, it would be with us still. But to treat explicit preaching against slavery and in praise of benevolence as the sufficient cause of the widening circles of humanitarian reform activity that history records in the century after 1750— and not to ask why such preaching emerged then and why the message was warmly received—would be to beg the most vital questions. Prescription is certainly a proximate cause, but nothing bars us from inquiring into the cause of a cause: what unleashed this avalanche of prescription? What enabled an avalanche of words to trigger in turn a flood of emotion and expressive action? The rule of reciprocity that the Golden Rule embodies is so central to moral judgment that everything else that can be said by way of prescribing moral duty is gilding the lily. The idea of reciprocity was not new; it had been available in the form of biblical precept for at least two millennia, and by itself it provided an adequate *prescriptive* basis for devoting one's entire life to the liberation of slaves. If prescriptions of moral duty had been enough, the history of opposition to slavery would have begun long before the eighteenth century. That it did not suggests that the cause of the sudden surge of humanitarian activism in the eighteenth century was not fundamentally a matter of prescription, no matter how indispensable prescription may have been to the outcome.

A more likely place to look for the answer to our question lies in the conventions that define personal agency, set practical limits to responsibility, and broadly determine specific interpretations of abstract moral prescriptions like the Golden Rule. We cannot literally do for every suffering "other" what we would have others do for us, and without conventional guidelines to limit and specify our responsibilities, we would not know what it means to "be good." The conventions that prevail in Western culture today enable us to feel that we live by the Golden Rule even though we actually render aid to only a minuscule fraction of the world's needy people—only that fraction so centrally located within our sphere of causal influence that not to help them would seem abnormal, a departure from the level of care that we routinely achieve in our everyday affairs. Our ancestors were also guided by convention, but, because the fabric of everyday affairs in which we are enmeshed is very different from the one they knew, we have no reason to think that the causal conventions that shape our operative limits of responsibility today are the same ones that prevailed two centuries ago. The causal imagination feeds on the recognition that things could be other than they are and that we know how to alter them. Behind every observation that "$x$ causes $y$" is a hypothetical annihilation in which $x$, the cause, is imagined not to exist: "in the absence of $x$, no $y$" is the violent fantasy from which each judgment of causal relationship springs. This hypothetical violence comes more readily to us than to our ancestors. We live in a society that is rife with change, that preens itself on the range of options it holds out to each of its members, and that routinely puts in human hands dramatic powers to come, go, move, do, build, destroy, and otherwise transfigure the world that were scarcely dreamed of before the eighteenth century.

If, as I suppose, the conventions that prevailed before the eighteenth century confined what people thought they could do within much narrower limits than ours—if, in other words, their conventionally defined sphere of causal influence excluded much that ours now includes—there would be nothing surprising in their failure to take action against slavery and other evils that we construe as remediable. This difference between their conventions and ours would explain why even the most scrupulous moralists could acknowledge the misery of slaves and even feel a passive sympathy for them without feeling any obligation to take action against the institution that made them miserable—all the while being sincerely devoted to the Golden Rule. Just as causal conventions allow us to have clear consciences today about the starving strangers and earthquake victims whom we omit to help because they are "too far away," so, I suggest, a different set of conventions once made the misery of slaves seem equally far out of reach. Before substantial numbers of people could feel outraged by the very existence of slavery and take action designed to uproot it (which, again, is not at all the same thing as feeling passive sympathy or protesting particular instances of mistreatment, attitudes that leave the institution itself unchallenged), they had to be able to impute to themselves historically unprecedented powers of intervention and to perceive hierarchical social arrangements and institutional structures not as reflections of God's will or manifestations of nature's own order but as contingent, malleable phenomena open to human influence and correction.[44] This is just another, more familiar, way of saying that an upheaval had to occur in the conventions governing the attribution of causation and responsibility. One result of upheaval would have been to transform what had been perceived as "necessary evils" into remediable ones, thereby imposing on certain sensitive souls a compelling sense of obligation to remedy miseries that had in all prior human history evoked no more (and usually less) than passive sympathy, even from the most scrupulous and compassionate moralists.

Does this scheme of explanation make human beings "passive automata wholly programmed by 'society,' " as Davis suggests?[45] Certainly not. We do not detract from the honor due those hardy souls who first perceived slavery as a remediable evil by observing that equally compassionate people in previous centuries did not respond to the same facts in the same way, or by suggesting that people could not have responded as the reformers did until they felt, accurately or not, that they had knowledge of cause-and-effect relations sufficiently complex and far-reaching that they could readily imagine a course of practical action capable of uprooting one of the most ancient and interest-bound institutions in their society. To say that it took a shift of causal conventions to push people over this threshold and place slavery (and much else) on the agenda of remediable evils, making possible the collective action historians call "humanitarianism" does not reduce humane sentiments to something lower or undermine in any way the subjective sense of freedom to choose between perceived options that we all normally feel. The only vantage point from which my scheme must appear comparatively deterministic is that of a reader who (boldly) believes that mankind is free not only to choose between perceived options but also to choose which options to perceive, for my causal explanation extends only to what people perceived the outer limits of their responsibility to be, not to the choices they made in light of that perception.[46]

44. As Davis observed in his first volume on slavery, the middle years of the eighteenth century "represented a turning point in the history of Western culture. To both religious and secular writers the period brought an almost explosive consciousness of man's freedom to shape the world in accordance with his own will and reason. As the dogmas and restraints of the past lost their compelling force, there was a heightened concern for discovering laws and principles that would enable human society to be something more than an endless contest of greed and power. This quest for moral assurance led inevitably to examinations of inequality, sovereignty, and servitude"; Davis, *Problem of Slavery in Western Culture*, 485.
45. Davis, "Reflections on Abolitionism," 802.
46. Ashworth fears that my scheme falls victim to "technological determinism" because it does not allow for the possibility that people might first feel responsible for suffering and then seek means (technologies) for doing something about it. Ashworth fails to recognize that no one can "feel responsible" (operatively responsible,

To contend that the moral perceptions that were constitutive of humanitarianism did not exist before the eighteenth century and could not have become available until certain historical conditions were met is no more deterministic, in the ordinary sense of that word, than observing that a person cannot jog while seated, play bridge without a deck of cards, perform a lifesaving tracheotomy without medical training, or understand what inflation is without having lived in a monetary economy. To ask that our moral judgments and perceptions be independent even of conditions like these would be to ask for a sort of freedom that the world cannot deliver and that we do not need.

Nothing has seemed more shocking to my critics than my suggestion that the capitalist marketplace had something important to do with the establishment of these cognitive preconditions for the emergence of the humanitarian sensibility. Their astonishment is ironic, since the role I assign to capitalism is a good deal smaller and less direct than the one Davis assumes. Instead of treating the antislavery movement (or at any rate, its acceptance by the powerful) as a refraction of class interest, unconsciously aiming at the legitimation of a new, ostensibly free, system of labor discipline, I argue that the market merely had the incidental effect of expanding the sphere of causal perception within which everyday affairs proceeded, pushing people over a threshold of perception such that the most sensitive moralists among them no longer found passive sympathy an adequate response to the misery of slaves. The point of departure for my argument was the conviction prevalent among historians that the concomitance of capitalism and abolitionism, though paradoxical, was not coincidental. Taking for granted the existence of some connection, I set out to rethink what it might be, other than class interest. My conclusion that capitalism contributed to the freeing of the slaves "only a precondition, albeit a vital one" does not assign capitalism a very large role in the emergence of the humanitarian sensibility.[47] Had there not already been a debate in progress over the relationship between

---

as opposed to feeling passive sympathy) for suffering whose knowledge of cause-and-effect relations is so limited that he or she cannot imagine any course of action that would relieve the suffering. Responsibility presupposes possession of some threshold level of recipe knowledge, and the entire point of my scheme is to account for the crossing of that threshold. It is of course true that once a person feels responsible, he or she is then free, within limits, to seek appropriate means to relieve the pain, but the very fact of feeling responsible means that the critical threshold that should interest us historically has already been crossed. See Ashworth, "Relationship between Capitalism and Humanitarianism," 820.

47. Haskell, "Capitalism and the Origins of the Humanitarian Sensibility, Part 2," 563.

capitalism and antislavery, I am not at all sure that I would have assigned capitalism a role even that large, for, unlike many of the participants in this longstanding controversy, I have no interest at all in chalking up points "for" or "against" capitalism.

From my perspective, the question that most needs answering concerns the history of causal perception: why did social problems that once appeared intractable take on, in the eighteenth century, an appearance of unprecedented plasticity? Capitalism enters the picture only insofar as it helps answer that question. After centuries during which the misery of slaves was treated with indifference, or at most as a necessary evil, something produced an outward shift in the conventionally defined sphere of causal perception, such that some unusually acute moral reasoners began finding it easy to imagine a course of action leading to the destruction of slavery—so easy that not to embark on it seemed a dereliction of moral duty. What was it that produced this crucial expansion of the sphere of causal perception within which people assessed their responsibility for the suffering of strangers?

My crucial claim in this regard is that the market was one of the major factors in the expansion of causal horizons. Pivotal though the claim is, Davis and Ashworth put up surprisingly little resistance to it. As Davis says, "there can be no doubt that the market tended to teach people to keep their promises and attend to the remote consequences of their acts."[48] This concession is more important than Davis recognizes. Given the dependence of "ought" on "can," and "can" on conventions of causal attribution, the tendency of the market to widen causal horizons gives us a way of accounting for the concomitance of capitalism and abolitionism that relies neither on naive concepts of moral progress nor on class interest cunningly disguised as altruism. Capitalism and humanitarianism seem antithetical—and their concomitance puzzling—because of the divergence of the sentiments on which each rests. Capitalism fosters self-regarding sentiments, while humanitarianism seems other-regarding. What can account for the parallel development in history of two such opposed tendencies? The mystery fades considerably once we recognize that, in spite of their divergent properties, capitalism and humanitarianism also have something important in common: both presuppose the existence of wide causal horizons. Both depend on people who attribute to themselves far-reaching powers of intervention. Neither can flourish unless it can enlist the energies of people who display a strongly self-monitoring disposition, people who routinely allow their behavior in the present to be shaped by obligations incurred in the distant past and by anticipations of consequences that lie far in the future. Peo-

48. Davis, "Reflections on Abolitionism," 811.

ple who dwell only in the present and attribute to themselves little power to alter the course of events live in a world that cannot sustain either a market-oriented form of life or the acute sensations of moral responsibility that Nietzsche derisively associated with the "bad conscience" of the humanitarian reformers. And, although humanitarianism has no means of bringing into existence the type of "conscience-ridden" personality it needs, capitalism, through the disciplinary mechanism of the market, has a very considerable power to do just that.

It would, of course, be absurd to credit the market with the power of bringing this personality type into existence by itself. The point of my previous article was to show that capitalism and humanitarianism both presuppose a population imbued with the habit of remote causal attribution and therefore that their concomitance can be accounted for without construing humanitarianism as a reflex of class interest. I did not claim that capitalism was the sole source of the humanitarian sensibility. Humanitarianism and the personality capable of sustaining it were the outcome of a "civilizing process" that extended over many centuries and resulted at least as much from religious and political developments as from anything economic. Christianity's definition of the person as a potentially immortal, but immaterial, soul, temporarily housed within a corruptible, material body, is eloquent testimony to the antiquity and the centrality in Western culture of the aspiration toward overcoming the self and transcending impulse. No market ever held out any reward for delay of gratification that could compare with that which Christianity held out to those who could learn to live for the future: eternal salvation.

At a completely different level of analysis, Norbert Elias has made a strong case for the importance of geographically extensive monopolies of physical force. Only the emergence of such monopolies in the medieval period, he contends, permitted the crystallization of networks of functional dependence within which social constraints could achieve enough force and steadiness to be internalized as self-restraint. "The moderation of spontaneous emotions," he argued, "the tempering of affects, the extension of mental space beyond the moment into the past and future, the habit of connecting events in terms of chains of cause and effect—all these are different aspects of the same transformation of conduct which necessarily takes place with the monopolization of physical violence, and the lengthening of the chains of social action and interdependence. It is a 'civilizing' change of behavior."[49] The political rigors of living at court and taking part in courtly intrigue no doubt did more to convert warriors into calculating courtiers

49. Norbert Elias, *Power and Civility: The Civilizing Process*, vol. 2, Edmund Jephcott, trans. (New York, 1982), 236.

than either religion or any economic institution of the age could, and yet Elias recognizes that what life at court once did to induce foresight in a handful of warrior aristocrats was, in the eighteenth and nineteenth centuries, extended to a much larger sector of society by the trade networks and functional dependencies of an increasingly interdependent economy. Even then, of course, the market could shape personality to its needs only within limits established by traditional religion and morality and only within a framework of legal order and comparative political stability supplied by the state.

The market reinforced the long-term drift of Western culture toward vigorous self-surveillance and far-flung causal horizons, and these tendencies were magnified still further by contemporary events such as the scientific revolution of the seventeenth century, the dramatic technological feats of the next two centuries, and the eruption of political revolutions in France and North America. Nothing could have done more to stimulate the causal imagination or to dispel illusions of immutability (sides of the same coin) than the sight of a world of ranks turned topsy-turvy. But revolutionary acts presuppose a high degree of confidence that the world is open to alteration, and the humanitarian sensibility did not make its first appearance in 1776 or 1789. As Karl Marx observed, capitalism had long been teaching, in a subtle yet compelling way, much the same lesson about mutability that revolution taught: "All that is solid melts into air, all that is holy is profaned."[50]

Although Davis and Ashworth accept the idea that the market helped expand causal horizons, they seem not to understand that this effect in itself sheds much light on the concomitance of capitalism and humanitarianism and establishes a linkage between "base" and "superstructure" that does not rely on the concept of interest. I contend that the market, by expanding causal horizons, helped bring into existence a perceptual world in which some people—those who would have been distinguished for their exceptional conscientiousness in any case—began defining their own responsibility for suffering so broadly that they, unlike their equally scrupulous predecessors in earlier generations, could no longer witness the misery of slaves with merely passive sympathy. Attributing to themselves great powers of intervention, they also found themselves exposed to acute sensations of guilt and responsibility-by-omission for evils whose causes had previously seemed inaccessibly remote to everyone, even the most sensitive moralists.

50.  Marx quoted in Marshall Berman, " 'All That Is Solid Melts into Air': Marx, Modernism, and Modernization," *Dissent*, 25 (Winter 1978): 54–73.

In contrast to this explanation, in which the idea of a perceptual threshold figures prominently, Davis and Ashworth seem to believe that, in my view, the market acted unilaterally and mechanically to bring about a general improvement in the morality of those subject to its influence, converting sinners into saints. They impute to me a theory in which the market functions like a source of benign radioactivity: the closer a person is to it and the longer exposed, the greater the dosage of humane impulses—no matter what the person's values, character, religious convictions, ethical commitments, gender role, material interests, or state of mind. This is the theory that Davis evidently has in mind when he contends that my scheme cannot explain the presence of women in the antislavery movement (because they were comparatively uninvolved in the market) and suggests that my theory should lead us to expect slavetraders to have been converted to the antislavery cause (because they were directly involved in market transactions).[51]

I took considerable pains in my original article to guard against this sort of misinterpretation, especially in the "case of the starving stranger," where the idea of humanitarianism as a threshold phenomenon is developed at some length. It was the "radioactive" view of the market's function that I was rejecting when I wrote that "the argument presented here is not that markets breed humane action but that in the particular historical circumstances of late eighteenth-century Anglo-American culture the market happens to have been the force that pushed causal perception across the threshold that had hitherto made the slaves' misery (and much other human suffering) seem a necessary evil."[52] That was also the view I meant to reject when I stressed that John Woolman's pioneering antislavery work presupposed both exceptionally wide causal horizons and exceptional moral standards, and yet again when I acknowledged that most of those whose horizons expanded took the occasion only as an opportunity to pursue self-interest at a higher pitch.[53]

That slavetraders did not become abolitionists and that women often did would tend to disconfirm an explanatory scheme which held that markets uniformly induce humane behavior in those most closely exposed to them, regardless of all other influences. But the scheme I set forth holds no such thing. In view of the longstanding identification of femininity with com-

---

51. Davis, "Reflections on Abolitionism," 812.
52. Haskell, "Capitalism and the Origins of the Humanitarian Sensibility, Part 2," 563.
53. Haskell, "Capitalism and the Origins of the Humanitarian Sensibility, Part 1," 353–59; "Capitalism and the Origins of the Humanitarian Sensibility, Part 2," 565–66, 562–63.

passion and moral recititude, I see nothing at all surprising or disconfirming about the prominence of women in the antislavery movement (or about the prominence of people of deep religious convictions, of a comparatively rigid moral temperament, or of a fairly high level of aggressiveness and self-confidence). For women as well as men, the key question remains why indifference and passive sympathy for slaves gave way in the eighteenth century to active opposition to the institution of slavery. Anyone seeking the answer to that question would have to take the stereotype of the separate spheres very literally indeed to think that women were not influenced by the market (or that men were not influenced by the domestic sphere). To say as Davis does that women "were not subject to . . . market discipline" is to construe the cultural impact of the market too narrowly.[54]

As for the idea that the market had the power to transform callous people into ethically sensitive ones, or slavetraders into abolitionists, I am unable to find any statement in my essay remotely capable of encouraging such a preposterous inference. Of course, the market did not exist in a vacuum or act on its subjects unilaterally—nothing in the universe of human affairs does. The market was only the keystone for an entire way of life, one in which radicals could be as deeply immersed as entrepreneurs and about which women could become as conversant as men. Like other complex institutions, the market determined nothing rigidly but channeled conduct by encouraging some perceptions and discouraging others. Like poems and rainy days, the experiences it induced were open to a range of interpretations, and the interpretation given to them varied with the personal history of the interpreter. Quakers, prosperous artisans, and other members of the middle class were among the earliest to adopt this way of life, and it is no coincidence that it was from among these groups that some of the earliest antislavery leaders emerged, but a person did not have to cut deals, sign contracts, dispatch bills of lading, or mobilize a work force in order to see the world in an altered perspective and experience the heightened sense of agency that is relevant to my form of explanation. Nor today is it necessarily airplane pilots and computer operators who best grasp the revolutionary cultural implications of the innovations they superintend. The

54. Davis, "Reflections on Abolitionism," 812. To see how easy it would be to exaggerate the gender specificity of the market's impact on culture, one need only think of the centrality of the concepts of covenant and contract in English political philosophy and religion. A recent important work on religion is David Zaret, *The Heavenly Contract: Ideology and Organization in Pre-Revolutionary Puritanism* (Chicago, 1985). For a very broad construction of the cultural impact of the market, see Jean-Christophe Agnew, *Worlds Apart: The Market and the Theater in Anglo-American Thought, 1550–1750* (New York, 1986).

market did not make anyone "good." The market does not help explain why some people conducted themselves morally but why moral conduct was redefined in some circles to include root-and-branch opposition to slavery, a problem previously construed as intractable.

Of the three efforts Davis makes to test my thesis empirically, the first two, concerning women and slavetraders, seem to me very wide of the mark, but the third is more interesting. Assuming that Holland was a strongly market-oriented society, Davis takes the weakness of the antislavery movement in Holland to be an argument against my thesis. His point is well taken: if the advance of a market-oriented way of life is what pushed Britons and Americans over the threshold into a new moral universe, why was the same effect not felt in Holland? The Dutch case is well worth further exploration, but we must begin by noting that it poses no more of a problem for me than it does for Davis. He, after all, *should* find it puzzling that the Dutch bourgeoisie passed up the opportunity to legitimize wage labor, accumulate moral capital, and bolster its own self-esteem by attacking slavery. If Anglo-American capitalists were unconsciously attracted to antislavery agitation because it "gave a certain moral insulation to economic activities less visibly dependent on human suffering and injustice," why did Dutch capitalists not feel the same attraction?[55]

From both Davis's vantage point and my own, the Dutch case can fairly easily be distinguished from the Anglo-American one by pointing to the decidedly paternalistic temper of Dutch political life and to the very marginal role that slave labor played in the Dutch economy. Relying only on the same essay that Davis cited by the Dutch historian P. C. Emmer, we can see that the slave trade to the Dutch colonies in the New World had nearly ceased as early as 1773, not because of agitation but because of diminishing returns. About 36,000 slaves lived under Dutch control when emancipation came in 1863, and in the 1840s the trade between the principal slave colony, Surinam, and the Netherlands amounted to only about 1.5 percent of the Dutch gross national product. Even when Dutch consumers drank slave-grown coffee sweetened with slave-produced sugar, they were relying largely on imports from plantations beyond the control of their government. In the in-

---

55. Davis, *Problem of Slavery in the Age of Revolution*, 251. Davis might argue that it was not capitalists generally who sought to legitimize wage labor but industrial capitalists, and that the Dutch bourgeoisie was predominantly mercantile. Before one could assess such an argument, one would need to know more about the Dutch economy than has been brought forward so far. Merchants need wage labor, too, and it would not be at all easy (judging from what Davis has written in *Problem of Slavery in the Age of Revolution*) to show that Anglo-American abolitionists owed more to industrial than to mercantile wealth.

terval running from about 1800 to 1813, slavery was a "purely academic issue in the Netherlands" because during those years all of the Dutch slave-holding colonies were controlled by the British.[56]

There may be some sense in which the Dutch deserve their reputation as a market-oriented people, but, if so, their political culture in the era of abolition was curiously lacking in the liberalism that is generally taken to be the paramount political expression of market culture and capitalist hegemony. Emmer reported that "the ideology of political and economic liberalism found few adherents in the Netherlands" and noted that in 1840 the king was so determined to resist popular initiatives of any kind that he refused even to receive a petition by the British Anti-Slavery Society—one that was accepted by all the other monarchs of Europe except the Sultan of Turkey. The king seems to have been not so much concerned to defend slavery as to retain control over its eradication, for, although the details of compensation were drawn out, emancipation was taken for granted as an inevitability by the government after 1844 and by slaveowners as well after 1852.[57] My thesis would be severely challenged by evidence of a truly market-oriented society whose members continued to see slavery as nothing worse than a necessary evil, but that is not what the Dutch represent. On the contrary, support for slavery seems to have evaporated in spite of the absence of any strong, indigenous antislavery movement. The Dutch case is an odd one, and further investigation may demonstrate that it is a genuine counterinstance, but the evidence brought forward thus far is too ambiguous to do my thesis any significant harm. Indeed, in the absence of political agitation, what else could account for the abandonment of slavery in the Dutch colonies if not a pervasive sea change in moral perspective?

Momentarily shedding his antipositivist robes, Davis complains in the closing pages of his essay that my form of explanation "has no predictive power." Frustrated by my untroubled acknowledgment that not everyone exposed to the market was transformed by it into an abolitionist—indeed, that for many people an expansion of causal horizons meant only that self-interest would be pursued on a grander scale—Davis says that "this very softness shields Haskell from serious empirical attack." For Davis, it is a sign of the lamentable evasiveness of my explanation that "Haskell can claim that nothing is proved by the failure of slavetraders to become humanitarians."[58]

56. P. C. Emmer, "Anti-Slavery and the Dutch: Abolition without Reform," in *Anti-Slavery, Religion, and Reform: Essays in Memory of Roger Anstey*, Christine Bolt and Seymour Drescher, eds. (Folkestone, Kent, 1980), 80–83, 88–89, 84.
57. Emmer, "Anti-Slavery and the Dutch," 85, 87, 80.
58. Davis, "Reflections on Abolitionism," 811.

This complaint reflects not only a failure to recall what the argument is about—why two developments as dissimilar as capitalism and humanitarianism emerged in close historical conjunction—but also a failure to grasp the character of a threshold explanation. Surely, Davis does not really expect historians to explain the conduct of human beings more fully than a chemist can explain the motion of molecules—yet, when a chemist explains the boiling of a pot of water by saying that at certain threshold values of pressure, volume, and temperature, water will begin to undergo a change of state, becoming a gas instead of a liquid, we do not reject the explanation because some of the water in the pot remains a liquid, nor do we complain about the chemist's failure to tell us which individual molecules will break through the surface and enter the atmosphere—it is enough to know that some (those with the greatest velocity) will do so.

Although we have no analog in the study of human affairs to the thermometers, gauges, and scales that enable the chemist to predict when the change of state will begin, that does not prevent us from realizing that we are dealing with a threshold phenomenon and that it was only natural for the line to be crossed at a time when the market was powerfully reshaping everyday life to its needs. Being skeptical about moral progress, scholars must assume that people who lived before the eighteenth century were about as insightful and capable of moral choice as people are today. We know that they recognized that slaves suffered and also that they acknowledged the force of a moral prescription that required them to do for others what they would want done for themselves. I am not trying to account for an instantaneous or universal triumph of antislavery opinion, for, even at the moment of emancipation, some people favored the retention of slavery, many were indifferent, and most probably continued to feel only the passive sympathy that had for so many centuries marked the outer limits of response. Missing from this picture, however, is an expansion of the perceived limits of human agency and responsibility—one sufficiently far-reaching to account for the emergence of a determined network of activists and a gradual shift of opinion in their direction. Without attributing to the market any power whatsoever to make bad people good, we can see that the premium the market paid for forethought and all the other habits of remote causal attribution could easily have supplied the missing piece, completing the picture, and creating a world of wide causal horizons in which slavery would appear to some people as a remediable and intolerable indignity.

What most disturbs both Davis and Ashworth is, perhaps, not the supposed determinism or limited predictive capacity of my explanation but rather its counterintuitive character. Davis's own account has a counterintuitive touch insofar as it depicts bad capitalism giving rise to good antislavery sentiment, but then its final twist, in which antislavery is shown to be shot through with hegemonic implications, confirms the reader's intuitive expectation that bad causes should produce bad effects. In contrast, my explanation requires the reader to believe that the market had one decidedly good effect, and this idea will be counterintuitive for those who are committed to the view that the market is a bad thing. Up to a point, I have no quarrel with those who criticize the market. As I acknowledged very fully in my original essay, "the market" was the favorite rhetorical resource for several generations of people intent on playing down concerns about the public interest and legitimizing the pursuit of self-interest. There may be a touch of romanticism in Davis's lament for the "older, paternalistic notions of responsibility" (which could, of course, be extremely intrusive and never hinted of any general obligation to help strangers), but there can be no doubt that appeals to the automatic functioning of the market often served to justify cold and callous relations between contracting parties, including especially those between employers and employees.[59] If the market shrank responsibility in this respect, my critics ask, how can it be said to have expanded responsibility in any other?

The answer is obvious: complex institutions like the market have multiple and contradictory effects that defy any sort of reconciliation. So, for that matter, does so common a substance as water, which cooks or cools, gives life or takes it away, enables distant transport or destroys whole towns and villages, depending on its amount, its temperature, its relation to bodily orifices, and so on. Why would anyone expect the effects of the market to be any less diverse and contradictory than those of water? And what point would there be in trying to sum up its overall impact, as if each bad effect came tagged with a minus sign and each good one with a plus? Does the scalding of John somehow cancel out or negate Mary's cooling bath? Or a thirst-quenching drink make up for a devastating flood? Because these effects have no common denominator, we have no choice but to deal with them discretely, which means that bad causes may well lead to good effects.[60]

Both of my critics seem to fear that by saying something good about the market we forfeit the right to indict the evils associated with it. I give us all greater credit for mental agility than this fear implies. Ashworth is even more insistent than Davis that the good effects I have attributed to the market could only be justified by some sort of calculus that would tote up all the market's good and bad results and show that its overall impact on morality

59. Davis, "Reflections on Abolitionism," 811.
60. Compare with Ashworth's complaint that Woolman's humane sentiments are "negated" by the example of Daniel Defoe; Ashworth, "Relationship between Capitalism and Humanitarianism," 818.

was good.[61] The project appears to me both futile and irrelevant. There is nothing illogical about attributing to the market two distinct effects: it authorized the more aggressive pursuit of self-interest in business affairs and, by expanding the horizon of causal perception, it also encouraged in some people strong feelings of guilt and anger about suffering that had previously aroused no more than passive sympathy. One would not be surprised to find individuals in whom both effects were expressed simultaneously and whose behavior toward others might accordingly meander between rigorousness in regard to people perceived as contractual equals and tenderness in regard to those—like slaves—who were perceived as suffering through no fault of their own. This is, in fact, not a bad description of a common Victorian stance toward others. Knowing that, by some overall measure, the market was, on the whole, good or bad would add nothing to our understanding of this contradictory scene. We know that water is, on the whole, good, in that life cannot continue in its absence. But this awareness does not diminish the importance of knowing that floods, drownings, and scaldings are bad. By the same token, even if we were to conclude that the market's effects on the whole were bad, this would not diminish the importance of knowing that one of them was good.

Although I have tried to demonstrate that the humanitarian sensibility can be linked to capitalism without relying on the much-overworked concept of class interest, I took pains in my original article to acknowledge that interest functioned as an indispensable concept in human affairs, and I noted in particular that "interests exert an important influence on belief through what [Max] Weber called 'elective affinity.' "[62] My aim has not been to supplant the concept of interest—an unthinkably bizarre project—but to supplement it and suggest that its explanatory power may be exaggerated. In his response to my essay, John Ashworth often seems to assume that my disapproval of Davis's sort of explanation, which wraps interest in a cloak of self-deception, must extend to all forms of explanation based on interest, including his own. But this is not quite so. I find much to agree with in Ashworth's essay. In its best moments, it bears a resemblance to Weber's approach, which, while denying the crude thesis that interests directly determine consciousness, acknowledges that, through the process of "elective affinity," people do adopt ideas and values that are loosely suited to their interests. Ashworth's understanding of the role of interest is not consistent,

61. Ashworth, "Relationship between Capitalism and Humanitarianism," 817.
62. Haskell, "Capitalism and the Origins of the Humanitarian Sensibility, Part 1," 342; Richard Herbert Howe, "Max Weber's Elective Affinities: Sociology within the Bounds of Pure Reason," *American Journal of Sociology*, 84 (1978): 366–85.

and I am not at all persuaded by his claim that antislavery can best be understood as a product of class interest, but my objections have more to do with execution than the type of explanation he is recommending.

In a curious maneuver near the beginning of his argument, Ashworth nearly succeeds in obscuring its merits (and its kinship with that of Weber) by announcing that his aim is to rehabilitate the discredited notion of "false consciousness." This term has a very checkered history and no certain referent, but it is often associated with the very view Weber was attacking, one that treats consciousness as epiphenomenal. This, it turns out, is not at all what Ashworth means. He means by the term only that historical actors always act on an "incomplete" perception of reality (never mind all the questions that could be raised about the singularity and objectivity of "reality" and the "completeness" of our own perception) and that historians are entitled to assign to historical acts meanings other than those the actors had in mind.[63]

Why Ashworth maintains that the assertion of these familiar propositions requires the resurrection of false consciousness is not clear to me. He evidently imagines that I wish to confine the meanings of acts to those which the actors themselves held, but this is simply not true. When I explain humanitarianism in terms of a shift of causal conventions, I am obviously assigning to the actions of the reformers meanings very different from the ones they had in mind. Ashworth apparently mistakes my concern with cultural availability for the outlandish view that only the actor's meanings count. It is of course vital to ascertain the range of meanings culturally available to past actors so that we do not mistakenly impute to them a view of the world and an understanding of self that they could not have had. But this concern to avoid anachronism in no way prevents us from contrasting the meaning the act had for the actor with the meaning that it has for us, which may be very different because we view it in retrospect and see it in light of our different experiences and priorities. Indeed, ascertaining cultural availability is the indispensable groundwork for any such distinction, and only by maintaining this distinction scrupulously can we prevent history from being a bag of tricks played on the dead.

Disregarding, then, the unfortunate connotations of false consciousness, we can see in Ashworth's proposal a scheme of explanation that bears comparison to the approach that Weber developed most fully in *The Protestant Ethic and the Spirit of Capitalism*.[64] Weber did not employ the notion of self-deception and neither does Ashworth, who is no more persuaded by

63. Ashworth, "Relationship between Capitalism and Humanitarianism," 814–15.
64. Max Weber, *The Protestant Ethic and the Spirit of Capitalism*, Talcott Parsons, trans. (New York, 1958).

this aspect of Davis's interpretation than I am. Ashworth agrees with Davis, as I do, that some of the consequences of reform served the hegemonic interests of the reformers, but unlike Davis, he treats these consequences as unintended—just as I do. Neither consciously nor unconsciously, in Ashworth's view, did any significant number of reformers intend, by attacking slavery, to advance their own interests. Here again, his treatment parallels that of Weber, who insisted on a very close relationship between the spread of Protestant religious doctrines and the advance of capitalism but who strongly denied that ministers or their parishioners had ever *intended* anything other than the glorification of God.

It is at the next stage of the argument that Ashworth parts company with both Weber and me. Although he does not regard the hegemonic consequences of reform as in any sense intended, Ashworth does believe that they must be viewed as a product of class interest. In contrast, I had argued that the very idea of "pursuing class interest," or being "moved" by it, implies intentionality, at least of an unconscious character. "To say that a person is moved by class interest is to say that he *intends* to further the interests of his class, or it is to say nothing at all."[65] This was a strong assertion and not one I would want to detach from its original argumentative context and set up as a general methodological imperative, but it does accord with Weber's practice in *The Protestant Ethic*: in his view, the contribution that Protestantism made to the advance of capitalism was neither intended nor the result of class interest. Weber held that it was a fortuitous conjunction, not any causal dependence of values on interests, that brought capitalism together with a religious ideology capable of breaking down the traditional psychological barriers that had hitherto blocked economic advance.[66]

Ashworth says at one point, in a very un-Weberian manner, that "a person is moved by certain ideals that have *grown out of* class interest" (emphasis added).[67] If the relationship between interests and values was truly like that of the acorn to the oak or the caterpillar to the butterfly, so that one grows out of the other, we would have grounds for saying that interest is the "major factor" in explaining both values and whatever outcomes they lead to in action. But the metaphor "growing out of" notoriously exagger-

65. Haskell, "Capitalism and the Humanitarian Sensibility, Part 1," 347.
66. "For those to whom no causal explanation is adequate without an economic . . . interpretation, it may be remarked that I consider the influence of economic development on the fate of religious ideas to be very important and shall later attempt to show how in our case the process of mutual adaptation of the two took place. On the other hand, those religious ideas themselves simply cannot be deduced from economic circumstances"; Weber, *The Protestant Ethic and the Spirit of Capitalism*, 277 n.84; see also chap. 2.
67. Ashworth, "Relationship between Capitalism and Humanitarianism," 815.

ates both the objectivity of interest and the determinateness of the influence that it exerts on our thinking. It was in part to protest that sort of exaggeration that Weber turned to the much looser and more ambiguous metaphor of "elective affinity."

The question of how much class interest explains is finally one of degree, for neither Weber nor I deny that interests and values tend to go together and to be mutually reinforcing. In fact, my own scheme, by treating people's perceptions of both interest and moral obligation as elements of the cognitive style appropriate to a market-oriented way of life, suggests a connection between values and interests that is even more intimate than the word "affinity" implies—namely, a common origin in a set of causal conventions. But I do not believe that the values of the movement against slavery were generally produced by class interest or that the movement can be best explained in its terms. And if we focus on Ashworth's practice rather than his methodological pronouncements, neither does he—at least, not all the time.

Ashworth says that he is going to show, contrary to my argument, that the reformers were moved by class interests, even though they had no intention of advancing those interests. But the scene he actually paints for us depicts people being moved not by class interests but by consciously held values and ideals, such as the importance of personal autonomy, the primacy of conscience, the sanctity of the family, and the like. True, Ashworth makes a case for the idea that these values and ideals were, in turn, related to the class interest of the reformers, but the relation he draws is not very strong, and, even if we accepted his claim at face value, it would not follow that the reformers, in attacking slavery, were "pursuing class interest" or that antislavery could be best understood as an expression of class interest. That antislavery values and bourgeois interests are not wholly unrelated goes without saying, as does the existence of affinities between them. But that is not what the debate is about. Ashworth has evidently set out to prove that class interest is "the major causal factor," the principal explanation of the movement against slavery, and in this he does not succeed.[68]

Consider the structure of his argument. He contends that the commodification of labor that attended the advance of capitalism provoked, in the middle and upper levels of society, a twofold reaction: a heightened ideological commitment to a cluster of values centering on the priority of individual conscience and the sanctity of the family and, in close association with these values, a general search for ways of setting limits to the wholesale

68. See Ashworth, "Relationship between Capitalism and Humanitarianism," 823–28, 815.

legitimation of self-interest that the triumph of capitalism seemed to threaten. Because a strong conscience was commonly thought capable of anchoring moral judgment in the bedrock of divine law, and home and family were widely understood to be refuges from competition within which disinterested love could survive and flourish, these values were, appropriately enough, held aloft by those leading the battle to confine self-interest within manageable boundaries. As these ideological commitments gathered strength, the institution of slavery, which disrupted families and substituted the self-indulgent whims of a slaveowner for the sacred authority of conscience, came to appear ever more evil and anomalous. Finally, inspired by the vision of bounded liberty and conscientious conduct that the struggle to come to terms with wage labor had indirectly set in motion, the middle and upper classes felt obliged to rid their society of slavery, in what might be described as a paroxysm of ideological consistency. The ideals of family and conscience that they had come to venerate they sought to translate into reality, not only in their own lives, which would be unsurprising, but also in the lives of the slaves—which Ashworth should find much more surprising than he does.

In fact, I find this explanation unpersuasive (at least in its present, abbreviated form) on several different levels. Ashworth fails to establish a strong enough connection between class interests and ideology, on the one hand, and between ideology and antislavery action, on the other, to justify his conclusion that antislavery ought to be understood mainly as an expression of class interest. Still more vulnerable are certain of his assumptions. He imputes to human beings a greater thirst for consistency between values and practices than I believe they display, and he correspondingly underestimates the ease (and sincerity) with which even the most passionately held values can be interpreted so as to seem in conformity with a wide variety of practices. Most serious of all, Ashworth offers no explanation for what I regard as the defining characteristic of the rise of humanitarianism as a historical event—the extension to strangers of levels of care and concern that were previously confined to family, friends, and neighbors. No doubt slavery was an outrage against ideals of conscience and family, but it was an outrage perpetrated against the slaves, not the reformers whose behavior we are trying to explain. The reformer's own domestic tranquility obviously was not imperiled by the existence of slavery and neither was the reformer's fidelity to conscience, except insofar as he or she chose to construe the extension of benevolence to slaves as one of the demands of conscience. Ashworth gives us no reason to think that reformers could not have cultivated these values within their own circles, while leaving slaves bereft of them, just as democratic and republican values had been cultivated within the free populations of ancient Athens and colonial Virginia—or, for that matter, just as the values of hearth and home were cultivated on many an antebellum plantation. By taking it for granted that people who learn to venerate conscience and the family will naturally seek to extend those blessings from those who are near and dear to the most lowly and distant of strangers, Ashworth not only simplifies his task, he literally assumes away the central problem for which we seek an explanation.

This is not to say that Ashworth's account is without merit. I strongly agree with his suggestion that abolition was part of a broader effort to tame the market by setting limits to the pursuit of self-interest. Ashworth evidently imagines that the existence of such an effort is evidence against my thesis, but my argument has never depended on the claim that the preponderance of the market's effects on morality was good. I claim only that the market helped push people across a critical threshold of perception; whether it was on the whole good or bad may be a lively political question, but it is irrelevant to the question of historical causation that concerns us here. Having myself written about some of the quite different forms that this countermovement against the market took in the latter half of the nineteenth century, I can heartily endorse Ashworth's suggestion that the celebration of conscience, the veneration of family life, and the repudiation of slavery ought to be viewed as three aspects of a many-sided campaign to restore moral authority in the face of the market's de-moralizing impact on traditional practices.[69] Much of the history of England and America in these years could be written in terms of this wide-ranging effort at containment, some aspects of which were first described by Karl Polanyi in *The Great Transformation*, a book Ashworth does not mention but in which he would find much support for this part of his argument.[70]

Although I agree that the ideology of antislavery drew strength from these concerns about the widening orbit of legitimized self-interest in capitalist society, the relationship between this ideology and the class interests of those who embraced it is much more ambiguous than Ashworth allows. In a footnote, Ashworth applauds a statement I made in my original article warning that the concept of interest is elastic—so elastic that there is lit-

69. Ashworth, "Relationship between Capitalism and Humanitarianism," 822. See my essay "Professionalism versus Capitalism: R. H. Tawney, Emile Durkheim, and C. S. Pierce on the Disinterestedness of Professional Communities," in *The Authority of Experts: Studies in History and Theory*, T. L. Haskell, ed. (Bloomington, Ind., 1984), 180–225; and *The Emergence of Professional Social Science: The American Social Science Association and the Nineteenth Century Crisis of Authority* (Urbana, Ill., 1977).
70. Karl Polanyi, *The Great Transformation* (New York, 1944).

erally no human act that cannot be construed as self-interested.[71] But he proceeds inadvertently to formulate what deserves to become the classic textbook illustration of the dubious practice I was warning against, by contending that a campaign to inhibit the pursuit of interest was itself an expression of interest. What can one say? Interest can never be ruled out as an explanation of behavior: measures taken to restrain self-interest may in fact have benefited some people more than others, and it is not inconceivable that some of the beneficiaries—whether deliberately, self-deceptively, or by way of "elective affinity," or even "false consciousness"—anticipated the benefit and joined the containment effort in order to achieve that benefit. But the scenario puts a heavy strain on the idea of interest. We can easily imagine a campaign against self-interest that would erect barriers selectively so as to favor the interests of the campaigners, but the campaign that Ashworth describes does not display any obvious biases. The interest he imputes to the campaigners is that of avoiding social "collapse"—an interest not confined to any one class.[72] Even if an entrepreneurial class were to conclude that its self-interest required the erection of barriers against the pursuit of interest, would not other, non-entrepreneurial, classes reap the principal benefits? Instances like this, in which people can be said to be pursuing interest even as they oppose its pursuit, should at least alert us to the elasticity of the concept and point toward the double illusion under which much contemporary scholarship labors: that interest is the only thing that explains human behavior and that, once historians have linked acts with interests that might plausibly account for them, there is nothing left to explain.

Every link in the chain by which Ashworth tries to attach antislavery to class interest is open to objection. Consider first the provocation that is supposed to have set the entire process in motion—the emergence of a class of propertyless laborers, deprived of access to the means of production and forced to sell their labor power on the market. Ashworth is very eager that his readers take this to be the cutting edge of capitalism, rather than anything as general and abstract as "the market," partly, perhaps, because it has a robust Marxian flavor and partly because it permits him to claim that his explanation solves the supposedly knotty mystery of why the abolitionists "selectively" went to the aid of slaves rather than helping exploited workers generally: the problem of legitimating wage labor, he claims, was what they were really grappling with from the very beginning.[73] This claim

71. Ashworth, "Relationship between Capitalism and Humanitarianism," 815 n.6.
72. Ashworth, "Relationship between Capitalism and Humanitarianism," 822.
73. Ashworth, "Relationship between Capitalism and Humanitarianism," 822.

might be plausible if the values that Ashworth describes offered any likely solution to the problems faced by a ruling class seeking to legitimate wage labor. We could understand why the rise of a new class of unruly laborers would inspire fear of crime or revolution or provoke anxiety about the future of republican institutions. But why would it lead specifically to the veneration of family life, the exaltation of conscience, and a general preoccupation with the dangers of self-interest? These are reactions suitable to people whose eyes were fixed not only on the commodification of labor and the problem of controlling an underclass but on the broader problems created by the general breakdown of taboos on the pursuit of self-interest and consequent spread of competitive relations throughout society. "The market" is a term of art referring to this very phenomenon, and, when Ashworth actually addresses the task of explaining the middle-class preoccupation with self-interest, he repeatedly speaks of it as a response to "the spread of the market" rather than wage labor—apparently unaware that this undercuts his concluding exclamation that "it was precisely because of the spread of wage labor that they attacked slavery in the way they did."[74]

Even if we could agree that reformers' heightened concern for conscience and family stemmed from their anxieties about wage labor rather than the market, Ashworth has given us no adequate reason to think that these values were novel enough or determinate enough in their implications for action to account for the attack on slavery. He argues that the increasing number of wage-laborers, hitherto viewed as a slavish class unfit for citizenship in republican society, set in motion a massive shift of attitudes and practices. People searched for and found "new supports for individual morality and the social order" in three things: the family, the home, and individual conscience. "None had previously been ignored," Ashworth assures us, "but all came to be redefined." He goes on to say that, "in societies that had redefined them or were in the process of redefining them, slavery came to appear as a greater and greater evil. Thus a small but growing number of influential individuals were sensitized to the evils of slavery. As they viewed their own society differently, they initiated a new hostility to slavery (and other evils, too) and led the humanitarian movement."[75] Much hinges on just what this redefinition of family and conscience consisted of.

74. Ashworth, "Relationship between Capitalism and Humanitarianism," 822–23, 828. The commodification of labor and the spread of "the market" are not two distinct things between which we must choose; the former is a particular case of the latter and one that it may be important to bring to the forefront in certain contexts. My usage follows that of Polanyi (for whom the countermovement was specifically aimed at containing "the market") and C. B. Macpherson, *The Political Theory of Possessive Individualism: Hobbes to Locke* (Oxford, 1964).
75. Ashworth, "Relationship between Capitalism and Humanitarianism," 822.

Ashworth tells us only that the family lost its economic primacy as a center of production and that both family and conscience gained a new significance as counterweights to the growing force of self-interest. Exactly what it was about these surprisingly familiar and undramatic redefinitions that suddenly "sensitized" people to the evils of an institution that had been tolerated for centuries is none too clear. Ashworth merely asserts, without explaining, that "the heightened concern for the soul and the individual conscience, nourished within the family circle, *necessarily* intensified concern for slavery, which disrupted family ties and offered many temptations and opportunities for the slaveholder to sin" (my emphasis).[76] Evidently, we are expected to believe that, as middle-class people grappled with the problem of wage labor by appealing (never mind the mismatch between means and ends) to the values of disinterestedness, individual conscience, and domesticity, the growing disparity between their high ideals and the lowly life of the slave became so great that they could not stand it any longer.

This conclusion vastly overestimates the determinateness of values and the force of prescriptions. Values are prescriptions: when we value conscience, we embrace a prescription that tells us that the good life consists of attention to an inner voice, one that promises to bring us into conformity with the dictates of universal moral law. When we value hearth and home, we embrace a prescription that identifies the good life with the pleasures of the domestic sphere, as opposed to the cold world outside, and defines duty and fulfillment largely in terms of nurturing the next generation. Nothing in the values named by Ashworth specifies to whom these prescriptions apply; even the most ardent devotees of family and conscience need not feel any obligation to extend these blessings to slaves, or to neighbors, or to the residents of the next town, or to anyone beyond the circle of their closest associates.

Although these prescriptions regarding family and conscience were highly characteristic of middle-class people during the era of abolition, they were not distinctive. They were neither new at that time nor unique to that class. Conscience, in particular, has for centuries stood close to the heart of Christian teachings, and, if we were to look for a plateau when its importance was notably increased, the Reformation of the sixteenth century would be a better candidate than anything that happened in the eighteenth or nineteenth centuries. Family values, too, have had a long history. What redefinition of conscience and family in the eighteenth century could possibly account for the failure of earlier versions of these values, or any others, to provoke hostility to slavery? How could even redefined versions of open-

---

76. Ashworth, "Relationship between Capitalism and Humanitarianism," 827.

ended values like these, which specify nothing inherently about their application, accomplish more toward the overthrow of slavery in a few decades
than had been accomplished over a period of two millennia by the biblical
injunction "Do unto others as you would have them do unto you"? The
Golden Rule is the prescription of prescriptions, and it not only told people
what the good life was but also to whom it should be extended. If that was
not enough to inaugurate the history of active opposition to the institution
of slavery, nothing in the realm of prescription could have done so.

Ashworth loses sight of the central questions. How are we to account for
Davis's finding that practically no one before the eighteenth century saw in
slavery anything worse than a necessary evil? Why at that time did people
who were, by individual disposition, probably no more compassionate or
scrupulous than their ancestors decide that an institution their ancestors
had found tolerable was instead an intolerable evil and set about its destruction? I believe that they did this because of a shift of conventions, which
prompted them to evaluate their responsiblity for suffering within an unprecedentedly broad arena and therefore to feel responsible for suffering
that previous generations had perceived as inaccessibly remote. Ashworth
can only suggest that their family-nurtured ideals of conscientious behavior
rose to such stratospheric heights that they could no longer bear for slaves
not to share in them.

It is especially ironic that Ashworth thinks that my scheme of explanation ignores changes in morality.[77] Here, Davis is closer to the mark. He sees
that the most problematical and disturbing aspect of my explanation is precisely that it puts morality in motion, by giving it roots that run no deeper
than convention. What Ashworth mistakes for a failure to recognize the
historicity of morality is instead my insistence that prescription and practice
not be naively lumped together, as if we could predict how people will act
once we know what prescriptions they embrace. There is no one-to-one relation between prescription and practice; what people do is not merely an
unfolding of the values they embrace. Of course, moral practices change:
no one could write about the rise of antislavery or the emergence of the humanitarian sensibility who doubted this. Prescription also changes, but not
in any way that could explain the emergence of the humanitarian sensibility. To explain that development, we must take into account changes in
the tacitly understood conventions that shape the way prescriptions are interpreted and reconciled (sometimes very circuitously) with practices. That
is what my original essay strove to do, and that is what Ashworth's alternative leaves entirely out of account.

77. Ashworth, "Relationship between Capitalism and Humanitarianism," 819.

Was there anything revealingly selective about the decision of abolitionists to attack chattel slavery rather than labor exploitation generally? One might think that the question could be shelved in view of Davis's concession ("in theory," at least) that an abolitionist sincerely opposed to all forms of oppression might nonetheless have given priority to the slave trade and chattel slavery as "the most flagrant and remediable crimes against humanity."[78] What is there to explain when people choose to attack the most "flagrant" and "remediable" of the "crimes" before them, instead of doing something else? Problems that can be described in terms this strong naturally take priority. Davis has also acknowledged that "everyone knew that white workers were not really slaves." Since no one has ever thought that mistaken identity was an issue, I interpret this to mean that everyone also knew (taking both material and non-material conditions into account) that the plight of wageworkers—an extremely heterogeneous category—was not as severe as that of slaves. Davis has also allowed that the reformers, whatever their shortcomings, "have been vindicated by history: morally, they were right." Surely, history has also vindicated their sense of strategic priorities: as the *National Anti-Slavery Standard* remarked, "the first work of the reformers . . . is to establish universally the right of man to himself." The problem of slavery "underlies all other reforms . . . [for] there can be no universal reform . . . even no partial reform . . . in a nation that holds one-sixth of its people in bondage."[79]

These considerations suggest to me that, although there may be something puzzling about the abolitionists' attitudes toward wage labor and toward the poor generally, there is nothing at all puzzling about their selection of slavery as the problem of highest priority. Ashworth, however, laments my "retreat" from the "crucial" issue of "the selectivity of the abolitionists, their concern with chattel slavery rather than . . . wage slavery." Surprisingly, he concludes that on this point I have practically "noth-

78. Davis, "Reflections on Abolitionism," 800. Davis believes that an abolitionist who thought like this would have left a written record of regrets about the tendency of attacks on slavery to obscure the abusive treatment of wage-laborers. I wonder. One common reaction to political opponents who try to cast doubts on one's motives is simply to ignore them, on the theory that base canards should not be dignified by a reply.
79. Davis,"Reflections on Abolitionism," 809, 810; John R. Commons, *et al.*, eds., *A Documentary History of American Industrial Society*, 10 vols. (New York, 1958), 7: 219. There has been no clear resolution of the immiseration controversy, but for purposes of argument I have assumed in everything that follows that no important difference existed between slaves and free workers at the level of the material conditions of life. No doubt some wage earners were as bad off as slaves, but the heterogeneity of the category "wage labor" makes it very likely that the group as a whole was better off materially than were slaves.

ing to say. . . . Search Haskell's article as we may, we will find nothing that helps answer this question."[80]

Taken at face value, this is a most disheartening response for it suggests that Ashworth has entirely missed the point of my essay, which from start to finish revolved around the problem of selectivity. The keystone of Davis's interpretation in *The Problem of Slavery in the Age of Revolution* was his claim that "as a social force, antislavery was a highly selective response to labor exploitation," one which—not unintentionally, but as a result of an unconscious hegemonic interest about which the reformers deceived themselves—"gave a certain moral insulation to economic activities less visibly dependent on human suffering and injustice."[81] Against this claim by Davis of an unconsciously intended selectivity on the part of the reformers, I have argued that, in a world that overflows with suffering, all humane acts are unavoidably selective. Because no possibility exists of acting unselectively, the fact that the reformers went to the aid of slaves rather than exploited wage-laborers cannot logically be taken to imply any sort of intention, conscious or otherwise, to "morally insulate" the exploitation of wage labor. To say (in the absence of more specific evidence) that the reformers unconsciously intended to perpetuate this or any of the multitude of other evils they left unrelieved is not essentially different from saying that a person who sends a contribution to Oxfam instead of Amnesty International displays an ominous indifference to torture—or that a person who makes the opposite choice thereby reveals a heartless disregard for hunger. The conclusion does not follow, except on the fallacious proposition that "if you are not for us, you are against us." As long as the question of selectivity is posed in hopes of inferring unconscious intentions, then, it is a question *mal posée*.

Ashworth, unlike Davis, rules out unconscious intentions from the start. This puts the question of selectivity on a different, and I think less vulnerable, footing, but the difference comes at a cost, and not all readers will think the cost acceptable. Davis posed the question of selectivity in hopes of inferring unconscious intentions; Ashworth returns to it for the sake of highlighting what he takes to be the reformer's "false consciousness" or, more exactly, the incompleteness of their grasp of reality. Instead of assuming that the reformers knew in their hearts that wageworkers were victims

80. Ashworth, "Relationship between Capitalism and Humanitarianism," 815–16. If selectivity were a problem at all, it would be as much a problem for Ashworth as anyone. Why would the same idealization of family and conscience that supposedly drove middle-class people to liberate slaves not also have driven them to ameliorate the lot of immiserated wageworkers?
81. Davis, *Problem of Slavery in the Age of Revolution*, 251.

of exploitation and that the reformers failed to render aid because they hid that knowledge from themselves, Ashworth assumes that reformers were blinded to the facts of exploitation by their class position. In Ashworth's view, it was the nature of their "involvement in society" that kept them from understanding the real conditions of working-class life, and he takes pains to stress that this is "not a matter of self-deception" but of class-induced ignorance.[82]

This explanatory strategy has the considerable virtue of making it unnecessary to postulate the existence of unconscious intentions (empirically undemonstrable, anyway), yet it retains the claim that the reformers' conduct was governed by their class position—which, at first glance, seems to be the same thing as saying that it was governed by class interest. Like any strategy, however, this one entails certain costs. By conceding that the reformers did not know, either consciously or unconsciously, that they should have gone to the aid of "wage slaves" as well as chattel slaves, Ashworth locates the hegemonic effects of antislavery agitation squarely in the category of unintended consequences. As such, neither the reformers nor anyone else bears responsibility for them. The reformers acted in ignorance, and, although their ignorance resulted from their privileged class position, it is not at all clear how any person or group could be thought blameworthy for failing to perform a duty of which, for whatever reason, they were genuinely ignorant. Ashworth's account has a blander tone than Davis's, and necessarily so, for, in the absence of intentionality and blameworthiness, words like "social control," "class oppression," and "hegemony" lose their bite.[83] It was presumably for this reason that Raymond Williams warned Marxists that, by withdrawing too far from the claim that there is a "process of determination," they risked emptying "of its essential content the original Marxist proposition. . . . Intention, the notion of intention, restores the key question, or rather the key emphasis." In order for an interpretation to be called "Marxist," Williams believed it should at least depict the "organization and structure [of society] . . . as directly related to certain social intentions, intentions by which we define the society, intentions which in all our experience have been the rule of a particular class."[84]

Anyone hoping to defend Ashworth's strategy may have second thoughts at this point and want to reopen the question of just how "ignorant" the

---

82. Ashworth, "Relationship between Capitalism and Humanitarianism," 815.
83. The paradoxical coexistence in the Marxian tradition of moralism with doctrines deeply subversive of the very idea of morality is the subject of Steven Lukes, *Marxism and Morality* (New York, 1985).
84. Raymond Williams, "Base and Superstructure in Marxist Cultural Theory," *New Left Review*, 82 (1973): 7.

reformers were. Perhaps false consciousness produces a sort of ignorance over which people have some control; perhaps it is all a matter of degree; perhaps they could have overcome their class-induced blindness if only they had tried harder. But every step in this direction leads back toward self-deception or some functional equivalent. We mean, by self-deception, a form of ignorance that is self-inflicted and for which the self can be held partly responsible, on the theory that whatever the self can do, it has at least some power to undo. Any modification of false consciousness that would entitle Ashworth to say "they ought to have known better" would be vulnerable to all the same objections that we have already registered against self-deception.

We are now in a better position to appreciate the brilliance of Davis's formulation and see how much was at stake in it. By treating the hegemonic effects of antislavery as a result of intentions that were unconscious, Davis avoided the conspiratorial and reductionist overtones that plagued Eric Williams's interpretation of abolitionism, and yet Davis also retained a strong enough element of intentionality both to account causally for the reformers' comparative indifference to the problems of wage labor and to hold them at least ambiguously responsible for the consequences of that indifference. In contrast, Ashworth can account causally for their indifference—the nature of their "involvement in society" obscured from them the realities of the wage earner's situation—but he has no basis for imputing responsibility. Ashworth's account has victims but no villains, for he attributes the shortcomings of reform to the distortions of consciousness (something we "all possess to a greater or lesser degree") that come from our having to occupy a single vantage point in society, from which the whole can never be apprehended in its entirety.[85] The only villain is the human condition.

Ashworth's abandonment of intentionality may make his interpretation unacceptable in some quarters, but I have no objections on this point. I have argued all along that the hegemonic consequences of antislavery were unintended. The disagreement between Ashworth and myself lies elsewhere, in the reason for the abolitionists' comparative indifference to the suffering of wage earners and the poor. I have no doubt that their attitudes were shaped in part by their social position, but I am not persuaded that this is the main or the most useful explanation. I would distinguish, moreover, between class position and class interest, as two separate and possibly contradictory kinds of influence on perception and ideology. Ashworth lumps them together as if there could be no important difference between them: having accepted the idea that values grow smoothly out of interests, he

85. Ashworth, "Relationship between Capitalism and Humanitarianism," 815.

naturally supposes that interests themselves grow out of class position in an equally regular fashion. There is no justification for these assumptions.

It is undoubtedly true that the reformers, because they came preponderantly from a single, affluent sector of society, had a limited experience of life and made errors when they generalized, as we all must, from their own experience to that of others in their society. Their vision was, then, influenced by their class position, just as Ashworth claims. But this is not at all the same thing as saying that their blind spots were induced by, or served, class interest. The wants, desires, and passions that drive conduct no doubt take shape within the confines of the particular perspective that a person's social position affords, but they can originate anywhere. As Jon Elster has shown, there is no reason to assume that the interests shaped by position necessarily function to reinforce that position or even that the beliefs shaped by interest necessarily serve that interest. These are matters for empirical investigation, not sweeping generalization. Wishful thinking induced by interest, for example, can be fatal to the interest that induced it, and a taste for conspicuous consumption can fritter away the wealth that sustains the taste. The idea that a social situation always induces beliefs that are favorable to the ruling class or conducive to the perpetuation of the status quo is no more plausible than the idea that bad causes always give rise to bad effects, or *vice versa*.[86]

Is it possible, in spite of everything I have said to the contrary, that the comparative insensitivity of the abolitionists to the needs of wage labor was the result of class interest? Of course. Interest can never be ruled out. There is no human act so incontrovertibly disinterested that it cannot be construed as self-interested by enclosing it within a suitable interpretive framework.[87] But the ease with which any sophomore can perform this trick should make us skeptical of its value. Trying to explain events without referring to interests would be absurd, but we can take note of the infinite elasticity of the concept and the obsessiveness of our reliance on it and then develop a certain skepticism in the presence of those of every political persuasion who take it to be the sole proper terminus of explanation.

Let me close with a concrete example of selectivity, partly to bring these abstract issues into tighter focus and partly to satisfy Ashworth's curiosity about how I would explain the abolitionist's comparative unconcern with wage labor. The example is one my critics ought to find congenial, for it

86. Jon Elster, *Sour Grapes: Studies in the Subversion of Rationality* (Cambridge, 1983), 141–66. See also Robert W. Gordon, "Critical Legal Histories," *Stanford Law Review*, 36 (January 1984): 57–125.
87. Haskell, "Capitalism and the Origins of the Humanitarian Sensibility, Part 1," 351 n.32.

lends itself readily to an interpretation in terms of class interest. My aim is not to show that such an interpretation is flatly erroneous—no such demonstration could ever succeed, in my view—but rather to display in a specific case the tendency of explanation-by-interest to terminate inquiry prematurely.

The views of the American abolitionist Wendell Phillips are especially pertinent, because, in spite of his patrician origins, he ultimately came to believe something quite close to what Davis and Ashworth assume that all of the abolitionists would always have believed if their judgment had not been distorted by class interest. In 1871, when Phillips presided over a Labor Reform convention that declared war on the entire system of wage labor, alleging that it "enslaves" the working man and "demoralizes" and "cheats" both him and his employer, he construed the problems of labor in a way that is basically familiar to us today—that is, in a way that sees through the formal liberty of abused wageworkers and situates their problems on a continuum with those of chattel slaves, acknowledging differences in degree, perhaps, but not in kind.[88]

Phillips had not always thought that it made sense to compare wage earners and slaves, much less to lump their problems together as variations on the single theme of labor exploitation. Before the Civil War, like most humanitarian reformers of his generation, Phillips had found the very idea of "wages slavery" to be "utterly unintelligible," at least in the American context. In a remarkable statement in 1847, he acknowledged that manufactured articles were often the products of "unrequited labor" and that complaints against capital and monopoly were well justified in England and Europe, but things were different in America. Between the free laborers of the North and the slaves of the South, he drew a distinction so total as to stagger the imagination of any twentieth-century reader:

> Except in a few crowded cities and a few manufacturing towns, I believe the terms 'wages slavery' and 'white slavery' would be utterly unintelligible to an audience of laboring people, as applied to themselves. There are two prominent points which distinguish the laborers in this country from the slaves. First, the laborers, as a class, are neither wronged nor oppressed: and secondly, if they were, they possess ample power to defend themselves, by the exercise of their own acknowledged rights. Does legislation bear hard upon them? Their votes can alter it. Does capital wrong them? Economy will make them capitalists. Does the crowded competition of cities reduce their wages? They have only to stay at home, devoted to other pursuits, and soon diminished supply will bring the remedy. . . . To

88. Wendell Phillips, *Speeches, Lectures, and Letters,* 2d ser. (Boston, 1894), 152.

economy, self-denial, temperance, education, and moral and religious character, the laboring class, and every other class in this
country, must owe its elevation and improvement.[89]

These are obviously the words of a man who defined the self and its relation to the world in a manner that is extremely formalistic by present standards. Phillips seems not to have recognized any distinction between the
form of freedom and its substance. He seems to have believed that a person
who is physically and legally unconstrained is as free as any human being
ever can be. Some of what he said resembles twentieth-century laissez-faire
conservatism, but the resemblance is largely spurious, and even a reckless
conservative today would be unlikely to assert in public, as Phillips unhesi-
tatingly did, that workers need only practice "economy" in order to become
capitalists in their own right, or that low wages can be raised by staying at
home, or that self-denial, the ballot box, and good character form a sure
path to advancement. These assertions are shot through with implications
of a strongly formalist character, and everything turns on what we make of
this alien element in Phillips's thinking.

The more alien an idea is, the easier it is to dismiss as ideology, but if we
resist this temptation and take what Phillips said as an expression of the way
the world once looked to an acute and certainly conscientious observer, we
immediately discover that his attitude in 1847 toward wage labor is not at
all perplexing—once we grant him his formalist premises. No matter how
unrealistic we may think these premises, once adopted, they lead naturally
and consistently to the conclusion that "wages slavery" is a contradiction in
terms.

The cast of Phillips's mind will not be unfamiliar to students of Victorian
culture in England and America. He wrote as if a normal, healthy, adult self
was an uncaused cause, a pure point of origin, a kind of cornucopia in which
purposeful activity arose out of nothing and surged into the world. To be a
person, in this view, was only incidentally to be a material body, caught up
in nature's endless fabric of cause-and-effect relations and fully subject to
all the natural processes of growth, disease, and decay. The heart of per-
sonhood lay in the will, and the will, though not necessarily supernatural,
was uncanny. The self formed a pure point of origin through its mysterious
capacity of "willing," of almost magically transmuting the evanescent, in-
ward, and private experience of desire and choice into the concrete, outward,

89. Phillips quoted in John R. Commons, *A Documentary History of American
Industrial Society*, 7: 220–21. See also Daniel T. Rodgers, *The Work Ethic in Industrial America, 1850–1920* (Chicago, 1978), 32; and Richard Stott, "British Immigrants and the American 'Work Ethic' in the Mid-Nineteenth Century," *Labor
History*, 26 (Winter 1985): 86–102.

and public phenomenon of action. More mysterious still, the resulting external acts produced consequences that corresponded with, or satisfied, the internal desires—or, at least, could do so if the will allowed itself to be guided by the dictates of reason and knowledge.

The self's ability to trigger causal chains and set events in motion meant that it was very much *in* the world, and yet, because it was always the producer, never merely the product of any antecedent chain of natural causation, it was not quite *of* this world. Every merely natural cause is a transitive link in a chain and can be construed both as cause of what it produces and the effect of some link antecedent to it—which, in turn, can be seen as the effect of some cause still more remote, and so on indefinitely. But the self in the act of willing was seen as a new, non-transitive, causal beginning, independent of everything but the First Cause and His providential order—a very special sort of dependence that even predestinarians insisted did not dilute in the least the self's responsibility for whatever it willingly did.[90] In the world of formalism, the self's every act was deemed voluntary insofar as will was in it, and scarcely anything other than direct physical coercion was thought capable of displacing the will and emptying an act of its voluntary character.

Formalism assigned such a high level of autonomy to the will that the context within which the will formed faded into the distant background, making nearly all deliberate acts appear voluntary. Circumstances, the stuff of environmentalist interpretations of behavior, counted for very little in judging what the self was responsible for. The self was responsible for whatever its activity led to, almost without regard to the circumstances surrounding choice and action. The formalist had no difficulty in recognizing that the will actively assessed its environment and inclined toward one act rather than another *in light of* various circumstantial factors, but to assign these factors causal significance and treat them as the explanation of what the self did would have been to deprive the self of the uncaused character that made it what it was. The cause (and therefore the explanation) of what people did was their choosing to do it, not the circumstances surrounding the choice. We of the twentieth century impute to circumstances a power to mold and induce choice—virtually to cause it and certainly to explain it—that mere circumstances could not possess in a formalist's eyes.

These are the conventional premises defining selfhood and governing the

90. "Man is entirely, perfectly and unspeakably different from a mere machine, in that he has reason and understanding, and has a faculty of will, and so is capable of volition and choice; . . . so that he has liberty to act according to his choice, and to do what he pleases . . . [and so is fully worthy of] praise . . . [or] punishment"; Jonathan Edwards, *Freedom of the Will* (New Haven, Conn., 1957), 370.

allocation of praise, blame, and responsibility that I believe Phillips and most members of his generation shared. They account for what we perceive as his curious insensitivity to the plight of exploited wageworkers and the poor. As seen from our (not necessarily superior) vantage point, Phillips and his contemporaries were blind to an entire range of environmental factors that powerfully influence conduct yet leave people formally free to do as they please. Where we see a deceptive form of freedom, lacking substance, they saw a large and sunlit realm of authentically voluntary choice.

To a person who sees the world as Phillips did in 1847, the difference between a free worker and a slave is not a matter of degree but of quality. Phillips imputed to free workers—a class "neither wronged nor oppressed" and equipped with "ample power to defend themselves"—a degree of autonomy so great that their problems were not commensurable with those of slaves. Free workers, unlike slaves, were masters of their own fate. Even by our twentieth-century standards, there is an irreducible element of voluntariness in even the most fated of contractual arrangements: the free worker can, at a cost, always say "no" and refuse the employment contract. For a formalist, the perceived cost approximates zero because the conditions impelling the employee to accept undesirable conditions of work are assigned little weight.

Because wage earners were thought free to rise or fall to whatever social position corresponded to their inner merit, those who found themselves in a state of misery had little besides themselves to blame. Formalist assumptions did not prevent decent people like Phillips from feeling passive sympathy for a pauper or playing the Good Samaritan in particular cases by "lending a hand" to a person "down on his luck." But there could be no general attack on the institution of wage labor or any systematic attempt to reform the institution (indeed, it could not even be perceived in a causal role), as long as reformers saw the world through lenses that made most of the poor appear to be deeply complicitous in their own suffering. Because formalists perceived the causes of suffering to lie largely in the victims' own apparently unimpeded choices (ultimately, in defects of the will), the only general remedy for their misfortunes was to help them perfect the arts of self-mastery and educate them about the predictable consequences of their actions. The lessons of "economy," "self-denial," "temperance," and "education" thus stood at the head of Phillips's list of priorities. We must struggle to appreciate that, to him and to most members of his generation, this thin gruel was not only an adequate prescription for social improvement but a trenchant identification of what on formalist premises were the vital nutrients of progressive change.

Although, on formalist assumptions, immiserated wage earners were the cause of their own misery, slaves could not possibly be cast in the same causal role.[91] The status of chattel property shrinks to the vanishing point every hint of voluntariness, making the slave the perfect victim, a person whose misery even in formalist eyes is untainted by any suspicion of complicity. It is for this reason that the concern for slavery displayed by Phillips's generation of reformers could be more wholehearted and vehement than their reaction to most other forms of suffering. In the eyes of an observer who makes little or no distinction between formal and substantive freedom, legally free workers bear a large measure of responsibility for their own plight, but the suffering of slaves, being wholly involuntary, is the responsibility of everyone who has any power to stop it.

We can see, then, that the different treatment Phillips accorded to slaves and wage laborers did not result from a discrete bias against wage laborers but from a system of conventional assumptions that colored his and his generation's thinking about all human conduct. This is not the place to sort out the connections between this set of assumptions and the rise of capitalism, or between those two developments and the great upheaval in the conventions governing causal attribution that made reformers of formalists like Phillips (by expanding causal horizons and thereby overcoming the chilling effect of their extravagant concept of voluntariness) and then helped shatter formalism itself. It is indeed true that formalism, like opposition to slavery, "cannot be divorced from the vast economic changes" of the eighteenth and nineteenth centuries, but neither can it be understood as a reflex, however unconscious or indirect, of those changes.[92] No doubt it insulated entrepreneurs against the barbs of conscience and public opinion as they drove hard bargains with workers too poor to "stay at home," waiting for wages to rise. But it had many effects that were not at all congruent with the needs of capitalism and may even have obstructed its path.

The formalist cast of mind was not something capitalism brought into existence. Six hundred years before Phillips was born, Thomas Aquinas defined the outer perimeter of voluntary action no less extravagantly than Phillips did. In an image that Hobbes would borrow four hundred years

---

91. Here I may understate the extravagance (in our eyes) of the formalist concept of voluntariness, for at a more abstract level the question of whether people could ever be thought to have voluntarily renounced their freedom and chosen to become slaves was taken very seriously by several generations of rights theorists, beginning in the early sixteenth century. At a more prosaic level, one of the principal rationales for the legitimacy of slaveowning construed the slave as originally a captive in war, who might well choose slavery over death. See Richard Tuck, *Natural Rights Theories: Their Origin and Development* (Cambridge, 1979), 3, 49, 54, 100; and Davis, *Problem of Slavery in Western Culture*, 117–20.

92. Davis, "Reflections on Abolitionism," 806.

later, and that Aristotle had employed more ambivalently a millennium and
a half earlier, Aquinas, the great codifier of Christian doctrine, insisted that
even a man at sea, who chooses to throw his possessions overboard rather
than risk death in a storm, is acting voluntarily. "That which is done
through fear is voluntary," said Aquinas. "The will cannot be compelled to
act . . . violence cannot be done to the will."[93]

We sense how truly alien to our own experience the perspective of formalism is when we see how literally Aquinas believed that the willing self
was a new causal beginning, a pure point of origin. Turning a radically blind
eye to all the environmental factors that (in our eyes, at least) shape the will
and tailor life's opportunities to the imperatives of a particular social order—to all the factors, in other words, that create a gap between the form
and the substance of freedom—Aquinas denied that there was anything at
all outside the self, anywhere in God's created universe, that could move the
will, other than its own object (the "apprehended good") and the gentle art
of persuasion.

> Now it is a law of providence that everything is moved by its proxi-
> mate cause. . . . But the proximate moving cause of the will is the
> apprehended good, which is its object, and the will is moved by it as
> sight is by color. Therefore no created substance can move the will
> except by means of the apprehended good—in so far, namely, as it
> shows that a particular thing is good to do; and this is *to persuade*.
> Therefore no created substance can act on the will, or cause our
> choice, except by way of persuasion.[94]

We are the heirs today of a revolt against formalism that bore fruit in the
years 1880–1920 and inaugurated the modern era in social thought.[95] To ex-

93. Aquinas and Aristotle, unlike Hobbes, recognized that the seafarer's act is of a
"mixed kind" and that there is a sense in which it is involuntary. But both assigned
clear priority to the sense in which it is voluntary, just as Hobbes did. *Basic Writings
of St. Thomas Aquinas*, Anton C. Pegis, ed., 2 vols. (New York, 1945), 2: 234, 231;
*The Nichomachean Ethics of Aristotle*, D. P. Chase, trans. (New York, 1911), 44–
45 [Book III]; Thomas Hobbes in *British Moralists, 1650–1800*, D. D. Raphael, ed.,
2 vols. (Oxford, 1969), 1: 55 [*Leviathan*, chap. 22].
94. *Basic Writings of St. Thomas Aquinas*, 2: 168–69 [Summa Contra Gentiles,
Book III, chap. 88].
95. Morton White, *Social Thought in America: The Revolt against Formalism*, expanded edn. (Boston, 1957); H. Stuart Hughes, *Consciousness and Society: The
Reorientation of European Social Thought, 1890–1930* (New York, 1958); Talcott
Parsons, *The Structure of Social Action: A Study in Social Theory with Reference
to a Group of Recent European Writers* (New York, 1937); James T. Kloppenberg,
*Uncertain Victory: Social Democracy and Progressivism in European and American
Thought, 1870–1920* (New York, 1986); Haskell, *Emergence of Professional Social
Science*.

pect people who lived prior to this intellectual watershed to share our antiformalist concept of freedom and responsibility is to project into an age
importantly different from ours the deceptively familiar features of our
own world. It is also to underestimate the genuine historical novelty of antiformalism, one prophetic stream of which first struggled into existence in
the thought of Owen, Fourier, Marx, Engels, and a cadre of others, who
were the first to criticize the highly abstract and autonomous characteri-
zation of the self and its relation to the world that came to be known in the
nineteenth century as individualism. To find that the abolitionists defined
freedom formalistically and were therefore more sympathetic to slaves
(whose lack of independence made them perfect victims) than to impoverished wageworkers (whose formally defined freedom meant that they always bore some responsibility for their own misery) is merely to reaffirm
that the likes of Owen and Marx were truly harbingers of a new age who
construed the world in ways that were profoundly unconventional, which is
to say, culturally unavailable to most people of their era.

Given the antiquity of formalism and its centrality in the Christian tradition, the question we need to ask about Wendell Phillips is not why he
"selectively" attacked slavery and ignored the plight of wage-laborers in
1847, but why, a few decades later, he and many others abandoned the premises of formalism and adopted a far less robust concept of the self that put
the entire problem of responsibility and reform in a dramatically new light.
As long as we are mesmerized by the idea of interest, this question cannot
even come up.

If we asked Davis and Ashworth why Phillips changed his mind between
1847 and 1871, we would likely receive an answer that treats twentieth-
century antiformalist assumptions not as anything mediated by convention or emergent in history but simply as reality. Davis's answer would
presumably explain how Phillips managed to stop deceiving himself about
formalistic assumptions that, unconsciously, he had always known were unrealistic. Ashworth—perhaps after hesitating momentarily at the thought
of a change of values without any corresponding change in the interests they
supposedly grew from—would presumably strive to show how Phillips
managed to break the grip of "false consciousness" and began seeing things
in their true light. From both vantage points, Phillips's initial opinion requires explanation, since it was an error, but his later opinion would not
seem to merit an explanation because, when people give up error for truth,
there is nothing to explain. In contrast, if we take the role of conventions
seriously, put interest to one side, and do not press the all-too-human claim
that our own views correspond with reality, Phillips's opinion in 1871 can

be seen as part of a cultural transformation of far-reaching significance, one that we cannot hope to understand until we have charted the entire course of that upheaval in the conventions defining selfhood and governing the allocation of praise, blame, and responsibility that began in the eighteenth century.

# Part 3

## THE DEBATE CONTINUED

# Chapter 9

# Capitalism, Class, and Antislavery

*John Ashworth*

One of the most urgent problems confronting historians today is to relate changes in ideas and consciousness to economic and material change. Articles in *The American Historical Review* have attempted to find connections between the rise of capitalism and the growth of humanitarian sentiment, particularly in regard to slavery.[1] Although the debate was sparked by a lengthy article by Thomas Haskell, it is to David Brion Davis that credit belongs for rekindling interest in this subject. Indeed no other tribute need be paid to Davis than to observe that the entire modern debate over the antislavery movement and its social origins is conducted with constant reference to the interpretation set forth in his two great works *The Problem of Slavery in Western Culture* and *The Problem of Slavery in the Age of Revolution*.[2] Although it is clear that both Haskell and I are critical of some of the views expressed in these volumes, it is, I hope, equally clear that neither of us can claim to be anything more than, as Haskell puts it, a stowaway on board Davis's vessel, each having the temerity to suggest a change of course.

I should like to assess and review some of the arguments that Davis originally proposed, as well as some of the replies he has made to his critics, but it will perhaps be convenient if I begin by considering again the objections

1. Thomas L. Haskell, "Capitalism and the Origins of the Humanitarian Sensibility," 2 parts, *AHR*, 90 (April 1985): 339–61; (June 1985): 547–66; John Ashworth, "The Relationship between Capitalism and Humanitarianism," *AHR*, 92 (October 1987): 813–28; David Brion Davis, "Reflections on Abolitionism and Ideological Hegemony," *AHR*, 92 (October 1987): 797–812; Haskell, "Convention and Hegemonic Interest in the Debate over Antislavery: A Reply to Davis and Ashworth," *AHR*, 92 (October 1987): 829–78.
2. Davis, *The Problem of Slavery in Western Culture* (Ithaca, N.Y., 1966); Davis, *The Problem of Slavery in the Age of Revolution, 1770–1823* (Ithaca, N.Y., 1975).

I made to the change of course that Haskell proposed in his original article. To most of these objections he has offered, as one would expect, substantive and substantial rejoinders, all of which deserve the closest analysis. To one of them, however, he has said nothing. In response to Haskell's claim that the market promotes humanitarianism, I offered the American South as an example of a society that was market-oriented but nevertheless lacked a powerful humanitarian movement. As everyone knows, antislavery in particular receded in the last decades of the antebellum South, precisely at a time when the market was increasing in importance. When considering the case of Holland, Haskell observed in his reply that his thesis "would be severely challenged by evidence of a truly market-oriented society whose members continued to see slavery as nothing worse than a necessary evil." Should we then conclude that the South did not have "a truly market-oriented society"? If so, then the history of that region will have to be rewritten. If not, is Haskell's thesis "severely challenged"? It seems to me that Southern society here lends itself to an analysis that emphasizes hegemony and is extremely difficult to understand without it. I shall return to this later.[3]

A second objection that I made to Haskell's interpretation concerned the contradictory effects of the market. I noted, as he himself had done, that the market might produce, not an increased concern for the public interest, but a greater dedication to the selfish pursuit of private gain. I also pointed out that even if the market did, as Haskell claimed, create an enhanced awareness of causal relations, the result might have been the opposite of the one he posited. That is to say, it would have been logical to agree with Daniel Defoe that the complex web of interdependencies produced by the market was so delicate that it must not be tampered with. In this way the market would have had a paralyzing effect.[4]

Haskell's response was an interesting one. He accepted that the market might have different and contradictory effects, just as water might either save life (by ending a drought, for example) or take it away (in the event of flooding perhaps). He insisted, however, that this in no way weakened his interpretation. I argued that "if one demonstrates that factor $f$ tends both to produce and to prevent result $r$, then to make $f$ a significant cause of $r$, one must show that the productive effects are greater than the preventive ones." Haskell, however, replied that such a project "would be both futile and irrelevant," since both effects could be shown to exist even in a single individual and certainly within an entire society. Hence, he maintained, the

3. Ashworth, "Relationship between Capitalism and Humanitarianism," 818; Haskell, "Convention and Hegemonic Interest in the Debate over Antislavery," 857.
4. Ashworth, "Relationship between Capitalism and Humanitarianism," 817–18.

positive effects that he identified have causal force and explanatory power regardless of the weight of the opposing ones.[5]

How are we to assess this claim? The way to evaluate it is by returning to the question we are both seeking to answer. If Haskell's interpretation set out to explain why certain individuals mounted a humanitarian crusade against evils like slavery, then it is true that no consideration of contradictory effects was needed to confirm the relationship he postulated. But without such a consideration Haskell was discussing individuals, or groups of individuals, rather than a society. For if we re-pose the question so that we ask why a *society* generated a powerful and successful movement against social abuses such as slavery, then it is clear that the kind of project I requested, but which Haskell so scathingly dismissed, is not only relevant but quite indispensable. If we wish to explain the growth of antislavery at a societal level by reference to the market and yet accept that the market both encouraged and deterred humanitarian sentiment, then we are logically required to demonstrate that one set of effects was greater than the other. To return to Haskell's analogy: if we discovered that people were living longer in a particular African country, it would be insufficient to explain this solely by reference to water. We would need to show that the beneficial effects of water were greater than the destructive ones. In other words, we would need to show that the water saved more lives by ending droughts than it took away by flooding. Until we did so, we could not expect our explanation to command widespread acceptance.

There are thus two different questions being discussed here, one concerning individuals, one concerning societies. Sometimes Haskell wrote as if he were confining himself to the first, more limited one. But this is, from his own point of view, inadvisable. Are we to believe that the process by which the reformers were motivated does not help us understand how the broad social change was effected? Not only does this appear unlikely, it reduces considerably the claims Haskell made. Or rather it ought to reduce them. For Haskell at times appeared to believe that he had answered the wider question as well as the narrower one. Consider the final paragraph of his original article:

> Within little more than one long lifetime after Woolman wrote, slavery, an ancient institution from which millions of people profited, directly or indirectly, was completely overthrown in North

5. *Ibid.*, 817; Haskell, "Convention and Hegemonic Interest in the Debate over Antislavery," 860. Haskell also misunderstood my purpose here, perhaps because he took my terms "positive" and "negative" to mean good and bad respectively. My concern was not with the desirability or otherwise of market-inspired changes but with their overall effect. I was using "positive" to mean causal of a particular effect and "negative" to mean causal of the opposite effect.

America and the British empire. In spite of the enormous interests at stake, the rarity, even among abolitionists, of notions of racial equality, and the availability in England and America of a political-legal culture strongly oriented to the defense of property rights, surprisingly few people were willing to defend those who owned property in slaves. Thus, an institution, which, had it been evaluated in purely technical terms, might have represented a solution to the problems of labor discipline that modernizers everywhere confronted, was abruptly abandoned. This astounding reversal of fortunes does not testify to the importance of "interests," which could as easily be said to have favored the opposite outcome, or to the autonomous power of high ideals, which are, in themselves, compatible with many levels of passivity and activism. What it shows instead is the force of the conventions that govern causal perception and moral responsibility, without which we would not know what our interests are or what it means to be responsible.[6]

Clearly this is the conclusion to an article that set out to consider why certain societies abolished slavery. I believe that Haskell is well advised to maintain this, the larger of the two claims for "the conventions" upon which he focuses our attention. But in so doing, he will have to confront more fully than he has yet done the problem I noted. Just as societies are not reducible to the individuals who compose them, so societal changes cannot be explained solely by reference to the individuals who urge them.

Perhaps the major criticism I leveled against Haskell's interpretation, however, concerned his treatment of values and morality. At times Haskell seemed to recognize that values had changed regarding slavery, an institution which had once been "routinely defended and hardly ever condemned outright." Yet when the starving stranger analogy was used, a subtle shift in argument occurred, so that the problem was apparently not to explain a change in morality but instead to account for the translation into action of preexisting moral commitments. I then wondered whether the assumption underlying this error was that values in general change when the conventions concerning their application alter. Since it is obvious that this causal process can easily be reversed, I was led to accuse Haskell of a tendency to "technological determininism." To this Haskell made the following reply: "Ashworth fears that my scheme falls victim to 'technological determinism' because it does not allow for the possibility that people might first feel responsible for suffering and then seek means (technologies) for doing something about it."[7]

6. Haskell, "Capitalism and the Origins of the Humanitarian Sensibility, Part 2," 566.
7. Haskell, "Capitalism and the Origins of the Humanitarian Sensibility, Part 1,"

This, of course, was not at all the argument that I offered. I did not speak of a feeling of responsibility, but rather of a prior belief that slavery was something that should be viewed as an evil. Haskell's use of the word "responsibility," however, allowed him to slide some way back to his favorite theme of "recipe knowledge." He took another step in this direction when he emphasized that this "responsibility" was to be understood as an "operative" one. By this time he had moved so far from the actual criticism I offered that he was able simply to reaffirm his original thesis: "Ashworth fails to recognize that no one can 'feel responsible' (operatively responsible, as opposed to feeling passive sympathy) for suffering whose knowledge of cause-and-effect relations is so limited that he or she cannot imagine any course of action that would relieve the suffering. Responsibility presupposes possession of some threshold level of recipe knowledge, and the entire point of my scheme is to account for the crossing of that threshold."[8]

It is clear that Haskell's reply did not even begin to meet the objection raised, but it is also clear from what he says elsewhere that the explanation for his lack of interest in changing morality was different from what I had supposed. It lay instead in his understanding of the Golden Rule and of Western society's commitment to it.

According to Haskell, Western man is committed (at the level of prescription) to the Golden Rule, by which one is exhorted to "do unto others as you would have them do unto you." To this he attaches enormous importance. For "the rule of reciprocity that the Golden Rule embodies is so central to moral judgment that everything else that can be said by way of prescribing moral duty is gilding the lily." As a result any changes that took place in the realm of values can safely be ignored by the historian concerned to explain the rise of antislavery. As Haskell confidently put it: "If that [the Golden Rule] was not enough to inaugurate the history of active opposition to the institution of slavery, nothing in the realm of prescription could have done so." The problem then, according to Haskell, is to explain how the rise of capitalism led people to translate their commitment to the Golden Rule into action in novel ways from the eighteenth century onward.[9]

For this reason Haskell developed the lengthy comparison with the starving stranger in the twentieth century and explored the reasons why, despite our belief in the Golden Rule, we do not immediately go to his aid. After all, we would ourselves desire such aid if we were starving. He then located our

---

339; Haskell, "Convention and Hegemonic Interest in the Debate over Antislavery," 851 n.46.

8. Haskell, "Convention and Hegemonic Interest in the Debate over Antislavery," 851 n.46.

9. Haskell, "Convention and Hegemonic Interest in the Debate over Antislavery," 849, 867.

failure to act outside the realm of values. Yet this is a gross oversimplification, resulting from an extremely narrow and one-dimensional view of values. While it is true that most people might affirm a general commitment to the Golden Rule if they were questioned about it, it is equally true that they might affirm a commitment to other values which determine or limit its application. For example, the need for a parent to provide care for a child is equally well entrenched in Western culture, and yet it might very well conflict with the requirement to go to the aid of a starving stranger. More generally, a commitment to the values of Western capitalism—self-help, individualism, the nation—and to its goals—wealth, power, consumption—can, and does, undermine concern for the starving in the third world. So we need a full and empathic understanding of the ideas, beliefs, and assumptions of the individuals involved. Haskell, however, in his treatment of the starving stranger as well as his discussion of the humanitarian movement of the eighteenth and nineteenth centuries, abandoned discussion of values far too quickly in order to focus our interest on the ways in which highly abstract moral commitments are put into practice. He then emphasized recipe knowledge and "convention" in order to explain why we do not go to the aid of the starving stranger. The deficiencies of this view, however, become apparent if we ask why people do not employ a recipe that is familiar to us all: bequest. It is easy to arrange for one's wealth to be disposed of after one's death, and there are even a few individuals who donate it to third world charities. Why is this not more common? A major reason is that it conflicts with other values that Western men and women espouse. Haskell might reply that this brings us back to the realm of "convention," and it is true that "convention" does not encourage the practice. But to say this is merely to say that the practice is uncommon because it is uncommon. "Convention" in this context (as so often when he used it) has no explanatory power.[10]

10. Haskell, "Capitalism and the Origins of the Humanitarian Sensibility, Part 1," 354–61. These difficulties with the Golden Rule point to another problem in Haskell's work. Although his articles show an awareness of the extent of suffering in the world today (as well as in the past) that I personally find admirable, there is no recognition that much of this is directly consequent upon the operation of the prevailing social system. To put it slightly differently, suffering is often consequent upon exploitation, and exploitation is often functionally necessary for a given set of social structures. Thus if slavery generates a large portion of the wealth that supports a society and sustains a specific class, then to attack it will be to court the most determined opposition of that class and of large numbers of people who have an ideological or material stake in the maintenance of that society. Similarly, a proposal to bring all the resources of the West to bear on the problem of third world poverty would engender the most ferocious opposition from those who argue that such an effort would create massive social and economic dislocation. Such opposition con-

Haskell took pains to demonstrate that interpretations which stress "interests" are unsatisfactory because there is no action that cannot be so construed and because, as he claimed, such interpretations will tend to close off further discusssion prematurely.[11] Yet ironically these deficiencies are precisely those that his own view entails. The Golden Rule is compatible with almost any set of values, ranging from the most to the least humane. Consider, for example, the treatment of prisoners. It would be quite logical for someone to oppose prison reform on the grounds that if he had been found guilty of a specific crime, he would himself expect to be treated harshly. As far as the starving stranger is concerned, a logical, if not particularly admirable, response from an exponent of the Golden Rule would be to the effect that in a similar situation, he would expect, not people thousands of miles away, but rather his own government, or father, or children to come to his aid. In other words, the Golden Rule is utterly elastic. It is surprising that Haskell needs to be reminded of this, for we need look no further than Davis's *Problem of Slavery in Western Culture* to see that its exponents could even excuse slavery. "Both Catholics and Protestants," Davis noted, "were able to reconcile slavery with the Golden Rule by piously affirming that masters should treat their bondsmen as they themselves would be treated, should they have the misfortune of becoming slaves." The extraordinarily heavy emphasis Haskell placed on the Golden Rule thus led him to terminate his discussion of values far too early, to look prematurely to "convention," and, as we shall see, to miss the significance of some of the shifts in values that his own work identified.[12]

As David Brion Davis showed, slavery had been "associated with certain religious and philosophical doctrines that gave it the highest sanction." The attack upon it throughout the Western world thus represented a dramatic revision of these accepted truths. It is, to say the least, curious that Haskell believes that because of the existence of the Golden Rule, changes in values play no part in explaining this revision. Indeed his own work suggested otherwise. Noting the increase in promise-keeping that occurred from the late eighteenth century on, he argued that this encouraged "new levels of scru-

---

stitutes a major reason why these reforms are not attempted. It is at this point that the elasticity of the Golden Rule (as well as other maxims) allows it to assume a shape that permits the maintenance of the status quo. To understand the failure to act in terms of "convention" is, to say the least, unsatisfactory.

11. Haskell, "Capitalism and the Origins of the Humanitarian Sensibility, Part 1," 351 n.32; Haskell, "Convention and Hegemonic Interest in the Debate over Antislavery," 872.

12. Davis, *Problem of Slavery in Western Culture*, 308. We should note that the irony in this passage is present because Davis detected self-deception. Haskell, however, would not accept this.

pulosity in the fulfillment of ethical maxims."[13] Why it did not also encourage the development of new ethical maxims, which might have
antislavery implications, we were never told. In my response to Haskell I
claimed that an adequate explanation for the emergence of antislavery
would need to pay special attention to the growth of wage labor, and Haskell
confirmed this when he declared that capitalism requires a "sovereign individual," one "whose freedom would continue to be conditioned by his
promises." For otherwise "the individual cannot be said to possess his capacity to perform labor at some future time, or to be free to dispose of his
labor to others for due compensation." It is remarkable that Haskell did not
realize that this self-possessed individual is the antithesis of the slave. The
most valuable part of Haskell's analysis is that which dealt with changing
values, but he did not draw the conclusion that was staring him in the face.
As Davis put it: "Haskell failed to see that thinking causally, keeping promises, learning to calculate and compute, and taking responsibility for the remote consequences of one's actions is precisely the kind of behavior that
slavery proscribed. How could a slave be expected to keep all promises or
make reasonable choices? Slavery stood in direct opposition to all the virtues inculcated by the market." Davis argued—I believe correctly—that
the inculcation of these virtues was very much in the interests of the capitalist class. Haskell, however, has a peculiar approach to the question of interests, one which creates great difficulties and which ultimately, I think,
cripples his attempt to understand social change. I shall return to this
later.[14]

In his original article, Haskell claimed that a series of changing practices
led to new applications of the Golden Rule. This prompted a third criticism
of his analysis: it failed to explain the selectivity of the abolitionists, their
concern with slavery rather than with wage labor. Haskell then met this
criticism with a cogent examination of the views of American abolitionist
Wendell Phillips. Phillips, he noted, subscribed to a highly formalistic view
of freedom, which allowed him to conclude that even a pauper, since he was
not subjected to the coercion a slave faced, was "free." Phillips, Haskell concluded, "seems to have believed that a person who is physically and legally
unconstrained is as free as any human being ever can be." Thus formalism
explains the abolitionists' emphasis on the evils of slavery rather than the
problems of wage labor.[15]

13.  Davis, *Problem of Slavery in Western Culture*, ix; Haskell, "Capitalism and the
Origins of the Humanitarian Sensibility, Part 2," 555.
14.  Ashworth, "Relationship between Capitalism and Humanitarianism," *passim*;
Haskell, "Capitalism and the Origins of the Humanitarian Sensibility, Part 2," 553;
Davis, "Reflections on Abolitionism and Ideological Hegemony," 812.
15.  Ashworth, "Relationship between Capitalism and Humanitarianism," 815–16;

At this point, all readers were doubtless wondering what it was that explained formalism. They were perhaps especially keen to see how a view that was so obviously of benefit to the capitalist class could be explained without referring to interests. But, if so, they were to be greatly disappointed. For, instead of an explanation, Haskell, in what was by far the weakest part of his rejoinder, presented an extraordinary set of non sequiturs and red herrings, the effect of which (since clearly there was neither conscious nor unconscious intention involved!) was simply to obfuscate the issue.

First he asked whether, "in spite of everything I have said to the contrary," it was possible that "the comparative insensitivity of the abolitionists to the needs of wage labor was the result of class interest." The answer was surprising: "Of course. Interest can never be ruled out." But at this point Haskell returned to the argument he made in his original article to the effect that all actions, even the most altruistic, can be explained in terms of interest. I originally welcomed this argument in that it did invite historians to be more careful than they sometimes are in their use of the term "interest." I never had any suspicion that it would be used to claim that all interpretations emphasizing interests should be seen as utterly vacuous. Yet this is apparently the claim Haskell was making, for after acknowledging that interest "can never be ruled out," he added that "there is no act so incontrovertibly disinterested that it cannot be construed as self-interested by enclosing it within a suitable interpretive framework." However, "the ease with which any sophomore can perform this trick should make us skeptical of its value." Here it was Haskell who had performed the conjuring trick, though one unlikely to impress any readers who had difficulty imagining a history of human society that gives no explanatory weight to interests.[16] Perhaps for this reason, Haskell, once again forced to recognize that the example of Phillips "lends itself readily to an interpretation in terms of class interest," quickly changed tack and claimed that an "explanation by interest" tends "to terminate enquiry prematurely." But it clearly did not have this effect on his own "enquiry," since he soon announced that "this is not the place to sort out the connections between this set of assumptions [formalism] and the rise of capitalism." This would indeed be news to his readers, most of whom had, I suspect, formed the opinion that a primary purpose of the original article was to show the inadequacy of an interpretation based on class interests and to suggest an alternative. For David Brion Davis and for me, the selectivity of the abolitionists here is a clue to the im-

Haskell, "Convention and Hegemonic Interest in the Debate over Antislavery," 872–78.
16. Haskell, "Convention and Hegemonic Interest in the Debate over Antislavery," 872.

portance of class interests in the development of antislavery in particular and of humanitarianism in general. Haskell, however, seemed to want to refute the argument while ignoring the evidence presented in support of it.[17]

In fact, there is no reason to believe that an emphasis on class interest will terminate the enquiry prematurely, and it may even be that Haskell himself was not convinced that it would. For he next argued that some of the tenets of formalism preceded the development of capitalism and even went so far as to quote Saint Thomas Aquinas. He then concluded that "given the antiquity of formalism and its centrality in the Christian tradition," we should hardly be asking why Phillips " 'selectively' attacked slavery and ignored the plight of wage-laborers in 1847." Again the reasoning was defective. Aquinas, of course, was so little an abolitionist that, in Davis's words, "at times . . . [he] suggested that the principle of slavery was part of the governing pattern of nature." So a dilemma confronts Haskell. If formalism can include within it a defense of slavery, Phillips's selectivity cannot be explained by reference to formalism. And if formalism cannot encompass slavery, why cite defenders of slavery as if they embraced its essential tenets? The answer is, of course, that Haskell was out to disable all interpretations based on class interest.[18]

Even this did not exhaust his arguments against a class-interest interpretation. He also suggested that formalism "had many effects that were not at all congruent with the needs of capitalism and may even have obstructed its path." What these effects were we were not told, but even if they had been identified, Haskell's case would still not have been established. For he was now shifting attention away from causes to consequences. Even if the consequences were partly dysfunctional for capitalism, this would in no way preclude the possibility that class interests go far toward explaining the emergence of formalism. Haskell elsewhere actually stated that "there is no reason to assume that the interests shaped by class position necessarily function to reinforce that position or even that the beliefs shaped by interest necessarily serve that interest." This statement alone demonstrates the danger of refuting a claim about causes by evidence concerning consequences.[19]

The most extraordinary part of Haskell's reply, however, came when he noted that Wendell Phillips subsequently changed his view of the condition

17. Haskell, "Convention and Hegemonic Interest in the Debate over Antislavery," 872, 876.
18. Haskell, "Convention and Hegemonic Interest in the Debate over Antislavery," 876–77; Davis, *Problem of Slavery in Western Culture*, 94.
19. Haskell, "Convention and Hegemonic Interest in the Debate over Antislavery," 876, 872.

of the wage-laborer and concluded that he was indeed exploited. This interesting reversal of opinion on Phillips's part was one that the historian may well wish to explain. For some reason, however, Haskell claimed that neither Davis nor I would be interested in explaining it. Apparently I (and Davis too) believe that "when people give up error for truth, there is nothing to explain." In my reply to Haskell, I put forward what was intended as the beginnings of an interpretation of the rise of humanitarian movements like temperance and antislavery. Davis, for his part, has devoted volumes to these subjects. Has Haskell formed the impression that we are both in favor of alcoholism and slavery?[20]

Why did the quality of Haskell's argumentation plummet here? In his original article he sought to demonstrate that an interpretation which stressed class interest needed to show that the pursuit of class interest was intended. The intention might be conscious or it might be unconscious, but, in Haskell's words, "to say that a person is moved by class interest is to say that he *intends* to further the interests of his class, or it is to say nothing at all." My task was to show that this view was, quite simply, wrong. In his rejoinder, Haskell very sensibly abandoned this position. Such at least would seem to have been his purpose when he wrote that "this was a strong assertion and not one I would wish to detach from its original argumentative context and set up as a general methodological imperative." Yet it was apparent that he could see no way of integrating class interests into his scheme—or any other—if they were not furthered either intentionally or by chance. Hence he was uncomfortable with them, even while he recognized that they could not be ignored.[21]

It would be a mistake to deny, however, that this is a major theoretical problem. It is one that Davis also failed to resolve. Unlike Haskell, Davis was convinced that class interests played a major role in the emergence of humanitarianism, but he too did not see how they could be furthered other than by intention or by chance. Hence he made the following claim: "If we have empirical evidence that a group of historical actors believed they were advancing the interests of all humanity when they were actually advancing the interests of a special class, we can justifiably speak of self-deception." If Davis meant by this that such "empirical evidence" is sufficient to make the

20. Haskell, "Convention and Hegemonic Interest in the Debate over Antislavery," 878. There is, of course, no reason why one should not explain the origin of ideas one accepts. Antiformalism I would explain (roughly) in terms of the growth of large collectivities, cities, units of production, and so on, dwarfing the individual.
21. Haskell, "Capitalism and the Origins of the Humanitarian Sensibility, Part 1," 347; Haskell, "Convention and Hegemonic Interest in the Debate over Antislavery," 862.

case for self-deception, the statement is simply false. There is another way in which to theorize the furthering of class interests.[22]

In my reply to Haskell, however, I did not engage in such theorizing. I took my cue from his assertion that for someone to be moved by class interest, an intention must be present. In this context, I wrote that "one can say that a person is moved by certain ideals that have grown out of class interest," and then argued that this might still be the case when there was no intention of promoting class interest.[23] In response to Haskell's counter-assertion, I wanted to show that ideas *could* in certain circumstances promote the interest of certain groups or classes without any intention, conscious or otherwise, being present. I had no wish to imply that all ideas should be so viewed. If the sentence above can be read as Haskell has read it, it can also be read in the way I intended, and the rest of the article, I believe, supports the second reading. Indeed, when I went on to advance an alternative view, I made no claim that all the ideas or ideals I was considering should be understood as having simply and unproblematically "grown out of" class interest. My alternative interpretation was merely the briefest attempt to show that there was another way of linking humanitarianism and capitalism in terms of a shift in values occasioned by the latter and giving rise to the former. Although class interest is certainly involved in this process, I did not, because of the complexity of the subject, theorize it at this point. Most of Haskell's objections to my argument disappear when this is recognized. Since I perhaps failed to clarify my position on this question, I shall return to it later.

Before I do so, however, it may be appropriate to consider the alternative interpretation I advanced in the light of the criticisms it might attract. It is important to demonstrate that such an interpretation is not vulnerable to the objections that can be made to Haskell's scheme. At the risk of oversimplifying, I shall attempt to represent diagramatically the different positions we are taking on the origins of antislavery and humanitarianism generally. Diagrams 1 and 2 illustrate our different interpretations.

First, the problem of selectivity. I argued that the economic changes associated with capitalism caused a shift in values which in turn made slavery appear much worse. The legitimation of wage labor encouraged a perception of the conscience and of the family as supports for a new social order.[24] The

22. Davis, "Reflections on Abolitionism and Ideological Hegemony," 802.
23. Ashworth, "Relationship between Capitalism and Humanitarianism," 815.
24. Note in this connection Seymour Drescher's remark that Manchester, a town of the uprooted, was particularly "moved by Clarkson's focus on the peculiar terrors of the slave trade: loss of kin, hearth and community." Drescher, *Capitalism and Antislavery* (London, 1986), 72, 267–68.

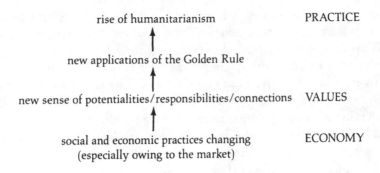

rise of humanitarianism        PRACTICE

↑

new applications of the Golden Rule

↑

new sense of potentialities/responsibilities/connections    VALUES

↑

social and economic practices changing        ECONOMY
(especially owing to the market)

Diagram 1.   Haskell's position

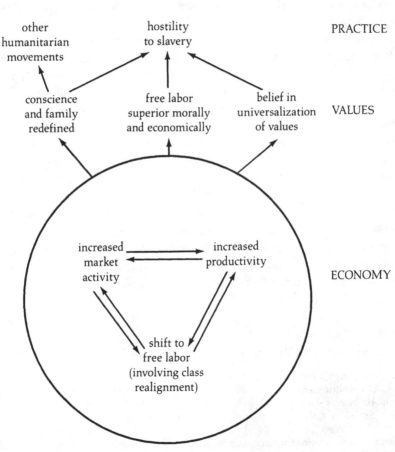

Diagram 2.   Ashworth's position

act of selling labor power was viewed, we might say, formalistically—that is, as a free and unconstrained exchange between two consenting parties. Thus we may follow Haskell in explaining the selectivity of the abolitionists, their concern with the miseries of the slave rather than those of the wage-laborer, by reference to formalism. But we can depart from him in viewing formalism as, in good part, an expression of class interest. It is true that formalism cannot be explained as a simple, direct reflex of class, since a highly complex series of mediations was involved. But, as we shall see, class interest must nonetheless play a key role in the explanation.[25]

Similarly, the problem Haskell encountered with the Golden Rule, arising from its elasticity, is absent from an interpretation that emphasizes much more specific values. The belief that all men should operate with formalistic freedom, but guided by family and conscience, implies a great deal—antislavery, temperance, Bible promotion, and so on—and reformers typically embraced all these (and other) projects. But these values are not infinite in their application.

Next we need to consider the overall societal shift away from slavery. There is no reason to assume that whatever was the primary motive of abolitionists was the primary consideration of the legislators who actually abolished slavery. On the other hand, it would be strange if some of the same factors were not present in each group. In fact, it seems likely that, in the United States at least, the same factors were present but in different proportions. Thus abolitionists believed that slavery had detrimental effects on economic performance, though this was not their major concern. On the other hand, the Republican party, whose triumph in 1860 was the signal for secession, Civil War, and eventually abolition, was made up of men who disliked slavery on moral grounds but who were nevertheless far more likely to stress its economic effects.[26] In each case, the relationship between slave and slaveholder, rather than the mere existence of the market, was at the center of attention. Thus there is reason to believe that similar causes were at work both in promoting abolition as a reform movement and in bringing about the actual destruction of slavery.

In his rejoinder, Haskell raised a series of objections to my interpretation. Most of them were directed against the view that analysis can move simply and unproblematically from class position to class interests to values. Any-

25. Ashworth, "Relationship between Capitalism and Humanitarianism," 821–28.
26. On abolitionism, see, e.g., Ronald G. Walters, *The Antislavery Appeal: American Abolitionism after 1830* (Baltimore, 1976); on the Republicans, see Eric Foner, *Free Soil, Free Labor, Free Men: The Ideology of the Republican Party before the Civil War* (New York, 1970). As I observed in my earlier essay, a complete explanation of the relationship between capitalism and humanitarianism must take full account of the different economic effects of wage and slave labor.

one who takes this view would be well advised to pay close attention to Haskell's remarks on this subject, but since it is a view I have always rejected, no further discussion is needed here. Of more importance is his claim that the process I describe cannot explain the growth of humanitarianism in general or antislavery in particular. Haskell's critique is in two parts. First, he denies that the emphasis on conscience and the family was sufficiently novel or potent in its effects to explain the emergence of the humanitarian movement. Second, he asks why "the rise of a new class of unruly laborers" should "lead specifically to the veneration of family life, the exaltation of conscience, and a general preoccupation with the dangers of self-interest?" These, he asserts, "are reactions suitable to people whose eyes were fixed not only on the commodification of labor and the problem of controlling an underclass but on the broader problems created by the general breakdown of taboos on the pursuit of self-interest and consequent spread of competitive relations throughout society." All of which is to reaffirm, not the importance of wage labor, but instead the role of the market.[27]

On this last point we are not in complete disagreement, for I do believe that the existence of a market for labor will result in greater market activity generally.[28] Capitalism, if it is defined so as to require the existence of wage labor, is likely to create a need for restraints, some but not all of which will concern the need to subdue the underclass. If it is Haskell's intention to argue that these restraints are not reducible to class antagonisms, then we are in agreement. If it is his intention to claim that they can be understood without a heavy emphasis on class and class conflict, then we are not. In order to explain the link between wage labor and the values of domesticity and conscience, I shall refer to Paul E. Johnson's recent study of religious revivalism in the United States. Since the mechanisms involved are subtle ones, it will be necessary to spend some time restating the argument of this excellent study. My purpose is not, of course, to assess the empirical data Johnson presents, but rather to satisfy Haskell's doubts about the relationships I am postulating.

*A Shopkeeper's Millennium* is a study of revivals in Rochester, New York, in the 1830s. It deals with temperance at some length but hardly at all with antislavery. Nevertheless, the links between abolitionism and both Evangelicalism and the revival have been well established. Moreover, it is the emergence of specific values and their relationship to the growth of wage labor that are of most concern here. In this connection, Johnson notes that

27. Haskell, "Convention and Hegemonic Interest in the Debate over Antislavery," 865–66.
28. One of the effects of a market for labor is a deepening of the division of labor. This in turn entails more market transactions.

"the 1820s witnessed the beginnings of large-scale manufacturing in American cities," and that "with it came attempts to subject farm boys and preindustrial artisans to the discipline and monotony of modern work." To fight this battle, masters frequently used religious weapons, and "their most favored means of combating drunkenness, spontaneous holidays, and inattention to work were the temperance society, the Sunday school, and the revival." As a result "the crucial first generation of industrial conflict in this country was fought largely along religious lines."[29]

The task for the masters was to promote Christian self-control, partly because they themselves needed to establish a reputation for honesty and reliability, but also because of the transformation in the nature of work and in the spatial distributions in the city. As production increased in pace, scale, and regularity, so conviviality between masters and workers diminished. The practice of consuming alcohol at work was discontinued, and workers ceased to live at their place of employment. Traditional social relations were breaking down and being replaced by newer ones. After work "masters walked down quiet side streets and entered households that had seceded from the marketplace. Separated from work and workingmen, they and their wives and children turned the middle-class family into a refuge from the amoral economy and disorderly society outside its doors." One result was a "new ethos of family life." Yet "every night the sounds of quarrels, shouting, and laughter from the poorer quarters invaded their newly secluded domestic worlds." The new ethos called for "standards of discipline, self-control, and domesticity that banned liquor." It was one that had grown out of "the new relationship between master and wage earner."[30]

The role of evangelical religion in the process was of vital importance. In effect, it absolved the masters of responsibility "by teaching that virtue and order were products not of external authority but of choices made by morally responsible individuals." The task of the Christian gentleman was now not to govern his men in the manner of the traditional patriarch but instead "to educate them and change their hearts." In this sense "the Rochester revival served the needs . . . of entrepreneurs who employed wage labor" and "evangelicalism was a middle class solution to problems of class, legitimacy, and order generated in the early stages of manufacturing." Not only did the new values function "as powerful social controls"; they also, in their emphasis on the spiritual freedom and autonomy of every man, "enabled masters to present a relationship that denied human interdependence as the realization of Christian ideals."[31]

29. Paul E. Johnson, *A Shopkeeper's Millenium: Society and Revivals in Rochester, New York, 1815–1837* (New York, 1978), 6.
30. *Ibid.*, 8, 25, 57, 53, 60, 106.
31. *Ibid.*, 111–12, 137–38.

Johnson is careful to point out that these entrepreneurs were not involved in a conspiracy to construct a religion to meet their economic and
social requirements. Rather, they experienced the problems of disobedience
and disorder as religious ones and sought religious solutions. (We might go
so far as to employ the terminology Haskell finds so deeply displeasing and
claim that their consciousness was, in this respect, a false one.) The new
religion taught that traditional "relations of direct dependence" actually
"prevented underlings from discovering the infinite potential for good that
was in each of them." Johnson's concluding lines are worth quoting in full:

> Workingmen who continued to drink and carouse and to stay away
> from church were no longer considered errant children; they were
> free moral agents who had chosen to oppose the Coming Kingdom.
> They could be hired when they were needed, fired without a qualm
> when they were not. Thus a nascent industrial capitalism became
> attached to visions of a perfect moral order based on individual free-
> dom and self-government, and old relations of dependence, servility,
> and mutuality were defined as sinful and left behind. The revival
> was not a capitalist plot. But it certainly was a crucial step in the
> legitimation of free labor.[32]

Johnson's work makes it easy to perceive the connections that Haskell is
so reluctant to admit, since the growth of wage labor, with its attendant
problems, is the prime mover in the entire process. But unlike Davis, Johnson makes no claim that the masters have engaged in self-deception. On the
contrary, he credits them with the utmost sincerity. They were responding
to problems they experienced as religious ones, and they devised religious
and moral solutions. Although Johnson does not deal with antislavery at all,
it is quite apparent that the view of humanity entailed by the evangelical
revival made slavery abhorrent. The masters were clearly motivated by class
interest, but it was an interest mediated most obviously through the prism
of religion. If we were to assume that similar individuals were prominent
in the abolition movement, then we would not be committed to the view
that abolition was a simple reflex of class interest. But we would necessarily
conclude that class interest was a major causal force.

Finally, Haskell raised another objection to my interpretation when he
claimed that it "vastly overestimates the determinateness of values and the
force of prescriptions." Thus he asked why a veneration for home and conscience should lead to a concern for slaves, since "nothing in the values
named by Ashworth specifies to whom these prescriptions apply; even the
most ardent devotees of family and conscience need not feel any obligation
to extend these blessings to slaves, or to neighbors, or to the residents of the

32. *Ibid.*, 140–41.

next town, or to anyone beyond the circle of their closest associates." Haskell believes the process I am describing is one that involves no less than "a paroxysm of ideological consistency."[33]

Why Haskell should find such a process so curious is itself curious. The idea of an ideological spill-over is quite familiar to historians and need provoke no feeling of astonishment. Thus, to cite a single example, Bernard Bailyn in *The Ideological Origins of the American Revolution* speaks of the "contagion of liberty" and shows how the rhetoric and the values generated by the revolutionary struggle made Americans increasingly critical of many practices and institutions in their own states.[34] It is perhaps because Haskell is mesmerized by the Golden Rule and the inability of any human being fully to act upon it (given the necessity for selectivity) that he grossly *underestimates* the determinateness of values. As we have seen, men and women may embrace other values that are not so elastic.

The belief in the universality of what we can term formalistic values should itself be treated as an idea in need of explanation. Rather than describing the move from prescription to practice in terms of "convention," it is better to recognize that practice itself has an ideational component.[35] How are we to explain the confidence in formalism that was a hallmark of the mid-Victorian mind? The answer to this question is obviously a complex one, but it is apparent that in the nineteenth century there were good reasons for the belief that values were universally applicable. The great material transformations of the era encouraged the idea that the riddles of human existence had been solved. The resulting confidence made for the view that the values of the age were universally valid. All classes and all races in the North, and indeed elsewhere, could progress with them, so the maltreatment of the slaves was all the more inexcusable. This confidence and optimism are in no sense reducible to class interest, and they were shared by other groups than simply the employers of labor. But is it not apparent that it was particularly consonant with the interests of a particular class? Are we really to believe that this consonance was fortuitous? It is at last appropriate to examine the theoretical questions involved in interpretations that stress class interest.

First, a definition. Class interests may be defined as lying in the preservation or the betterment, either directly or indirectly, of the material con-

33. Haskell, "Convention and Hegemonic Interest in the Debate over Antislavery," 867, 863.
34. Bernard Bailyn, *The Ideological Origins of the American Revolution* (Cambridge, Mass., 1967), 230–319.
35. In other words it may be necessary to collapse the distinction (upon which Haskell builds the entire structure of his argument) between prescription and practice.

ditions enjoyed by a class relative to another class. Such interest may be furthered indirectly by political or ideological means, or even by conceding a material loss so as not to suffer a larger one. Thus we are dealing with a broad category of activities and processes and only rarely will an emphasis on class yield predictions. That is to say, we are concerned with explanatory rather than predictive power. And even if we are able to conclude that class interest is a major causal factor, the explanation will not then be at an end. For we need also to identify the process by which those interests come to be advanced and then go on to explain the process itself.

There are several ways in which class interests can be furthered. First and most obviously, they may be promoted as a result of the conscious intention of the agent. Little more needs to be said on this subject. Second, an agent may realize a goal that he believes to be unrelated to class but which is nonetheless a function of an ideology structured by class interest. To illustrate this, let us return to the possibly apocryphal story of Marie Antoinette telling the impoverished citizenry of Paris to eat cake. In my original article I noted that it was her position in society which had occasioned her failure to realize that the Parisian poor could not afford cake. The deception was not a self-deception but a socially induced one. Let us pursue this a little further—and into the realm of fiction—in order to come to grips with the problem of the unintended promotion of class interests. We are in the Paris of 1789 and the poor, still seeking bread, take violent action. Marie Antoinette, baffled by their refusal to alter their eating habits, concludes that they are quite unreasonable men and women with whom nothing can be done and reluctantly orders the National Guard to open fire upon them. She wishes to preserve order and sees her action as in the interests of all classes and not especially of her own. She has no conscious or unconscious intention of furthering a class interest. Can we say nonetheless that she is, in good part, "moved by class interest"? Indeed we can. In the first place, her original error, attributable largely to class position, is uncorrected partly because it is in her interest to retain that position. She tends to discountenance evidence that might rectify the error but which at the same time might raise disturbing questions about the nature of the society she wishes to preserve. In the second place, the decision to open fire on the rebellious masses is caused by a commitment to "order" that is, to say the least, heavily impregnated with class interest. For it is clearly in Marie Antoinette's interest to define social disorder in terms of unruly crowds, whereas the interest of the poor might well lie in defining it in terms of mass hunger and starvation. All of which is to say that individuals can act in accordance with an ideology that bears a clear imprint of class interest but perceive their actions as being in the general interest or even in no particular interest at all. Such actions are common; indeed one might argue that the most successful tyrants are those who rule primarily in the interests of a dominant class but whose propaganda asserts that they serve the general interest. And the most successful of all are often the ones who, without any self-deception, believe their own propaganda.

The story I have just cited is, of course, a fictional one. Let me offer as a second example the anti-union propaganda that is so prevalent in Britain, the United States, and indeed throughout the Western world in our own times. Let us imagine a situation in which certain groups take the lead in condemning the pursuit of self-interest collectively by union actions such as strikes. They argue that such action is morally indefensible since it results in coercion of both employers and of those workers who would prefer not to strike. The anti-union campaign is successful and strikes are banned. The campaigners believe that they have advanced the general interest and actually benefited all groups, including labor. There is no intention of furthering a class interest. Nevertheless, it is easy to see that the attempt to confine the pursuit of self-interest to individualist channels is part of a morality that in turn is structured by class interest. The example is analogous to that of Marie Antoinette. Once again, the values concerned bear the imprint of class interest, and whether this is or is not recognized by the actor is a separate and subordinate question.

It is perfectly true that the actions of Marie Antoinette or of the anti-union campaigners are not the only ones compatible with class interest. But this will only count against a class-interest interpretation if it is assumed that such interests dictate a single course of action. And such an assumption can be seen to be unfounded as soon as we recognize that it is not predictions but explanations after the event which we are seeking. A full explanation would need to show how and in what way the actions chosen were based on a set of values impregnated with class interest. In other words, we need to proceed from interests to ideas and values and then to actions. It is true that this task will often be a large and complex one; but to say this is merely to repeat that Haskell is quite mistaken when he assumes that an emphasis on class closes off discussion prematurely.

There is a third route by which class interests may be furthered. Certain outcomes may be unsought by anyone, yet benefit one class at the expense of others. The benefit might be entirely fortuitous, or it might have a structural cause. Let us consider an example of this process. Let us suppose that overseas demand for a specific product suddenly falls and unemployment ensues. Although a minority of employers suffer, wages fall, and the strength of employers relative to employees increases. This outcome was not what anyone intended, nor is it inherent in any individual's goal. Yet it is not a random one. It proceeds instead from the greater structural power of the employer, which protects him from adversity and allows him to augment his power still further. Society can be viewed as a prism through which intentionate actions pass on their way to becoming outcomes. Some are blocked entirely, some are refracted and transformed, others pass through undisturbed. This is obviously a complex process, but in each case the interest of various classes can *sometimes* play a decisive role.

It may now be worth comparing this approach with Haskell's. Haskell appears to believe that an outcome which is unintended is radically indeterminate. After referring to the unintended consequence of a Hank Aaron home run (a spectator receiving a new baseball), he asserts that "if the aim of furthering capitalist hegemony entered into the intentions of the abolitionists no more significantly than the aim of gift giving figured in Aaron's mind as he swung at the ball, we would not feel that humanitarianism had anything important to do with the rise of capitalism—not, at least, so long as we assume that class interest is the only way to link the two."[36] Yet we have seen that unintended outcomes, like values, often bear a clear imprint of the social structure in which they occur. In ignoring this, Haskell makes an error that neatly complements his earlier one concerning intentions. Just as intentions may be generated by class interest but be experienced by the agent in entirely different terms, so the outcome of an agent's action may be unintended by anyone, including himself, yet be the consequence in large part of the pursuit, within society, of class interests. Thus, to repeat, unintended out-comes, like values, often bear a clear imprint of the social structure in which they occur.[37]

Let us return for a moment to Marie Antoinette. Her decision to employ the National Guard against the rebellious masses results not in the reestablishment of order but instead in a full-blown revolution. One consequence of the revolution is the execution of certain aristocrats, one of whom is none other than Marie Antoinette. With hindsight it becomes apparent to all that her action was not optimal either for herself or for her class. An important conclusion follows. Just as class interest may be advanced intentionally or unintentionally, so actions taken may be functional or dysfunctional for the class that takes them.

It is now possible to consider the role of class interest in the alternative

36. Haskell, "Capitalism and the Origins of the Humanitarian Sensibility, Part 1," 347.
37. It may also be worth noting that in capitalist societies (and in certain others) that social structure can only exist and be reproduced if class interests are pursued. On this and related matters, my thinking has been shaped above all by Roy Bhaskar. See Bhaskar, *The Possibility of Naturalism* (Brighton, 1979).

interpretation that my original article offered. First, there was no suggestion that class interest was pursued by abolitionists and other humanitarians directly either via conscious motivation or self-deception. Nor was
there any claim that humanitarianism was the only response given a certain
class interest, nor that it was the optimal response. I did not, and do not
claim that if class interest is a major cause of an action, the outcome must
*necessarily* favor that interest. Instead, I emphasized the causal force of ideology and values closely associated with, but not to be read off from, class
interests. For ideology is deeply influenced by past traditions, by the state
of technology, by chance, by climate, by religion, and by many other considerations. Some of these influences are, in turn, connected to class interest, others are not. Even those that are so connected can hardly ever be
*reduced* to class interest. Finally, ideology is deeply influenced by the interests of other groups besides classes. Yet when all these qualifications have
been made, it is surely apparent that any attempt to explain humanitarianism without a heavy emphasis on class interest is doomed. Humanitarians and mainstream abolitionists assumed that the relations between
capitalist and laborer were, or could be made, harmonious. As Johnson suggests, the values of the reformer were structured by the interests, and rooted
in the practices of, an emerging bourgeois class.

Before leaving this subject, let us consider outcomes a little further. Here
Haskell made a good point when he claimed that the question of whether
beliefs produced by class interest will further that interest is an empirical
one.[38] There is no reason to assume that classes (and in this they resemble
individuals) always succeed in promoting their own interest, even when
they set out to do so. But he pushed a good point too far. For outcomes are
not quite so indeterminate as he believes. There is a likelihood of some "fit"
between actions and outcomes, especially where a dominant class is concerned. Why is this? Clearly a full answer is impossible here but some suggestions can be offered. First, there will generally be a tendency for a
social system to reproduce itself ceteris paribus. Thus the intention of a
dominant class will always be to sustain itself, and its disproportionate
power will help here. Second, there will be feedback if the intended goals
are not attained or if outcomes have the unexpected consequence of diminishing that interest. As a result, actions will be altered and practices revised.
Again the disproportionate power of a dominant class will help. Third, the
dominant class can present itself as the defender of the general interest, and

38. Haskell, "Convention and Hegemonic Interest in the Debate over Antislavery,"
872.

thus of values like "freedom" and "order," and this posture will help it to secure its goals.

Finally, let us consider hegemony, Davis's use of the concept, and its place in the explanatory scheme I am proposing. Though it was employed by Lenin, the term "hegemony" is identified particularly with Antonio Gramsci, who began to use it in the 1920s in order to explain the failure of revolution in the West following the Bolshevik seizure of power. Unfortunately, as one analyst put it, "it has become one of those fashionable political catchwords which is often invoked but seldom properly defined or submitted to close scrutiny." At its core is the idea of leadership—intellectual, moral, and cultural—exercised by a class so as to produce a significant measure of consent on the part of those governed and dominated by that class. Gramsci himself did not spell out the necessary conditions for hegemony, and it is clear that he recognized that the extent to which hegemonic values pervade a society, and the enthusiasm with which they are held, can vary. In an extreme case, the entire population might embrace the dominant values as ideal ones; at the other extreme, people might believe them to be deficient but acquiesce in them out of fear that any alternative would surely be worse. There are thus different degrees of hegemonic control, and only rarely will hegemony lead to the complete ideological incorporation of the lower classes.[39]

The concept of hegemony was thus designed to shed light on the failure of revolution; the goal was to explain the stability of certain regimes. Gramsci did not believe that hegemony was a characteristic of all societies, and it is probable that he doubted whether it existed before the rise of the bourgeoisie. This has not prevented scholars from seeking to apply the concept to other states and societies. Thus Eugene Genovese has made the entirely plausible claim that slaveholders exercised hegemony over the antebellum South. As a result, in the last few decades before the Civil War, it became impossible even to discuss the question of slavery in large parts of the South.[40] It is, of course, true that historians do not discharge their duties simply by identifying hegemony; we still need to know how it is established, how pervasive it is, and how enthusiastically hegemonic values are held. For the Old South most of these questions are, in my opinion, still

39. Joseph Femia, *Gramsci's Political Thought* (Oxford, 1981), 23. See also Walter L. Adamson, *Hegemony and Revolution: A Study of Antonio Gramsci's Political and Cultural Theory* (Berkeley, 1980); Anne Showstack Sassoon, *Gramsci's Politics* (London, 1980).
40. Eugene O. Genovese, *Roll, Jordan, Roll: The World the Slaves Made* (New York, 1974), esp. 25–49. Yet it is worth noting that, even here, there was also the threat—and sometimes the reality—of violence.

unanswered. Yet the concept of hegemony can, it seems, be productively applied here; indeed, it is hard to see how the consensus on slavery that existed there can be seen in any other terms.

Davis's use of "hegemony" is considerably more problematic, however,
and it has attracted powerful criticism from some scholars, most notably
Seymour Drescher and Thomas Haskell.[41] Davis wished to show that "British abolitionism," while serving "conflicting ideological functions" nonetheless "helped reinforce . . . the hegemony of capitalist values," at least
in the years from 1790 to 1823. He then spelled out some of the hegemonic
consequences of the crusade against slavery. First, he claimed that in defining slavery as unacceptable, abolitionists gave sanction to "less barbarous
modes of social discipline." Second, he suggested that analogies with chattel slavery "may . . . have retarded the development of a vocabulary that
could depict more subtle forms of coercion, oppression, and class rule."
Third, he argued that antislavery gave the elite in Britain an opportunity to
"demonstrate their commitment to decency and justice." The assault on
slavery thus "bestowed moral legitimacy on the reformed Parliament, British society, and the British character."[42]

How are we to assess these claims? The three effects Davis mentions are
plausible enough, and although their importance might be questioned, I see
no reason to dispute their existence. But Davis makes other claims, which
are far less persuasive. Thus he cites, as offering "invaluable support" for
"the hegemonic thesis," the fact that antislavery had mass appeal in parts
of Britain and was popular with elites and ordinary men and women alike.
Why should this be taken as either a cause or a manifestation of hegemony?
To equate hegemony with cross-class agreement is to devalue the term considerably. Similarly, he maintains that the very term "wage slavery" was
hegemonic in its effect, a claim that, as Thomas Haskell has showed, is
easily discredited.[43]

Let us for the moment agree, however, that abolition had certain effects
that were hegemonic. It does not, of course, follow that this was its overall

41. Seymour Drescher, "Cart Whip and Billy Roller: Antislavery and Reform
Symbolism in Industrializing Britain," *Journal of Social History*, 15 (September
1981): 3–24; Drescher, *Capitalism and Antislavery*, 135–61; Haskell, "Convention
and Hegemonic Interest in the Debate over Antislavery," 829–36.
42. Davis, "Reflections on Abolitionism and Ideological Hegemony," 797; *Problem
of Slavery in the Age of Revolution*, 466–67; "Reflections on Abolitionism and Ideological Hegemony," 809, 805, 810. It should perhaps be added that Davis maintained
that his thesis concerning hegemony should be applied to Britain only; see "Reflections on Abolitionism and Ideological Hegemony," 798.
43. Davis, "Reflections on Abolitionism and Ideological Hegemony," 808, 809;
Haskell, "Convention and Hegemonic Interest in the Debate over Antislavery," 835.

effect. Davis himself acknowledges that antislavery "bred a new sensitivity to social oppression"; it "ultimately taught many Englishmen to recognize forms of systematic oppression that were closer to home."[44] Unless "hegemony" is to be robbed of all explanatory value by being stretched to include anything that does not actually encourage revolution, these consequences must be reckoned as counter-hegemonic.[45] And if they are so reckoned, then the contradictory consequences of antislavery will have to be weighed so as to determine the overall effects of the movement. Davis concludes that the abolitionists themselves "helped to strengthen the invisible chains being forged at home."[46] This statement leaves us in no doubt as to his view of the overall impact of antislavery. But nowhere does he present an argument to support this conclusion.

Yet Davis does not limit his argument about hegemony to the consequences of abolition. He claims that the causes of antislavery are also to be understood in terms of hegemony. Such at least would seem to have been his intention in asserting that abolitionism was "always related to the need to legitimate free wage labor." Clearly, as Haskell has observed, much depends on what is meant by "related to."[47] In the same way, when Davis says that "the continuing evolution" of "an international antislavery opinion" "reflected the ideological needs of various groups and classes," he does not explain further what he means by "reflected." Davis's critics have assumed that the causal connection he detects between antislavery and hegemony is a strong one. Drescher has interpreted him to mean that abolitionism was intended to divert attention from exploitation at home, but Davis himself is clearly unhappy with this notion.[48] In what sense, then, is the relationship a causal one?

It must be said that even a close reading of Davis's work does not make this question easy to answer. Before we seek an answer, however, it may be worth making a general point about causation. When historians ask what caused an event, they are normally looking for one or more phenomena without which the event would not have occurred. There is thus an implicit comparison with a past in which the said event failed to materialize. For example, when we seek to explain the origins of World War I, we are searching

44. Davis, *Problem of Slavery in the Age of Revolution*, 455, 467–68.
45. See Haskell, "Convention and Hegemonic Interest in the Debate over Antislavery," 835.
46. Davis, *Problem of Slavery in the Age of Revolution*, 456.
47. Davis, "Reflections on Abolitionism and Ideological Hegemony," 798; Haskell, "Convention and Hegemonic Interest in the Debate over Antislavery," 830–31.
48. Davis, *Problem of Slavery in the Age of Revolution*, 42; Drescher, "Cart Whip and Billy Roller," 4; Davis, "Reflections on Abolitionism and Ideological Hegemony," 805.

for causal factors in the absence of which no world war would have taken place. The question being asked is (approximately): "Why World War I at this time rather than peace?" Let us now change the question so that it reads: "Why World War I at this time rather than an atomic war?" Plainly the answer will now be very different, centering presumably on the state of weapons technology in 1914 and demonstrating why nuclear weapons had not yet been developed. The two questions are, of course, quite dissimilar; the answers given to the second would be most odd if given to the first.

If we now return to Davis and antislavery, there is reason to believe that much of the time he is answering a question that is neither the one his critics are addressing nor the one with which they believe he is concerned. Instead of "Why the success of antislavery?" Davis's question often seems to be "Why was antislavery, rather than some other movement, successful?" Certainly this seems to be the implication of the following passage: "The crucial question, therefore, was not why groups of enlightened British, French, and Americans attacked slavery from the 1760s to the 1780s but why this single reform cause, which attracted significant radical support in the early 1790s and which some conservatives denounced as a Jacobin front, won growing acceptance in the early nineteenth century from British political and social elites otherwise obsessed with the fear that social reform would open the gates to revolution."[49]

In the context of this question, an emphasis on hegemony seems entirely appropriate. If we wish to understand why a movement that aimed to destroy slavery was successful in a way that one aiming at a wholesale reorganization of British society (say by destroying wage labor) could not have been, then the hegemonic control of the ruling classes in Britain is likely to be of primary significance. An analogy may be appropriate here with the ability of the slaveholding classes in the Old South to prevent a serious attack on slavery. Yet an answer to this question clearly will not take us far toward an explanation of the first, more difficult and more fundamental question. We still need to know why antislavery (rather than indifference to, or support for, slavery) flourished. And historians are entitled to doubt whether "hegemony," despite its usefulness as a concept, can supply the answer. For if he wishes to make "hegemony" a major causal factor, Davis will need to explain the processes or mechanisms at work. As yet he has identified only one: self-deception. And as Haskell has shown, this concept raises more questions than it answers.[50] Davis's scheme, with its emphasis on hegemony, can thus help explain why an attack on slavery, rather than

49. Davis, "Reflections on Abolitionism and Ideological Hegemony," 798.
50. Haskell, "Capitalism and the Origins of the Humanitarian Sensibility, Part 1," 348–55.

on other evils, succeeded, but is less successful in telling us how the fundamental reforming impulse was generated, whereas Haskell's, insofar as it rejects class interests, is unable to account for the selectivity of the abolitionists.

How then can we summarize the relationship between antislavery and hegemony? As far as consequences are concerned, it is still an open question whether, overall, antislavery furthered or modestly hindered hegemony. But there is little reason to believe that the emergence, the spread, or the ultimate success of antislavery can be explained in terms of hegemony. Nevertheless, there may be a more indirect relationship between the two. I have argued that antislavery is to be explained, in part, in terms of a shift in values resulting from the spread of wage labor. These values made slavery appear increasingly intolerable, and they spread beyond the middle classes, whose experience they most directly reflected. Can we say therefore that the forces that established the hegemony of the bourgeoisie were also those that gave rise to the humanitarian movement and destroyed slavery?

Let me conclude with a brief assessment of the contributions of Haskell and Davis to our understanding of the relationship between capitalism and antislavery. Unfortunately, Haskell minimizes the role of class interests in the growth of antislavery either because he defined them so narrowly as to exclude them or because he claims that any alternative definition makes the concept so elastic as to be unserviceable as an explanation. He also effectively excludes values, since he holds that the Golden Rule renders all discussion of them irrelevant. He is thus left with "convention," an under-analyzed category that contains much of the class interest and some of the values whose importance he fails to appreciate. One of the most valuable parts of Haskell's work indeed concerns the emergence of new attitudes and values, some of which, it is clear, prescribed hostility to slavery. His other invaluable contribution lies in his criticisms of some of Davis's work, in particular of Davis's use of the concepts of "hegemony" and "self-deception." Yet although I have doubts about the processes he identifies, Davis's general conclusions seem to me to have withstood criticism. Can we doubt that "slavery stood in direct opposition to the virtues inculcated by the market, the virtues that English employers and ratepayers wished to instill in the English working class?" We must surely agree that antislavery "cannot be divorced from the vast economic changes that were intensifying social conflicts and heightening class consciousness."[51] The interpretation I have tried to advance has sought to strengthen these, Davis's general conclusions, even while dissenting from major parts of his analysis.

51. Davis, "Reflections on Abolitionism and Ideological Hegemony," 812, 806.

Chapter 10

# The Perils of Doing History by Ahistorical Abstraction

*A Reply to Thomas L. Haskell's AHR Forum Reply*

David Brion Davis

In a debate of this kind, which is not addressed to a specific proposition agreed upon by all parties, there is always a danger that the participants will talk past each other. Thomas L. Haskell has been centrally concerned with questions of personal agency and individual moral responsibility, exemplified by his invocation of the Golden Rule and the starving stranger. His model of the emerging humanitarian sensibility leaves no space for mediating structures or institutions between abstract market forces and individual cognition. By contrast, I have assumed that economic forces are only part of a multicausal process that includes cultural heritage, religious and political transformations, and the initiative of unique individuals embedded in unique social situations. I have been especially preoccupied with ideologies, or forms of *collective* moral perception and discourse that first sanctioned human bondage and then singled it out for attack.

In *The Problem of Slavery in Western Culture,* I analyzed the cultural and intellectual heritage that led to the eighteenth-century moral indictment of human bondage and then provided a referential framework for the great nineteenth-century controversies over slavery in various parts of the world. In *The Problem of Slavery in the Age of Revolution,* I described some of the specific religious and political developments that made antislavery a major issue in America and especially in Britain. It was my attempt to explain this momentous transformation in moral values that provided Haskell

I want to thank various friends who read drafts of this essay and who gave me invaluable criticism and advice. My indebtedness to the following people does not imply that they agree with my arguments or bear any responsibility for what I say: Seymour Drescher, Stanley L. Engerman, Robert P. Forbes, Richard Fox, David Hollinger, Lewis C. Perry, Michael Salman, Amy Stanley, Sean Wilentz, and C. Vann Woodward.

with a historiographical vessel to board, as "a rude stowaway" in his disarming phrase, since he wished to navigate by a different star. We should look to the impact of a capitalistic market, Haskell maintained, if we wish to understand the new habits of thought that transformed moral conventions and made it possible for abolitionists to go to the aid of suffering slaves. In response, I fell into a defensive posture of trying to clarify my own position and correct certain misrepresentations. However necessary this may be, the time has now come to examine Haskell's main thesis with greater care.

Haskell is so fluent as a writer and so skilled as a debater that one easily loses sight of the distance between his supple constructs and historical reality. His continuing conflation and reification of the "market" and "capitalism" is far removed from time and space. Haskell never indicates how his own vaguely defined market revolution differed from earlier stages of merchant capitalism, such as Europe's "commercial revolution" of the mid-tenth to the mid-fourteenth centuries, or the spectacular expansion of trade and colonial settlement from the mid-fifteenth to the mid-seventeenth centuries.[1] Did these earlier breakthroughs in long-distance trade, credit, and banking alter human character at least in thriving commercial centers and lead the Genoese, Venetians, and Lisboans to adopt higher standards of promise keeping and expand their limits of moral responsibility? Since the growth of a world market was a continuing process that took place in various stages, can Haskell point to a synchronized development of humanitarianism or abolitionism as Europeans' understanding of causation gave new efficacy to the Golden Rule?

Surely the market was more "the keystone for an entire way of life" in the fifteenth-century Mediterranean, the birthplace of modern plantation slavery, than in many inland rural homesteads and towns in early nineteenth-century America, including those in regions like Vermont, which nourished passionate support for antislavery. Randolph A. Roth's meticulous study of social reform in antebellum Vermont casts serious doubt on the importance of the market as a stimulus to abolitionism in the Connecticut River Valley of Vermont: "In the towns studied intensively," Roth

1. For examples of the impact of the market and long-distance trading in the medieval Mediterranean world, see Robert S. Lopez, *The Commercial Revolution of the Middle Ages, 950–1350* (Englewood Cliffs, N.J., 1971); Lopez, "Market Expansion: The Case of Genoa," in *Su e giù per la storia di Genova* (Genoa, 1975), 45–62; Rodney Hilton, "The Transition from Feudalism to Capitalism," *Science and Society*, 17 (1953): 340–48; Center for Medieval and Renaissance Studies, University of California, Los Angeles, *The Dawn of Modern Banking* (New Haven, 1979); Charles Verlinden, *The Beginnings of Modern Colonization: Eleven Essays with an Introduction*, Yvonne Freccero, trans. (Ithaca, N.Y., 1970).

writes, "abolition appealed most strongly to rural Calvinists. . . . Only one of the movement's leaders came from a Calvinist church in the marketing and manufacturing centers in Woodstock, Windsor, and St. Johnsbury townships. One-fifth of all the abolitionists identified were also leading Antimasons. . . . It was in areas strongly supportive of Antimasonry, areas away from the Connecticut River, that abolitionist societies formed."[2] But such specific references are out of keeping with Haskell's approach. Places, names, dates, and contexts are notably rare in the ninety-three pages accorded to Haskell by *The American Historical Review*. Few, if any, historians have published so many assertions backed by so little empirical evidence.

Haskell conveys no sense of capitalism as a system of specific social relations. He virtually ignores the new social world created when merchant capitalism was being transformed by industrialization. Although Haskell builds his entire argument on the emergence of a new kind of market from roughly 1750 to 1850, he says remarkably little about *industry* and is as vague about dates as he is about geography. Does he have in mind the kind of markets to which the young William Wilberforce was exposed—the North Sea timber trade out of Hull? Or the West India trade in provisions and manufactured goods from Anthony Benezet's Philadelphia? Or the commercial and credit markets of the Netherlands, which combined extensive intercontinental trade with highly efficient agriculture and a cottage industry devoted to refinishing or processing imported goods for later export?[3] Did such markets have the same effect on cognition as the workshops and factories of Lancashire, where in the 1780s a new kind of mechanized industrialism suddenly appeared side by side with abolitionism's first demonstration of mass appeal? How does one equate the "market" influence of Manchester with that of rural and village environments that also gave rise to strong abolitionist activism in Britain and the United States? As Seymour Drescher asks: "Were the slave traders of eighteenth-century London

2. Randolph A. Roth, *The Democratic Dilemma: Religion, Reform, and the Social Order in the Connecticut River Valley of Vermont, 1791–1850* (Cambridge, 1987), 164, 179–80 (quotation from p. 180).
3. For the Dutch market economy, to which I shall shortly turn, see especially Joel Mokyr, *Industrialization in the Low Countries, 1795–1850* (New Haven, 1976); C. R. Boxer, *The Dutch Seaborne Empire, 1600–1800* (New York, 1965); Jan de Vries, *The Economy of Europe in an Age of Crisis, 1600–1750* (Cambridge, 1976); Maurice Aymard, ed., *Dutch Capitalism and World Capitalism* (Cambridge, 1982); Jonathan Israel, *Dutch Primacy in the World Trade, 1585–1740* (New York, 1989); Simon Schama, *The Embarrassment of Riches: An Interpretation of Dutch Culture in the Golden Age* (New York, 1988); J. G. Van Dillen, "Economic Fluctuations and Trade in the Netherlands, 1650–1750," in *Essays in European Economic History, 1500–1800*, Peter Earle, ed. (Oxford, 1974), 199–209.

and Liverpool less cognitively aware of the long-term consequences of slave dealing than the Quaker brewers and bankers?''[4]

In a highly significant concession, Haskell admits that his thesis "would be severely challenged by evidence of a truly market-oriented society whose members continued to see slavery as nothing worse than a necessary evil." This concession, one should note, presupposes a direct causal relationship between a society's becoming "market-oriented" and its viewing slavery as something "worse than a necessary evil." After assuring us that the Dutch do not represent such a case, Haskell considers an alternative hypothesis in the related footnote: "Davis might argue that it was not capitalists generally who sought to legitimize wage labor but industrial capitalists, and that the Dutch bourgeoisie was predominantly mercantile. Before one could assess such an argument, one would need to know more about the Dutch economy than has been brought forward so far."[5]

I would amend this hypothesis in two ways. First, I would reject any suggestion of economic determinism: I have never sought to claim that antislavery *had* to rest on the vindication of industrial wage labor; I argued only that in early industrial Britain, it did serve such a function for certain classes. Second, I would delete "industrial capitalists" as the legitimators of wage labor and substitute "various aspiring groups, including skilled workers, who lived in a society undergoing industrialization." Although capitalist entrepreneurs would ultimately reap disproportional benefits from the legitimization of wage labor, they would tend initially to be less sensitive to the issue than artisans, small-scale producers, journalists, religious leaders, and others eager to make sense of a world in rapid transition. Ideological hegemony is rarely imposed from the top down: it is an uneasy compromise created by various competing interests in search of legitimacy and mutual recognition.

One of the objectives of my chapter on the Quakers was to show how, as British Quakers began to shift their activities from merchant to industrial enterprise, they became increasingly attuned to distinctions between "free" and "slave" labor. This is not to imply, I hasten to add, that Quakers and other early entrepreneurs became hostile to chattel slavery *because* they saw such testimony as a means of legitimizing the kind of clockwork labor discipline instituted in the mills of Josiah Wedgwood, the creator of the world-famed cameo of the chained black slave kneeling under the words "Am I Not a Man and a Brother?" Yet the synchronized appearance of

4. Seymour Drescher, *Capitalism and Antislavery: British Mobilization in Comparative Perspective* (New York, 1987), 21.
5. Thomas L. Haskell, "Convention and Hegemonic Interest in the Debate over Antislavery: A Reply to Davis and Ashworth," *AHR*, 92 (October 1987): 857.

Wedgwood's abolitionist logo and his Etruria mill, with its futuristic methods for maximizing production and eliminating waste or moments of idleness, was something more than accident.[6] Both were parts of a new system that redefined rewards, punishment, and the kind of undeserved "suffering" that ought to arouse the sympathy of strangers. I was thinking of a transformation of consciousness and basic categories of understanding when I pointed to ideological links between the spread of antislavery doctrine, as a kind of self-evident truth, and the industrialization that first took hold in northern England—and some decades later in New England.[7]

As for the Netherlands, there can be no doubt that it perfectly fits Haskell's model of a "truly market-oriented society whose members continued to see slavery as nothing worse than a necessary evil." Among the authorities I have already cited, there is much disagreement about the relative or absolute decline of the Dutch economy in the later eighteenth century. But if the Dutch economy in the seventeenth and eighteenth centuries was not market-oriented, it would be difficult to find another society that could fit the description. During this period, Holland had the most diversified trade of any nation on the Continent; though some parts of the country remained relatively backward, Holland was the one nation in which commercial agriculture and finishing trades were closely tied to global commerce and banking. By the mid-eighteenth century, one-third of the assets of the Bank of England were in Dutch hands. The Netherlands was so prosperous and wage levels were so high that the fear of luxury and material corruption—

6. David Brion Davis, *The Problem of Slavery in the Age of Revolution, 1770–1823* (Ithaca, N.Y., 1975), 460.
7. "We may never learn precisely why people became abolitionists, and the fact is we do not need to know what brings individuals to a movement in order to understand the movement itself. We can suspend the question of motivation and ask, instead, what there was in a social and cultural situation that gave a reform its style, its particular set of concerns and solutions. I have taken that approach and attempted to find the resonance between the most persistent themes in antislavery literature and conditions in antebellum America. . . . My interest . . . has been in the interplay between personality, culture, and environment. I attempt to get at that through an analysis of perception—of what it was abolitionists saw in slavery and of how what they saw reverberated with their own social situation. Perception is an important matter because people do not always see what is *there*. They see what their values, attitudes, and preconceptions prepare them to see. When a new view of an old institution arises . . . it marks social and cultural shifts of great significance," says Ronald G. Walters (*The Antislavery Appeal: American Abolitionism after 1830* [Baltimore, 1976], xii–xv). I agree that our respect for abolitionism should not be diminished by our knowledge that in the United States the movement gave moral validation to laissez-faire economics and prepared the way for an "entente with late nineteenth-century industrialism" (*ibid.*, p. xvi).

what Simon Schama calls "the embarrassment of riches"—become a dominant theme in Dutch culture.[8]

At various times in the seventeenth century, the Dutch had dominated the Atlantic slave trade. It was not by accident that the first ship that delivered African slaves to Virginia hailed from Holland. Although the Dutch share of the international slave trade declined in the eighteenth century, it was only in the Fourth Anglo-Dutch War (the war of American independence) that the British greatly weakened the Dutch slave system. Even so, from 1790 to 1795 the Dutch transported well over eight thousand slaves from Africa to Surinam, Demerara, and other New World colonies.[9] The fact that the slave trade was becoming far less important to the Dutch economy than to the economy of England might plausibly have provided a greater opening for abolitionists. Dutch traditions of religious and political toleration, reinforced by the pervasive desire to prove that the nation had not become mired in luxury and self-indulgence, would seem to furnish preconditions for a strong abolitionist movement.

Yet all studies, including the recent book by Johannes Menne Postma, agree that Holland must have teemed with the most powerful antibodies to ward off the antislavery infection—perhaps in small part because of its English origin. Despite decades of exposure to the Enlightenment's critique of chattel slavery, Postma concludes:

> Most of the eighteenth-century Dutch literature that dealt with the slave trade and slavery was apologetic; it tended to condone and defend the slave trade. All the arguments used elsewhere, such as biblical endorsement, were also displayed by Dutch writers. Most expressed the belief that the blacks were much better off in the colonies as slaves than as free men in Africa. Others argued that Africa could not feed all its people anyway, making forced emigration a blessing in disguise. Some went so far as to claim that slaves were often grateful for the passage provided by European ships.[10]

How are we to explain the fact that the nation that may have contained the most literate, prosperous, enlightened, and "market-oriented" population in the world produced only a handful of largely imitative antislavery tracts? Or the fact that, even after England had virtually forced the Netherlands to end the slave trade, "many Dutch subjects and a significant ele-

8. This depiction of the Dutch economy is drawn from the works cited in footnote 3.
9. For statistics on the Dutch slave trade, see Johannes Menne Postma, *The Dutch in the Atlantic Slave Trade, 1600–1815* (Cambridge, 1990), 284–303, 308–61.
10. *Ibid.*, 292–93.

ment of the country's economy continued to be wedded to the plantation system in the West"?[11] The Netherlands failed to free the nation's colonial slaves even in 1848, when the revolutions of that year opened the way for the French and Danish edicts of emancipation. Despite the economic marginality of the Dutch slave colonies, emancipation was delayed until 1863, the year that began in the United States with Abraham Lincoln's famed Emancipation Proclamation (an "unintended consequence" of the Civil War for which Lincoln later received considerable moral credit).

Obviously, I cannot provide a solution to the Dutch enigma in an essay of this kind, even if I have shown that the Netherlands meets Haskell's test of a "truly market-oriented society whose members continued to see slavery as nothing worse than a necessary evil." The best works on British and American abolitionism suggest that a serious student of the Dutch enigma should begin with a comparison of British and Dutch religious ferment and political culture, subjects Haskell conspicuously ignores.[12] What distinguished Britain and the United States from the Netherlands and other Continental countries was a symbiosis of popular evangelicalism and political dissent. As for more indirect preconditions, industrialization appears more promising than Haskell's vague "market." The Netherlands, for all its precocity in merchant capitalism, fell well behind even Belgium in industrialization. It was the difference in the timing of industrialization that most sharply distinguished the British from the Dutch economy. And the appearance in Holland of anemic antislavery voices coincided with the country's delayed industrialization.

But one should be wary of drawing facile connections or of reducing the appearance of abolitionism to a "base" of industrialization. Industrialization, like Haskell's even more pervasive market behavior, leapt from one nation to another; abolitionism became a powerful force, even for a brief period, in only three or possibly four countries.[13] In view of the rapid spread of capitalism in the nineteenth century, why was concerted opposition to slavery so rare? Even in the softest and most qualified formulation of his thesis, Haskell fails to specify "the particular historical circumstances of late eighteenth-century Anglo-American culture" that allowed the market

11. *Ibid.*, 293.
12. Even scholars as far separated ideologically as Robin Blackburn and Robert William Fogel agree that the triumphs of abolitionism in Britain and the United States must be explained in political, not economic terms. See Blackburn, *The Overthrow of Colonial Slavery, 1776–1848* (London, 1988); Fogel, *Without Consent or Contract: The Rise and Fall of American Slavery* (New York, 1989).
13. I am referring to Britain, the northern United States, Brazil in the 1880s, and France in 1848.

to become "the force that pushed causal perception across the threshold that had hitherto made the slaves' misery . . . seem a necessary evil."[14]

Because Haskell conflates abolitionism with the "unprecedented wave of humanitarian reform sentiment [that] swept through the societies of Western Europe, England, and North America in the hundred years following 1750," he greatly exaggerates abolitionism's universal appeal.[15] In the United States and even in Britain until 1830, the main consequence of "humanitarian reform sentiment" was not emancipationism but the campaign to ameliorate and improve the treatment of slaves. The Presbyterian minister Timothy Flint described one aspect of this change when he took note in 1826 of the "growing desire among masters to be popular with their slaves."[16] Any causal explanation of abolitionism, as distinct from this desire to reform the slave system, must take account of the continuing weakness or nonexistence of antislavery movements in the Continental maritime nations; the continuing resistance from all quarters to Britain's efforts to suppress the criminal slave trade in the various seas of the world; and the ferocious hostility that abolitionists encountered in the northern United States, where even Lincoln's Emancipation Proclamation evoked widespread disapproval. It is one thing to explain the ideological transformation that brought most enlightened peoples to repudiate traditional religious and philosophical justifications for slavery; it is quite another to account for the early antislavery actions of an extremely conservative British government (1799–1807), or the popular enthusiasm in 1833 that led one out of every seven British adults to sign an emancipationist petition.[17]

Haskell is right when he finds "at the heart" of our disagreement "a different way of formulating the relationship of consciousness and society."[18]

14. Thomas L. Haskell, "Capitalism and the Origins of the Humanitarian Sensibility, Part 2," *AHR*, 90 (June 1985): 563. Haskell's statement of his argument on this page, that "capitalism supplied only a precondition" and that "no one need be surprised that the subsequent history of capitalist societies has not been greatly distinguished by humanitarian achievements," not only weakens his thesis but seems wholly at odds with the hard version of his argument, which appears, for example, when he admits that his thesis "would be severely challenged by evidence of a truly market-oriented society whose members continued to see slavery as nothing worse than a necessary evil" (Haskell, "Convention and Hegemonic Interest in the Debate over Antislavery," 857).
15. Thomas L. Haskell, "Capitalism and the Origins of the Humanitarian Sensibility, Part 1," *AHR*, 90 (April 1985): 339.
16. Quoted in Peter Kolchin, *Unfree Labor: American Slavery and Russian Serfdom* (Cambridge, Mass., 1987), 128–29.
17. Fogel, *Without Consent or Contract*, 227.
18. Haskell, "Convention and Hegemonic Interest in the Debate over Antislavery," 836.

Yet his continual misunderstanding of my position is the direct result of his attempt to impose on my work his own simplistic framework of "base and superstructure." He assumes that we both share an obsolete and quasi-Marxian conviction that the primal cause of antislavery is to be found in market capitalism, and that we then differ in the weight we assign to such "superstructural" reverberations as social convention and class interest. In Haskell's eyes, even political liberalism can be explained quite simply as "the paramount political expression of market culture and capitalist hegemony."[19] This is a kind of ethically inverted Marxism, in the sense that Haskell celebrates the alleged by-products of capitalism that Marx generally condemned.

My *Problem of Slavery in the Age of Revolution* took on strategic importance for Haskell's project to vindicate the capitalist market from "the rich nineteenth-century folklore about avaricious landlords and piratical factory owners . . . the metahistorical imagery of a class of me-first bourgeois individualists."[20] In one unguarded moment, Haskell even proclaimed: "Historically speaking, capitalism requires conscience and can even be said to be identical with the ascendancy of conscience."[21] Haskell knew that I am not a Marxist and that my book tends "to play down class interest (even while finally embracing it)." That meant, however, that if Haskell could discredit what he called "the most penetrating and sophisticated example" of "the social control interpretation"—the view that class interest was the only or major link connecting "the rise of capitalism" with humanitarian reform—then he would also have demolished all the Marxian and fellow-traveler accounts that purport to show "how supposedly disinterested reforms actually functioned to advance bourgeois interests."[22] Haskell clearly believed that such accounts had gained immense and unwarranted popularity; his attack on me, if initially prefaced with words of respect and praise, soon revealed the colors of a true believer's war.

Ironically, while I have always sought to avoid any suggestion of single causes or of historical determinism, I have often been criticized for assigning primacy to ideas and culture—to what Haskell would classify as superstructure. To understand the emergence of highly diverse manifestations of antislavery sentiment by the mid-eighteenth century, as well as their subsequent development, I insisted that one must examine specific religious,

19. *Ibid.*, 857.
20. Haskell, "Capitalism and the Origins of the Humanitarian Sensibility, Part 2," 549.
21. *Ibid.*, 552.
22. Haskell, "Capitalism and the Origins of the Humanitarian Sensibility, Part 1," 341–44.

political, literary, and philosophical developments that were related to new conceptions of freedom and thus to new social possibilities, but that no one has connected in any intelligible way to class interests or other ingredients of a structural "base." Although I took some pains in *The Problem of Slavery in Western Culture* to disavow the earlier idealist view of antislavery as a teleological force, immanent in Plato or primitive Christianity, I emphasized the importance of cultural constructs inherited from the past, such as Noah's curse of Canaan, the belief in original sin, the noble or innocent savage, and natural rights. I also pointed to the complex convergence, in Anglo-American history, of religious perfectionism, primitivism, rationalism, and the cult of sensibility, as well as to the functions antislavery came to serve for various groups in particular religious and political contexts.

It was this latter theme that led me to give some consideration, in *The Problem of Slavery in the Age of Revolution*, to the explosive issues of class interest and hegemony. Before turning to that debate, however, I need to stress the continuities and congruence between the two volumes. From Haskell's summaries one would never suspect that the second volume begins with a fairly long restatement of the first volume's major themes, or that it includes sustained discussions of legal, religious, and political developments that are not directly connected to class interest or to any economic "base." Nevertheless, as I have already indicated at the beginning of this essay, the first volume addresses the origins of antislavery opinion and the second volume is more concerned with the active acceptance, rejection, modification, and implementation of antislavery measures by specific groups of people at specific times.

Far from being a recent revision of my position, as Haskell suggests, concocted in 1987 in response to his own *American Historical Review* essay of 1985, my distinction between the conditions that governed the origins of antislavery thought and its reception among various governing elites owed much to Moses I. Finley's review of my first volume early in 1967. Surprisingly tolerant of my "history of ideas—more precisely, of ideology," Finley also made some sobering remarks that influenced my subsequent plans:

> "By the early 1770s [Davis writes] a large number of moralists, poets, intellectuals, and reformers had come to regard American slavery as an unmitigated evil." It is only a little unfair to remind Professor Davis of Jim Farley's remark, towards the close of Adlai Stevenson's first presidential campaign. Someone at a party was being jubilant over the fact that nearly all intellectuals were for Stevenson. "All sixty thousand of them," retorted Farley. Moralists, poets, intellectuals, and reformers did not destroy slavery. The Civil

War did that. . . . Nothing did or could happen until . . . moral
fervor became translated into political and military action, and how
that came about cannot be answered by the history of ideas. Nothing is more difficult perhaps than to explain how and why, or why
not, a new moral perception becomes effective in action. Yet nothing
is more urgent if an academic historical exercise is to become a significant investigation of human behavior with direct relevance to the
world we now live in.[23]

Unfortunately, the overall design of my work has been obscured in this
debate by Haskell's misunderstandings and misleading use of quotations.
When I previously used the term "misquoted me," I was actually referring
to Haskell's manipulation and misinterpretation of quotations, a practice he
now repeats and elaborates in order to support his claim, "I did not misquote him." The controversial passage, taken from the introductory chapter
of *The Problem of Slavery in the Age of Revolution* and now quoted by Haskell in italics, makes two distinct points: (1) *"The emergence of an international antislavery opinion represented a momentous turning point in the
evolution of man's moral perception, and thus in man's image of himself"*;
(2) *"The continuing 'evolution' did not spring from transcendent sources:
as a historical artifact, it reflected the ideological needs of various groups
and classes."*
It was no doubt confusing to use the word "evolution" to refer both to a
change in "man's moral perception" and to a continuing and subsequent
stage in antislavery's development. But in the second sentence, contrary to
Haskell's reading, the pronoun "it" plainly refers to the grammatical subject of that sentence, "the continuing 'evolution,' " not to the subject of the
*first* sentence, "the emergence of an international antislavery opinion."
Even apart from syntax, my distinction between emergence or origins and
continuing evolution is underscored by the third sentence of the paragraph,
which Haskell omits: *"The explanation must begin, however, with the heritage of religious, legal, and philosophical tensions associated with slavery—
or in other words, with the ways in which Western culture had organized
man's experience with lordship and bondage"* (emphasis added).[24]
Yet how did Haskell summarize and interpret these words?

23. Moses I. Finley, "The Idea of Slavery," review of *The Problem of Slavery in
Western Culture,* by David Brion Davis, *New York Review of Books,* 26 January
1967, 6–9. Since in 1952 I was one of the intellectuals who had worked and voted
for Stevenson, Finley's use of Farley had a special bite. I should add, however, that
my *original* research design, strongly influenced in the late 1950s by Karl Mann-
heim and Talcott Parsons, had envisioned a shift from "cultural heritage," conceived
largely as intellectual history, to a "theory of action," oriented to political, sociological, and ideological "functions."
24. Davis, *Problem of Slavery in the Age of Revolution,* 42; Haskell, "Convention

Unlike Foucault, Davis was confident that humanitarianism, or at any rate its antislavery component, represents an authentic and "remarkable shift in moral consciousness . . . a momentous turning point in the evolution of man's moral perception and thus in man's image of himself." Like Foucault, however, Davis insisted that the new sensibility "did not spring from transcendent sources." Rather its origin, he said, lies in "the ideological needs of various groups and classes."[25]

When faced with evidence of obvious distortion—of substituting "new sensibility" and "origin" for my "continuing 'evolution,'" and the predicate "lies in" for my "reflected," which carries a wholly different meaning—Haskell takes refuge in obfuscation:

The words I had enclosed in quotation marks accurately reproduce Davis's language. It is evidently my use of the word "origin" in place of "continuing 'evolution'" that he objects to, yet in his own text, the latter term presumably refers back to the previous sentence in which he spoke of the "emergence" of international antislavery opinion.[26]

---

and Hegemonic Interest in the Debate over Antislavery," 831. The controversial paragraph, I should point out, leads to a summary of the main themes of *The Problem of Slavery in Western Culture* (Ithaca, N.Y., 1966), a book that seeks to explore "the heritage of religious, legal, and philosophical tensions associated with slavery," as well as "the emergence of an international antislavery opinion" in the seventeenth and eighteenth centuries. Technically, as I have now tried to make clear, Haskell does not misquote me. But his use of quotations frequently distorts the plain meaning of my text. To give only one other example, in summing up my discussion of self-deception, Haskell writes: "[Davis] says that we can justifiably speak of self-deception whenever a group of historical actors 'believed they were advancing the interests of all humanity when they were actually promoting the interests of a special class.'" "This," Haskell triumphantly proclaims, "is not a workable test of self-deception." But it is not a workable test precisely because Haskell omits the crucial phrase with which my sentence begins: "*If we have empirical evidence that* a group of historical actors believed they were advancing the interests of all humanity when they were actually promoting the interests of a special class, we can justifiably speak of self-deception" (Haskell, "Convention and Hegemonic Interest in the Debate over Antislavery," 838; Davis, "Reflections on Abolitionism and Ideological Hegemony," *AHR*, 92 (October 1987): 802 [emphasis added]).
25. Haskell, "Capitalism and the Origins of the Humanitarian Sensibility, Part 1," 344.
26. Haskell, "Convention and Hegemonic Interest in the Debate over Antislavery," 832. On p. 830 of the same essay Haskell misrepresents me again when he claims that I am now eager to make a distinction between the origins of the antislavery "*movement*" and its acceptance among various governing elites, whereas I actually used the phrase "antislavery *sentiment*" (emphasis added), since I was referring to the period *before* antislavery movements got underway (Davis, "Reflections on Abolitionism and Ideological Hegemony," 798).

On what basis can one presume that an "origin" or "emergence" is synonymous with a "continuing evolution"? To extend the biological metaphor, is the genetic mutation of a new organism synonymous with the specific, historical conditions of natural selection that permit the continuing evolution of that organism? Can the two phases of development be explained in the same way and same language? I use this biological figure only as a means of illustration, not as a model. And I freely admit that my distinction between the rise of antislavery sentiment in the mid-eighteenth century and its later translation into political action needed more elaboration at that particular point in the book. Yet my distinction was not only valid but took obvious physical form in two separate volumes, integrally related but addressed to the quite different questions raised by "origins" and "continuing evolution."

Haskell's eagerness to find expressions of the "social control" heresy leads to a misreading of the central themes of *The Problem of Slavery in the Age of Revolution*, especially with respect to complex links between religion and economic interest. He cites page 251, for example, when he describes the "keystone" of my "interpretation" as the "claim that 'as a social force, antislavery was a highly selective response to labor exploitation,' one which—not unintentionally, but as a result of an unconscious hegemonic interest about which the reformers deceived themselves—'gave a certain moral insulation to economic activities less visibly dependent on human suffering and injustice.' "[27]

Totally baffled by this garbled and hardly coherent passage, I turned to page 251, wondering if I could have written such nonsense there. The cited page actually contains no summing up of my themes, no "keystone." It is specifically about the effort of Anglo-American Quakers to interpret "each step toward a total disengagement from slaveholding as a tangible sign of growing religious purity." After discussing the importance of the Quaker example to Christians of other faiths, I reject "the simplistic thesis that Quaker abolitionists were governed by 'economic interest' in the sense that they stood to profit from the destruction of the slave trade or a weakening of the plantation system." Contrary to Haskell's presentation, nothing at all is said at this point in the book about self-deception or unconscious hegemonic interest. For me, at least, the central sentence of the page, which does state one of the themes of the book, reads as follows: "To moralists and reformers of other faiths, the Quakers demonstrated that testimony against slavery could be a social correlative of inner purity which seemed to pose

27. Haskell, "Convention and Hegemonic Interest in the Debate over Antislavery," 869.

no threat to the social order—at least to that capitalist order in which the Quakers had won so enviable a 'stake.' " The example of this page brings out a curious aspect of Haskell's distortion of my position: here as elsewhere he wholly ignores my continuing emphasis on religious issues, religious meanings, and religious motivations.

Perhaps because Haskell remains so aloof from the loamy soil of historical narrative—the specific people, groups, actions, dates, movements, and contexts to which I refer in both my book and *AHR* reply—he confuses and conflates abstract words, particularly "hegemony" and "ideology." Although I defined my understanding of ideology in the preface of the book and in my *AHR* essay,[28] Haskell stubbornly equates "ideology" with "hegemony" and uses them as interchangeable terms. As a result of this misunderstanding, he continues to insist that a book that *is* centrally concerned with ideology is no less preoccupied with hegemony: "Far from devoting only a 'few pages' of *The Problem of Slavery in the Age of Revolution* to the hegemony argument, Davis organized much of the book around it."[29]

"Hegemony," which derives from the Greek word for "leader" and in ordinary parlance means no more than a dominant influence or authority over others, can become ideological when an ideology helps a group or class to win and sustain dominance over other people. The term "ideological hegemony" clearly cannot refer to a group that may have an ideology but that lacks or does not achieve hegemony. Yet Haskell asserts that "to say that abolitionism is in some degree explicable in terms of the need to legitimate wage labor is to say that it is, in that same degree, hegemonic."[30]

Haskell's error, which pervades much of his discussion, becomes evident as soon as we ask whose need is being legitimated? Haskell orbited at too high an altitude to see that "the abolitionists" were made up of very different kinds of people working in extremely different political contexts, and

---

28. Davis, *Problem of Slavery in the Age of Revolution*, 14–15; "Reflections on Abolitionism and Ideological Hegemony," 799. The first definition reads as follows: "I have used 'ideology' to mean an integrated system of beliefs, assumptions, and values, not necessarily true or false, which reflects the needs and interests of a group or class at a particular time in history. By 'interest' I mean anything that benefits or is thought to benefit a specific collective identity. Because ideologies are modes of consciousness, containing the criteria for interpreting social reality, they help to define as well as to legitimate collective needs and interests. Hence there is a continuous interaction between ideology and the material forces of history. The salient characteristic of an ideology is that, while it is taken for granted by people who have internalized it, it is never the eternal or absolute truth it claims to be. Ideologies focus attention on certain phenomena, but only by arbitrarily screening out other phenomena in patterns that are not without meaning."
29. Haskell, "Convention and Hegemonic Interest in the Debate over Antislavery," 830.
30. *Ibid.*

that the British Quakers, for example, were Dissenters who had little influence on lawmakers. Although the Quakers' late eighteenth-century assault on the ownership of human souls ultimately helped to legitimate the commodification of wage labor, the Anglo-American Quakers cannot be said to have enjoyed "hegemony." Certainly the desire to legitimate free manual labor was not confined to a small elite—indeed, traditional elites tended to look with contempt on *all* forms of manual labor. As the nineteenth century progressed, entrepreneurs and master craftsmen in both Britain and North America sought to legitimate wage labor as a just and consensual form of reciprocity. Yet the ideal of *free* labor, as distinct from both chattel and "wage slavery," appealed to artisans and workers of varying degrees of skill who, faced by the disintegration of the traditional craft-apprenticeship system, were eager to dignify manual labor and to dissociate it from the ancient stigma of subservience. Up to a point, the desire of skilled workers to dignify manual labor could and did play into the hands of entrepreneurial politicians, business leaders, journalists, and political economists who wanted to assure wage-laborers that they were ennobled by a competitive labor market.[31] But in the United States it was only when a national working class finally emerged, after the Civil War and after slave emancipation, that antislavery ideology succeeded in validating the view that a voluntary contract exemplified "equivalence," the polar opposite of the slave-master relation.[32]

By misinterpreting my references to ideology as the "hegemonic argument," Haskell can ignore the fact that I do not discuss the concept of hegemony until the reader has trekked 349 pages through *The Problem of Slavery in the Age of Revolution*, or 63 percent of the text. At that point, I quoted the Italian Marxist Antonio Gramsci, as well as the conservative sociologist Peter Berger. I can recall that at that moment in writing my book, Gramsci's concept of ideological hegemony and Berger's insights into collective and self-deception offered an exciting clue, consistent with the evidence, that promised to shed light on a very specific historical problem in British history. As I defined the problem in the *AHR Forum*: Why was it that "this single reform cause [abolitionism], which attracted significant radical support in the early 1790s and which some conservatives denounced

31. By far the most comprehensive and insightful study of this subject is Jonathan A. Glickstein, "Concepts of Free Labor in Antebellum America: Volume One" (Ph.D. dissertation, Yale University, 1989). For a no less brilliant analysis on the level of social history, see Sean Wilentz, *Chants Democratic: New York City and the Rise of the American Working Class, 1788–1850* (New York, 1984).
32. A masterful exploration of this subject is Amy Dru Stanley, "Contract Rights in the Age of Emancipation: Wage Labor and Marriage after the Civil War" (Ph.D. dissertation, Yale University, 1990).

as a Jacobin front, won growing acceptance in the early nineteenth century from British political and social elites otherwise obsessed with the fear that social reform would open the gates to revolution."[33]

Although the word "hegemony" appears only seven times in my text following this brief discussion, the mention of Gramsci became literally a red flag, and for some readers I instantly became a "Gramscian" (though never a "Bergerian"). The Gramscian use of "hegemony" may be so highly charged and so subject to misunderstanding that a different term needs to be found.[34] However, when I read the seventy-five pages of printed transcripts from the Rice University Center for Cultural Studies recording the remarks made by Thomas Haskell and various commentators at a 1987–88 seminar series, I was especially struck by Haskell's following statement:

> I have always insisted and agreed with Davis that the attack on slav-ery had hegemonic consequences. The question of whether it had hegemonic consequences or not is really not at issue. I agree that it had hegemonic consequences of putting wage labour in a favourable position. There's no doubt about that. But the question is, How do you get from that consequence, which one can witness on this pro-jective screen, without any trouble, one can see clearly how signifi-cant it is in the legitimation of wage labour. . . . How do you get from that to the production of the antislavery rhetoric and action? Did they in any meaningful sense become abolitionists and attack slavery for the sake of achieving that consequence?[35]

33. Davis, "Reflections on Abolitionism and Ideological Hegemony," 798. It was only after I had finished the book and had applied the "hegemonic argument" to the particular British case that I wrote in the introductory chapter the sentence that Haskell triumphantly quotes: "Much of this book will be concerned with the ideo-logical functions and implications of attacking this symbol of the most extreme subordination, exploitation, and dehumanization, at a time when various enlight-ened elites were experimenting with internalized moral and cultural controls to establish or preserve their own hegemony" (*Problem of Slavery in the Age of Revo-lution*, 49). A careful reading of this sentence will reveal that it does not say, as Has-kell suggests, that much of the book will be organized around "the hegemony argument."

34. As John Patrick Diggins points out, Gramsci's concept was anticipated in many respects by Adam Smith, Alexis de Tocqueville, and Thorstein Veblen, among others (Diggins, "Gramsci and the Intellectuals," *Raritan: A Quarterly Review*, 9 [Fall 1989]: 129–52).

35. Rice University Center for Cultural Studies, *Discussion: Locating Moral Sen-sibilities, The Haskell Debates* (18 January, 1988), 1987–1988 Seminar Series: Moral Sensibilities in Cultural and Historical Context (n.p., n.d.), 10. This is a much stronger concession, it seems to me, than the more hedged statement Haskell made in his 1985 essay: "This is not to deny that some effects of the attack on slav-ery furthered bourgeois interests. The consequences of the antislavery movement that Davis called 'hegemonic' are real enough, but we have not been given any ade-quate reason to think they were produced by class interest, by a desire for hegemony,

I must confess that upon reading the first five sentences, my initial re-action was to ask what all the other rhetoric had been about. I had cau-tiously tried to limit "the hegemonic argument" to a phase of British abolitionism that coincided with the political and economic dominance of a very small, generally repressive, and counterrevolutionary elite, since I was all too aware of the *antiabolitionist* venom of various United States elites in the 1830s and 1840s. I also knew that in both Britain and the United States, antislavery acquired truly radical characteristics, spawning or serving as a model for other movements that challenged inequalities and prevailing forms of domination. Antislavery helped to undermine many forms of he-gemony even if, with regard to industrial wage labor, it ultimately served hegemonic functions. Haskell appeared, at least in 1988, to grant even more than I had claimed. If the "hegemonic consequences" of antislavery were no longer an issue in 1988, no histories of the movement had pointed to such consequences, so far as I know, before the publication of my *Problem of Slavery in the Age of Revolution*.

As for the last part of Haskell's statement, I know of no historian who has even hinted that, "in any meaningful sense," men and women became abolitionists for the sake of putting wage labor in a favorable position. The very thought must seem absurd to any one who knows the sources. I have repeatedly insisted that I have little interest in individual motivation, a shadowy subject even for the most insightful biographers blessed with the most revealing evidence. I have tried to show how *collective* symbol systems can both widen and limit a people's sense of moral responsibility. When a particular moral problem moves from the margins to the center of public attention, there is a shift in the criteria of plausibility that involves, not "so-cial control" in any narrow, elitist sense, but a change in what common sense decrees as right or wrong. Whatever terms one uses to describe this process must be capable, with respect to abolitionism in the early industrial age, of accounting for the fact that the very first issue of William Lloyd Gar-rison's *Liberator* castigated northern workingmen's parties for trying "to enflame the minds of our working class against the more opulent, and to persuade men that they are contemned and oppressed by a wealthy aristoc-racy"; that in 1847 Wendell Phillips preached that northern workers who complained of poverty could blame only their own failure with regard to "economy, self-denial, temperance, education, and moral and religious character"; and that even after the Civil War, Phillips defended the sacred-

---

or by any other form of intention, conscious or unconscious. They belong mainly to the category of unintended consequences" (Haskell, "Capitalism and the Origins of the Humanitarian Sensibility, Part 2," 547).

ness of labor contracts and proclaimed that, thanks to slave emancipation, the "struggle for the ownership of labor" had at last been overcome.[36]

At times Haskell claims that he, too, is not concerned with "individual episodes of human kindness and decency," but rather with "a sustained, collective pattern of behavior in which substantial numbers of people regularly act to alleviate the suffering of strangers."[37] Such statements are hard to reconcile, however, with Haskell's continuing emphasis on individual charity and his traditional Christian image of the suffering or starving "stranger," whose agonies never result from oppressive actions or institutions. Since Haskell's "recipe knowledge" is so geared to the effects of technology on individual acts of charity, he can give us the astonishingly ahistorical example of an American citizen selling his car to raise funds in order to fly to Phnom Penh or Bombay and feed a starving stranger. I call this ahistorical because, for all of Haskell's talk about airplanes increasing our feeling of responsibility, he never once recognizes the direct "causal connection" between actions taken by the U.S. government and the miseries suffered in Cambodia, or for that matter in Bombay after the backfiring of our well-intentioned efforts to aid India's agricultural production (to say nothing about the maimed and starving strangers of Bhopal).[38] If John Ashworth and I have disappointed Haskell by not giving much attention to his "case of the starving stranger," it is because the example is irrelevant to the history of abolitionism—or to more contemporary instances of massive oppression, exploitation, and suffering.

I grant that John Woolman, one of the few historical figures whom Haskell mentions, represents a transition between traditional Christian charity and antislavery protest. But Woolman was a lone figure, a saintly man who was never part of an abolitionist movement. Early abolitionists such as Granville Sharp, Thomas Clarkson, William Wilberforce, and James Stephen were acutely aware of national and governmental complicity in the crimes of the slave trade, and of the plea of "unintentionality" as a means of absolving the nation from guilt. James Stephen, whom Haskell confuses with Sir James Stephen, the son of the abolitionist, insisted that his quarrel

---

36. Quoted in Jonathan A. Glickstein, " 'Poverty Is Not Slavery': American Abolitionists and the Competitive Labor Market," in *Antislavery Reconsidered: New Perspectives on the Abolitionists*, Lewis Perry and Michael Fellman, eds. (Baton Rouge, La., 1979), 203–4; and in Stanley, "Contract Rights in the Age of Emancipation," 98. Although Phillips and a few other abolitionists are rightly credited with supporting labor reforms, Phillips's conceptions of freedom and consent were fairly rigidly molded by antislavery doctrine.
37. Haskell, "Convention and Hegemonic Interest in the Debate over Antislavery," 848.
38. Haskell, "Capitalism and the Humanitarian Sensibility, Part 1," 354–55.

was not with "those who *conduct* the system," that is, with individual planters, but with the *system* itself. His view of an unreformable system that necessitates ghastly oppression for the benefit of competitive proprietors and consumers represents a different conceptual world from the Golden Rule and the starving stranger.[39]

Moreover, the British abolitionists' "recipes" for intervention were emphatically not, as Haskell would have it, "of sufficient ordinariness, familiarity, certainty of effect, and ease of operation that . . . failure to use them would constitute a suspension of routine, an out-of-the-ordinary event, possibly even an intentional act in itself."[40] From the time that Clarkson risked his life by gathering information about the outfitting and records of slave ships on the docks of Liverpool, the British abolitionists' methods for abolishing the slave trade and then slavery itself (not aiding individual slaves, except in rare circumstances), were usually novel, difficult, and quite unpredictable. Often unfamiliar with the traditional practice of politics, they quickly became skilled at relatively new political techniques such as mass petitioning, interrogating candidates for office, and organizing hundreds of local abolitionist societies for both men and women. After 1835 the same points apply to the United States, where abolitionists were in a more desperate position as a persecuted minority who were literally driven to innovation and radical experiment.

Where, then, does this leave us? The debate initiated by Haskell's essay has exposed lacunae in my own account and has forced me to reconsider the endless complexities of ideology and social change. My own sense, however, is that Haskell's critique has not undermined the original thesis, even if that thesis is now more precisely bounded in time and space. I would still maintain that a hostility to slavery, largely religious and philosophical in origin, had little chance of having any practical effect until it became incorporated into the political culture of the British governing elite. While recognizing the appeal of antislavery to a significant number of aspiring artisans and shopkeepers, as well as the way radical reformers continued in both Britain and America to invoke abolitionist precedents, it still seems sound to say that the growing power of antislavery in early industrial Britain was at least partly a function of the fit between antislavery ideology and the interests of an emergent capitalist class. Today I am more aware of how little we know about the character of British "political culture" in the years from Pitt to Canning. Still, I am convinced now, as in 1975, that the growth and triumphs of antislavery had the long-term effect, regardless of the aboli-

39. David Brion Davis, *Slavery and Human Progress*, 171–72.
40. Haskell, "Capitalism and the Humanitarian Sensibility, Part 1," 358.

tionists' intentions, of legitimating and morally sustaining the new industrial capitalist order.

I actually think there is much truth in W. E. H. Lecky's often-quoted assertion that "the unwearied, unostentatious, and inglorious crusade of England against slavery may probably be regarded as among the three or four perfectly virtuous acts recorded in the history of nations."[41] But in the 1990s it would be naïve not to add that such a crusade inevitably helps to valorize and redeem the particular social order from which it springs.

41. W. E. H. Lecky, *A History of European Morals: From Augustus to Charlemagne* (New York, 1876), 1: 161.

# Index

Aaron, Hank, 123–24
Abingdon, Earl of, 67
Abolition: and capitalism, 161, 228, 235–36; and class interest, 4, 12, 110, 118, 279; economic justification for, 74; and hegemony, 161–62, 201–2, 286–87, 306; and labor discipline problem, 171; moral basis of, 195; religious sources of, 4, 11, 162; rhetoric of, 9; and social oppression, 172; universal appeal of, 297; and wage slavery, 125–26. *See also* Antislavery movements; Emancipation; Manumission, private
Abolition Bill (Great Britain, 1807), 163
Abolition Committee (London), 34, 48, 84, 93n
Abolitionists: American, 192–98, 296; attitudes toward wage labor, 247–49, 270; class interest of, 251, 271; ethical conventions of, 124–25; motivation of, 294n, 306; self-deception of, 120; techniques of, 308; women as, 178–79, 209, 231
Abolition societies, 30; composition of, 50–52
Act of Settlement (England, 1662), 77
"Address on Slavery" (Lee), 43
African colonization, 33n, 100
African Company (Great Britain), 36
African Institution (London), 57, 202; sponsors of, 205
"Age of Contract," 145, 146, 152
Alcoholism, 278, 279

Alexander I (emperor of Russia), 40, 59
Alger, William, 193
Allen, William: early life of, 53–54; philanthropic activities of, 55–56, 63; scientific interest of, 55–56; ties with liberal reformers, 57–59
American and Foreign Anti-Slavery Society, 193
American Revolution. *See* Revolution, American
Amis des noirs (Paris), 34, 50, 98; declaration of principles, 66
Amnesty International, 221, 248
Anglo-Dutch War, Fourth, 295
Annet, Peter, 87
Anstey, Roger, 69, 109
Antiformalism, 258
Antislavery literature, 32–33, 37, 47, 84–92; free laborers in, 168; ideological function of, 87–88; and liberal values, 72; in the Netherlands, 178
Antislavery movements: and British hegemony, 1, 70–71; and causation, 288; and class interest, 4, 12, 110, 118, 181–82, 238, 271–72, 279; and economic theory, 72; emergence of, 1, 113; and English middle class, 81; and English poor, 77–79; in France, 34, 50, 66, 98; and humanitarian reform movements, 107–8, 297; ideology of, 95, 204, 241–42; international opinion concerning, 203–4, 300–301; and labor market, 78–79; and labor movements, 120–21, 248; le-

311

Burke, Edmund, 55, 68, 74, 82;
 opposition to slave trade, 76, 78
Burt, John, 154
Burton, Daniel, 93, 96
Buxton, Thomas Fowell, 48, 173,
 174
Byllesby, Langton, 173

Calvin, John, 21, 217
Calvinism, 23, 114; and abolition,
 292
Capitalism: and abolition, 161,
 228, 235–36; and antislavery
 movements, 8, 11, 71, 109, 117,
 155, 177, 289; and class relations, 7, 10–11; and conscience,
 143–44, 298; cultural history
 of, 11; definition of, 10, 190;
 and emergence of antislavery,
 1–2; ethics of, 59; exploitation
 under, 8; and humanitarianism,
 108, 110, 115, 125, 136–37,
 147, 180, 183, 205, 228, 237,
 274, 297n; industrial, 2, 12;
 Marxist definition of, 191n;
 merchant, 292; as moderating
 force, 139–40; morality of, 9;
 in northern United States, 9;
 and paternalism, 139; and Protestantism, 239; and Quakerism, 45, 114; rise of, 1, 108,
 110, 176, 205, 271–72, 283,
 298; and social relations, 292;
 and wage laborers, 190–91
*Capitalism and Slavery* (Williams), 1–2, 69, 161
Capitalists: Dutch, 9–10, 293–94;
 hegemony of, 5, 117; Quaker,
 45, 60–61, 114
Capital punishment, 58
Cartwright, John, Major, 92
*The Case of Our Fellow Creatures,*

*the Oppressed Africans* (Lloyd),
 37
Castlereagh, Robert Stewart, Vis-
 count, 163
*Catechism on the Corn Laws,* 80
Causality, 127–32, 144, 153, 208,
 219, 287–88; and humanitari-
 anism, 148, 238; and the mar-
 ket, 156, 177, 189, 228, 230;
 and moral responsibility, 160;
 in pre-industrial age, 225;
 Woolman's treatment of, 159
Cavendish, John, Lord, 36
"Charity" (poem by Cowper),
 88–92
Chartists, 173
Chattel slavery. *See* Slavery, chattel
Christianity, 229, 272, 299; effect
 of on slavery, 18, 20, 24, 25,
 38n, 58n; and self-control, 278
Christie, Ian, 82
Churchman, John, 39–41
Church of England, 56
Civil War, American, 252, 276,
 285, 299
Clapham Sect, 87
Clarkson, Thomas, 31n, 33, 34,
 45, 73n, 307; essays of, 78–79,
 164; investigation of slave
 ships, 308; retirement of, 85n;
 support for French Revolution,
 98
Class interest, 112, 164, 176–77,
 179, 273, 280–83; and antislavery movements, 4, 12, 110,
 118, 181–82, 238, 243, 271,
 272, 279; and humanitarianism, 115–16, 130, 273, 284;
 ideology of, 284; and labor discipline, 227; of reformers, 113,
 240, 249, 250–52; and self-
 interest, 111, 183

Dutch: in America, 35; antislavery activities of, 233, 293; as capitalists, 9–10; emancipation by, 234, 296. *See also* Netherlands

Dutch West India Company, 28n

*Econocide* (Drescher), 109
Eddy, Thomas, 49
Eden, Sir Frederick Morton, 79
*Edinburgh Review*, 79–80
Elective affinity, 111, 237, 243
Elias, Norbert, 136–37, 139, 229–30
Elster, Jon, 251
Emancipation, 66; by the Dutch, 234, 296; economic justification for, 74, 81; effect of on working class, 304; French edict of, 98–99, 296; politics of, 175; West Indian, 69, 70, 77, 102n, 113, 163. *See also* Abolition; Manumission, private
Emancipation Act of 1833 (Great Britain), 174–75
Emancipation Proclamation (U.S., 1863), 296, 297
Emmer, Peter C., 178, 233
Engels, Friedrich, 172, 258
Enlightenment, European, 22, 51, 149; and colonial planters, 25–26
*Essay on the Impolicy of the African Slave Trade* (Clarkson), 73n
*Essay on the Slavery and Commerce of the Human Species* (Clarkson), 78–79
*An Essay on the Treatment and Conversion of African Slaves in the British West Indies* (Ramsay), 33, 34, 95–97
*Essay Upon Projects* (Defoe), 150
Estwick, Samuel, 94–95
Etruria mill, 294

Evangelical movements, 23–24, 40, 76, 114, 170, 223; and antislavery movements, 34, 279, 296; and growth of wage labor, 277–78
Evans, Thomas, 172

Factory owners, American, 198n
Factory system, 62, 101, 116, 181; in Lancashire, 292
Family: as center of production, 191; effect of slavery on, 197–98, 241; middle-class, 278; nineteenth-century, 195–98; and rise of abolitionism, 191, 241, 274, 276; veneration of, 244–45
Farley, Jim, 299, 300n
Femininity, traditional values of, 231–32
Feminists, 215
Finley, Moses I., 299–300
First Bank of the United States, 49
Fladeland, Betty, 162n
Flint, Timothy, 297
Follen, Eliza Lee, 193
Foner, Eric, 5n
Foot, Jesse, 164
Formalism, 253–58, 280; emergence of, 272; and rise of capitalism, 270–72
Foster, Stephen S., 196
Fothergill, John, 42
Fothergill, Samuel, 41; mission through the South, 42
Foucault, Michel, 108–9, 139n, 203, 301
Fourth Lateran Council (1215), 139n
Fox, Charles James, 76
Fox, George, 27n
Fox, Joseph, 59
Fox, William, 98–99

Revolution, French, 56, 76, 162, 230; and antislavery movements, 84, 85
Revolution, Industrial, 162, 164, 165
Reynolds, Richard, 57
Rhode Island: antislavery movement in, 41; slave trade in, 28n
Rice University Center for Cultural Studies, 305
Rochester revival, 277–78
Rockingham Whigs, 82–83, 92
Roman law, 18
Romilly, Samuel, 58, 78
Roth, Randolph A., 291
Rousseau, Jean-Jacques, 168
Royal African Company, 28n, 159n, 223
Rush, Benjamin, 30, 35; cooperation with Benezet, 40n; correspondence with Granville Sharp, 58n; correspondence with J. C. Lettsom, 62

Sadler, Michael Thomas, 78n
St. Domingue insurrection, 97–98
Sanson, Philip, 34, 47
Savery, William, 40
Schama, Simon, 295
Seamen, English, 73, 95
Sectarians, 21
Self-control: and Christianity, 278; and the market, 153
Self-deception, 13, 118–22, 166–67, 237, 250, 274, 288–89; and antislavery movement, 136; and class interest, 112, 284; definition of, 217; and ethical conventions, 124–25; and hegemony, 200, 205; and intentionality, 208–12; of masters, 279; and moral responsibility, 120–21; proof of, 182; and risk

aversion, 211; socially induced, 281; universality of, 215
Self-interest, 13, 23, 192, 237; and abolitionism, 180; in abolition of slave trade, 70; in classical republicanism, 191; and class interest, 111, 183; and false charity, 74–75; and family ties, 197, 244; legitimation of, 241–43; and the market, 185, 192, 237; in master-slave relationship, 100; and slavery, 73–75
Sensibility, cult of, 76, 85, 179, 299
Seven Years' War, 25; Quakers in, 22, 28n, 35–36
Sexism, 167
Sharp, Granville, 33, 43n, 46, 47, 92–94, 307; correspondence with Benjamin Rush, 58n; on Quakers, 57; on St. Domingue insurrection, 98; on slavery and labor, 99–100
Shay, John Michael, 30n
Shelburne, Lord, 76
*A Shopkeeper's Millennium* (Johnson), 277–79
Sierra Leone, colonization of, 33n, 100
*Las Siete Partidas* (legal code), 133n, 223
Simeon, Charles, 58
Skidmore, Thomas, 173
Slaveholders: French, 98; hegemony of, 285–86; legal rights of, 94; morality of, 158; Quaker, 22, 27n–28n, 29n, 37, 61, 302; southern, 288; West Indian, 99
Slavery: in antiquity, 17–20, 188; in British West Indies, 1, 41, 49, 163–64, 175; and divine retribution, 166; economic defense of, 72; economics of,

Starving stranger, analogy of, 127–28, 219, 231, 266–69, 290
Stephen, James, the elder, 85–87, 99, 165–66, 168, 210
Stephen, James, the younger, 307
Stevenson, Adlai, 299, 300n
Stowe, Harriet Beecher, 193–94, 197
Strauss, Leo, 218
Sugar trade, 54; overproduction in, 69; profitability of, 73
Sunday markets, 171
Sunday Schools, 278
Supply and demand, laws of, 138, 186
Surinam, slave colony at, 233, 295

Tarleton, Banastre, Colonel, 69
Technological determinism, 266
Technological innovation, 230; and moral responsibility, 128–29, 188, 221, 226n
Temperance, 192, 198, 253, 255, 278, 306
Temperley, Howard, 109, 132, 181
Test and Corporation Acts (Great Britain), 92
Thelwall, John, 86, 87n
The Theory of Moral Sentiments (Smith), 1, 23, 75
Thomas Aquinas, Saint, 21, 256–57, 272
Thompson, E. P., 54, 85, 118
Thompson, Thomas, 94n
Thornton, Henry, 55, 90
Thoughts and Details on Scarcity (Burke), 79
Timber trade, 292
Torts, 144, 146
Torture: judicial, 139n; of slaves, 170
Townsend, Joseph, 78–79
Trial by ordeal, 139n

Truman, Hanbury & Co., 48
Two Dialogues on the Man-Trade (pamphlet), 92n

Uncle Tom's Cabin (Stowe), 193–94, 197
Unitarianism, 206
United States: antebellum period of, 192; labor in, 9, 52, 175, 190; municipal life in, 51–53
Universalism, 93n
Utilitarianism, 65, 74–76, 85, 101, 170

Vaux, George, 42
Vegetarianism, 125–26, 183
Vermont, social reform in, 291–92
Village culture, preindustrial, 170
Villeins, 18
Virginia, antislavery in, 178
The Virginia Gazette (periodical), 26
Virginia General Assembly, 43
Voltaire, 28n
Voluntarism, 222, 256–57

Wage labor, 9, 198–99, 241, 254; and antislavery movements, 5, 164–66, 181, 213–14, 251, 270; and conscience, 277; growth of, 190; legitimation of, 4, 202, 243–44, 274, 287, 293, 303–5; in the Netherlands, 233; spread of, 192, 289; symbolism of, 59–64; in United States, 9, 190
Wage slavery, 173, 286; and chattel slavery, 115, 120, 124–26, 174–76, 190, 249, 252, 304; Wendell Phillips on, 148n
Wage slaves, 207, 247; fear of revolution by, 172. See also Poor

Walker, Thomas, 83, 92–93
Wallace, George, 92
Waln, Robert, 49
Walters, Ronald G., 294n
Walvin, James, 87n, 121n
Warfare, 125–26
*The Wealth of Nations* (Smith), 1,
23, 72, 75, 97, 159
Weber, Max, 6, 11, 108, 111, 139,
237–40; historical sociology of,
7; on the market, 140–41
Wedderburn, Robert, 172
Wedgwood, Josiah, 42, 293–94
*The Weekly Magazine or Edin-
burgh Amusement* (periodical),
26
Weld, Theodore Dwight, 193
Wellington, Duke of, 163
Wesley, John, 23, 24, 46
Western culture: bondage in, 19,
300; conventions of, 224; self-
surveillance of, 229–30; use of
Golden Rule, 267–69
West India Committee, 100
West Indies, British, 1–2, 32;
slavery in, 1, 49, 75n; sugar
trade in, 54
Weston, James, & Dillwyn (firm),
47

Whig Party (Great Britain), 82–
83, 95; view of abolitionists,
180, 184, 187
White, Edward, 97
Wilberforce, William, 34, 76, 128,
163, 168, 172, 292, 307; friend-
ship with William Allen, 55;
parliamentary campaigns of,
82, 165; philanthropies of,
100–101; preservation of paternalism, 78; on Quakers, 57–58
Williams, Eric, 1–2, 69–70, 119,
161, 180–81; interpretation of
abolitionism, 250
Williams, Raymond, 117n, 118,
249
Women: as abolitionists, 178–79,
209, 231–32; flogging of, 171
Woods, Joseph, 47, 48
Woolman, John, 24, 28, 146, 156–
60, 186, 231, 265, 307; friends
of, 40–41; on Golden Rule,
157; life-style of, 59–60; mission through the South, 42
Workhouses, 78
World War I, origins of, 287–88
Wray, Sir Cecil, 36
Wright, Henry C., 196
Wyvil, Christopher, 82, 92

CPSIA information can be obtained
at www.ICGtesting.com
Printed in the USA
JSHW041048080721
16688JS00001B/15